Alexander William Doniphan

MISSOURI BIOGRAPHY SERIES
WILLIAM E. FOLEY, EDITOR

Alexander William Doniphan in uniform as he appeared at the time of his Mexican-American War expedition into the Southwest, 1846–1847. From an antebellum engraving. Photo accession no. 009116, courtesy of the State Historical Society of Missouri, Columbia.

Alexander William ❧ Doniphan

Portrait of a Missouri Moderate

ROGER D. LAUNIUS

UNIVERSITY OF MISSOURI PRESS
Columbia and London

Library of Congress Cataloging-in-Publication Data
Launius, Roger D.
   Alexander William Doniphan : portrait of a Missouri moderate /
   Roger D. Launius.
      p.   cm. — (Missouri biography series)
   Includes bibliographical references (p.) and index.
   ISBN 0-8262-1132-1 (alk. paper)
      1. Doniphan, Alexander William.   2. Generals—United States—
Biography.   3. United States. Army—Biography.   4. Politicians—
Missouri—Biography. 5. Mexican War, 1846–1848—Campaigns.
6. Mormons—Civil rights—United States.   7. Missouri—Biography.
I. Title. II Series.
E403.1.D6L39   1997
973.6'2'092—dc21   97-15906
[B]   CIP

∞™ This paper meets the requirements of the
American National Standard for Permanence of Paper
for Printed Library Materials, Z39.48, 1984.

Designer: Mindy Shouse
Typesetter: BOOKCOMP
Printer and binder: Thomson-Shore, Inc.
Typeface: Book Antiqua

For I. L. P.

Contents

Preface

THE ESSENCE OF American civilization has always been the ability to appreciate a diversity of opinion, even when holding specific ideals, and to find a position somewhere in the middle that all can accept. Alexander William Doniphan—Missouri attorney, military figure, politician, and businessman of the nineteenth century—epitomized that unique attribute of United States culture and politics throughout most of his life. For more than fifty years, from the 1830s to the 1880s, Doniphan was active in a variety of affairs in the state and always represented a moral position tempered by moderation. Never just a "deal cutter" who would blow with the political wind, Doniphan held firm to several underlying principles throughout his life, including loyalty, hard work, the sanctity of the republic, and commitment to Christian charity. These attributes brought him marked success, and in the process he gained fame and fortune. The key to Doniphan's importance was his persistent moderation on the critical issues of his day. He represented the middle ground of American politics and society, neither radical in pressing for change nor reactionary in seeking to maintain the status quo. It is this aspect of his life that most intrigues me and which I most want to understand.

It was his time as the commander of the Mexican War First Missouri Mounted Volunteers assigned to the Army of the West that most shaped Doniphan's life, and one point where he represented moderation. In 1838 Doniphan had become a brigadier general of the Missouri State Militia, and when the United States entered the war with Mexico in 1846 he was elected to command the first enlistees from his home state. They departed Fort Leavenworth in June 1846, and by August his men had reached Santa Fe, where the Mexican government surrendered without a battle. While other parts of the army pushed on toward California, Doniphan's men remained in Santa Fe with orders to pacify or defeat hostile Indians and establish a government acceptable to Congress, and only then to push southward into Chihuahua, Mexico.

Doniphan quickly created a code of organic laws for the new territory and began actions to subdue the Indians of the region. Late in the year Doniphan's men marched for El Paso del Norte, and on Christmas Day camped near the city at a place called El Brazito. They soon learned that a Mexican army was approaching, and by the time the Mexicans attacked, Doniphan's men had moved into defensive positions. After a short fight, from 40 to 50 of the Mexicans were killed and 150 wounded. Doniphan's troops only counted 7 wounded.

A few days later Doniphan's column marched into El Paso del Norte, where it rested before moving on to Chihuahua. On February 28, 1847, Doniphan was nearing Chihuahua when he encountered a sizable Mexican force of several thousand near the Sacramento River. He engaged this force, defeating it, and then occupied Chihuahua City. Eventually Doniphan's force joined Zachary Taylor's army at Buena Vista before returning home. In one year, Doniphan's men had traveled more than thirty-five hundred miles by land and another thousand by water, fought two major battles in Mexico, established an Anglo-American-based democracy in New Mexico, and paved the way for the annexation of the territory that became New Mexico and Arizona.

After this success "Doniphan" was a household name in Missouri and much of the rest of the United States. That he did not parlay this into high political office is one of the important questions any historian should ask. The answer seems to be that he simply did not wish to do so. Some of his reasons were personal; his health was never good after his return from Mexico and his family suffered tragedy that debilitated him. Also, seeking office would have forced him to compromise his convictions and to engage in the politics of extremism. Accordingly, he represented the soul of moderation within his state throughout the years of the sectional conflict. Such moderation might have hindered whatever political aspirations Doniphan might have held, but it staked out an important place in the national political spectrum. Had more people occupied it the United States might have avoided the Civil War.

Although he never held an elective office more prestigious than that of state legislator, Doniphan was a persistent player in the antebellum politics of Missouri. A Whig by both inclination and affiliation, he was an early endorser of using political power for the betterment of society. He and his fellow Missouri Whigs battled the state's Democratic Party throughout the antebellum years over the role the government should play in fostering the welfare of its citizens. When the Whig Party collapsed under the weight of the issues of slavery and the sectional conflict that ensued, Doniphan saw firsthand how the power of government could be used to alter society, and in ways he did not endorse. He sought to moderate in the 1850s and 1860s the extremism he perceived around him, taking a pro-Southern and proslavery stance but remaining a firm advocate of the Federal union throughout the Civil War years. Until the very last minute in 1861 Doniphan tried to help negotiate a compromise that would preserve both the Union and the dignity of all sides. His failure to do so represented the greatest political disappointment of his life.

Doniphan might have decided to fight in the Civil War—either side would have been pleased to have him because of his experience and heroic status as the Mexican War commander of the First Missouri Mounted Volunteers—but he chose moderation again. His commitment to the Union prohibited him from taking up arms against it, and his allegiance to friends and institutions of the South prevented him from aiding in the putting down of the rebellion. In the end Doniphan did probably the only thing that his conscience would allow: he served as a state claims agent for the widows and orphans of butchered soldiers.

The moderation that Doniphan's life represented speaks to the present crisis in American politics at the end of the twentieth century. As extreme positions seem increasingly to be advanced, less and less room in the middle for interchange and compromise seems possible. Doniphan was appalled by similar development in the 1850s and 1860s, and his perspective might instruct Americans today. I am prompted to respect, if not often to agree with, the positions of Alexander William Doniphan.

If history has any true meaning for most people, and I believe it does, it is not because information gained from it can be used in a game of Trivial Pursuit but because it can help individuals to understand who they are and how they came to be that way. Most important, perhaps it can illuminate the present by drawing useful comparisons and perspectives. These are applied history goals, and I aspire to them. There is no point in examining the past without the desire to understand more effectively who we are. At a fundamental level the objective of the historian must be to serve the present, although the methodologies are indirect.

More important, history can not only serve the present but also help illuminate the future. Although few people think of historians as having anything important to say about the future, I would argue that history in fact offers us the best approach we have for understanding the shape of things to come. This is not because history provides a road map to the unknown world ahead and not because a knowledge of the past will keep us from repeating its mistakes. Rather, I would suggest that history is the discipline that can best help us to deal with the inexorable change that is so much a part of our world. It will help us to identify the deep continuities that link the past and present and pave the road to the future. Because we are all moving on a train called *continuity*, a study of history will help us understand the present and make our approach to the future a bit more tolerable. Doniphan's career provides a useful means of exploring past perspectives and political peccadillos. His life may help to provide information useful in developing a paradigm for present action, for clearly many of the general problems and issues with which he dealt have resurfaced in a variety of ways since his time.

As with any book, numerous debts were incurred over the course of the production of *Alexander William Doniphan*. I acknowledge the support and encouragement of a large number of people associated with the study of Missouri history and the developments of the "middle period" and want to thank many individuals who materially contributed to the completion of this project. Of course, I would never have taken this project on except for the encouragement and ideas provided by the editor of the Missouri Biography Series, William E. Foley, by the director of the University of Missouri Press, Beverly Jarrett, and by Press staff Jane Lago, Julie Schroeder, and Clair Willcox. The Missouri State Archivist, Kenneth H. Winn, also aided in more ways than he might ever know.

In addition, several individuals read all or part of this manuscript or otherwise offered helpful suggestions: Lavina Fielding Anderson, Alma R. Blair, Peter J. Blodgett, Donald Q. Cannon, Kimball Clark, Paul M. Edwards, R. Kenneth Elliott, Robert B. Flanders, Michael H. Gorn, Charles J. Gross, John E. Hallwas, Iris F. Harris, Perry D. Jamieson, Warren E. Jennings, Stanley B. Kimball, Stephen C. LeSueur, Perry McCandless, F. Mark McKiernan, William E. Parrish, Isleta L. Pement, Louis W. Potts, Michael S. Riggs, Randy Roberts, Ronald E. Romig, W. B. Spillman, and Phillip Thomas Tucker. My thanks are also gratefully given to the staffs of the Missouri State Archives, Jefferson City; Missouri Historical Society, St. Louis; State Historical Society of Missouri, Columbia; Western Historical Manuscript Collection, University of Missouri–Columbia; Jackson County Historical Society, Independence, Missouri; Archives of the Museum of New Mexico, Santa Fe; State of New Mexico Records Center and Archives, Santa Fe; Special Collections, William Jewell College, Liberty, Missouri; Reorganized Church of Jesus Christ of Latter Day Saints Library-Archives; Archives of the Church of Jesus Christ of Latter-day Saints; Huntington Library; Brigham Young University Library; National Archives and Records Administration, Washington, D.C.; and Kansas State Historical Society. I also wish to acknowledge a research grant from the Religious Studies Center of Brigham Young University, which provided travel funds for this project. Without the assistance of these people and institutions this book could not have been completed.

Alexander William Doniphan

1

The Young Lawyer

FOR AN ENTERPRISING young man in the Jacksonian era, no place in the United States excited more ambition than the recently created state of Missouri. The far western fur trade and the Santa Fe trade with Mexico promised huge profits for those willing to take huge risks, and the opening of rich bottomland along the Missouri River made plantation-style agriculture possible. St. Louis, located near the confluence of the Missouri and Mississippi Rivers in the eastern part of the state, was the new state's largest town with more than five thousand people, while Independence on the Missouri River near the western border was a burgeoning boomtown catering to the frontier economy. Steamboats plied the state's rivers carrying goods to the growing and scattered population, and the roads filled with caravans heading hither and yon on commerce. In many respects Missouri as a political entity in the United States was the result of American entrepreneurs from the East coming there to engage in business and ending up possessing the land as well. Andrew Jackson, the Tennessean who had become president in 1829 and whose name defined the age, would have been pleased. Missouri was a tangible expression of the American dream.[1]

Alexander William Doniphan, known as Will to his friends, came inexorably to Missouri with all its opportunities, prejudices, promises, and chances. Born of Celtic stock on July 9, 1808, in Mason County, Kentucky, the youngest son of Virginians Joseph Doniphan and Anne Smith, young Doniphan epitomized the Jacksonian entrepreneur. He was a man of talent

---

1. Dale L. Morgan, *Jedediah Smith and the Opening of the West,* 19–23; William E. Parrish, Charles T. Jones Jr., and Lawrence O. Christensen, *Missouri: The Heart of the Nation,* 66–74; James R. Shortridge, "The Expansion of the Settlement Frontier in Missouri."

and ambition who rose above his class through determination, talent, and not a little luck. He received a good education, as well as specialized training in the law—then, as now, an especially significant means of advancement in society—and he made opportunities for himself to enter elite groups on the Missouri frontier.[2]

Doniphan was not born to wealth, although he could not and did not claim a log cabin background. Doniphan's father was a Revolutionary War veteran, serving as an enlistee between 1776 and 1779, when he apparently followed Daniel Boone to Boonesboro, Kentucky. Joseph Doniphan taught school in Boonesboro for a short time, and his son always thought him the first schoolteacher in the region. He then returned to Virginia and reenlisted in the Army, where he served until the siege of Yorktown in 1781. In 1785, still in Virginia, Joseph Doniphan married Anne Smith, and in 1790 their first child, George, was born.[3]

Joseph Doniphan, by then with a small family, returned to Kentucky in the early 1790s and settled in Mason County at a place called Kenton's Station, five miles west of Maysville in the central part of the state. In Mason County the Doniphans prospered. He became a farmer of reasonable stature, evidenced by the fact that by 1810 his household included eighteen slaves and one white employee. At the time of his death in 1813, Joseph Doniphan was also sheriff of Mason County.[4]

While much of Doniphan's childhood remains murky, he seems to have enjoyed a serene youth. He was the youngest of ten children; eighteen years separated him from his oldest brother, George, so he only knew his older siblings as adults. This was brought home to him on March 12, 1813, when Joseph Doniphan died suddenly and the boy was sent to live

2. Although historians have tended to call Doniphan by his first name, evidence indicates that to his friends he was "Will." His correspondence is usually signed "A. W. Doniphan" except when written to close friends and relatives, when it is signed "Will." Moreover, Doniphan's published writings use his entire name, "Alexander William Doniphan," in identifying the author. See A. W. Doniphan to Emma Doniphan, [no month and day] 1875, Alexander William Doniphan Papers, Missouri Historical Society, St. Louis, [Doniphan Papers]; A. W. Doniphan to Abiel Leonard, January 23, 1843, Abiel Leonard Collection, Western Historical Manuscript Collection, Columbia, Mo.; and Alexander William Doniphan, *Address by Col. Alexander W. Doniphan, Delivered in Liberty, Mo., June 5, 1872, on the Occasion of the Celebration by the People of Clay County, of the 50th Anniversary of the County's Establishment.*

3. A. W. Doniphan to D. C. Allen, "Sketch of Life," 1, Doniphan Papers; William B. McGroarty, ed., "William H. Richardson's Journal of Doniphan's Expedition," 195; "Alexander W. Doniphan," in Howard L. Conard, ed., *Encyclopedia of the History of Missouri*, 2:295; Raymond W. Settle, *Alexander William Doniphan: Symbol of Pioneer Americanism*, 2.

4. Hugh P. Williamson, "Colonel Alexander W. Doniphan—Soldier, Lawyer and Statesman," 180; Doniphan to Allen, "Sketch of Life," 1, Doniphan Papers; McGroarty, ed., "Richardson's Journal," 195; Mason County, Ky., Population Schedules for the Third Federal Census, 1810, National Archives, Washington, D.C.; G. Glen Clift, *History of Maysville and Mason County, Kentucky*, 1:411.

with his oldest brother at Augusta, Kentucky, so that he could receive a proper education. Joseph Doniphan's will provided adequately for his young son, bequeathing to him a slave boy named Steven and a part of the family farm, where his mother and the other children remained. The inheritance of a slave, moreover, signified his family's basic acceptance of the racial system of the South. Doniphan, therefore, never challenged the institution of slavery in antebellum Missouri and owned slaves until the Civil War. He always accepted the basic arguments of racial inferiority of dark-skinned people, and may have thought that slavery was not just an economic institution that benefited white America but also a positive development for the enslaved race. Certainly he would not have been alone in such a perception.[5]

The inheritance Doniphan received from his father also allowed him to pursue an education. Richard Keene, his tutor at a school in Augusta, substantially affected Doniphan's development. Keene, described by Doniphan as "a learned but eccentric Irishman," had come to America as a fugitive of the Irish rebellion of 1798. He forced Doniphan to study the ideas and philosophies of the Enlightenment—engendering a commitment to republican ideals, a belief in reason and moderation, and a respect for the rights of others. Perhaps most important, he taught young Doniphan the techniques of effective public speaking. Keene pushed Doniphan to study the works of the great poets because of their use of language to move people. Keene told him that "Through knowledge of the poets could alone come the precise meaning of words, the perfect pronunciation of them, the melody of speech, and the majestic declamation of the orator."[6]

At age fourteen Doniphan enrolled in Augusta College, from which he graduated with distinction four years later. Although this educational experience also proved valuable, it did not make the lasting impression on Doniphan that had his tutelage under Keene. Only in the area of oratory did he remember any significant impact from his college years. Dr. Henry B. Bascom, a minister famed for his eloquence in the pulpit, taught Doniphan at Augusta both the power of rhetoric to sway audiences and the complexity of reasoning necessary to every jeremiad. These were lessons Doniphan never forgot, and he put them to masterful use throughout his legal career. In antebellum Missouri no one developed a greater reputation as a persuasive attorney. Doniphan's longtime friend, confidant, and business partner, D. C. Allen, expressed the opinion that

5. A. W. Doniphan to D. C. Allen, February 4, 1874, Doniphan Papers. The perceptions of white nineteenth-century America toward blacks has been analyzed in William Stanton, *The Leopard's Spots: Scientific Attitudes toward Race in America, 1815–1859*, and George M. Frederickson, *The Black Image in the White Mind*.
6. Doniphan to Allen, "Sketch of Life," 2, Doniphan Papers.

Doniphan was "eloquent beyond description, and without doubt entitled to be classed among the greatest orators that ever lived."[7]

Following graduation from Augusta College at age eighteen, Doniphan took six months off and leisurely studied ancient and modern English literature before continuing his formal studies. In 1827 he began reading law in the office of Martin P. Marshall, the brother of Supreme Court Justice John C. Marshall. D. C. Allen recalled that Marshall

> required his pupil to read and carefully study portions of the clas-
> sical authors of the English language. . . . It was, as Mr. Marshall
> phrased it, to fructify and chasten the pupil's imagination and give
> him wings for more arduous flights. Secondly, he required him to
> read the histories of England and America and cognate works, so
> that he might see, historically, the evolution of our system of law.
> And, thirdly, he required of him a most careful study of those text-
> books of the law which were then considered necessary in order
> to gain admission to practice.[8]

After two years of apprenticeship, in 1829 Doniphan joined the bar in Kentucky. He then crossed the Ohio River and petitioned the Ohio Supreme Court for admission to the bar in that state as well. He was not yet twenty-one years old.

The newly minted attorney was an imposing figure. Tall, muscular, and powerful looking, Doniphan stood six feet, four inches tall. When he stood rock-ribbed and fully erect Doniphan towered over most other people. A shock of thick auburn hair covered his head and until it finally turned gray in the 1860s many observers commented on it as a striking feature of the lawyer. Doniphan also had the charisma to command everyone in a room without their resentment. D. C. Allen described him as "well proportioned, altogether dignified in appearance, and gentle in his manners . . . his bright hazel eye[s] discerning, keen and expressive." Doniphan never balded. While he was clean shaven early on, from the 1850s he wore a beard, which was especially fashionable during the Civil War era, and then later a goatee. Doniphan also wore his hair long; daguerreotypes sometimes show it riding his collar with locks combed back from his forehead.[9]

Indicative of Doniphan's presence, while attending the Washington Peace Conference in February 1861, a last-ditch effort to mitigate the secession of the slave South, Doniphan met president-elect Abraham Lincoln. Lincoln apparently was quite impressed with Doniphan who

---

7. D. C. Allen, "Colonel Alexander W. Doniphan—His Life and Character," in William Elsey Connelley, ed., *Doniphan's Expedition, and the Conquest of New Mexico and California,* 18.

8. Ibid., 21.

9. Ibid., 27.

was by then a legendary frontier lawyer and Mexican-American War commander. "And this is Colonel Doniphan who made the wild march against the Navajos and Mexicans," Lincoln remarked. "You are the only man I ever met," he added, "who in appearance came up to my previous expectation."[10]

The young lawyer cut a dashing figure on the frontier. His impressive bearing, powerful physique, handsome features, and dynamic character made him especially attractive to women, with whom he very much enjoyed socializing. He wrote to a friend in St. Charles, Missouri, about their mutual interest in one young woman in June 1836. John Chauncey had asked Doniphan to speak with her on his behalf and ascertain if she might be interested in developing a relationship. Chauncey asked Doniphan to help because he was more experienced in "the habit of whispering soft things in the ears of the fair ones." Despite accepting Chauncey's compliment, Doniphan corrected his friend's expectations. "I have never yet bowed at the shrine of beauty & lov[e]liness or appealed to so *fair* a tribunal," adding that since recovering from illness "I have not spent even one delicious moment in the company" of women. He told Chauncey that "as I have been acting as attorney for others during some years I shall in that capacity attend to this delicate affair with fidelity & with all the powers of persuasion that I can master."[11]

After his admittance to the bar, Doniphan went on an extended trip through the south central states before setting up his practice. During this period he decided to go to Missouri. In this decision, Doniphan was undoubtedly motivated by several factors. First, he was probably influenced by the experiences of his father, who went to the frontier and took advantage of opportunities for fame and fortune present there. Second, Doniphan may have been influenced by the example of General Andrew S. Hughes, an idol of Doniphan's since he first met him in 1824, who had moved to western Missouri to become an Indian agent in the Platte country.[12]

Finally, and this may have been the driving reason, Doniphan felt drawn to the Missouri frontier because of the opportunity awaiting a determined, ambitious young American. And there is no doubt about Doniphan's ambition. He saw waves of people moving westward across the United States, part of the "Greater Virginia migration stream," and those migrants from the Upper South found the "rough unglaciated hill country of the Ohio Valley and Missouri entirely familiar in kind,

10. Ibid., 39.

11. A. W. Doniphan to Capt. John Chauncey, June 11, 1836, Harold B. Lee Library, Special Collections, Brigham Young University, Provo, Utah.

12. Francis Frazee Hamilton, *Ancestral Lines of the Doniphan, Frazee, and Hamilton Families*, n.p.; Doniphan to Allen, "Sketch of Life," 2–3, Doniphan Papers; Doniphan, *Address*, 11–12.

and they readily worked their way into the coves and recesses of the Ozarks." Marked by the removal of the Indians to the west of Missouri, the full impact of the transportation revolution, and the emergence of market economies, Doniphan recognized that this young state offered tremendous opportunity. Most immigrants were attracted by the prospect of abundant land at minuscule prices. Missouri had such land, good land along the Missouri River snaking westward across the middle of the state, and, since the area was a slave state, southerners especially felt attraction to it. Most settlers in the area came from other slave states, especially Kentucky and Tennessee, and they would require legal services.[13]

Doniphan arrived in St. Louis in March 1830 ready to make the state his own. The move proved a boon to his career. During the decades between 1830 and 1860 the state's population grew nearly tenfold, from 140,455 in 1830 to 1,182,012 in 1860. Most inhabitants in 1830 lived along the eastern border near the Mississippi River, or in isolated pockets along the Missouri River in the center part of the state. That changed during the next thirty years as the state became more settled. After an April 19, 1830, appearance before the Missouri Supreme Court at Fayette for a license to practice law, Doniphan first went to Lexington, located on the south side of the Missouri River in the central western part of the state. One of its more populous communities with nearly two thousand residents, Lexington was the seat of Lafayette County and a logical place for an attorney to set up shop. It was also a growing commercial center, a transshipment point for merchandise, mules, wagons, and other goods destined for the Santa Fe trade.[14]

At that time Lexington was also a logical base for traveling around the Missouri Fifth Judicial Circuit. This circuit extended along both sides of the Missouri River to the western boundary of the state, an area of more than twenty-five hundred square miles. Doniphan spent many days every month on the circuit with representatives of the court trying whatever cases brought to it as it passed from town to town. The courts often convened in crude surroundings, usually a tavern or a small log courthouse.[15]

In an 1872 address Doniphan reflected on a typical day of travel on this judicial circuit:

> Nearing the close of a weary day's travel on horseback, nothing was more cheering than the sight of the curling smoke of

13. D. W. Meinig, *The Shaping of America: A Geographical Perspective on 500 Years of History*, Vol. 2, *Continental America, 1800–1867*, 229.

14. Doniphan to Allen, "Sketch of Life," 3, Doniphan Papers; William Young, *Young's History of Lafayette County, Missouri*, 1:310; R. Douglas Hurt, "Planters and Slavery in Little Dixie."

15. Doniphan to Allen, "Sketch of Life," 2–3, Doniphan Papers; Doniphan, *Address*, 11–12.

a cabin, with no fear of refusal—even to a stranger. Alighting, most probably the sturdy host was preparing his gun, ramrod and ammunition for the morrow's hunt. The bright, cheery housewife, in home-spun dress, often of the inevitable Tennessee stripe, would be busily engaged in preparing the evening meal for the returned hunter. Often have I met with the accident of a dinner as the juicy venison ribs were roasting before a bright, wood fire in the ample fire place. . . . If the host was from Tennessee—as was often the case—he would easily glide into a social chat by asking about General Jackson. . . . We were not then a nation of readers; few journals reached the country;—hence the inquiries. It would have been unkind not to have gratified their patriotic anxiety, and I never failed to do so, either from my own limited store of reliable information, or more frequently, from the ample stores of youthful imagination. The rule was: horse well cared for, comfortable night, smoking breakfast, and nothing ever to pay. Indeed, the most delicate diplomacy was required in making the offer so as to avoid giving offense to your generous entertainer. For twenty years after my arrival, I do not remember paying a bill at a farm house.[16]

The next day, Doniphan went wherever the court gathered, performed his duties, then traveled to the next location when that session concluded.

Although the travel was grueling and the surroundings casual, Judge David Todd presided over the Fifth Judicial Circuit Court with a formal bearing, and demanded the same formality of the attorneys participating in its proceedings. Some of these early lawyers included Abiel Leonard, Robert W. Wells, David R. Atchison, and Thomas C. Reynolds. These colleagues all became significant political figures in Missouri and Doniphan developed close ties to each of them. Doniphan accepted the role of the young, inexperienced, and deferential attorney while traveling on this circuit in 1830. In most instances, and in all situations where the case was serious, he assumed a secondary position by helping the senior attorneys on the circuit. In these instances he prepared background materials, took depositions, and prepared briefs for the trial lawyers who carried the brunt of the work in the courtroom. When he handled a case by himself, most likely it was some civil suit over lost hogs, failed payments of promissory notes, or legal claims to land or other property. In the process he lived a meager lifestyle since fees from secondary cases and as an assistant were never great. At least the lifestyle befitted the type of work Doniphan usually did on the frontier circuit.[17]

Doniphan's first break on the judicial circuit came when Abiel Leonard asked him to assist with a murder case. Doniphan at first refrained from

16. Doniphan, *Address*, 5.
17. Doniphan to Allen, "Sketch of Life," 2–3, Doniphan Papers; Doniphan, *Address*, 11–12.

participating, and only after Leonard assured him that he was ready for it did he agree to help. While the details of this case are unknown, those who witnessed the case said that the young lawyer's "conduct in this trial was modest, and gave evidence of the dawning of the reputation as a criminal lawyer which he afterward attained." Doniphan learned much about his craft from this murder trial, and he soon developed an excellent record as a defense attorney on capital cases. He wrote in later years that this case was memorable because he made his "first speech in defence of a criminal charged with murder he had ever heard, never having witnessed a trial for murder before."[18]

For three years Doniphan worked out of Lexington, having an office on the courthouse square, but spending much of his time on the circuit working for whatever he could get from his clients. He recalled in 1872 that he "regularly attended the courts in ten counties. The formation of new counties often changed the courts, (but not their number,) in which I practiced." More often than not, however, during those early years he received barter rather than cash for his services. In this way he built a modest legal practice, became familiar with Missouri law and culture, and earned a reputation as a solid and ambitious attorney. But he could not break into the upper echelon of lawyers working in the western part of the state.

Farther up the river, near the Indian territory, land claims and all manner of other civil court actions were being argued, but mostly by lawyers other than himself. For instance, another young Kentuckian named David Rice Atchison, who later became one of Doniphan's closest personal friends and staunchest political rivals, first practiced before the court in Liberty, Clay County, during the August 1830 term. Although about the same age as Doniphan, with a similar background and capabilities and catering to the same clientele, Atchison dealt with many more cases than Doniphan and received greater remuneration for his work. The major difference between the two (or so it seemed) was that Atchison had settled in Liberty in 1830 and was therefore better known by the citizens than the itinerant Doniphan who only visited Liberty during the sessions of the court.[19]

Doniphan clearly wanted a greater share of the legal work available. He had been willing to show deference for a time to the older and more established attorneys on the Fifth Judicial Circuit, but after three years he believed he had paid his dues and deserved greater opportunities. As a

18. *History of Clinton County, Missouri,* 450; Doniphan to Allen, "Sketch of Life," 4, Doniphan Papers; James Williams, *Seventy-five Years on the Border,* 30–31, 130–31; Doniphan to Emma Doniphan, [no day and month] 1875, Doniphan Papers; Henry Clay McDougal, *Recollections, 1844–1909,* 37; *Liberty Weekly Tribune,* February 20, 1847.

19. Doniphan, *Address,* 5–6; William E. Parrish, *David Rice Atchison of Missouri: Border Politician,* 6–7.

result, in May 1833 Doniphan packed up his belongings and moved to Liberty. There he joined an elite cadre of attorneys, including Atchison, who were already practicing law on the state's western border. For the next thirty years Doniphan made Liberty his home, and his economic and political fortunes became inextricably tied to it.[20]

When the twenty-five-year-old Doniphan arrived in Liberty it was still a small town in its infancy, but everyone recognized it as well positioned to become a major outpost on the western frontier. The seat of Clay County, created in 1830 just to the north of the Missouri River, the county abutted the Platte country reserved for the Sauk and Fox and Iowa Indian tribes just to the west. In 1830 Clay County had a population of 5,338, of which only about 300 resided in Liberty, but the town was growing rapidly and its influence beyond the county was significant. For one thing, Liberty served as the shopping site of choice for the families of nearby Fort Leavenworth, established about thirty miles to the west in 1827 in Kansas. The officers and their families often visited Liberty and participated in its public gatherings and parties. Like Lexington had been earlier, the western Missouri towns of Liberty, Independence, and St. Joseph became during the 1830s rapidly expanding commercial centers and transhipment points for goods destined for the frontier. That growth, coupled with the prospect of opening even more territory to the west—especially the Platte country—made Liberty inviting to Doniphan. Doniphan admitted late in life that especially the attraction of an "early annexation of the Platte Country to the state and growth of Jackson [County] induced him in May 1833 to remove to Liberty."[21]

Most of the people living in Clay County, like Doniphan, were from the South, especially Kentucky, Tennessee, Virginia, North Carolina, and Maryland. Although he may have been much better educated and more refined than most of the people on that frontier, Doniphan found that he had a great affinity for them. He understood, appreciated, and accepted the culture and institutions that they had transplanted from the older South. This included several ingredients, but the most outwardly apparent was chattel slavery. Missouri had been admitted to the Union in 1821 with slavery intact after a bitter political struggle and compromise. Despite the acrimony of this fight in Washington, only a handful of people in Missouri in the antebellum era questioned either the legality or the morality of the institution.[22]

20. Doniphan to Allen, "Sketch of Life," 3, Doniphan Papers; Doniphan, *Address,* 1–3; Shortridge, "Expansion of the Settlement Frontier," 74–78.

21. Doniphan, *Address,* 1–3, 24; Judge Joseph Thorp, *Early Days in the West: Along the Missouri One Hundred Years Ago,* 60–64; Eugene T. Wells, "The Growth of Independence, Missouri, 1827–1850"; Doniphan to Allen, "Sketch of Life," 5, Doniphan Papers.

22. The standard work on the Missouri Compromise is Glover Moore, *The Missouri Controversy, 1819–1821.*

Certainly very few in Clay County did so. Slaveholding generally followed the river systems in the state, and by far its largest concentration was along the Missouri River from Callaway County westward to Clay County. The rich bottomlands surrounding the rivers provided an excellent environment for plantation-style agriculture where hemp for rope and tobacco became profitable crops. Slaves made up almost 15 percent of the state's population in the 1830s, but they accounted for something over 30 percent in Clay County. Most of the large slaveholders, however, were not the type of large planters seen in the deep South; there most owned fewer than ten slaves and worked together with them on their land. Indeed, the majority of Missourians owned fewer than five slaves. After he became successful in the practice of law in the 1840s Doniphan was in this category, owning a small number of slaves throughout the antebellum period, apparently either hiring them out or using them for domestic work. As early as 1840 he owned three slaves, and the number rose to five by 1860. Doniphan was also an eloquent spokesman for slavery as a social and economic institution. While serving in the state legislature between 1836 and 1838, for example, he actively upheld the rights of slaveholders to their property as opposed to other issues at stake like free speech and human rights.[23]

Other aspects of southern culture also appealed to Doniphan. For example, he was an avid sportsman and enjoyed hunting and fishing in the Missouri forests and streams. He and Atchison went hunting together on occasion, Doniphan commenting in later years that Atchison was especially "fond of hunting, and very successful as a hunter." They might have been more successful attorneys, he recalled, had they stayed in their offices more and out in the woods or at parties or in political caucuses less.[24] Doniphan also enjoyed card games and just about any form of gambling, horse racing, and evenings sitting in taverns with friends. On one occasion in February 1834, Doniphan and Atchison were enjoying a game of cards called "Bragg" when the sheriff came in and caught them in the act of betting "a large sum of money," twenty-five cents. Since gambling was technically illegal, the sheriff arrested them and brought them to trial in what could only have been seen as a huge joke. The local judge, a friend and fellow lawyer named Amos Rees, fined Doniphan and Atchison each $5.25 for their lawbreaking.[25]

23. Doniphan to Allen, "Sketch of Life," 4–6, Doniphan Papers; Doniphan, *Address*, 1–8. Clay County, Mo., Population Schedules for the Sixth Federal Census, 1840, 22; and Clay County, Mo., Slave Schedules for the Eighth Federal Census, 1860, 30, both in National Archives, microfilm located in the Missouri State Archives, Jefferson City, Mo. *Journal of the House of Representatives of the State of Missouri at the First Session of the Ninth General Assembly, November 29, 1836*, 383; Gordon E. Finnie, "The Antislavery Movement in the Upper South before 1840," 336.

24. *History of Clinton County*, 441–42.

25. "Record Book 2," February 1, 1834, 126, Circuit Court, Clay County Courthouse, Liberty, Mo.; Connelley, ed., *Doniphan's Expedition*, 370.

Another aspect of southern society that Doniphan especially enjoyed involved service in the militia. In the early 1830s, David Atchison had formed a militia company known as the Liberty Blues. He was its commander, holding the rank of captain, and Doniphan served in it first as an enlistee and later as an officer. The volunteer company mustered for drill three times a year, and every time it was a celebration. The members would gather in Liberty with their families, march around in the sun for a while, and then have a picnic with food and not a little drink. Doniphan remained a part of some militia force in Missouri for the next twenty years.[26]

Only occasionally did this militia force have to take the field for operations. One such instance took place in June 1836 when the Clay County militia mobilized for the "Heatherly war." This began when Brigadier General Henry Atkinson, U.S. Army commander at Jefferson Barracks near St. Louis, heard that two white men had been murdered by renegade Indians on the Grand River in northwestern Missouri. He directed Lieutenant Colonel Stephen Watts Kearny, commanding the First Regiment of Dragoons at Fort Leavenworth, to investigate the incident. Missouri governor Daniel Dunklin also learned of the murders and called out a force of two hundred militia to track down the Indians. The militia marched along the border of the Platte country in search of hostile Indians, although they failed to find any.[27]

Kearny had more success, discovering that the killings had taken place after a group of outlaws called the "Heatherly gang," named for three brothers who formed its nucleus, had tried to sell whiskey to an Ioway Indian hunting party in the Platte country. When they refused to buy, the gang stole the Indians' horses while they slept. The Indians tracked the horses into Missouri and in the ensuing fight three whites died. The Indians involved in the controversy surrendered to Kearny, but he released them after promises to appear in court. Kearny tried to calm the local population in western Missouri, explaining that the Indians had been blameless in the incident. Far from hostile, he said, the Indians acted only to recover their property from a bunch of outlaws.[28]

Doniphan's role in the Heatherly war was quite small. Although a private in the militia, because of his education and training he served

26. Thorp, *Early Days in the West*, 65–66; *Missouri Intelligencer and Boon's Lick Advertiser*, March 8, 1834; Settle, *Alexander William Doniphan*, 7. On southern society and the martial spirit, see Bertram Wyatt-Brown, *Southern Honor: Ethics and Behavior in the Old South.*

27. The story of the Heatherly war, along with reproduced documents from the War Department, can be found in Willis B. Hughes, "The Heatherly Incident of 1836." On the Heatherly gang, see "The Heatherly Family of Missouri."

28. Hughes, "Heatherly Incident of 1836," 164. Stephen Watts Kearny to Henry Atkinson, July 21, 1836, and Matthew Duncan to Stephen Watts Kearny, July 21, 1836, both in Steven Watts Kearny Letters, War Records, Adjutant General's Office, Letters Received (213 Atkinson 1836), RG 94, National Archives.

as an aide to Colonel Samuel C. Allen. He recorded his experience nearly forty years later:

> In June or July 1836 the Heatherly war commenced & terminated in 18 days for the boys from Clay. In what was then Carrol[l] County & now is Grundy or Mercer perhaps near the line of G & M. There were sparsely settled districts of rough pioneers—of whom perhaps the most degraded was a family named Heatherly— . . . The old woman was the moving spirit—a she fiend—smart, . . . & veng[e]ful & near the motive power of the whole family. In June of 1836 a part of the Iowa tribes of Indians then living not far from St. Joseph (before the addition of the Platte Country to the State) made a friendly excursion along the line between Iowa . . . & Mo as far East as to be about north of the Heatherly settlement. The Heatherly's father, mother, sons & son-in-law availing themselves of the alarms that usually proceed from incursions even of friendly Indians into or near scattered & unprotected settlements—raised a false alarm as to the vicinity & war like purposes of these Indians & during the excitement that (the H's) murdered Dunbar & another man with whom they had some difficulty & also for the purpose of stealing from them—and then fled into the nearest settlement raising the hue and cry that the Iowas were killing, scalping & robbing their settlement & they were flying for life.
>
> Brig. Gen. Thompson then of Ray ordered out one Co from Carroll & 2 from Ray & Clay each. . . . The County of Clay sent two companies one commanded by Capt. D.R. Atchison & one by Capt. Smith Crawford & Coln S. Allen commanded the battalion in person. They were ordered by Genl Thompson to march due north near the West boundary of the State to the north boundary of Mo . . . & so home again—either from facts ascertained by Genl Thompson or very soon after (but I think the former) the whole Heatherly gang was arrested & indicted in Carroll County for murder—some of them were sent to the Penitentiary—I do not think any were hanged. They were kept in jail perhaps a year or more—I went to see them at their request once in jail & of all my experiences in criminal cases I never met any thing approximating this gang of Gipsies, half breeds and full blooded murderers & thieves & the old woman impressed me as the most perfect Hecate [a mythological sorceress or witch] that this continent ever gave birth to.[29]

It was an incident that veterans of the group remembered for years and recalled at every reunion.

After coming to Liberty in 1833, Doniphan shared law offices with David Atchison and at least one other attorney, probably Amos Rees,

---

29. Doniphan to Allen, February 4, 1874, Doniphan Papers. Doniphan also told a similar story about the war in an affidavit prepared on October 2, 1858, and he recorded the daily events of the conflict in a campaign diary (Hughes, "Heatherly Incident of 1836," 176–78).

on the square in the center of town. Atchison, only a year older than Doniphan, was a little like a big brother during those early years in Liberty. Highly successful in his career, he shunted work to Doniphan whenever possible. Later, when Doniphan's practice had taken off and he no longer needed Atchison's assistance, he still conferred with him on points of law "more frequently than I did anyone else." Doniphan said of his associate that he "had a clear logical mind; had studied law well, and kept up with his profession by constant reading, when he was not engaged actively out of doors. . . . the position he took in any case he sustained with ability, and when he was on the right side he rarely failed of success."[30]

Just about the same might have been said of Doniphan. By the latter part of 1833 he had established himself as a young lawyer of promise in western Missouri. Doniphan still did not have many clients and lived a simple existence, but his determination to succeed sustained him. Doniphan's reputation as an attorney would be made, like so many other lawyers, by taking a high-profile case and performing in the spotlight of public attention. That opportunity proved golden for Doniphan, and it came to him in the form of a disliked little religious group in nearby Jackson County expelled from their homes in the fall of 1833. For the next six years Doniphan's career intertwined with that the Church of Jesus Christ of Latter Day Saints, the Mormons.

The first Mormons had settled in the Blue River section near present-day Kansas City in the summer of 1831. Joseph Smith Jr., the Mormon prophet, sent large numbers of church members into Jackson County where they believed they would help usher in the triumphal Second Coming of Christ and the advent of the millennial reign by building a community from which Christ could rule the world. The largest Mormon group was concentrated along the Brush Creek valley of the Blue River, but a cadre of Mormons also settled around Independence, where they opened several businesses. This Mormon community grew rapidly during the next two years, numbering more than twelve hundred by the summer of 1833. Their growing numbers ensured that they would have political and economic power, and that troubled many early Jackson Countians.[31]

Josiah Gregg, an Independence-based Santa Fe trader, sounded the ominous note of many non-Mormons when he opined that at the rate the

---

30. *History of Clinton County*, 441–42.
31. The most important work on this subject remains Warren A. Jennings's dissertation, "Zion Is Fled: The Expulsion of the Mormons from Jackson County, Missouri"; from which he published "The Expulsion of the Mormons from Jackson County, Missouri," and "The City in the Garden: Social Conflict in Jackson County, Missouri," in F. Mark McKiernan, Alma R. Blair, and Paul M. Edwards, eds., *The Restoration Movement: Essays in Mormon History*, 99–119.

Saints immigrated into the county, "they would soon be able to command a majority in the county, and consequently the entire control of affairs would fall into their hands." This prospect petrified Jackson Countians and a few decided to do something about it. This resulted in a violent expulsion of the Mormons from Jackson County in the fall of 1833, and Doniphan signed on as attorney for the embattled religious sect.[32]

Doniphan knew little about the Mormons at first, but he came to loathe their anti-democratic tendencies within a relatively short period. At the same time, Doniphan cherished the principles of the American Constitution and defended Mormon rights to life, liberty, and property. Pledged to give representation even to those guilty, Doniphan also thought that the Mormons had suffered illegal and immoral actions.

Doniphan sought justice for a persecuted minority, but he never endorsed the Mormon defense of being persecuted solely because of their religion. Instead, he recognized that they embodied a religious ideal that was at odds with the American republic. He agreed that violence aimed at the Mormons could not be tolerated in a republic of law and enlightenment. The Saints, he believed, had a right to live peaceably. Any crimes against the Saints had to be redressed, and Doniphan not only thought he was the man who could do it, but he also believed he could build himself a reputation as a great lawyer in the process.[33]

After the Mormons began to experience violence in Jackson County, the sect's leaders petitioned Missouri Governor Daniel Dunklin to redress their grievances. While the governor recognized the great wrongs perpetrated on the Mormons, he expressed concern about how to correct it. According to Mormon leader Newel K. Knight, the governor "stated that he desired to maintain law and order in the state, and was willing to do anything in his power to assist in the protection of the Saints."[34]

Daniel Dunklin had gained the governorship in 1832 on the Democratic ticket. As a competent politician who understood his state's political characteristics, he tried to deal with the Mormon crisis without alienating his political base. As he wrote in August 1834, "I have no regard for the Mormons, as a separate people; & have an utter contempt for them as a religious sect; while on the other hand I have much regard for the people of Jackson County, both personally and politically; they are, many of them, my personal friends, and nearly all of them are very staunch Democrats." Dunklin did, however, have a strong sense of responsibility and closed his

32. Josiah Gregg, *The Commerce of the Prairies*, 165.
33. On the sources of conflict between the Mormons and other Americans, see Kenneth H. Winn, *Exiles in a Land of Liberty: The Mormons in America, 1830–1846*, 85–100; and Marvin S. Hill, *Quest for Refuge: The Mormon Flight from American Pluralism*, 69–98. See also David Grimstead, "Rioting in Its Jacksonian Setting"; and Michael Feldberg, *The Turbulent Era: Riot and Disorder in Jacksonian America*.
34. Newel K. Knight, "Autobiography," 79.

letter by stating, "These are all secondary considerations when my *duties* are brought into question."[35]

A noncommittal answer came from Dunklin regarding help for the Mormons. He suggested that they carry their complaints to the courts, the proper place for settling difficulties between all citizens. He asked the Mormons on October 19, 1833, to "make a trial of the efficacy of the laws; the judge of your circuit is a conservator of the peace. If an affidavit is made before him by any of you, that your lives are threatened and you believe them in danger, it would be his duty to have the offenders apprehended and bind them to keep peace."[36]

The Latter Day Saints then prevailed upon four attorneys—Doniphan, David R. Atchison, Amos Rees, and William T. Wood—while attending the fall 1833 term of the Fifth Judicial Circuit Court in Independence to act on the Mormons' behalf. They responded on October 28, agreeing to accept the Mormons as clients, but with some unusual specifications. They asked that each receive $250 for handling the case, to be paid in advance. "We have been doing a practice here among these people, to a considerable extent," the lawyers wrote, "and by this engagement we must expect to lose the greatest part of it, which will be to all of us a considerable loss. . . ." For the $1,000 split among them the attorneys agreed to handle all of the Mormon complaints as a group. Doniphan and his associates apologized for the large fee they were charging, "but the circumstances here involved make it necessary" since they did not expect to have many other clients for some time afterward. "We prefer to bring your suits as we have been threatened by the mob," they wrote, "we wish to show them we disregard their empty bravadoes." Doniphan and company then threatened that if the Mormons did not accept their terms, they could "be engaged in the opposite side in all probability."[37] The next day, Mormon official Edward Partridge agreed to the four attorneys' terms, telling them he would pay them within six months after beginning work.[38]

Doniphan, Atchison, Rees, and Wood had no sooner begun work for the Mormons than the Jackson County situation took a turn for the worse.

35. Daniel Dunklin to Joel Haden, August 14, 1834, Daniel Dunklin Papers, Western Historical Manuscript Collection.

36. Daniel Dunklin to Edward Partridge et al., October 19, 1833, in Joseph Smith Jr., "History of Joseph Smith," *Times and Seasons* 6 (April 1, 1846): 880.

37. A. W. Doniphan to W. W. Phelps and LDS Leaders, October 28, 1833, W. W. Phelps, Collection of Missouri Documents, MS 657, Church of Jesus Christ of Latter-day Saints, Archives [LDS Archives], Salt Lake City, Utah. Joseph Smith Jr., *The History of the Church of Jesus Christ of Latter-day Saints,* 1:424–25, gives the date of this letter as October 30, 1833, but the original reads October 28, 1833.

38. Edward Partridge to Doniphan et al., October 29, 1833, W. W. Phelps, Collection of Missouri Documents, LDS Archives. Joseph Smith, while accepting the help of Doniphan and his colleagues, took the opportunity to chastise them for their pursuit of riches at the expense of the Mormons (Smith, *History of the Church,* 1:424).

Indeed, the decision to engage these lawyers, signaling that the Mormons intended to remain in Jackson County and to prosecute anti-Mormons, probably helped to spark violence. In late October 1833 anti-Mormons in the county demanded that the Latter Day Saints leave Jackson County immediately. Knight wrote:

> From the 31st of October until the 4th of November [1833], there was one continual scene of outrages of the most hideous kind. The mob collected in different parts of the county and attacked the Saints in most of their settlements, houses were unroofed, others were pulled down, leaving women and children, and even the sick and the dying exposed to the inclemency of the weather. Men were caught and whipped or clubbed until they were bruised from head to foot, and some were left upon the ground for dead. The most horrid threats and imprecations were uttered against us, and women and children were told, with cursings, that unless they left the country immediately they should be killed.[39]

Never pacifistic, the Mormons vowed to fight back. And they did on November 4 when the Saints and the Missourians fought a ruinous skirmish on the eastern side of the Blue River. One Mormon and two Missourians died in the fighting and several received injuries.[40]

Because of this battle Missouri militia Lieutenant Colonel Thomas Pitcher, also a respected Independence business leader, went with troops on November 5, 1833, to the main Mormon settlements and forced the Mormons to give up their arms. Within a short time twelve hundred Mormons began leaving the county, now having no way to protect themselves. Most went to Clay County, across the Missouri River to the north, but some also settled in nearby Ray, Lafayette, and Van Buren Counties.[41]

Doniphan and the other three lawyers provided three types of assistance to the Mormons, all typical of the services routinely furnished by attorneys both then and now. First, they served as mediators carrying messages between the Mormons and the state executive branch. Many of the communications between Governor Dunklin and the Mormon leaders passed through the hands of one of the four lawyers. The fact that they were all politically connected within the state, especially Atchison and

39. Newel Knight, "Autobiography," 80.
40. John P. Greene, *Facts Relative to the Expulsion of the Mormons or Latter-day Saints, from the State of Missouri, Under the "Exterminating Order"*, 11; "History of Persecution," *Times and Seasons* 1 (January 1840): 33–34; "From Missouri," *Evening and Morning Star* 2 (January 1834): 125; F. Mark McKiernan and Roger D. Launius, eds., *An Early Latter Day Saint History: The Book of John Whitmer*, 94; *Jeffersonian Republican*, December 21, 1833.
41. *Missouri Intelligencer and Boon's Lick Advertiser*, December 14, 1833, December 16, 1833; *Missouri Republican*, November 22, 1833, December 6, 1833, December 20, 1833; John Corrill, *A Brief History of the Church of Jesus Christ of Latter Day Saints (Commonly Called Mormons, Including an Account of their Doctrine and Discipline, with the Reasons of the Author for Leaving the Church)*, 19–20.

Wells, helped to ensure that the religious group received a hearing in the executive branch. Second, at the same time, they served as a liaison between the Mormons and the Jackson Countians, working on a settlement agreeable to all parties. Finally, the most substantive service they provided involved prosecuting cases against the Jackson Countians who had done violence to the sect.

In acting as the Mormons' legal counsel, Doniphan and his colleagues operated within a narrow set of parameters established by the church. The most important constraint was the Saints' refusal to abandon their property in Jackson County because of its religious significance, even if fully reimbursed. Joseph Smith told the membership that God would punish those who sold their property. The Mormon leadership told Doniphan and his associates to "use every lawful means" to secure reinstatement of the Saints back on their property in Jackson County.[42]

The clearest explanation of Mormon demands for settlement of the crisis was stated in a letter to the governor on December 6, 1833, that Doniphan and his colleagues helped to draft. It said:

> in behalf of our society, which is so scattered and suffering, we, your petitioners, ask aid and assistance of your Excellency, that we may be restored to our lands, houses, and property, and protected in them by the militia of the state, if legal, or by a detachment of the United States Rangers, which might be located at Independence, instead of at Cantonment Leavenworth, till peace can be restored. This could be done, probably, by conferring with the President, or perhaps with Colonel Dodge. Also, we ask that our men may be organized into companies of Jackson Guards, and be furnished with arms by the state, to assist in maintaining their rights against the unhallowed power of the mob of Jackson county.
>
> And then, when arrangements are made to protect us in our persons and property (which cannot be done without an armed force, nor would it be prudent to risk our lives there without guards, till we receive strength from our friends to protect ourselves), we wish a court of inquiry instituted, to investigate the whole matter of the mob against the "Mormons" . . .[43]

As a result of these requirements the Mormons placed Doniphan, Atchison, Rees, and Wood in a very tight box that demanded achievement of nothing less than complete victory on every point. Under normal circumstances, attorneys might have worked out an agreement for the Jackson Countians to purchase the Mormon property and improvements from them, but the restrictions imposed by the Mormons ensured that no compromise resulted.

---

42. Joseph Smith to Edward Partridge, December 5, 1833, quoted in Smith, "History," *Times and Seasons* 6 (June 1, 1845): 912–14.

43. W. W. Phelps et al., to Daniel Dunklin, December 6, 1833, quoted in ibid., 915.

Doniphan and Atchison, the principal attorneys working on the case, opened negotiations with the Missouri Attorney General, Robert W. Wells, in the latter part of November 1833. Wells gave Doniphan reason to believe that the state would support restoration of their property, the principal demand the Mormons made. He told Doniphan in a November 21 letter that "if they decide to be replaced in their property, that is, their houses in Jackson county, an adequate force will be sent forthwith to effect that object."[44] This proved an unfortunate letter, for Wells did not speak for the governor and made it sound like the state would send troops into Jackson County to reinstate the Mormons on their land. That does not seem to have really been a possibility.

More successful were the efforts to discover what had happened in Jackson County and to fix responsibility. Governor Dunklin directed John F. Ryland of Lexington, judge for the Fifth Circuit Court, to conduct an investigation of the late unpleasantness. On November 24 he contacted Doniphan and his associates to see if their clients would press charges. If so, Ryland outlined a plan for the case's adjudication. He indicated a willingness to convene a court in Jackson County at any time, and wanted to move promptly to limit poor public relations for the state. Ryland specifically expressed his belief that it was "a disgrace to the state for such acts to happen within its limits."[45]

Amos Rees, the recipient of Ryland's letter, immediately contacted Doniphan, and they met with Robert Wells about the possibility of a court in Jackson County. Between the state, the lawyers, and the Mormons they agreed to postpone a case in the county until the situation cooled down a bit. The Mormon A. S. Gilbert summarized his church's position on this: "Some of our principal witnesses would be women and children, and while the rage of the mob continues, it would be impossible to gather them in safety at Independence."[46] As a result, they set a court date for the February 1834 term in Independence. Doniphan worked during the winter to find witnesses and prepare a case for presentation at the February term, but he ran into constant problems. Many Mormons feared returning to Jackson County, especially since the locals threatened violence. "It is my opinion from present appearances," A. S. Gilbert wrote to the governor just after the first of the year, "that not one fourth of the witnesses of our people, can be prevailed upon to go into Jackson county to testify."[47]

44. Robert W. Wells to A. W. Doniphan and David R. Atchison, November 21, 1833, W. W. Phelps, Collection of Missouri Documents, LDS Archives.

45. Daniel Dunklin to John F. Ryland, November 24, 1833, in Smith, "History," *Times and Seasons* 6 (June 1, 1845): 912.

46. A. S. Gilbert to Daniel Dunklin, November 29, 1833, quoted in ibid., 912–13.

47. A. S. Gilbert to Daniel Dunklin, January 9, 1834, quoted in Smith, "History" *Times and Seasons* 6 (July 15, 1845): 962–63; *Edward Partridge v Samuel D. Lucas et al.*,

Because of this, Dunklin provided a militia force to keep order. Despite the fact that military power would be required to ensure the conduct of judicial proceedings, Dunklin naively believed that the court could settle the affair. He told the Mormons that "Justice is sometimes slow in its progress, but is not less sure on that account." The Liberty Blues, a militia unit of fifty men commanded by Captain David Atchison, received the order to provide security at the Independence court proceedings, and that was a fortunate choice for Doniphan. Although Atchison had to recuse himself from the legal proceedings, his presence ensured more stability than if an unproven commander and unit had been present.[48]

The court convened on Monday morning, February 24, 1834, with Judge Ryland on the bench, but little more than a public demonstration of opposition to Mormon claims took place. The day before, Atchison's Liberty Blues had met the Mormon witnesses at Everett's Ferry on the banks of the Missouri and marched to within a mile of Independence where they camped in a woods for the night. "The night was passed off in warlike style," a Mormon witness, W. W. Phelps, wrote, "with the sentinels marching silently at a proper distance from the watch fires."[49] The next morning Atchison took the Mormon witnesses into Independence and sequestered them in the tavern of Samuel Flournoy, where they awaited the court. A mob assembled at the courthouse, however, and the state's representatives had to decide whether to proceed with the hearing despite the possibility of violence or to wait until the situation had been defused. Atchison apparently wanted to proceed, confident that his Liberty Blues could ensure order, but Ryland and Attorney General Robert Wells, who was present at the court as a representative of the governor, decided to postpone. About midmorning they visited the Mormon witnesses and told them, according to Newel Knight, "that all hope of a criminal prosecution was at an end. Thus were the officers of the civil law, even when supported by the military, awed by a mob, and the great promises of the governor and Judge Ryland fell to the ground, and the strong arm of justice became weak and fell powerless to her side."[50]

Doniphan and the other Mormon attorneys decided to file a continuance to bring the case before the court in the fall of 1834. Thereafter, Doniphan asked Atchison to escort the witnesses back to Clay County. They marched in quick time through Independence to the tune of "Yankee Doodle" to impress the crowd gathered to heckle the Mormons in their

---

"Amended Declaration to the Circuit Court of February Term, 1834, n.d., MS 629.1, LDS Archives.

48. *Missouri Intelligencer and Boon's Lick Advertiser,* March 8, 1834; Parrish, *David R. Atchison,* 10–11; Warren A. Jennings, "Importuning for Redress."

49. "Dear Brethren, February 27, 1834," *Evening and Morning Star* 2 (March 1834): 139.

50. Newel Knight, "Autobiography," 90.

quest for justice. Doniphan did not let the matter drop there. At the October 1834 term of court in Independence, he proceeded with a trespass case that Edward Partridge had filed for an assault committed in the summer of 1833. Ryland remained the circuit judge in charge of adjudicating the case and a persistently fair voice in the Mormon affair. Doniphan obtained a change of venue for the case from Jackson County to Ray County on May 26, 1835, from Ryland, since at no time were the settlers in the county willing to allow a judgment to go against citizens who had engaged in violence against the despised Mormons. The Mormons still sought legal damages in 1836, but by that time the matter had been largely forgotten and the only adjudication that actually came to settlement, though not in the Mormon favor, was a state supreme court case in 1839. Doniphan's efforts on behalf of the Mormons, although ultimately unsuccessful, proved sufficiently aggressive to satisfy his clients.[51]

In his capacity as Mormon legal counsel, Doniphan also participated in an attempt to resolve the Jackson County problem through mediation on June 16, 1834. At that time Zion's Camp, a paramilitary group of Mormons from Ohio and other parts of the East, entered Missouri with the intention of reinstalling the Saints on their Jackson County lands. Since legal efforts had failed to gain redress, the Mormons raised a force of about two hundred armed volunteers to march to Missouri. Zion's Camp would reinstate the Mormons of their land and protect them from further attack. Missourians thought it an army of invasion and it only exacerbated the conflict. Doniphan had his hands full negotiating some settlement when this force arrived and destabilized the tenuous situation in the summer of 1834.

In this desperate environment, Ryland brought both sides together in Liberty to negotiate a peaceful settlement. In so doing, Ryland responded to a mandate from Governor Dunklin, who desperately sought a compromise with which everyone could live. Dunklin let both sides know of his commitment to resolving the Jackson County controversy and expected both protagonists to support the efforts of his emissary, Judge Ryland. Ryland then contacted both the Mormons and the Jackson Countians and told them about a proposed meeting set for Monday, June 16, 1834, at the courthouse in Liberty. Ryland applied classic democratic principles to this crisis. He sought to sit both sides down to hammer out an agreement that all could accept, even if not enthusiastically; instead of having a winner and a loser, there would be two near winners. The pragmatic politician

51. Missouri Circuit Court (5th Circuit), Legal Proceedings of *Edward Partridge v Samuel D. Lucas et al.*, MS 899, LDS Archives; A. W. Doniphan to George Woodward, September 2, 1835, MS 11861, LDS Archives; State of Missouri, "Subpoena of Missouri Circuit Court for Samuel D. Lucas," November 3, 1835, MS 2966, LDS Archives; Missouri State Supreme Court Records, Missouri State Archives.

engages in such "trade-offs" every day, accepting half a loaf as better than none and probably intending to go back for more at a later time.

The Jackson Countians began preparing for this compromise attempt with a meeting on June 9 to elect a delegation. Samuel C. Owens, a prominent Independence businessman and political leader, served as its head. By the time of this planning meeting the Jackson Countians had been warned by the governor that they should support Ryland's compromise attempts, specifically "by purchasing the lands of the Mormons, and paying them for the injuries which they have sustained." The Jackson Countians apparently agreed to this compromise, in the process admitting that they had been wrong in their actions in 1833 and agreeing to make restitution.[52]

The Mormons, however, balked at this compromise. Ryland asked the Mormons to agree to sell their Jackson County lands at double the appraised value and to take the proceeds and move elsewhere. It was a generous offer, Ryland believed, one that everyone could agree to and then get back to a normal life. The Mormons, however, refused to sell their property in Jackson County. As the Mormon John Corrill wrote, it would be "like selling our children into slavery."[53]

By ruling out of hand any proposal that allowed the Jackson Countians to make a cash settlement, the Mormons ensured that their attorneys could not successfully close the case. The refusal to compromise, seen by the Mormons as a virtue, led them into repeated difficulties thereafter. Their belief that they had a lock on truth and innocence led to numerous nearly irreconcilable confrontations with the federal and state governments of the nation. This was only the first such instance, and it placed Doniphan in the unenviable position of having to settle a case in which the Mormons would accept nothing less than total victory. As a result they got nothing.

On June 16, 1834, nearly a thousand people gathered in Liberty from throughout Jackson and Clay Counties. They swarmed into the courthouse, filling the seats, standing in the aisles, and overflowing into the yard. A larger number of Mormons, in addition to those designated to represent the sect, were present, as was the committee from Jackson County. Judge Ryland came from his home in Richmond to observe but not to preside; Judge Joel T. Turnham of Clay County was chosen to moderate. Doniphan also appeared, seated in the back of the room. Ryland, as the initiator of the meeting, addressed the assembly on the necessity of bringing the conflict to a halt before one side or the other caused further bloodshed. According to the June 18 *Missouri Intelligencer*

52. *Daily National Intelligencer,* July 2, 1834; *Missouri Intelligencer and Boon's Lick Advertiser,* June 21, 1834.

53. John F. Ryland to A. S. Gilbert, June 10, 1834, and John Corrill to John F. Ryland, June 14, 1834, both in Smith, "History," *Times and Seasons* 6 (January 15, 1846): 1088–89.

and Boon's Lick Advertiser, "He informed the committees of the respective parties that it was not his province, as a high judicial official to dictate to them the terms upon which they should settle this subject; nevertheless . . . he advised them [of] the necessity of regarding the laws of the land." He also pointed out the consequences should the two groups fail to reach an understanding. Because of Zion's Camp, and its threat of possible violence, Ryland cautioned that the time for a peaceful solution could slip away and that both sides should employ their best efforts to preserve order in western Missouri.[54]

Despite these conciliatory words, it soon became obvious that neither the Mormons nor the Jackson Countians were much interested in compromise. Non-Mormon Joseph Thorp recalled, "Our friends from Jackson were very rabid." The Jackson Countians confirmed Thorp's assessment by interrupting the proceedings with rowdiness and threats of violence should Zion's Camp enter their county. During the commotion that ensued, the Reverend M. Riley, a Baptist minister in Clay County, stood and insisted that the Jackson Countians had been right in the first place and that the Mormons should also be expelled from Clay. This brought more noise, and few heard Judge Turnham call for order in the resulting pandemonium. "Let us be republican," he shouted, barely above the din, "let us honor our country and not disgrace it like Jackson County. For God's Sake don't disfranchise or drive away the Mormons. They are better citizens than many of the old inhabitants."[55]

Alexander William Doniphan, who had been sitting quietly during most of these proceedings, suddenly arose and walked with solemn resolution to the front of the courtroom, shoving his sleeves up and stretching to his full six-feet four-inch height as he went. In a booming voice he seconded the opinion of Turnham, advocating the rights of the Saints and opposing "Judge Lynch and mob violence." "The Mormons have armed themselves," he said, "and if they don't fight they are cowards. I love to hear that they have brethren coming to their assistance, greater love can no man show, than he, who lays down his life for his brethren." Doniphan's speech quieted the uproar for only a short time, however. By late afternoon little had been accomplished and the meeting adjourned in disorder. The attempt at reconciling the differences between the Mormons and the Jackson residents had failed. Zion's Camp disbanded soon after, when its ranks thinned in an outbreak of cholera.[56]

54. *Missouri Intelligencer and Boon's Lick Advertiser,* June 18, 1834; Walter B. Stevens, *Centennial History of Missouri (The Center State): One Hundred Years in the Union, 1820–1921,* 2:106; Newel Knight, "Autobiography," 91.

55. Thorp, *Early Days in the West,* 78; Wilford Woodruff, Journal, July 8, 1834, LDS Archives; *Daily National Intelligencer,* July 9, 1834.

56. Thorp, *Early Days in the West,* 78; Smith, "History," *Times and Seasons* 6 (January 15, 1846): 1090; Roger D. Launius, *Zion's Camp: Expedition to Missouri, 1834,* 144–65.

In the end Doniphan could not assist the Mormons in their case against the Jackson Countians. His efforts proved sufficiently aggressive, however, that the Mormons—a notoriously difficult group to please—appreciated him. Indicative of this, Joseph Smith asked Doniphan to represent him and other Mormon leaders in the aftermath of the Mormon war in western Missouri in 1838.

Doniphan's representation of the Mormons did not seem to hurt his practice of the law, as he thought would happen when he accepted the case. Although difficult to quantify, there seems to have been a general sympathy for the plight of the Mormons at the hands of the Jackson Countians virtually everywhere outside that county. As a result, Doniphan garnered a reputation as a champion of liberty, a defender of cherished rights guaranteed by the Constitution, and a promoter of democratic virtues. Demand for his services rose after this case.[57]

That the case served as a springboard for obtaining additional clients was most important for Doniphan. Like modern attorneys making a name for themselves by taking a high-profile case, even if they have neither much prospect of gaining compensation for their work nor of winning, Doniphan's career benefited from the notoriety the Mormon case provided. Doniphan became a household name both in western Missouri and in Jefferson City. His first really big case won him the public's attention and remade him into a famous attorney known for upholding justice.

57. This is a difficult point to substantiate, but it appears to be the case judging from the many negative comments about nonmembers contained in the official *History of the Church*. If a nonmember befriended the Saints it was never enough help, and even if there was a record of support for the Mormons, but one instance in which they supported the other side, the person was condemned without qualification. This was especially true of political leaders who tried to deal with the Mormons as even-handedly as possible, giving a little and expecting a little in return.

2

Emergence of a Public Figure

IN THE FALL of 1834 difficulties with the Mormons subsided in western Missouri. Alexander William Doniphan continued as their legal counsel, but as their demands gradually diminished, he concentrated on other matters. Between 1834 and 1838 Doniphan burst onto the Missouri public scene and became a force in political affairs for the first time in his life. Much of this resulted from the fame he gained as attorney for the Mormons, but Doniphan parlayed this short-term fortune into long-term political influence, military and social position, and lucrative business deals. During this period he built an impressive law practice, invested in many business enterprises, obtained high rank in the state militia, became a leader in the nascent Whig Party in Missouri, served in public office for the first time, and built a web of friends and associates throughout the state.

Doniphan also married during this period, in the process gaining a set of relatives of powerful influence and wealth in the state. His relations proved important to him personally and politically throughout the remainder of his life. Also, by marrying well, Doniphan entered elite Missouri society, which opened doors to him that might have remained closed otherwise. In all, the mid-1830s represented an eventful period for an emergent public figure.

Doniphan, a skilled attorney, worked hard during these years to build a sizable law practice. The publicity from the Mormon case helped him attract new clients, and during the years that followed he frequently appeared before the Fifth Circuit Court as it traveled throughout the western part of Missouri. Beginning in 1842, Doniphan argued cases before the Missouri State Supreme Court regularly for the next thirty years.

Most of those cases were routine civil disagreements, but he demonstrated wide success in securing the judgments desired by his clients.[1]

In one case he brought to the supreme court, for example, Doniphan was attorney for the plaintiff in a civil suit over a bad debt that had originated during a land sale in Clinton County. In *Williamson P. Gibson v. John Livingston,* Doniphan argued successfully for Gibson to obtain the one hundred dollars owed by Livingston for an 1839 land purchase. Other cases also involving disputes over debts, land, and other property soon followed. In each case, Doniphan obtained judgments advantageous to his clients.[2]

Some of Doniphan's cases taken before the state supreme court were unusual. For instance, on a couple of occasions he argued cases for slaves seeking manumission and for free blacks. In 1843 Doniphan was the attorney for "John, a Mulatto," against James Affutt, over a bad debt in Lexington. Although court records show that race was not an ingredient in the case, it resonates as an example of a pattern seen in other legal practices by Doniphan to represent the dispossessed and accused. In several other examples, Doniphan showed compassion, perhaps laced with considerable paternalism, toward the plight of black Americans. On another occasion, he argued a case for freeing a slave manumitted by an owner at his death and whose heirs tried to keep him in servitude.[3]

If Doniphan proved an effective attorney arguing briefs before the state supreme court, he gained an even more impressive reputation as a criminal trial lawyer. After participating in his first murder case in 1830, as an assistant to Abiel Leonard, Doniphan went on to defend 188 people accused of that crime. He became quite successful in defending murder suspects; in an era when capital punishment was common, none of his clients received the death penalty, and he succeeded in gaining acquittal

1. It is nearly impossible to ascertain exactly the number of cases Doniphan handled in the circuit court. He apparently kept no records of them himself, and many of the counties do not have good records. For instance, the court records from Jackson County, one of the important places where he practiced and where historical materials have usually otherwise been well preserved, were destroyed. Additionally, in 1911 the Missouri State Capitol was destroyed by fire and many of its records were lost.

2. As examples, see *Williamson P. Gibson v John Livingston,* Box 30-A, Case 18, September Term, 1842; *John Wilson v Craven Calvert,* Box 31, Case 35, July Term, 1843; *Samuel C. Bowery v Isaac Higbee,* Box 36, Case 32, January Term, 1845, Missouri State Supreme Court; *John Little v Thomas Mercer,* Box 37, Case 7, January-October Term, 1845; *James G. Garred v William M. Macy and A. W. Doniphan,* Box 38, Case 30, January Term, 1845; *Moses W. Rouse v Frederick Dean,* Box 39, Case 2, July Term, 1845; and *State and Rel James Garland v George Kay, Isaac Cotton,* Box 39, Case 7, July Term, 1845, all in Missouri State Supreme Court, RG 600, Case Files, Missouri State Archives. See also A. W. Doniphan to Abiel Leonard, January 23, 1843, Leonard Collection.

3. *John, a Mulatto, v John Affutt,* Box 32, Case 28, July Term, 1843, Missouri State Supreme Court.

for many. In later years Doniphan regretted helping so many guilty people to escape justice, but in the midst of it he gave his entire energy. He firmly believed that the adversarial legal system was much superior to any other judicial structure, even if the occasional deserving party got away. With all its faults, Doniphan remained convinced that the best possible prosecution opposing the best possible defense made for the best possible justice.[4]

Doniphan never served as prosecuting attorney for any criminal case, concentrating on defense of those accused. He won fame for his ability to speak in public, and defendants hired him often to give the summation. Preparing the pleadings; gathering testimony, evidence, and documents; examining witnesses; and other similar duties he left to the other attorneys working on a case. He preferred a tag team effort, with Doniphan seizing upon a point by a witness and using it to develop a specific argument elaborated upon in his summation. When making his case at the conclusion of a trial, Doniphan tried to explain briefly why his client should be acquitted, hammering one main point repeatedly at the jury.[5]

Doniphan's success rested upon his always exceptional summations. These, he knew, mostly represented exercises in elocution since other members of the defense team had already presented the salient evidence, and he used them not just to make his point and persuade the jury but to make the jury feel empathy for the defendant. It represented drama at its best, the ability to move others with his words. These were, by every shred of documentation available, often superb orations capable of turning the jury in ways seemingly impossible to understand. David Rice Atchison, a friend of Doniphan's and fellow lawyer on the circuit, remarked that "I knew all the great men of our country in the earlier days—Clay, Webster, Calhoun, John Quincy Adams, Clayton, Crittenden, and others." But of Doniphan's oratorical skills, Atchison said, "I heard him climb higher than any of them."[6]

In essence, Doniphan was a debater rather than a scholar when it came to legal work. He argued plausibly, even his supporters said, but rarely deeply. He could make a case with grand eloquence, punctuated with flourishing metaphors and similes, but his colleagues did not confuse him with a legal genius. John W. Henry, a contemporary, rated Doniphan below Abiel Leonard, Henry S. Geyer, and a few other revered attorneys in terms of his knowledge and brilliance in the law, but he said Doniphan had no equal as an advocate. If accused of a serious crime, no one could

4. A. W. Doniphan to D. C. Allen, "Sketch of Life," 2–3, Doniphan Papers; W. B. Napton to W. E. Connelley, October 14, 1907, W. B. Napton Letters, Western Historical Manuscript Collection; D. C. Allen, "Colonel Alexander W. Doniphan—His Life and Character," in Connelley, ed., *Doniphan's Expedition*, 22; Settle, *Alexander William Doniphan*, 6–7; Doniphan, *Address*, 11–12.

5. Allen, "Doniphan," in Connelley, ed., *Doniphan's Expedition*, 24–27.

6. Quoted in R. Kenneth Elliott, "The Rhetoric of Alexander W. Doniphan," 12.

better address a jury than Doniphan. In frontier Missouri, where court was even more an adventure in theater than today, the oratorical display of attorneys served well, and Doniphan had that skill in abundance. While a few of his legal defense strategies might have been genuinely ingenious, Doniphan's fame as a lawyer rested squarely on his ability as a public speaker.[7]

Doniphan sometimes put too much of himself into these speeches and exhausted his strength in their preparation and delivery. On occasion he had to accept a physician's care at their conclusion because of the emotional and physical exertion that went into them. Doniphan recalled in later years that this type of work was for the young, and because of it he began to move outside the profession of the law in the 1850s, taking on few additional clients, and he left its practice altogether in the 1870s.[8]

One of Doniphan's early cases was the defense of Thomas Turnham, son of the former judge Joel Turnham who had tried to mediate the Mormon crisis in 1834. Turnham had been accused of murdering a man named Hayes, and the trial was held in the Clay County Circuit Court in November 1844. Doniphan first had his client released on a bail of eight thousand dollars—a substantial sum in the 1840s, but remarkable because bail for defendants in a capital case was almost unheard of at that time. Although a team of attorneys worked on the case, Doniphan took much more of a lead than normal. He nearly exhausted himself as he countered the prosecution's evidence against Turnham; then, in his summation, he took the offensive. In an eloquent speech, Doniphan turned the jury in favor of the defendant in spite of significant evidence that he was guilty. In the end, the best the prosecution could manage was Turnham's conviction of fourth degree manslaughter. The judge fined the defendant one hundred dollars and sent him on his way. When asked about Doniphan's role in the case, Joel Turnham remarked, "Sir, Aleck Doniphan spoke only forty minutes, but he said everything."[9]

Doniphan benefited from the respectability of the bar while he practiced law in antebellum Missouri. Probably nothing was more significant in giving him a leg up in the state. The popular idea that lawyers were men uniquely able to solve the practical problems of an emerging people on

7. Napton to Connelley, October 14, 1907, Napton Letters; *Missouri Argus,* May 14, 1840; A. J. D. Stewart, ed., *The History of the Bench and Bar in Missouri,* 385–86; Williams, *Seventy-five Years on the Border,* 30–31.

8. Allen, "Doniphan," in Connelley, ed., *Doniphan's Expedition,* 24–27; Williams, *Seventy-five Years on the Border,* 30–31, 130–31; A. W. Doniphan to Emma Doniphan, [no day and month] 1875, Alexander William Doniphan Collection, Western Historical Manuscript Collection [Doniphan Collection]; McDougal, *Recollections,* 37; *Liberty Weekly Tribune,* February 20, 1847.

9. Quoted in Allen, "Doniphan," in Connelley, ed., *Doniphan's Expedition,* 25–26.

the frontier held powerful appeal and reinforced Doniphan's rise. Most people considered Doniphan a "doer" rather than a "thinker." Doniphan personified the ideal image of the attorney as a human being of reason who stood on principal, a person who soberly dealt with facts, a man who courageously defended his client, and an individual who crusaded when appropriate.[10]

The mystique of the court enhanced this public image, building on a perception that the practice of law epitomized responsibility and dispassionate decision making. Historian Michael Grossman has concluded:

> The courtroom, with its raised dais, robed judges, code of deferential silence, jury box, and solemn trappings, became a symbol of the majesty and mystery of the law in a society that deified litigation as the most appropriate form of public conflict resolution. And the courtroom was a male domain, into which women—and other men—came primarily as supplicants. The rituals of law were thus dominated by a manly brethren of robed jurists and lawyer-acolytes.[11]

Without understanding or fully appreciating the aura that surrounded the legal profession, Doniphan benefited from it in furthering his own fortune in the 1830s.

Because of his success in the legal profession, Doniphan found himself with the wherewithal and the contacts to diversify his business activities beginning in the mid-1830s. He began to purchase land in western Missouri and to enter into partnerships for the development of communities. For example, the tax rolls of Clay County in 1838 suggest that Doniphan owned 160 acres of land and that the next year he purchased another 320 acres nearby. He also began buying up lots in Liberty both for his home and office and for investment. Doniphan continued to acquire land in Clay County for the next several years, some of it for renting to farmers, some for his own use, and some for development. Doniphan also entered land and business deals elsewhere. For instance, in 1841 he and William B. Almond purchased the Hamilton Ferry over the Platte River, plus all associated lands. Obviously an investment, it was only the earliest of many he would make in what became Platte County between Clay County and the Missouri River.[12]

10. This point has been made by Alexis de Tocqueville, *Democracy in America,* 1:48–56, 102–7, 247–50, 282–90; Daniel J. Boorstin, *The Americans: The National Experience,* 35–42.

11. Michael Grossman, "Institutionalizing Masculinity: The Law as a Masculine Profession," 141.

12. Missouri Tax Lists, 1836–1839, Clay County, 59 (old numbering), 424–25 (new numbering); Missouri Tax Lists, 1840–1845, 938, 1028, 1074–75, 1172, 1212, both in Missouri Historical Society; *Kansas City Times,* February 24, 1947; Platte County Deed Book A, 147, Missouri State Archives.

Doniphan, probably because of the business opportunities there, became an early and persistent advocate of the incorporation of the Platte region into Missouri. He had moved to Liberty in part because of the prospect of opening even more territory to the west; his longtime confidant D. C. Allen admitted that the "early annexation of the Platte Country to the state and growth of Jackson induced him in May 1833 to remove to Liberty." The Platte region had been excluded from the western part of Missouri in 1821. Previously, a line running north and south from the point where the Kansas River intersected the Missouri River had marked the state's western boundary; the official line started at meridian 17° 30'. Now the familiar triangle of northwestern Missouri, the area consists of about two million acres comprising the present counties of Platte, Buchanan, Andrew, Holt, Nodaway, and Atchison. It also became the site of one of the state's important urban areas, St. Joseph, where several major transcontinental routes emanated in the 1840s and 1850s, and the antebellum boom towns of Weston and Platte City.[13]

Missourians had long coveted the rich land between its western border and the Missouri River, especially because the Federal government had set it aside for the Iowas, Sauks and Foxes, and a few other Indian nations. As Howard I. McKee concluded: "Settlers along the western border of Missouri saw the policy of assigning lands to Indians in perpetuity as a frustration of their hopes to create new western states, the loss of access to Missouri River steamboat transportation, and the equally undesirable loss to white occupation of the fertile river bottoms, rolling prairies and mill sites in the Little Platte area." One of the many subtexts to this quest for the Platte country was its richness and ability to support large-scale plantation agriculture along the river bottoms. In a state with a large population of southerners, that represented a compelling vision of economic prosperity.[14]

Because of this desire for the Platte country, a series of congressional border wars took place during the first half of the 1830s. The Missouri delegation in Congress, especially Senators Thomas Hart Benton and Lewis F. Linn, led a sustained effort to reverse the Federal policy. The senators argued that as long as Missourians on the border lived within a few miles of the steamboats plying the Missouri River, they would routinely violate the reserved lands of the Indians to take their goods to a landing for trade. Likewise, they depicted the Platte as a region trapped and hunted out, and the Indians there as either dependent on Federal largesse or likely to cross the border into Missouri to steal cattle and

13. Doniphan to Allen, "Sketch of Life," 3, Doniphan Papers; Doniphan, *Address,* 1–3, 24; Thorp, *Early Days in the West,* 60–64; Howard I. McKee, "The Platte Purchase."
14. McKee, "Platte Purchase," 131; Shortridge, "Expansion of the Settlement Frontier."

other livestock from white settlers. However it might ignite, according to Missouri politicians, the border was a tinderbox awaiting a single spark to start a war.[15]

In his 1832 message to the Missouri General Assembly, Governor John Miller unabashedly called for incorporating the Platte territory into the state. "By annexing it to the state," he said, "the Missouri river would become our boundary, which would greatly protect that frontier from the invasion of hostile Indians, and prevent those questions of right to jurisdiction, which so often disturb the quiet of the country, and afford not only an excuse for, but a temptation to the commission of crime." The Missourians found several sympathetic people in Washington, but the problem of what to do with the Indians proved a bone of contention.[16]

A. W. Doniphan became involved in the process of acquiring the Platte country in the summer of 1835 when he attended a militia muster at the farm of Weakly Dale, three miles north of Liberty, where they discussed the issue. Andrew S. Hughes, retired general and Indian agent whom Doniphan had idolized since a youth, was the principal speaker at the meeting and he made a powerful case for annexing the Platte region. After discussion, those assembled agreed to form a committee to take action. They chose Doniphan, David R. Atchison, E. M. Samuel, Peter H. Burnett, and William T. Wood, all prominent attorneys or businessmen, to write a memorial to Congress. Wood wrote the first draft, with each committee member offering revisions. They each signed the final document and sent it to Missouri's delegation in Congress. Since earlier memorials to Congress had received little attention, one of the strategies discussed at this militia muster involved illegally settling on the territory. A few militia members did so, but apparently not Doniphan, and U.S. Army troops from Fort Leavenworth had to expel them from the Platte country.[17]

Doniphan keenly felt the importance of securing the Platte country for the state's economic development. He wrote a friend in mid-1836 about its possibilities: "We have now the strong assurances from our representatives that the preliminary steps for annexing the country west

15. These arguments were made in Thomas Hart Benton, *Thirty Years' View, or, A History of the Working of the American Government for Thirty Years, from 1820 to 1850 . . . by a Senator of Thirty Years,* 1:626; *House Reports,* 23d Cong., 2d Sess., Document 107, 2–9; McKee, "Platte Purchase," 133–34.

16. *Journal of the House of Representatives of the State of Missouri at the First Session of the Seventh General Assembly, 1832–1833,* 56. A detailed study of the process of Indian removal, with an emphasis on the sordid, can be found in R. David Edmunds, "Potawatomis in the Platte Country: An Indian Removal Incomplete."

17. Doniphan to Allen, "Sketch of Life," 2–3, Doniphan Papers; Allen, "Doniphan," in Connelley, ed., *Doniphan's Expedition,* 6–7; Doniphan, *Address,* 11–12; McKee, "Platte Purchase," 137–38; Floyd C. Shoemaker, "Clay County," 29; *History of Andrew and DeKalb Counties, Missouri,* 1:77, 114; *The Daily News History of Buchanan County and St. Joseph, Missouri,* 539; Parrish, *David Rice Atchison,* 15–16.

of us have resulted favorably & so soon as the Indian titles have been extinguished it will become an integral part of the State. When this is consummated it will open a fine field for speculation." He added that "it will increase the business, improve the society, add to the wealth & increase the prosperity of this County." Doniphan added that as a lawyer he did not understand business, but he knew that young men with investment capital could do well by putting it into businesses in western Missouri that would expand when the Platte opened to development.[18]

Quite right about the economic potential of opening the Platte region to white settlement, Doniphan recognized that the central obstacle involved persuading the tribes living there to resettle further west. The administration of Andrew Jackson was sympathetic to this effort. Doniphan and his associates expressed delight in the spring of 1836 when the president directed the government to make new treaties with the confederated tribes of Sauks and Foxes, Mdewakanton, Wahpekute, Wahpeton, Otoes, and Missouri Indians. With a good deal of coercion, government agents induced tribal leaders to relinquish their claims to the Platte country. As this took place, Doniphan also learned that Senator John M. Clayton, chair of the Judiciary Committee, presented a bill to extend Missouri's border to the river. The Senate passed it on May 14, 1836, with the House following on June 3, and Jackson signed it into law June 7, 1836.[19]

Next, the state had to ratify the action of Congress, and Doniphan became a key participant in the Missouri General Assembly's border extension. When the assembly met in November 1836 Doniphan had just been elected to the state house as a representative from Clay County—the first of three terms he served in the General Assembly—and as a freshman he offered enthusiastic support to the Platte annexation. Doniphan, appointed to a committee having to do with the state boundary, used his skills of persuasion to see the effort to completion. The committee successfully navigated through the legislature "An Act to express the assent of the State of Missouri, to the extension of the western boundary line of the State," passed on a vote of only forty-one in favor to twenty-nine opposed. Most of those who opposed represented districts in the eastern part of the state. After these actions, the president, Martin Van Buren, issued a proclamation on March 28, 1837, that solidified the annexation.[20]

Within a year of the congressional law, the only real losers in the Platte transfer, the Indian tribes, had left the territory. Somewhere between eight hundred and nine hundred Iowas and about five hundred Sauks and

18. A. W. Doniphan to Capt. John Chauncey, June 11, 1836, Harold B. Lee Library.
19. McKee, "Platte Purchase," 140–44.
20. *Journal of the House of Representatives . . . First Session of the Ninth General Assembly,* 56, 130; *Historical Listing of the Missouri Legislature,* 34; *Laws of the State of Missouri, Passed at the First Session of the Ninth General Assembly, Begun and Held at the City of Jefferson, November 21, 1836,* 28–29; McKee, "Platte Purchase," 146–47.

Foxes moved across the river into Kansas, along with several smaller Indian groups. To celebrate, western Missourians lit bonfires, held torchlight rallies, and cracked open numerous kegs. Doniphan, as one of the writers of the 1835 memorial and a member of the General Assembly that accepted the annexation, participated with his friends in this celebration. One tale about the festivities involved one of Doniphan's associates from the 1835 memorial. Peter Burnett supposedly rode "hell-bent-for-leather" from Liberty to the settlement of Barry, in what became western Platte County, with the news of annexation. After the announcement, the townspeople adjourned to the local "grocery" to imbibe. Burnett lost his tall hat in the commotion, but according to one eyewitness "more than one hat went up, like the Hebrew children, on that occasion."[21]

Doniphan's involvement in the Platte country annexation demonstrates the intersection of law, business, and politics so much a part of the rest of his career. Events in one aspect of his life often led directly to or from other aspects in an almost seamless tapestry of entangling relationships, concerns, interests, and ideas. His experience in the General Assembly in 1836–1838 showed this interweaving repeatedly. He was elected by an almost unanimous vote to replace his friend and associate David Atchison in the lower house of the state legislature in the summer of 1836. When he arrived at Jefferson City to take his seat at the Ninth General Assembly on November 21, 1836, Doniphan found it impossible to disaggregate the various sectors of his life. He generally followed the path of doing what he thought was best for Clay County. In so doing he often found, not surprisingly, that it suited him well both financially and professionally. Doniphan reflected late in life that he considered his many actions in politics both honorable and just, although he regretted that sometimes there were losers as well as winners in the decision-making process. He wrote that off, however, to the vicissitudes of life.[22]

The election of 1836 that brought Doniphan to the state capital for the first time clarified many of the subtle issues that had been a part of the governmental landscape in Missouri for several years. Before, there had been no real political parties in the state, but this changed dramatically with the election of 1836. Andrew Jackson, as president for the previous eight years, had built a powerful national political organization that had its Missouri component. Those who had disagreed with his policies had worked for years without real focus before this election. In 1836, however, a national anti-Jackson coalition emerged that later came to

21. *Missouri Argus,* August 8, 1837; Perry McCandless, *A History of Missouri,* Vol. 2, *1820 to 1860,* 116–17.
22. A. W. Doniphan to D. C. Allen, May 4, 1875; Doniphan to Allen, "Sketch of Life," 8–12, both in Doniphan Papers; Doniphan to Emma Doniphan, [no day and month] 1875, Doniphan Collection.

be called the Whigs. It ran three regional candidates—Daniel Webster of Massachusetts, Hugh L. White of Tennessee, and William Henry Harrison of Ohio—for the presidency against Jackson's hand-picked successor, Martin Van Buren, in the hope of preventing a clear majority and thereby throwing the election into the House of Representatives where one of its adherents might achieve victory. Since the nascent Whigs of Missouri could not agree among themselves on a candidate, they placed electors for both Harrison and White on the ballot. Van Buren carried the state and 170 of 294 electoral votes nationwide. Although defeated in the national election, a large number of those with whiggish beliefs, including Doniphan, entered office. More important, a party organization coalesced out of the election.[23]

The Whig Party that Doniphan joined in 1836 never represented a majority position in the state. Kentuckian Henry Clay, the "Great Compromiser" and one of the Whig ringmasters, became Doniphan's idol and drew him into the party more than any other single factor. Both his western heritage and his ideals appealed to Doniphan, as did Clay's agrarian background. Later Doniphan embraced Clay's aggressive championing of Federal measures to foster economic progress. Doniphan admitted that "I worshipped Clay as no man but him was ever worshipped by his followers."[24] Long after the collapse of the Whig Party in the early 1850s, Doniphan remained a proponent of its idea of government, industry, the nation, the economy, and society as a whole.

The culture of the Whigs that Doniphan adopted has been variously described as aristocratic, rational, paternalistic, and progressive, besides other more pejorative terms used by their political rivals. The Whigs, however, appear in retrospect as people trying to deal evenhandedly with practical political problems. They believed in moderation, self-restraint, and a "rational persuasion" that helped create a balanced political order, economic growth, and social harmony. They also shared an underlying conviction that the Jacksonian Democrats showed little common sense in dealing with the most divisive issues of the antebellum era: economic concerns, race relations, class tensions, and sectional rivalries.

Historian Daniel Walker Howe labeled the Whig Party the champions of the "positive liberal state."

> This ideal implied the belief that the state should actively seek "to promote the general welfare, raise the level of opportunity for all

23. McCandless, *History of Missouri,* 2:100; William J. Cooper Jr., *Liberty and Slavery: Southern Politics to 1860,* 187–91; Clarence H. McClure, "Early Opposition to Thomas Hart Benton"; Leota Newhard, "The Beginning of the Whig Party in Missouri, 1824–1840."

24. Settle, *Alexander William Doniphan,* 4; William B. McGroarty, ed., "Letters from Alexander W. Doniphan," 27.

men, and aid all individuals to develop their full potentialities."
The Democrats, by contrast, believed in a "negative liberal state,"
which left men free to pursue their own definition of happiness.
A great advantage of this distinction between the parties is that
it implies a connection between the economic and moral aspects
of Whiggery. In both cases, the Whigs believed in asserting active
control. They wanted "improvements" both economic and moral,
and they did not believe in leaving others alone.

Perhaps the most persistent aspect of the Whig worldview was the party's
resoluteness in using political power for the furtherance of its ideals.[25]
The Whigs throughout their existence expressed optimism about U.S.
economic progress, consolidation, and stabilization. They adopted as an
economic goal the creation of a mixed economy that made room for
industry, trade, business, and agriculture; that included entrepreneurs
both large and small; and where bourgeoisie and proletariat and any other
group could achieve justice and opportunity. They saw the need for government to foster the creation of both a climate and an infrastructure that
would further that mixed economy. The establishment of a government
bank with the power to regulate the money supply, and the building of
harbors and roads and making other internal improvements were only
specific efforts to foster the economy. While some of the Whig economic
programs were beneficial to only certain groups—such as a tariff directed
at protecting American industry—other efforts advanced the fortunes of
diverse groups. Through these programs, the Whigs sought to bring order
to the U.S. economy and to free it from dependency on the mercantilism of
Europe. The Whig economic ideal proved more inclusive than that held
by the Jacksonian Democrats with their emphasis on agriculture, hard
currency, and small business.[26]
The subject of economics did not excite grassroots political action in
the antebellum United States much more than it does now. Thus, the
Whigs became a strong political party that could seriously challenge
the Democrats in national elections only after they had articulated their
vision of American society and culture. Although they were optimistic
about the nation's economic prospects and could devise legislation to help
further it, they were wary of the problems inherent in achieving social
and moral balance. Inextricably tied to their idea of society was a sense of
commonality of interests between all Americans, whether yeoman farmer
or planter, factory worker or industrialist, professional or artisan. Pulling
together to enlarge national wealth would, they argued, eventually help
everyone. Equality of opportunity was a persistent theme in their rhetoric,

25. Daniel Walker Howe, *The Political Culture of the American Whigs*, 20.
26. Ibid., 299–300.

as they urged the electorate to exhibit greater thrift, industry, productivity, and independence.

Doniphan embraced this ideology and expressed it in concrete ways during his first term in the Missouri General Assembly. While Jacksonian Democrats were victorious in attaining most of the significant offices in the state—Lilburn W. Boggs became governor, Albert G. Harrison and John Miller went to the House of Representatives, and Lewis F. Linn was elected to the Senate—the Whig influence ran as an undercurrent in the 1836–1838 General Assembly. Doniphan and other Whigs in the legislature made it one of the most proactive of the antebellum era, fostering economic progress in the state. Historian James Neal Primm even called its first session the "great railroad and banking session of 1836–37." Although certainly not solely the result of Whigs such as Doniphan in the legislature, without their presence, the banking, internal improvement, and incorporation acts that emerged from the General Assembly could not have been passed.[27]

The first major action by Doniphan as a legislator that fit into the Whig mode of economics was the chartering of a state bank. Since Andrew Jackson's veto of a charter to continue the Second Bank of the United States in 1832, and its demise in 1836, Missouri businessmen had asked for the establishment of a state bank. Missouri Senator Thomas Hart Benton, nicknamed "Old Bullion Benton," distrusted banks altogether, and his faction of the Democratic Party stood with Andrew Jackson in condemning all banks and currency except specie. The Whigs, based largely in St. Louis and in other urban centers and including those like Doniphan in the west, favored an inflation of the currency with paper money to provide venture capital for continued economic growth. They also recognized that a bank could stabilize the economy through regulation of the paper money supply. Some Missouri Democrats—led by Governor Boggs, also from the western part of the state and with similar goals as Doniphan and the Whigs—also supported the creation of a state bank.[28]

On November 22, 1836, Lilburn Boggs asked the General Assembly to charter a state bank. He told the representatives that the state's economy

27. James Neal Primm, *Economic Policy in the Development of a Western State: Missouri, 1820–1860,* 33. It should be added that Robert E. Shalhope, "Thomas Hart Benton and Missouri State Politics: A Re-Examination," makes the case that the "Boons Lick Democrats" took control of the state Democratic machine in the 1830s and developed a doctrinaire philosophy based on oligarchy. But they were less at odds with the Whigs economically than Thomas Hart Benton's old Jacksonians. As a result, they supported the idea of a state bank with limited power, and the use of a modest amount of state resources for internal improvements and other programs that might benefit the economy.

28. On the Jacksonian bank war, see Robert V. Remini, *Andrew Jackson and the Bank War;* and William G. Shade, *Banks or No Banks: The Money Question in Western Politics, 1832–1865.*

could no longer operate only with specie. Boggs called for the creation of a well-overseen bank that would pay specie on demand for paper money, thereby providing the inflation needed to finance continued economic growth. Doniphan agreed with Boggs and voted in favor of chartering the Bank of the State of Missouri, an organization capitalized at five million dollars with the state owning a half interest. The bill moved swiftly through the General Assembly in the winter of 1836–1837, and Boggs signed it into law on February 2, 1837. Although the new bank was a conservative instrument, a compromise between Democratic and Whig economic ideals, it represented a significant turn in the state. It was also the first instance in which Doniphan affected money policy. In the post–Civil War era he would be especially significant in this arena as the president of a bank, the Ray County Savings Bank, in the western part of the state.[29]

Doniphan also served on the cutting edge of efforts in the 1836–1837 session of the General Assembly to incorporate a large number of new entities dedicated toward economic goals deemed of value to the Missouri population, something the Jacksonian Democrats had been loath to do because of fear of monopolies and other possible special privileges that might accrue to the corporations. Infused with new Whig representatives, however, the Ninth General Assembly showed a whiggish belief in the social value of far-reaching economic enterprises as worthy of public trust by incorporating eighty-nine new organizations, more than the previous six state legislative sessions combined. Each of these new charters contained language about the public good, thereby reflecting the Whig goal to enhance "the general welfare, raise the level of opportunity for all men, and aid all individuals to develop their full potentialities." The Whigs successfully argued that corporations could provide useful services, without exclusive privileges or unnecessary powers, if properly regulated for the public interest.[30]

Of these new corporations, the Whig ambition of fostering the development of a transportation infrastructure achieved reality through the chartering of twenty-nine railways or turnpikes. As a member of this General Assembly Doniphan and the other Whigs also helped to pass incorporation bills for fourteen insurance companies and six manufacturing and mining organizations. In every case the Whig aim of furthering the social good motivated passage. The St. Louis Gas Light Company, for example, would furnish inhabitants with coal and gas for fuel and

29. Primm, *Economic Policy,* 18–31; *Laws of the State of Missouri . . . 1836,* 11–24; *Missouri Argus,* December 23, 1836, December 30, 1836, January 13, 1837, February 17, 1837; John Ray Cable, *The Bank of the State of Missouri,* 103–19.

30. Dwight H. Brown, ed., *Corporations Chartered or Organized under the Territorial Laws and by Act of the General Assembly of the State of Missouri, 1803–1865,* passim; *Missouri Argus,* March 3, 1837. The quote on Whig attitudes is in Lee Benson, *The Concept of Jacksonian Democracy: New York as a Test Case,* 103.

operate in a manner "generally conducive to the public good." Doniphan was quite willing to grant a monopoly to the company, exempting it from all taxes for ten years, because of the social progress it would presumably foster.[31]

This overarching ideology for Doniphan's efforts in the General Assembly received its best proof in the chartering of the Marion City and Missouri Railroad Company. Although the railway existed far from Doniphan's power base in western Missouri and would not benefit his constituents directly, he viewed it as part of a larger set of "internal improvements" fostering economic and social progress. The bill passed easily, fifty-nine to twelve members in the lower house, with Doniphan in the majority. Most of the opposition came from Democrats in rural counties far removed from the action, but Whigs from everywhere supported the legislation.[32]

Although Doniphan and his Whig associates could not have passed such legislation by themselves, their support proved critical to the rise of a new brand of Democrats in the state, those who were less hard-money and agrarian and more business-minded, led by such politicians as Lilburn Boggs as governor and St. Louis businessman James B. Bowlin, principal architect of the state bank. The Whigs also had help from the exceedingly important western Democrat John C. Thornton, Doniphan's colleague in the House of Representatives from Clay County. A former judge of the county court of Ray County, Thornton had been a major force in the politics of the state since 1824. For ten straight years he had served as a representative in the General Assembly, and between 1828 and 1832 had acted as Speaker. Although a Jacksonian, Thornton was a firm "state's rights" advocate and had opposed the president's disavowal of South Carolina's Nullification Proclamation. This cost him his seat in the legislature in 1834, but he returned in 1836 and although a Democrat became Doniphan's mentor in the capitol.[33]

Thornton was supportive of Doniphan's most important "pet project" while in the General Assembly in 1836–1837, the creation of a "homeland" for the Mormons separate from everyone else in the state. Ever since the Mormon expulsion from Jackson County in 1833, Doniphan had unsuccessfully worked to gain recompense for their losses. While those efforts wound their way through the courts, many members of the sect had taken up residence in Clay County, where they had at first been welcomed.

31. *Laws of the State of Missouri . . . 1836,* 173–79; A. W. Doniphan to Abiel Leonard, August 28, 1836, Leonard Collection.
32. *Laws of the State of Missouri . . . 1836,* 253–60; *Journal of the House of Representatives . . . First Session of the Ninth General Assembly,* 260.
33. Raymond W. Settle, "Doniphan Notes and Miscellaneous Papers," 1:13–15, Raymond W. Settle Collection, William Jewell College, Special Collections, Curry Library, Liberty, Mo.

Soon, however, difficulties arose and the local residents wanted them to leave. By the spring of 1836, the antagonism had grown so pronounced that rallies began in Liberty and other places to drum up support for running them out of the county. Clay Countians became convinced that the Mormons "are flocking in here faster than ever and making great talk what they would do. A letter from Ohio [where Joseph Smith lived] Shows plainly that they intended to Emigrate here til they outnumber us. Then they would rule the Co[u]ntry at pleasure."[34]

These problems climaxed on June 16, 1836, when about one thousand residents assembled in Liberty to debate the "Mormon question." Samuel C. Owens, a ringleader in the Mormon expulsion from Jackson County three years earlier, addressed the crowd and, after telling some horror stories, urged the Clay people to get rid of the Mormons. As Joseph Thorp recalled the episode:

> They wrangled and jawed, till Colonel Doniphan, who had been a listener and thought their proposition rather too stringent, arose and began to shove up his sleeves, (his manner when a little warmed up), and commenced his remarks in a rather excited tone, when the chairman or someone called him to order, saying he was giving too strong vent to his feelings; that it was calculated to raise an excitement in the crowd, whose feelings were then almost ready to boil over. The Colonel pulled his sleeve up a little higher, and told him, "that was what he got up for—to give vent to his feelings."
>
> I wish I could give his speech, but if I recollect, he advocated the right of citizen and individual liberty, with individual responsibility, and was opposed to Judge Lynch and mob violence; was in favor of law and order; the law was made for the punishment of evil doers, and to protect the law-abiding, and should be strictly enforced.[35]

Although two years to the day after an earlier meeting about the Mormons had ended in riot, this time Doniphan succeeded in calming the citizens.

Doniphan and several other county leaders, including John Thornton, David Atchison, and William Wood, met on June 29, 1836, at the courthouse in Liberty to see if a solution could be worked out. Doniphan served on a committee to write an ultimatum to the Mormons. This statement concluded that the Mormons could not remain in Clay County because they were much too different from the other settlers. They asked that they leave voluntarily, offering to help them explore prospects on the Wisconsin frontier or in some other non-slave, unsettled territory. The Mormons responded to these efforts with a denial of any wrongdoing

34. A. Wilson and Emelia Wilson to Brother and Sister, July 4, 1836, in Durwood T. Stokes, ed., "The Wilson Letters, 1835–1849," 504.
35. Thorp, *Early Days in the West*, 80.

and asked to be left alone to live their religion. They did, however, accept the offer of help to find them new land.[36]

Doniphan worked with Mormon leaders in the summer of 1836 to negotiate a gathering spot for the sect in nearby Ray County. John Corrill was one of the principal Mormons involved in these efforts, seeking what he called a "resting place" from persecution. Corrill pledged that should the day come when "Ray County requires the 'Mormons' to leave it entirely, we [would] feel disposed to do so on our part and urge and advise our brethren to do the same." Such behavior paid off, and with the help of Doniphan, Atchison, and Amos Rees, the Mormons moved without opposition to unincorporated land attached to Ray County north of the already settled areas. The Mormons purchased property upon which they built their main settlement, the town of Far West, on August 8, 1836.[37]

Doniphan further helped this effort within the state capitol when he presented a petition on behalf of the Mormons for the creation of a new jurisdiction carved out of the unpopulated northern section of Ray County. It would be a reservation, similar to those of the Indians, on which to place the Mormons. Years later, Doniphan recalled that, as when Indians would flee the reservation, trouble erupted in northwestern Missouri between the Mormons and other Missourians when "they commenced forming a settlement in Davis [Daviess] county, when, under their agreement, they had no right to do."[38]

To organize these new counties, the House appointed Doniphan chair of a study committee and on December 17, 1836, it reported a bill to organize Caldwell and Daviess Counties from northern Ray County. This bill passed the House on December 23, the Senate agreed on December 27, and Lilburn Boggs signed it into law on December 29. It represented quite a Christmas present for the Mormons, and although nothing in the bill mentioned restrictions on who could settle where, everyone assumed that Caldwell County—which no one else wanted since it was not particularly rich or readily accessible to river transport—would be a reserve for the Mormons.[39]

36. Smith, *History of the Church,* 2:448–55.
37. Quote in Richard L. Anderson, "Atchison's Letters and the Causes of Mormon Expulsion from Missouri," 12–13; Max H. Parkin, "A History of the Latter-Day Saints in Clay County, Missouri, from 1833 to 1837," 270.
38. *Kansas City Journal,* June 12, 1881. Historian Walter B. Stevens even remarked in his *Centennial History of Missouri,* 2:108, that this "reservation" approach toward dealing with the Mormons was explicit and in return for home rule in Caldwell County, the Mormons were not to move beyond its borders without "permission of two-thirds of the residents of the township in which they desired to locate. This seemed to be a compromise that satisfied both sides."
39. *Laws of the State of Missouri . . . 1836,* 38–43, 46–47; *Journal of the House of Representatives . . . First Session of the Ninth General Assembly,* 86, 188, 219; Andre Paul Duchateau, "Missouri Colossus: Alexander William Doniphan, 1808–1887," 37. Im-

Doniphan's efforts to create a Mormon "homeland" were not quite as straightforward as he might have liked. On January 8, 1837, Doniphan wrote from Jefferson City to the Mormon W. W. Phelps that he had made some compromises to obtain passage of the legislation creating Caldwell County. Doniphan said that "The petition of the people of North Grand River, the statements of the citizens of Ray, the influence of her members, and the prejudices of [Smallwood] Noland [of Jackson County], [Lilburn] Boggs, Jeffery, McLelland, etc., were to be combatted. I did not succeed as you wished or as you might have expected, in fixing the boundaries of your county. In the first place, I was forced to report a bill making two counties north of Ray, instead of one." The boundary problem remained for some time, especially since the county created north of Caldwell was Daviess and it became a source of contention in 1838. Doniphan hoped that "In time, I hope you may add to its [the county's] limits, when prejudices have subsided and reason and common sense have again assumed the helm."[40] This unsettled issue helped foster problems later between Mormon and non-Mormon groups in the region. But for now it signaled a major step for the Mormons. It also enhanced Doniphan's reputation in Clay County, for he had solved a difficult problem with diplomacy and skill.

While Doniphan received acclaim for his efforts to help the Mormons, his motives may not have been entirely selfless. Although a man of strong ethics with an ideology of honor and moderation, he was also a savvy businessman. He had long identified his future fortune with the development of the Platte country, having purchased property there, and, after ousting the Indians from the territory, no one wanted to take a chance on the Mormons creating an even bigger problem. Thus, Doniphan also helped establish Caldwell County because he wanted to prevent the Mormons from settling in Missouri's attractive Platte region that Clay's non-Mormons wanted for themselves.[41]

Doniphan's first term in the General Assembly also involved him in issues that would affect him throughout his life. He fostered the passage of state laws for roads and highways, banking, the regulation of Indian

---

mediately after the passage of the act for organizing counties, between December 16, 1836, and January 20, 1837, the following counties were either organized or altered in some substantive way (usually to cut territory from them for new counties): Audrain, Benton, Caldwell, Daviess, Clark, Clay and Clinton, Greene, Livingston, Macon, Taney, Linn, Miller, Pulaski, Shannon, Van Buren (*Laws of the State of Missouri . . . 1836*, 44–55).

40. A. W. Doniphan to W. W. Phelps, January 8, 1837, Alexander William Doniphan Letters, LDS Archives.

41. Michael S. Riggs suggested that "the Mormons were given what was perceived to be the dross prairie country of Caldwell County as a diversion from the choice bottomlands of the Platte Country" (Riggs, "The Economic Impact of Fort Leavenworth on Northwestern Missouri 1827–1838: Yet Another Reason for the Mormon War?" 129).

affairs, and the slavery controversy. In every case, Doniphan reflected his southern heritage and his whiggish bent. Nothing showed this "whiggery" better than Doniphan's vote of "nay" to a resolution to tender to the outgoing president, Democrat Andrew Jackson, the Missouri General Assembly's "respect, esteem and best wishes for his future happiness at his retirement." The vote was fifty-one in favor, to Doniphan and eleven others against.[42]

Doniphan did not stand for reelection as a member of the Tenth General Assembly of Missouri in 1838. He had other affairs on his mind by that time, for on December 21, 1837, Doniphan married one of the daughters of John Thornton, his colleague in the state legislature from Clay County. Among other things, Doniphan had to make a living to provide for his new bride. Elizabeth Jane Thornton turned seventeen on their wedding day, and the two had a small double wedding at the Old School Baptist Church in Liberty, with Jane's sister Caroline and Oliver P. Moss.[43] D. C. Allen, Doniphan's longtime friend, recalled their marriage:

> It was a perfect union of heart and intellect. She was a highly intellectual, cultivated woman, and her grace of manner and charm in conversation made her a delight of society. Save when public duty or business imperatively demanded it, he and she were constantly united. At home or abroad they were together. They were both insatiable readers, and their evenings in literature will always stir delightful thoughts in the memories of their friends. He knew and loved no place like home, and neither the mystery of lodges nor the joviality of clubs had any power to draw him thence.[44]

Even allowing for separate spheres and the chivalry of the Victorian era, Allen's description of Doniphan's marriage seems overblown. Yet there is considerable truth in his assertions; Doniphan repeatedly gave up the public realm and authority of office to be near his wife and their children.

In 1875 Doniphan wrote to his cousin Emma, telling her a little about their relationship. His remarks show that he was paternalistic toward her, but also that he appreciated her and her abilities. Doniphan commented,

> . . . my wife was a lovely woman; I married her the day she was seventeen; I was glad she had no more education then the Common Schools of this frontier country then afforded; I desired to educate her myself—to form her mind and tastes—I was young, liberally educated, and energetic. I never read a book to myself (other than

42. *Journal of the House of Representatives . . . First Session of the Ninth General Assembly*, 373.

43. William M. Paxton, *Annals of Platte County, Missouri*, 549–51.

44. Marion Lucille Carr, *Marriage Records of Clay County, Missouri, 1822–1852*; Allen, "Doniphan," in Connelley, ed., *Doniphan's Expedition*, 29.

a Law work) during more than thirty years of married life; I read them all to her and with her, she often relieving me. You can form some idea of her culture when I say without immodesty that I have been a great student—almost a universal one.[45]

Alexander William Doniphan was twelve and one-half years older than his new wife, and he overshadowed her both physically and in his maturity and learning. It must have been a relationship in which he dominated in virtually all aspects; he believed in an unequal partnership. In 1872, he announced in a speech that when he first married, "There were then two distinct sexes. The short haired, hen-crowing hybrid had not been hatched. Affinities and counterparts—the adjuncts of free-love and woman's rights to run mad—did not disturb the peaceful dreams of the ladies in those days. They only asked to be women—not peers of men." Whether for this reason or others, Jane Doniphan was never a strong woman; frail and weak, she became a near invalid for much of her life.[46]

Less than a year after their marriage, on September 18, 1838, Jane Doniphan gave birth to their first child, a boy whom they named John Thornton, after her father and A. W. Doniphan's benefactor. Two years later, on September 10, 1840, they had a second son, Alexander William Jr. Doniphan was very attached to his sons. "I may say without vanity they were the most highly educated, [with] the most finished educations, of any boys of that age in the state besides the ordinary classical," he wrote to a cousin, "and scientific collegiate training, [and] each could speak and write French, Spanish, German, and Italian. . . . I had provided them with private teachers from childhood and never tasked them heavily, and required them to plough and to hoe when I feared study was enervating them." It nearly destroyed him when both sons, at different times and for different reasons, died in accidents while still youths.[47]

Without question the union of Alexander William Doniphan and Elizabeth Jane Thornton was more than a marriage based on love and passion. Having John Thornton as a father-in-law was advantageous to a young man seeking fortune and power. Thornton, a native of Kentucky like Doniphan, had come to Missouri in 1817 and had been a force in the politics of the state since before its admission to the Union. He had been a judge in Ray County, a longtime member of the state General Assembly, and a colonel in the Twenty-eighth Regiment of the Missouri Militia. Thornton's political and business connections were broad and useful to Doniphan. With his marriage to Jane Thornton, Doniphan was bound by kinship to some of the other "first families" of Missouri. John Thornton had married the daughter of Major General Stephen Trigg, another important leader

45. Doniphan to Emma Doniphan, [no day and month] 1875, Doniphan Collection.
46. Doniphan, *Address*, 11–12.
47. Doniphan to Emma Doniphan, [no day and month] 1875, Doniphan Collection.

Alexander William Doniphan, portrait by George Caleb Bingham. Photo accession number 020625, courtesy of the State Historical Society of Missouri, Columbia.

Elizabeth Jane Thornton Doniphan, portrait by George Caleb Bingham. Photo accession no. 020628, courtesy of the State Historical Society of Missouri, Columbia.

Alexander William Doniphan Jr., portrait by George Caleb Bingham. Photo accession no. 020626, courtesy of the State Historical Society of Missouri, Columbia.

John Thornton Doniphan, portrait by George Caleb Bingham. Photo accession no. 020627, courtesy of the State Historical Society of Missouri, Columbia.

in early Missouri. Besides Jane, Thornton's other children, six daughters and a son, also married into leading families in the state. Through this network, Doniphan had entrée into the homes and offices of some of the most important men in Missouri, and while it is difficult to measure the importance of this access, it seems unreasonable to conclude that it had no bearing on his later career. Of course, he had to make the most of this entrée, and Doniphan rarely disappointed those who associated with him during those ambitious years of the 1830s and 1840s when he foresaw great prospects in business, law, and politics.[48]

48. Settle, "Doniphan Collection, Notes and Misc.," 13–15, William Jewell College, Special Collections.

3

The 1838 Mormon War

A L E X A N D E R W I L L I A M Doniphan was practicing law in Liberty in the fall of 1838 when the governor mobilized the local militia unit to put down a rebellion by Mormons in northwestern Missouri. The Mormons settled in the especially created county of Caldwell in the summer of 1836, establishing Far West as the county seat, and by the spring of 1838 some ten thousand members lived in the county. The church controlled all the county offices, had its own state militia unit, and enjoyed near autonomy. When large influxes of additional Mormons came into the region and began settling outside the reserved county, however, it infuriated the non-Mormons and trouble began.[1]

In spilling over the borders of Caldwell County the Mormons violated what the non-Mormons, including Doniphan, believed was a pact; seeing them like Indians leaving a reservation, the local citizenry dealt with them in a similar manner. "It is true, that when the Mormons left this [Clay] county, they agreed to settle in, and confine themselves to a district of country, which has since been formed into the County of Caldwell, but they have violated that agreement, and are spreading over Daviess, Clinton, Livingston, and Carroll," wrote one Missourian. "Such a number had settled in Daviess that the old inhabitants were apprehensive that they would be governed soon by the revelations of the great Prophet, Joe Smith, and hence their anxiety to rid themselves of such an incubus." Doniphan and his fellow western Missourians always believed the trouble came as a result of Mormon violations of the agreement to remain in their reserved county.[2]

1. The standard work on the conflict is Stephen C. LeSueur, *The 1838 Mormon War in Missouri.*
2. *Western Star,* September 14, 1838, cited in *Missouri Argus,* September 27, 1838.

MASSACRE OF MORMONS AT HAUN'S MILL.

The Mormon War in 1838 had only two really violent episodes. The first was the Battle of Crooked River, in which a few on both sides were killed, and the Haun's Mill Massacre, depicted here, where Missouri militia attacked a Mormon settlement on October 30, 1838. This episode steeled Doniphan's resolve to bring the conflict to a speedy conclusion with the siege of Far West and the surrender of the Mormon leaders to state authority three days later. Photo no. 2–751, courtesy Library-Archives of the Reorganized Church of Jesus Christ of Latter Day Saints, Independence, Missouri.

Missourians also reacted against an apocalyptic fervor that swept the Mormon church in the summer of 1838 and led to the sometimes ruthless suppression of internal dissenters, enforced by a zealous group of vigilantes known as the Danites. These men forcibly expelled from Far West several prominent Mormon dissenters. The dissenters warned their neighbors that a growing militant spirit among the Mormons threatened western Missouri, and this helped to rekindle flames of anti-Mormonism before summer's end.[3]

Although isolated instances of violence had taken place earlier, on August 6, 1838, an election-day fight in Gallatin, Daviess County, triggered

3. Leland H. Gentry, "The Danite Band of 1838"; Corrill, *Brief History of the Church*, 30; Kenneth H. Winn, " 'Such Republicanism as This': John Corrill's Rejection of Prophetic Rule," in Roger D. Launius and Linda Thatcher, eds., *Differing Visions: Dissenters in Mormon History*, 45–75.

rapidly escalating hostilities that soon inflamed all of northwestern Missouri. Adhering to the unwritten but strongly held belief that Mormons were not to settle outside Caldwell County, non-Mormons in Daviess County forcibly kept a group of Mormons from the polls when they showed up to vote. News of the Gallatin riot quickly got back to Far West, prompting Joseph Smith to march to Gallatin with an armed force to protect his followers.[4]

When he arrived the next day at Adam-ondi-Ahman, the principal Mormon settlement in Daviess, Smith learned that his disciples were unhurt and reports of violence had been exaggerated. He did not withdraw, however. On August 8, Smith sent a group of men to the home of a prominent Daviess County resident, Adam Black, to ascertain the level of anti-Mormon sentiment in the county. They tried to force Black, a local judge, into signing a prepared statement disavowing any sympathy for violence against the Mormons and promising to uphold legal institutions in the state. When Black refused to be intimidated, standing on his judicial oath to uphold the law, Smith coerced him into signing the statement. No sooner had the Mormons returned to Adam-ondi-Ahman than Black and several associates swore out a complaint against Joseph Smith and key Mormon leaders that charged them with starting a war on the Missouri frontier.[5]

Local judge Austin A. King issued a warrant for Joseph Smith's arrest, along with his chief lieutenants, and on September 2, 1838, Smith contacted Doniphan and David Atchison to help him get out of the mess. The next day the lawyers rode to Far West, meeting with the Mormon prophet on the morning of September 4, 1838. Doniphan and Atchison agreed to continue as the principal attorneys for the Mormons, as Joseph Smith noted, because "They are considered the first lawyers in the Upper Missouri." Doniphan and Atchison also persuaded Smith and Sidney Rigdon, his chief lieutenant, to surrender and stand trial for the supposed crime. The Mormon prophet did not want to, but Atchison persuaded him by pleading it will be "my life for yours" if trouble erupted.[6]

Doniphan and Atchison arranged a hearing for September 7, in a grove a half-mile from the Daviess County line. Austin King heard the case and, aside from an unruly group of Daviess settlers who looked briefly like they wanted to make trouble, the case proceeded without incident. William P. Peniston represented the state while Doniphan and Atchison defended the Mormon prophet and his associates. Adam Black was Peniston's only witness, but Doniphan called several people to testify that the incident had

    4. Reed C. Durham, "The Election Day Battle at Gallatin"; Stephen C. LeSueur, "The Danites Reconsidered: Were They Vigilantes or Just the Mormons' Version of the Elks Club?"; LeSueur, *1838 Mormon War*, 59–64.
    5. This story is most ably told in LeSueur, *1838 Mormon War*, 65–67.
    6. George W. Robinson, "The Scriptory Book of Joseph Smith, Jr., President of the Church of Jesus Christ of Latter-day Saints in All the World," 77–78, LDS Archives.

been much less threatening than Black alleged. In the end, King decided that sufficient evidence existed to bind the Mormons over for trial on a misdemeanor. He set bail at $250 each and ordered that they appear at the next session of the grand jury.[7]

After the hearing Doniphan, Atchison, and the Mormons returned to Far West. When they arrived at the Mormon capital they found a small delegation of Missourians from Chariton, led by Sterling Price, investigating the situation. In one of his trademark exhortations Doniphan made a convincing case for Mormon innocence, convincing Price to lead his group back to Chariton to quiet their neighbors. At the same time Doniphan and Atchison went to Richmond to deal with anti-Mormon sentiment there.

The controversy might have ended there but for a run-in between armed groups of Mormons and non-Mormons. While Doniphan and Atchison traveled to Richmond, Mormon militia captured a wagonload of arms and a detail of three anti-Mormons in Daviess County. The episode inflamed sentiments in western Missouri once again, especially after a pro-Mormon court in Far West bound the men over for trial for smuggling arms to a mob. Both sides now appealed to the governor for assistance, alleging the other's wrongdoing.

Atchison, serving both as legal counsel for the Mormons and as major general commanding the third division of state militia, found a nasty situation brewing when he arrived in Richmond. While he and Doniphan had been working to lessen the tension in a potentially explosive situation, it now looked like they had failed. Judge King tried to defuse the situation, demanding that the Saints "turn the prisoners loose, and let them receive kind treatment; that the guns were government property."[8] King also offered advice to Atchison in his role as militia commander of Missouri's Third Division. He asked Atchison to "send a force, say of two hundred men, or more if necessary. Dispel the forces in Daviess, and all the assembled armed forces in Caldwell, and while there, cause those Mormons who refuse to give up, to surrender and be recognized, for it will not do to compromise the law with them."[9]

Atchison called out four hundred men, placing half of them under Brigadier General Doniphan's command and the rest under Brigadier General Hiram G. Parks of Ray County.[10] Atchison then dispatched

7. *Missouri Republican,* September 22, 1838; *Missouri Argus,* September 27, 1838.

8. Smith, *History of the Church,* B. H. Roberts, ed., 3:75.

9. *Document Containing the Correspondence, Orders, &c. In Relation to the Disturbances with the Mormons; and the Evidence Given Before the Hon. Austin A. King,* 28–29.

10. Doniphan was a brigadier general in the Missouri State Militia, but in 1846 as commander of the First Missouri Mounted Volunteers he was commissioned as a colonel in the volunteers of the U.S. Army. The army commission took precedence over the state rank. As a result, after the war with Mexico he was usually referred to as Colonel Doniphan, his correct rank, but occasionally also as General Doniphan. This

Doniphan and his force to secure the release of the three captives at Far West, traveling to Ray County to meet Hiram Parks for the deployment to Daviess County. By September 14 the militia was in the field and state leaders were sanguine of the ability of "Generals Atchison and Doniphan, as well as other gentlemen who have gone out, to bring this matter to a peaceable termination."[11]

On the morning of September 12, 1838, Doniphan took command of his troops and marched to the border between Clay and Caldwell Counties and then bivouacked near the Crooked River. He then proceeded on to Far West with only an aide, Benjamin Holliday, leaving his troops behind to avoid any possibility of inciting violence. "On arriving at that place," Doniphan wrote in his report to Atchison, "I found Comer, Miller and McHaney, the prisoners mentioned in your order. I demanded of the guard who had them in confinement to deliver them over to me, which was promptly done. I also found that the guns that had been captured by the Sheriff and citizens of Caldwell had been distributed and placed in the hands of the soldiery and scattered over the country; I ordered them to be immediately collected and delivered up to me." Doniphan then summoned his command to Far West and collected forty-two stand of weapons, returning them along with the three prisoners to Atchison's headquarters in Ray County. On the morning of September 14 Doniphan's force left Far West and moved northward into Daviess County where it encamped between the Mormons at their settlement of Adam-ondi-Ahman and a band of anti-Mormons gathered near Gallatin.[12]

The next day Atchison arrived at Doniphan's bivouac with troops from Ray County. Both immediately realized the Mormons' peril from anti-Mormon forces in the area. They agreed, as Doniphan later wrote to Holliday, that their action had to "prevent an engagement between a self-constituted *collection* or army of citizens from various counties then in Daviess and the residents of Adam-ondi-Ahman who had embodied under General Lyman Wight for self-defence." Their four hundred troops then dispersed the two rival forces in Daviess County, after convincing the anti-Mormons that those for which there were warrants would stand trial. On September 18 Doniphan and Atchison represented several Mormons accused of riot at a preliminary hearing at Netherton Springs in Daviess County. Some surly anti-Mormons showed up to intimidate the court, and according to the Mormon George A. Smith, had it not been for the

changed during the Civil War when his nephew John Doniphan became a colonel of volunteers in the Union army. Alexander William Doniphan thereafter usually was referred to as General Doniphan, his militia rank, and John Doniphan, as colonel.

11. *Missouri Argus,* September 27, 1838.

12. Doniphan's entire report to Atchison, dated September 15, 1838, is quoted in Rollin J. Britton, "Early Days on the Grand River and the Mormon War," 130–32.

"stern vigilance" of Doniphan and Atchison "probably none of us would have left the ground alive." An overstatement, no doubt, but the assertion bespoke the general seriousness of the situation. In the end, the court bound the Mormon defendants over to appear at the next term of the circuit court.[13]

This outcome apparently satisfied the non-Mormons and on September 20 Atchison reported to the governor that all hostile parties were returning to their homes. Atchison dispersed the troops under his command, leaving only one hundred under Hiram Parks in Daviess County to keep order. Atchison and Doniphan then returned to Richmond and reported to the governor that western Missouri had two armed camps ready to do battle. All they needed was a spark to start the conflagration. Even so, the governor ordered the discharge of Doniphan's troops from state service, effective September 23.[14]

The action proved premature. Two weeks after returning to Liberty, Doniphan received orders to raise a militia force to quell renewed disturbances between the Mormon and other settlers. Skirmishes between the two groups had taken place frequently during the first ten days of October 1838, and only a return of the militia could restore order.

Hiram Parks feverishly wrote to Atchison that he must send Doniphan immediately with troops from Clay County. Only if militia arrived in sufficient strength before either side could work up the nerve to attack the other, Parks believed, could bloodshed be prevented. "Should these troops [from Doniphan's command] arrive here in time," he added, "I hope to be able to prevent bloodshed. Nothing seems so much in demand here (to hear the Carroll county men talk,) as Mormon scalps—as yet they are scarce." Because of this, Atchison told Parks to summon Doniphan's troops from Clay, as well as troops from other counties, and to march for Mormon country.[15]

Meanwhile, the Mormons fortified Adam-ondi-Ahman for an extended siege. On October 14–15, Joseph Smith and Sidney Rigdon sent some

13. A. W. Doniphan to Major B. Holliday, April 5, 1850, Alexander William Doniphan Letters; George A. Smith, History, 49–50, both in LDS Archives; *Document Containing the Correspondence, Orders, &c.,* 159–63.

14. David R. Atchison to the Governor, September 20, 1838, in *Document Containing the Correspondence, Orders, &c.,* 27–28. Interestingly, Doniphan was mustered out of state service after having served from September 10 to 23, 1838. His pay for that service was $45.06, with a clothing allowance of $5.20, for a total of $50.26. See "Mormon War Militia Pay Voucher," November 9, 1841, Missouri Fire Documents Collection, Collection #2154, fld. 24, Adjutant General, Mormon War: Pay Accounts, 3d Division, Missouri Militia, Nos. 21–40, Officers; "State of Missouri to A. W. Doniphan, Brig. Gen., 1st Brigd., 3 Div., M.M." both in Missouri State Archives; and Parrish, *David Rice Atchison,* 21–22.

15. Parks to Atchison, October 7, 1838, *Document Containing the Correspondence, Orders, &c.,* 38.

four hundred troops from Far West into Daviess County, ostensibly to protect Mormons at Adam-ondi-Ahman. But the situation soon escalated. With Mormon militia entering Daviess County, it was only a matter of time before trouble began. On October 18 Mormon troops plundered and burned Gallatin and Millport, looting and burning about two dozen buildings, and then torching an unspecified number of non-Mormon farmhouses. The Mormon John Corrill thought his fellow churchmen had undertaken the violence as a preemptive strike. No matter how understandable their plight may have seemed before the Daviess County episode, most Missourians now viewed the Mormon military opera-tions as unnecessary. Doniphan always believed that regardless of who had started the conflict, the Mormons had at this point become the aggressors.[16]

Doniphan received the blame for this fit of violence in Daviess County. On the evening of October 15, 1838, he entered Far West at the head of a column of about sixty militia from Clay County and rendezvoused with another column from Clay that was bivouacked just outside the town. Al-though ordered to take the field a week earlier, Doniphan did not feel great haste to get there, preparing instead for a lengthy campaign in Daviess and Caldwell Counties. In Far West, Doniphan apparently renewed his acquaintance with Mormon leaders and explained the situation. He told the Mormon leadership that he believed many of the militia were sympa-thetic to the non-Mormons and might become mutinous. The Saints could not rely upon the Clay men for protection, Doniphan announced.[17]

What Doniphan next told the Mormons is dependent on which source one believes. According to Joseph Smith, Doniphan took him aside and ex-plained that a force of some eight hundred men was slowly traveling from Carroll to Daviess County with the intention of expelling the Mormons from Adam-ondi-Ahman. Smith stated matter-of-factly that Doniphan "ordered out one of the officers to raise a force and march immediately to what he called Wight's town and defend our people from the attacks of the mob, until he should raise the militia of his, and the adjoining counties to put them down."[18] Supposedly in response to Doniphan's direction, the Mormons formed a company and "took up a line of march for Adam-ondi-Ahman, . . . and the brethren were very careful in all their movements to act in strict accordance with the constitutional laws of the land."[19] In the Mormons' "First Appeal to Congress," they also declared that Doniphan told them that anti-Mormon "Cornelius Gilliam was raising a mob to

16. LeSueur, *1838 Mormon War*, 119–20; Corrill, *Brief History of the Church*, 38.

17. Smith, *History of the Church*, 3:454–56; LeSueur, *1838 Mormon War in Missouri*, 115.

18. Joseph Smith Jr., "Journal Extract," 1839, in Jessee, ed., *The Papers of Joseph Smith*, Vol. 1, *Autobiographical and Historical Writings*, 216; Greene, *Facts Relative to the Expulsion*, 20.

19. Smith, *History of the Church*, 3:162.

destroy their town; and advised them to place our guards to watch the movements of the mob. He also directed them to raise a company of Mormons and send them to Daviess County to aid their brethren there, against like depredations; as a mob was marching down upon them from Carroll County." As a result, every one of the later violent actions taken by the Mormons seems to have been justified by following the orders of Alexander Doniphan, a state militia commander and political leader. In essence, they were acting as legitimate state troops.[20]

This does not square with Doniphan's intent in meeting the Mormons nor is it likely that he ordered the Mormons to confront vigilantes. Doniphan almost certainly sympathized with the plight of the Mormons, but he did not order Mormon troops to Daviess County. The Mormons had planned and organized the expedition before Doniphan arrived; they even staged a formal send-off on October 15 at Far West several hours before Doniphan arrived in town. Even had he been present, Doniphan did not have authority to command militia from Caldwell County; it was not a part of his brigade. That might not have bothered the Mormons, who would probably have listened to him in a situation such as this, but Doniphan was one of the finest lawyers in the state and he knew very well the boundaries of his legal authority. There is no reason for him to have overstepped it in this case. Instead, when Doniphan learned that the Mormons were marching to Daviess County, he urged caution. "He recommended that, to avoid any difficulties which might arise," said Sidney Rigdon, "they had better go in very small parties without arms, so that no legal advantage could be taken of them." He also counseled them only to protect Adam-ondi-Ahman until they received official direction from the proper state authorities.[21]

However the Mormons came to commit these depredations, they riveted statewide attention on the conflict in western Missouri. Parks visited the Mormon encampment and roundly condemned their military activities in Daviess County; concluding that a state of near civil war was then in existence and that the Mormons were at fault for starting it. He also wrote to Atchison confiding his sense of helplessness in keeping order in the region. His small force of state militia generally sided with the non-Mormons and Parks admitted to Atchison that they "partake, in a great degree of the mob spirit, so that no reliance can be placed upon them."[22] Some Ray County troops, thinking Parks overly sympathetic to the Mormons, even refused to accept orders from him. "The militia have been called out to suppress the mob," E. A. Lampkin said about the Ray

20. "The First Memorial," in Clark W. Johnson, ed., *Mormon Redress Petitions: Documents of the 1833–1838 Missouri Conflict,* 112.

21. Affidavit of Sidney Rigdon, in Smith, *History of the Church,* 3:454–55.

22. Quoted in Parrish, *David Rice Atchison,* 22.

County units, "but I believe they intend helping to kill [the Mormons]."[23] So strained were loyalties among Doniphan's own militia that he marched them back to Clay County and disbanded them, reportedly labeling them "damned rotten hearted."[24]

With Mormon actions in Daviess County forcing out most of the non-Mormons, Joseph Smith's men returned to Far West thinking they had settled the controversy. As far as they were concerned, the Saints had protected themselves from lawless mobs. They also repeated the belief that they acted merely in response to orders from Doniphan, despite considerable evidence to the contrary. But the controversy did not end there. "I do not know what to do," Hiram Parks wrote to Atchison in near desperation. "I will remain passive until I hear from you. I do not believe calling out the militia would avail anything towards restoring peace, unless they were called out in such force, as to fright[en] the Mormons and drive them from the country. This would satisfy the people, but I cannot agree to it. I hold myself ready to execute as far as I can go, any order from you."[25] Mormon activities in Daviess County, coupled with a general anti-Mormon sentiment, led to increased tension that neither Doniphan nor Atchison could control despite their best efforts.

The Mormons prepared for confrontation, and they did not have long to wait. A Ray County militia force of about seventy men under the command of a Captain Samuel Bogart went to the Caldwell–Ray County border on October 23 with the mission, "to range the line between Caldwell and Ray counties, with your company of volunteers, and prevent, if possible, any invasion of Ray county by any persons in arms whatever." Bogart exceeded his orders, splitting up his command and traveling from house to house and disarming every Mormon he found on both sides of the county line. Word of these actions soon reached Far West, along with them apparently exaggerated stories of violence, plundering, and depredations on the part of Bogart's men.[26]

On the afternoon of October 24 a detachment of Bogart's men captured two Mormon spies, William Seeley and Addison Green, in Ray County. They took the men to Bogart's camp on the Crooked River, about fifteen miles southwest of Far West. The result was predictable. On October 25,

23. E. A. Lampkin to Thomas G. Bradford, October 14, 1838, Thomas G. Bradford Correspondence, Missouri Historical Society.

24. Joseph Smith Jr., "History of Joseph Smith," *Times and Seasons* 1 (May 1840): 98; Smith, *History of the Church,* 3:369.

25. Hiram Parks to David R. Atchison, August 21, 1838, in *Document Containing the Correspondence, Orders, &c.,* 47–48.

26. Samuel Bogart to David Rice Atchison, October 23, 1838, in *Document Containing the Correspondence, Orders, &c.,* 48; David Rice Atchison to Samuel Bogart, October 23, 1838, in *Document Containing the Correspondence, Orders, &c.,* 108; Johnson, ed., *Mormon Redress Petitions,* 473; Greene, *Facts Relative to the Expulsion,* 12.

1838, in an attempt to rescue Mormon spies, the two sides clashed. In the battle Mormon Apostle David C. Patten died along with two other Mormons and a member of Bogart's command. Several others on both sides received wounds. Although the Ray County militiamen were anti-Mormon in sentiment and could have been viewed as little more than a loose confederation of vigilantes, the battle changed the nature of the conflict by reinforcing the impression of widespread Mormon hostilities in northwestern Missouri.[27]

News of this battle traveled quickly throughout the state. The governor had had enough. On October 26 he directed the head of the Howard County militia, Major General John B. Clark, to raise two thousand troops and join Doniphan and Parks for a campaign in northwestern Missouri. Clark acted in some haste to begin his campaign, especially after he received a brief October 25 report from Amos Rees and E. M. Ryland that he must hurry to Richmond, for "These creatures will never stop until they are stopped by the strong hand of force."[28]

The situation grew more grim on October 27, 1838, when Boggs, no friend of the Mormons, issued the infamous "Extermination Order." Written to Clark as he began his march to Richmond, the communication declared that "The Mormons must be treated as enemies and must be exterminated or driven from the state, if necessary for the public good. Their outrages are beyond all description." He specifically directed Clark "to unite with General Doniphan, of Clay, who has been ordered with five hundred men to proceed to the same point for the purpose of intercepting the retreat of the Mormons to the north. The whole force will be placed under your command."[29]

Doniphan had not been idle throughout this period. He raised new troops and on October 26, along with Atchison and Parks, marched to prevent further bloodshed. Doniphan and Atchison wrote to U.S. Army Lieutenant Colonel R. B. Mason at Fort Leavenworth on October 27:

> We regret that the State of (the) country in Upper Missouri is such as to make it necessary for each man to become a soldier; and each town to be guarded to protect them from arson and plunder. The citizens of Daviess, Carroll, and some other northern counties have raised mob after mob for the last two months for the purpose of driving a community of fanatics, (called mormons) from those counties and from the State. Those things have at length

27. "History of Joseph Smith," *Times and Seasons* 1 (July 1840): 170–71; Thorp, *Early Days in the West,* 85–86; LeSueur, *1838 Mormon War,* 137–42.

28. Governor Lilburn W. Boggs to Major General John B. Clark, October 26, 1838, and Amos Rees and E. M. Ryland to Major General John B. Clark, October 25, 1838, both in *Document Containing the Correspondence, Orders, &c.,* 62–63.

29. Governor Lilburn W. Boggs to Major General John B. Clark, October 27, 1838, in ibid., 61.

goaded the mormons into a state of desperation that has now made them aggressors instead of acting on the defensive. This places the citizens of this whole community in the unpleasant attitude that the civil and decent part of the community have now to engage in war to arrest a torrent that has been let loose by a cowardly mob, and from which they have dastardly fled on the first show of danger.

The generals asked for Mason's assistance with additional arms necessary to restore order in northwestern Missouri. Mason, however, refused the request, pleading that he did not have authority to send troops into a state without an explicit request from the governor.[30]

Doniphan and his associates had better success raising troops in nearby Richmond, enlisting two companies of men. But those who volunteered ached to fight the Mormons and Doniphan had trouble controlling them. On October 28 he and Atchison wrote the governor informing him of their actions, but General Clark intercepted this missive and it never reached Boggs. Accordingly, Doniphan marched his force north to the Crooked River, about a mile south of the Caldwell County border, where he began patrolling for outriders. While in the field, Doniphan was joined by forces under Atchison and Brigadier General Samuel D. Lucas, from Jackson County, and he also received a full set of Clark's dispatches. Clearly, Clark would assume overall command of the operation and Atchison had been relieved of his command because of his apparent sympathy with the plight of the Mormons. After reading these messages, Atchison turned his command over to Lucas and returned to Liberty, ending his involvement in the war. Doniphan thought about resigning his command as well, and would have done so had he "not been persuaded by General Atchison and others that by remaining I might save the effusion of blood. . . ."[31]

The next day, fully under Clark's command and chafing from it, Doniphan took up the line of march to Far West. He found few Mormons on farms outside the city; they had retreated to Far West because of the threat of the "Extermination Order." Doniphan arrived there on the afternoon of October 30, leading a phalanx of two thousand troops from all over northwestern Missouri. Lucas followed closely with Jackson County militia. Doniphan pulled up short of Far West, bivouacking about a half mile from the main road into the city with his tents pitched in a formation that allowed the men to form a defensive perimeter in the event of attack. He posted guards about the camp and closed the road to the Mormon

30. Atchison and Doniphan to Mason, October 27, 1838; see also Mason's response to Atchison and Doniphan, October 28, 1838, both in LDS Archives. This was a classic states' rights issue and Mason was correct in refraining from involvement without the governor's request.

31. Doniphan to Major B. Holliday, April 5, 1850, Alexander William Doniphan Letters, LDS Archives.

stronghold with pickets. He also left word to form on his right in the event of trouble; the code word for action, he chuckled, would be "Bogart."

The day did not pass without excitement; when Doniphan's pickets glimpsed dust rising on the road from Far West, they became convinced that it was Mormon troops advancing to attack. Hurriedly Doniphan ordered his men to form on his right, but as they tried to do so he kept moving to get a better look at the perceived enemy. Not surprisingly, his men failed to form on his right as directed. Doniphan lost his temper and started swearing at them, and then threatened to use the blunt edge of his sword on the troops if they did not form a proper line for combat. When his aide yelled for him to stay still, Doniphan's troops formed on his right with almost textbook precision. It was, of course, an excellent example of Doniphan's lack of experience as a military commander and a lesson that did not escape him. The source of the dust turned out to be nothing more than a squad of Missouri militia driving cattle into camp for the commissary, but had it been an enemy the result could have been disastrous.[32]

As Doniphan busied himself on the evening of October 30 with preparations for battle, Smith quietly sent emissaries under the safety of a white flag into the militia camp with a message offering to meet and discuss compromise. These representatives informed Doniphan that many Mormons were willing to fight to the death if Smith ordered it, but most wanted peace. Doniphan told them that he had no wish to harm any innocent Mormons, but that he intended "to have a complete reorganization of society in the county before he returned and by the suffrages of the people it should be determined whether Caldwell would still be governed by priestcraft. . . ." He also agreed to postpone battle until a meeting could be held the next day between the leaders of the two groups. He promised to meet the Mormon leadership early the next morning.[33]

With first light on Wednesday, October 31, Doniphan got his men up and prepared to move toward Far West when elements of his command apparently saw some Mormons from outlying areas trying to sneak into Far West. Doniphan ordered his men to cut off their retreat and capture them. With Doniphan galloping ahead, his Clay men charged down a hill and across Goose Creek racing the Mormons to the city. It was a ragtag unit, however, as the militia spread out for nearly a mile as some had to secure their gear and saddle their horses before they could ride. Once again, it was a tactical blunder that could have led to Doniphan's troops being cut apart had the Mormons turned and attacked. They did not, and when they reached their own battle lines Doniphan pulled up. About one

32. Thorp, *Early Days in the West*, 87.
33. Reed Peck Diary, 1839, 103–9, photocopy in Marriott Library, Special Collections, University of Utah, Salt Lake City; Corrill, *Brief History of the Church*, 40.

hundred yards from the Mormon barricades, Doniphan waited for his troops to catch up and then formed into line for battle.[34]

A white flag soon appeared from Far West and Doniphan rode out to meet it with a small unit, affectionately referred to as the "Old Men's Company." Their experience made them more reliable and less likely to cause an incident, so he used them to form up between the two forces while he talked to the Mormon leaders. Who met with Doniphan and exactly what they said is unknown. Apparently it was a preliminary meeting, for Doniphan told them that any final decisions would have to await the arrival of Clark. After a short meeting, Doniphan retreated to the main militia line.[35]

A short while later under another flag of truce, Colonel George M. Hinkle, the Mormon commanding the Caldwell militia, met with Doniphan. Hinkle had been instructed by Smith to negotiate a treaty "on any terms short of battle" but it looked at first like that might be impossible.[36] General Lucas insisted on taking the lead, and Hinkle received little sympathy from him. He threatened the Mormons with extermination if they failed to surrender, and Hinkle had little choice but to cooperate. The two sides produced a rather one-sided agreement, not surprising under the circumstances, in which the Mormons admitted they had been at fault for starting and sustaining the conflict and that they would make full reparations. It required the Mormons

(1) To give up the leaders of the Church of Jesus Christ of Latter Day Saints to be tried and punished.

(2) To make an appropriation of the property of all who had taken up arms, for the payment of their debts, and indemnify for the damage done by them.

(3) That the rest of the membership of the church should leave the state under the protection of the militia, but should be permitted to remain under protection until further orders were received from the commander-in-chief.

(4) To give up their arms of every description, which would be receipted for.[37]

Lucas ordered the Mormon delegation to complete the surrender within an hour or he would level Far West. Hinkle persuaded him to wait twenty-four hours, however, provided Joseph Smith, Sidney Rigdon, and several other Mormon officials gave themselves up as hostages.

34. Thorp, *Early Days in the West*, 88.
35. Corrill, *Brief History of the Church*, 40–41; Peck Diary, 108–9; Thorp, *Early Days in the West*, 88.
36. George M. Hinkle to W. W. Phelps, August 14, 1844, in S. J. Hinkle, "A Biographical Sketch of G. M. Hinkle."
37. *Document Containing the Correspondence, Orders, &c.*, 73.

Adhering to the terms of the treaty, later in the day Smith and his lieutenants surrendered to the militia. Later, Smith claimed that Hinkle, on the pretext of treating with the militia leaders, had conspired to turn him over to his enemies. Smith said that when he reached them "instead of being treated with that respect which is due from one citizen to another, we were taken as prisoners of war, and were treated with the utmost contempt. The officers would not converse with us, and the soldiers, almost to a man, insulted us as much as they felt disposed, breathing out threats against me and my companions." Smith never forgave Hinkle for this perceived breach of dignity, and Hinkle has been roundly vilified in Mormon accounts of the episode as a traitor to the gospel.[38]

By all accounts the situation in the militia camp on the night of October 31 was grim. Upon seeing the prisoners, some of the troops closed around them and threatened to shoot them and "be done with it." Doniphan and several other officers rushed in on horseback, surrounded Smith and his colleagues, drew their swords, and drove back the vigilantes. He placed his "Old Men's Company," about ninety men, in charge of guarding the prisoners, but they proved unable to make them comfortable.[39] The guards, for instance, could not keep other troops from taunting the Mormons. Smith, who probably exaggerated, told of horrible conditions.

> I cannot begin to tell the scene which I there witnessed. The loud cries and yells of more than one thousand voices, which rent the air and could be heard for miles; and the horrid and blasphemous threats and curses which were poured upon us in torrents, were enough to appall the stoutest heart. In the evening we had to lie down on the cold ground surrounded by a strong guard, who were only kept back by the power of God from depriving us of life. We petitioned the officers to know why we were thus treated, but they utterly refused to give us any answer, or to converse with us.[40]

One of the prisoners, Sidney Rigdon, in poor health for many years, went into "apoplectic fits," which Lyman Wight said "excited great laughter and much ridicule in the guard and mob militia."[41]

The next morning, All Saints' Day 1838, was one of the most eventful in Doniphan's life. Early in the day, Lucas accepted the surrender of the Mormon stronghold of Far West. Ebenezer Robinson, a member of the Mormon troops, recalled that, at about ten o'clock in the morning, the approximately six hundred Mormon troops in Far West marched from

---

38. Smith, "Journal Extract," 1839, 438; LeSueur, *1838 Mormon War*, 175–77. LeSueur concludes that it was not so much a betrayal as a misunderstanding between the two over the details of the treaty.
39. *Missouri Republican*, December 24, 1838; Thorp, *Early Days in the West*, 88–89.
40. Smith, "Journal Extract," 1839, 438.
41. Lyman Wight affidavit, July 1, 1843, in Smith, *History of the Church*, 3:445.

behind their barricades onto a prairie south of town, where Doniphan's militia had formed "three sides of a hollow square, leaving the north side open, through which our little army marched, and formed a hollow square inside of the square of the army. They had their artillery stationed on the south side of the square, with their guns pointing to the north in such a manner that in case anything should occur, making it necessary to use them, they could rake us fore and aft, without endangering their own men." Hinkle led his men through this formality, in the process slighting Lucas by singling out the better-liked Doniphan to surrender his sword and pistols to rather than to the overall commander.[42]

Afterward, Lucas ordered his men to march into Far West and take control of the city. They searched for other weapons, in the process ransacking Mormon homes. The Mormons later described all manner of depredations committed by the Missourians in Far West. According to the Mormons, widespread plundering, violence, and even rape took place for days thereafter. Mormon Vinson Knight wrote that the militia "went from house to house, plundering, pillaging, and destroying, and even driving many helpless women and children from their homes, and committing deeds even worse than these in some instances." Certainly the troops got out of control—probably not to the extent alleged by the Mormons—but officers failed to keep their troops in order and the aftermath of the siege of Far West represents an undeniable black mark against the performance of the state militia.[43]

On the evening of the Mormon surrender, November 1, Samuel Lucas presided over a court-martial of the seven main Mormon leaders, including Joseph Smith. According to Lyman Wight, the outcome was predetermined. One of Lucas's lieutenants pulled Wight aside and told him that Smith would be executed for his alleged crimes against the state. "We do not wish to hurt you nor kill you, neither shall you be, by G——," Wight was told, "but we have one thing against you, and that is, you are too friendly to Joe Smith, and we believe him to be a G—— d—— rascal, and, Wight, you know all about his character." The militiaman asked Wight to turn state's evidence against Smith. Wight told him that he would be glad to tell the court about the Mormon leader. Thinking that they had the goods on Smith, Wight proceeded to tell them on the record that the Mormon prophet was the "most philanthropic man he ever saw, and possessed of the most pure and republican principles—a friend to mankind, a maker of peace; 'and sir, had it not been that I had given heed to his counsel, I would have given you hell before this time, with all

42. Ebenezer Robinson, "Items of Personal History of the Editor," *The Return* 2 (February 1890): 210; Oliver B. Huntington, "History of the Life of Oliver B. Huntington, also His Travels and Troubles," 35, Harold B. Lee Library.

43. Vinson Knight, "Autobiography," 99.

your mob forces.' " He also told the Missourians that " 'You may thank Joe Smith that you are not in hell this night; for, had it not been for him, I would have put you there.' " That was not what the Missourians wanted to hear and Wight became one of the chief prisoners placed on trial.[44]

By eleven o'clock in the evening, the court-martial was over and Joseph Smith, Sidney Rigdon, Hyrum Smith, Lyman Wight, Parley P. Pratt, George W. Robinson, and Amasa Lyman had been convicted of treason despite the fact that neither the Smith brothers nor Rigdon had been members of the militia and the court-martial had no jurisdiction over civilians. They were all to be executed for their supposed crimes. Lucas presided over the court-martial, but exactly who else participated is unclear. The best evidence indicates that between seventeen and twenty officers were members of the court-martial and each had voice and vote in the proceedings. Doniphan was present and vigorously argued on behalf of turning the prisoners over to civil authorities for trial, as did Hiram Parks and George Hinkle, but about two-thirds of the officers present voted for immediate conviction.[45] Wight recalled that he learned from a sympathetic officer, Brigadier General Moses Wilson, "I regret to tell you your die is cast; your doom is fixed; you are sentenced to be shot tomorrow morning on the public square in Far West, at eight o'clock." Wight reportedly answered, "Shoot, and be damned."[46]

Doniphan had disagreed with the court-martial's premise from the beginning, asserting that Smith and most of the other defendants were not members of the militia and were not subject to its disciplinary system. Additionally, the governor had not declared martial law and therefore normal civil authority still had authority to try criminals. Doniphan protested that the court-martial was as "illegal as hell." Undoubtedly, he argued, it robbed the Mormon leaders of their constitutional rights to due process of law. He just as vigorously opposed the verdict of the court-martial and the punishment to be exacted. When Doniphan heard this verdict he "arose and said that neither himself nor his brigade should have any hand in the shooting, that it was nothing short of cold-blooded murder; and left the court-martial and ordered his brigade to prepare and march off the ground."[47]

He then apparently went to the Mormon prisoners and told them of the verdict. Wight recalled that Doniphan pulled him aside and said, "Colonel the decision is a d—— hard one, and I have washed my hands against such cool and deliberate murder." Wight also said that there was

44. Lyman Wight affidavit, July 1, 1843, in Smith, *History of the Church*, 3:446.

45. Josiah Butterfield to John Elden, June 17, 1839, Josiah Butterfield Letters, Missouri Historical Society; *Times and Seasons* 1 (January 1840): 37; Eliza R. Snow, "Letter from Missouri, February 22, 1839."

46. Lyman Wight affidavit, July 1, 1843, in Smith, *History of the Church*, 3:446.

47. Sidney Rigdon affidavit, July 1, 1843, in ibid., 3:460.

considerable disagreement among the other senior officers about Lucas's decision. They were not prepared to be a party to what many others might well consider cold-blooded murder, "Extermination Order" or no. At their parting Doniphan shook Wight's hand and said, "Colonel, I wish you well."[48]

Just why Lucas ordered Doniphan to carry out the court-martial's sentence is unclear. He could have ordered another commander to do it. Instead, he sent to the Clay brigade commander about midnight a simple if foolish order. "Sir," it read, "You will take Joseph Smith and the other prisoners into the public square of Far West, and shoot them at 9 o'clock tomorrow morning."[49] Lucas must have realized by this time that his sentence was illegal and that may have been the reason he ordered Doniphan to carry it out. Doniphan, even if no one else, had made quite clear his belief that the proceedings were illegal. In directing Doniphan to pull the trigger on the Mormon leaders, perhaps Lucas saw a way out of the predicament. If Doniphan refused to execute the prisoners, as Lucas had reason to believe, at least Lucas would not have been forced to back down from his own position, and he might even be able to transfer any ensuing blame from himself onto the insubordinate Doniphan. That would certainly play well in Jefferson City where Lilburn Boggs breathed fire about the Mormons. And if Doniphan carried out the order, it would lend an air of dignity to Lucas's posture. Doniphan, well known and well respected as an attorney, had been working with the Mormons for many years. If he served as the instrument of execution, it would help justify Lucas's position and deflect any subsequent criticism.

Doniphan refused any part of it. He wrote to General Lucas: "It is cold-blooded murder. I will not obey your order. My brigade shall march for Liberty tomorrow morning, at 8 o'clock; and if you execute these men, I will hold you responsible before an earthly tribunal, so help me God."[50] Privately Doniphan, looking him "square in the eyes," told Lucas that "you hurt one of these men if you dare and I will hold you personally responsible for it, and at some other time you and I will meet again when in mortal combat and we will see who is the better man." Lucas reportedly responded, "If that is how you feel about it, they shall not be shot."[51] One of Doniphan's militia members, Peter H. Burnett, recollected that Doniphan

48. Lyman Wight affidavit, July 1, 1843, in ibid., 3:446; Wandle Mace, "Journal of Wandle Mace," 43, typescript in Harold B. Lee Library; Lyman O. Littlefield, *Reminiscences of Latter-day Saints*, 78.

49. *History of Caldwell and Livingston Counties, Missouri*, 137.

50. Ibid., 137; Lyman Wight affidavit, July 1, 1843, in Smith, *History of the Church*, 3:446.

51. J. Wickliffe Rigdon, "I Never Knew a Time When I Did Not Know Joseph Smith," 36.

received assurance prior to making his formal response to Lucas that "we of Clay County would stand by him."[52] As a result, Doniphan's mutiny had popular support.

Doniphan's measured departure threw the militia camp into an uproar. The willful insubordination of a superior officer has never been accepted readily by the military. It usually results at least in removal of the officer from his position, and in some cases much worse punishment is inflicted. Doniphan himself would not have accepted such displays from his junior officers. His willingness to place his head on a block over this issue can be explained only by a strong sense of integrity about the illegality of the proceedings. General Lucas's willingness to let Doniphan get away with such insubordination can only be explained by a similar understanding. It tells much about the perspective Doniphan brought to each of his endeavors. That his stand prompted Lucas to reconsider can be seen from Lucas's decision not to direct anyone else to carry out the executions and by his later denial that the court-martial had even been held.[53]

Instead of carrying out the execution, early on the morning of November 2, Doniphan formed up his troops in the most impressive fashion the Clay Countians could manage and marched through Far West before heading toward Liberty and the end of their military service. He made a show of leading his troops past the Mormon prisoners in view of Lucas. As he left, Hyrum Smith reported that Doniphan called out to them, "By God, you have been sentenced by the court-martial to be shot this morning; but I will be damned if I will have any of the honor of it, or any of the disgrace of it, therefore I have ordered my brigade to take up the line of march and to leave the camp, for I consider it to be cold-blooded murder, and I bid you farewell."[54]

Lucas, as if changing his mind, decided to send the prisoners to Independence, Missouri, under the guard of Moses Wilson's brigade. They left on November 2, two days before John B. Clark, who was supposedly in charge of the overall campaign, even arrived. In Independence, the Mormons could be brought before civil authorities and tried for their crimes. Lucas then made it clear to the remaining Mormons that they

52. Peter H. Burnett, *Recollections and Opinions of an Old Pioneer,* 63.
53. The Mormons have always, and justifiably so, remembered Doniphan fondly for his stand at Far West. Apostle Amasa Lyman declared that "From the execution of this merciless sentence we were saved by the opposition, to the same, of General Doniphan, and long may he live to enjoy the reward of the soul ennobling qualities that exalted him incomparably above the priest-ridden, bloody rabble around him" (Amasa Lyman, "Amasa Lyman's History," *Latter-day Saints' Millennial Star,* 27 [1865]: 535). Lucas, however, denied the court-martial in a letter to Governor Boggs on November 11, 1838, in *Document Containing the Correspondence, Orders, &c.,* 64.
54. "*Missouri v Joseph Smith,*" *Times and Seasons* 3 (July 15, 1843): 251.

were to leave the state with all possible speed. Doniphan again mustered out of state service in Liberty on November 5, 1838, after having been on active duty for eleven days.[55]

Doniphan's relationship with the Mormons did not end with the termination of his military service. Indeed, he became a celebrity for his tough-minded stand in favor of justice at Far West. Also, he received virtually no negative publicity then or after from Missourians for his insubordination to Lucas. Various politicians and community leaders praised Doniphan, Atchison, Parks, and other militia commanders who had stood up for fairness in the Mormon War even though most were unsympathetic to the sect. While Doniphan's fairness and sense of justice deserves applause, it also did not hurt his legal practice to be identified with a stand in defense of justice at the frontier community of Far West.

The young lawyer also enhanced his image by serving as Mormon counsel during their preliminary hearing in Richmond between November 12 and 29, 1838. Presided over by Judge Austin A. King, the Mormons have incorrectly referred to this as a trial, though it was actually a preliminary hearing to determine if there was sufficient evidence to indict anyone. Mormons have also universally condemned the proceedings as unjust and motivated by religious bigotry. Doniphan and Amos Rees served as the principal Mormon attorneys, but James S. Rollins of Columbia assisted, while Thomas C. Birch headed the prosecution. There were more than seventy defendants—Joseph Smith the most prominent of them—in one of the most spectacular cases ever to take place in the state.[56]

Birch's task was to marshal witnesses and establish the probability in law that the accused had committed crimes in three key areas. First, he sought to show that Mormon defendants had illegally raided non-Mormon settlements in Daviess County and destroyed property, plundered homesteads, and driven settlers away. Those identified as being involved in this activity could then be charged with, according to Sidney Rigdon, "burglary, arson, larceny, theft, and stealing."[57] Second, Birch endeavored to demonstrate that certain defendants had been involved

55. Doniphan collected pay amounting to $67.35 due him for his time. This included, interestingly enough, a subsistence allowance for one servant—probably a slave—that accompanied him on the Mormon campaign. See "Mormon War Militia Pay Voucher," June 3, 1841, Collection #2154, fld. 34, Adjutant General, Mormon War: Pay Accounts, 3d Division, Missouri Militia, 2d Addition, Nos. 1–7, Officers; and "Mormon War Militia Pay Voucher," November 10, 1841, Collection #2154, fld. 26, Adjutant General, Mormon War: Pay Accounts, 3d Division, Missouri Militia, Nos. 61–80, Officers, both in Missouri Fire Documents Collection, Missouri State Archives.

56. Johnson, ed., *Missouri Redress Petitions*, 37, 41–42, 46–47, 88–90, 115–16, 316–17, 349–50, 407–8, 663–64; Stephen C. LeSueur, " 'High Treason and Murder': The Examination of Mormon Prisoners at Richmond, Missouri, in November 1838"; Lucien Carr, *Missouri: A Bone of Contention*, 184.

57. Sidney Rigdon affidavit, July 1, 1843, in Smith, *History of the Church*, 3:463.

in the Crooked River incident where a pitched battle had taken place on October 25 and where several people died. Those indicted for participating in this action could then be held for murder and treason. Third, the prosecution wanted to establish the probability of treason on the part of the Mormon leadership. This contention, the most difficult task of the prosecution, turned on the goals of the Mormon church and the specific actions of its leaders to establish the political kingdom of God on Earth—a government separate from the United States.[58]

Richmond had a circuslike atmosphere on the day the proceedings began. Hundreds of Missourians poured into the community, mostly curious about the proceedings. Nonetheless, the court bristled with hostility and both witnesses and accused felt intimidated by the taunts and crude depictions of what they planned to do with the Mormons. One of the guards reportedly joked, "Shoot your Mormon, I have shot mine." Despite this predicament, King performed well in keeping order and preventing any gross obstruction of justice.[59]

Birch made a case against as many of the Mormons as possible. His star witness was Dr. Sampson Avard, the leader of the Danites, who turned state's evidence to avoid prosecution. After two days on the stand Birch had a significant amount of testimony against the ranking Mormons that established their involvement in Danite activities, suggested treasonous activities, and intimated that Smith had been involved in murder and other lesser crimes. When asked about the concept of Zion and book of Daniel 7:27—"And the kingdom and dominion, and the greatness of the kingdom under the whole heaven, shall be given to the people of the Saints of the Most High, whose kingdom is an everlasting kingdom, and all dominions shall serve and obey him"—Avard said that the passage foretold the destruction of all Earthly kingdoms and their replacement with God's. King apparently turned to the clerk and said, "Write that down; it is a strong point for treason." Doniphan could not take that and replied in his booming baritone, "Judge, you had better make the Bible treason."[60]

After Avard, the prosecution called another forty-one witnesses, twenty-one of whom were Mormons or dissenters from the sect. None of them provided much additional information, however. John B. Clark appropriately commented to the governor that "I will here remark that but for the capture of Sampson Avard, a leading Mormon, I do not believe I could have obtained any useful facts."[61] Virtually all of this testimony proved negative toward the church, and that offered by Mormon dissenters reflected their fundamental disenchantment with Smith's militant

58. This theme has been extensively documented in Klaus J. Hansen, *Quest for Empire: The Kingdom of God and the Council of Fifty in Mormon History.*

59. Robinson, "Items of Personal History," *The Return* 2 (March 1890): 234.

60. Parley P. Pratt affidavit, July 1, 1843, in Smith, *History of the Church,* 3:430.

61. *Document Containing the Correspondence, Orders, &c.,* 90.

policies. Following the examinations of the state's witnesses, Doniphan called seven more on behalf of the Mormons. He did not place any of the defendants on the stand because, according to Sidney Rigdon, Doniphan claimed "it would avail us nothing, for the judge would put us into prison, if a cohort of angels were to come and swear that we were innocent." But those who testified provided specific bits of information about individual defendants and their activities.[62]

According to Hyrum Smith, Doniphan had a difficult time getting pro-Mormon witnesses on the stand. He claimed that Doniphan submitted the names of forty witnesses, but King had them arrested and thrown into jail rather than allowing them to testify. They went through this a couple of times, each with a similar result, when Judge King asked the defense team, "Gentlemen, are you not going to introduce some witnesses?" Fed up with the proceedings, Doniphan arose and bellowed that "He would be ———— if the witness should not be sworn, and that it was a damned shame that these defendants should be treated in this manner,—that they could not be permitted to get one witness before the court, whilst all their witnesses, even forty at a time, have been taken by force of arms and thrust into that damned 'bull pen,' in order to prevent them from giving their testimony." Thereafter Doniphan asked seven witnesses to enter testimony.

Doniphan left no comments about this case, and Hyrum Smith's statements about witness intimidation and outright jailing seems so egregious as to be unbelievable, even if irregularities and bias found display. Although bias certainly erupted in the proceedings, it is more likely that Doniphan and his associates made a tactical decision not to tip the hand of their defense in preliminary hearings. King's inquiry involved an examination of the evidence amassed by the state to determine its sufficiency to warrant proceeding with indictment and formal court action. It was not a trial to prove innocence or guilt. Birch himself made this plain in his comment at one point in the proceedings that "this was not a court to try the case, but only a court of investigation on the part of the state."[63]

Had the state been unable to present much convincing evidence Doniphan might have decided to offer countervailing testimony with the intention of securing the dismissal of the cases against his clients at the inquiry. Since Birch developed an able prosecution, although probably without the depth and inclusiveness that he planned for the full-fledged trial, veteran criminal lawyer Doniphan decided that a lengthy defense

---

62. These testimonies are in ibid., Malinda Porter, 146; Delia F. Pine, 146–47; Nancy Rigdon, 147; Jonathan W. Barlow, 147–48; Thoret Parsons, 148; Ezra Chipman, 148; Arza Judd Jr., 148–49; Sampson Avard, 98–107; John Corrill, 110–13; James C. Owens, 113–14; John Cleminson, 114–17; Reed Peck, 117–21; W. W. Phelps, 121–24; Morris Phelps, 107–10; George M. Hinkle, 125–28; Jeremiah Myers, 132–33; John Whitmer, 138. Rigdon's quote is in *Times and Seasons* 4 (July 15, 1843): 277.

63. Hyrum Smith affidavit, July 1, 1843, in Smith, *History of the Church,* 3:419.

would prove counterproductive. He would save his arguments, based as they were on Mormon claims that they were conducting alleged criminal activities in self-defense, for the formal trial. Indeed, mounting a hefty defense at this time might even further incriminate his clients and he did not want to run that risk. It was better to wait until the formal proceeding. In this context, Doniphan's comment about "a cohort of angels" swearing to their innocence may have referred more to the preponderance of evidence against the Saints admitted to the proceeding rather than supposed prejudice by Judge King.[64]

Doniphan's strategy did not bring complete victory, but it achieved success in many of the cases brought before King's bench. When the proceedings ended on November 29, King released twenty-nine defendants for lack of evidence. He bound twenty-four Mormons over for trial on suspicion of arson, burglary, robbery, and larceny, but released them on bail. They immediately fled the state in the larger Mormon exodus, an outcome anticipated and fully acceptable to King and Doniphan. Five more went into the Richmond jail without bail, to await trial for murders committed during the shoot-out with the militia at Crooked River. Mormon kingpins—the Smith brothers, Sidney Rigdon, Lyman Wight, and two lesser leaders—King charged with treason and held without bail at the Liberty jail. The incarcerated men received a trial date of March 1839, the next term of the court.[65]

The Mormon leaders spent a horrendous winter in jail awaiting trial. They groused about the unfairness of it all, convincing themselves of the evil nature of the state of Missouri and the lack of justice present there. They complained of the overt bias of the Richmond court of inquiry and of the wickedness of Austin King. They even whined about Doniphan's inability to gain their immediate release and blamed him for conspiring with the Missourians to persecute the innocent Saints. Joseph Smith accused Doniphan of cowardice in defending the Saints. "They have done us much harm from the beginning," the prophet said of his lawyers, ridiculously asserting that "they are co-workers with the mob."[66]

64. This is the quite reasonable conclusion of LeSueur in "'High Treason and Murder,'" 21–22. The central question then becomes one of rectifying the Mormon affidavits made afterward with this argument. While there were some instances of abuse at the Richmond proceedings and anti-Mormonism was expressed throughout it, the Mormons were writing accounts of the episode after the fact to establish their complete innocence of any wrongdoing. They downplayed or ignored altogether any of their actions that might be incriminating and, in some instances, may have fabricated abuse on the part of the judge and his entourage.

65. Judge King's November 29, 1838, mittimus can be found in Smith, *History of the Church*, 3:214–15.

66. Joseph Smith Jr., "The Prophet's Epistle to the Church," March 25, 1939, in Smith, *History of the Church*, 3:292; Joseph Smith Jr., to the Church, March 20, 1839, in Jessee, ed. *Personal Writings of Joseph Smith;* Paul C. Richards, "Missouri Persecutions: Petitions

Doniphan did not let the matter rest after the November 25 decision to bring the Mormon ringleaders to trial. He filed a writ of habeas corpus that forced the circuit court to convene on January 25, 1839, under the direction of Judge Joel Turnham. Turnham was Doniphan's friend, but his impartiality was legendary and he demonstrated it in this case. Doniphan represented all of the Mormons in Liberty jail except Rigdon, who decided to act in his own defense. Doniphan was unable to secure his clients' release, but Rigdon put on a performance that would have won awards on Broadway. When called upon to address the court, Rigdon rose from a sick bed—perhaps a prop—to describe in his impassioned rhetorical style the persecutions of the Saints and the suffering that came from his service to God. Doniphan, who knew how to reach audiences with his words as well, recalled that "Such a burst of eloquence it was never my fortune to listen to, at its close there was not a dry eye in the room, all were moved to tears."[67] Rigdon was freed on the spot, and on February 5, 1839, he left for Illinois.

By March 1839 Doniphan was fed up with the courts in Missouri. The Mormon leaders should have stood trial in the March term, but the days passed and the docket did not include them. He petitioned for a change of venue but bureaucratic difficulties delayed its approval. Finally, in early April Judge King ordered the prisoners moved to Daviess County for a hearing before a grand jury—still not a trial—preliminary to a formal proceeding. On April 6 Joseph Smith and two others were taken to Gallatin and on the ninth they appeared with Rees—Doniphan does not seem to have been present at this court—before the grand jury. The grand jury indicted the defendants for all the crimes previously charged against them and bound them over for trial.

All this time Doniphan tried to obtain a change of venue from western Missouri to some other part of the state, challenging that the Mormon leaders could not get a fair trial there. During the grand jury investigation the venue change came through, and on April 15 the prisoners boarded a wagon for a trek across the state to Boone County. Accompanied by sheriff William Morgan and four deputies, the group made its way over the poor Missouri roads. The second night out, Morgan and his deputies drank so heavily they passed out. The Mormon prisoners took the opportunity to escape. Hyrum Smith and Lyman Wight both said that the escape had been engineered by Missouri officials to get rid of a public relations problem and a judicial embarrassment. That may well have been the

---

for Redress." Basic accounts of the experience in the jail are in Leonard J. Arrington, "Church Leaders in Liberty Jail"; Dean C. Jessee, " 'Walls, Grates, and Screeching Iron Doors': The Prison Experience of Mormon Leaders in Missouri, 1838–1839."

67. "Gen. Doniphan's Recollections of the Troubles of that Early Time," *Saints' Herald* 28 (August 2, 1884): 230; *Kansas City Journal,* June 12, 1881.

case, but if so the Daviess County residents never forgave the guards for allowing it. Morgan signed an affidavit swearing that the Mormon leaders had made their "escape without the connivance[,] consent[,] or negligence of myself or said guard." Daviess citizens did not believe him, however, and rode him through Gallatin on an iron rod. He died not long thereafter, presumably from injuries sustained in this episode. Another set of Mormons held in Columbia also escaped soon thereafter, lending credence to the idea that state officials allowed them to get away, thereby ending the whole unpleasant episode.[68]

Whether a conspiracy had been hatched by state officials or not, the escape of the Mormons solved a problem for Missouri leaders. The state made no serious attempt to pursue the Mormon escapees and they went east to Illinois and took up residence in the Mormon town of Nauvoo. Although Joseph Smith was a public figure and state officials knew his whereabouts, not until 1842 did they make an actual attempt to gain his extradition from Illinois (and then only because of an attempted assassination of by then ex-governor Boggs that most people laid at the feet of the Mormons). Doniphan's service on the case, therefore, ended after he led the defense of the last two Mormons charged by the state, King Follett and Luman Gibbs, held elsewhere. He secured their case's dismissal.[69]

Doniphan had not worked for free during this important case and his service on behalf of the Mormons proved quite lucrative. Although the fame associated with the very public episode probably amounted to more remuneration than he got from the Mormons, he and Rees received 1,079.86 acres of land in Jackson County for their legal services. At the time this amounted to nearly five thousand dollars. Joseph Smith had prophesied that Doniphan should not take that land because "God's wrath hangs over Jackson County," and Mormons have since pointed to the decimation of the county during the Civil War as the fulfillment of that prophecy. The land is presently in the center of Kansas City, and when Doniphan sold his portion of it several years later he received a handsome profit.[70]

---

68. LeSueur, *1838 Mormon War*, 241–44, quote from 244. Doniphan supported the effort of one of the deputies, Samuel Tillery, to be paid for his service during the movement of the prisoners between locations. He indicated that the deputies had done their duty and deserved payment for services rendered. See A. W. Doniphan to L. T. F. Thompson, n.d., Doniphan Collection.

69. LeSueur, *1838 Mormon War*, 255–56.

70. Edward Partridge and Lydia Partridge, to Alexander W. Doniphan and Amos Rees, November 28, 1838, [filed February 20, 1839], Book F, 202, consideration: $5,000, copy in LDS Archives; Junius F. Wells, "A Prophecy and Its Fulfillment."

4

Whiggery and the Mexican-American War

THE 1838 MORMON war propelled Alexander William Doniphan into Missouri's political limelight. His refusal at Far West to execute the Mormon leader gained notoriety as a representation of courage under pressure and grace in a graceless age. Doniphan, by all accounts, enjoyed the fame and power that came with his celebrity status in Missouri. And he used that stature both for his own welfare and for the furtherance of causes he held dear.[1]

Doniphan especially used his fame to further the Whig political agenda. Now that he had more entrée into the decision-making process, he continued to advocate the economic and social program set down by the Whigs under the leadership of Henry Clay. While opposition to the Jacksonian Democrats in Missouri had existed for several years, it was not until 1839 that this opposition united to organize a formal Whig Party for the state. Doniphan enthusiastically supported it, confirming that conspicuous whiggery would benefit the opposition's cause to elect state officers, enact legislation reflective of its economic and political agenda, and alter the nature of American society.[2]

---

1. His renown for this act has continued in Missouri to the present. On October 27, 1994, Missouri Governor Mel Carnahan proclaimed "Brigadier General Alexander W. Doniphan Day," to commemorate his refusal to execute Joseph Smith. In his proclamation the governor stated that Doniphan exhibited "strength of character, courage, and respect for the rule of law," and that the state intended to "recognize individuals who bring honor to the State of Missouri." See Mel Carnahan, "Proclamation," October 21, 1994; and Reed A. Chambers II, Trustee of the General Alexander W. Doniphan Memorial Trust, "News Release," October 27, 1994, both in Reorganized Church of Jesus Christ of Latter Day Saints, Library-Archives, Independence, Mo.

2. On the formation of the Whig Party in Missouri, see John V. Mering, *The Whig Party in Missouri*; and Newhard, "Beginning of the Whig Party"; both, however, are largely outdated and the state deserves a more modern study.

The Missouri Whig Party never reached parity with Jacksonian Democrats. Throughout its existence it always remained a minority organization, successful enough to achieve a consistent majority in only eighteen of the state's counties. It proved capable neither of electing majorities to the legislature nor of sending its candidates to the Governor's Mansion or Congress. It had more success, beginning in 1840, in opposing the hard money policies advocated by the Jacksonians. This provided investment capital and other resources to help diversify the economy. In Missouri it also stood for reform, territorial expansion, and the rights of property owners. In the 1840s, Doniphan embraced and sought to advance all of these issues.

Doniphan especially adopted Whiggery's advocacy of middle-class values and goals. Not really a party of aristocratic capitalists and planters, the Missouri Whig rank and filers were often small businessmen, freeholders, and young men seeking a larger slice of the American pie. Men of wealth led both parties, and poor laborers and farmers also swelled the ranks of both. The difference rested in between, as a sizable group of middle-class Whigs like Doniphan exerted strong influences on the party. Indeed, practically no Whigs in the state owned more than twenty slaves, an important measure of wealth in the antebellum South. Doniphan, well on his way to becoming a prosperous man by the time he became a force in Missouri whiggery, owned only three slaves in 1840 and five in 1860. Doniphan represented, therefore, a cadre of young Whigs in the 1840s who embraced a system of national economic development, a strong capitalist tradition that he believed would lead both to his personal and to the public's greater security and advancement. They also possessed a high-minded value system that emphasized democratic principles and responsibility. These people believed that their future, and the general welfare of the nation as a whole, did not lie in the hard money agrarianism of the Democrats. Nor did it lie with the amoral office-seeking and rascality that they believed present among too many Democrats within the state. In the end, Doniphan and his Whig comrades believed fundamentally in the principle of governmental responsibility in promoting the welfare of its citizens.[3]

Doniphan stumped in the 1840 election for both the Whig candidates and for the party's stand on the issues. Although approached about running for Congress, Doniphan refused, but he did accept the Whig nomination for a second term in the Missouri state legislature from Clay County.

3. McCandless, *History of Missouri*, 2:125–26; Edward Pessen, *Jacksonian America: Society, Personality, and Politics*, 216–18; Howe, *Political Culture*, 299–303; Richard P. McCormick, "Suffrage Classes and Party Alignments: A Study in Voter Behavior." Doniphan's slaveholding status is calculated from Clay County, Mo., Population Schedules for the Sixth Federal Census, 1840, 22; and City of Liberty, Clay County, Mo., Slave Schedules for the Eighth Federal Census, 1860, 30, both in National Archives.

The on again/off again nature of Doniphan's office seeking throughout his public career, and indeed of all of the Whig standard-bearers, helps to explain why the party was not as successful as might have been the case otherwise. Doniphan might have been governor, U.S. senator, representative, or a more powerful state political official had he been more interested in aggressively running for office when asked to do so by his party. As it turned out, he never served in any elected office more important than that of the Missouri General Assembly.[4]

The reasons for this hesitancy, which seemed endemic to Missouri Whigs throughout the party's existence, rested on three related problems. First, many of them accepted as truth the high moral note of an earlier era that "the office should seek the man" and not the other way around. Many disliked campaigning for office. Such a position, however, essentially thwarted the idea of political parties. Parties exist to attain political objectives. In order to do that they must develop agendas and sponsor successful candidates. This required a certain zealousness for office and party organization that most Whigs in Missouri either were unwilling to accept, or, of the few who did, lacked the facility to bring to fruition. In their view, politics was crass, and they wished not to soil themselves with it. In Missouri some people equated this whiggish ideal with snobbery, and refrained from supporting their candidates regardless of their attractiveness otherwise. "Evidently equating efficient party organization with sordid secularism and with the abhorred Democrats," wrote historian Edward Pessen, "many Whigs felt a revulsion toward party politics that no doubt explains some of their failures."[5]

Second, the Whigs failed to achieve party solidarity in Missouri, even though party leaders tried to enforce it. As often as not, Whig division contributed to the party's defeat at the polls. The Whigs, for example, failed to rally around a single candidate for the U.S. Senate in 1844. Had they done so Thomas Hart Benton, running for reelection as a Democrat, might have been defeated. He had enemies within the Democratic party, and with only a few defections the Whigs might have been successful. As it was throughout this period, the Whig state organization lacked enough structure to insure victory. Doniphan and the Whigs of Clay County, as an example, apparently had little contact with the Whigs in St. Louis. Fear of defeat within this weak organization may have persuaded some of the stronger Whig contenders to decline running for office.[6]

Third, the Whigs in Missouri faced an overwhelmingly strong Democratic party that from a very practical perspective proved almost impossible to defeat. The national Democratic organization was headed by

4. *Missouri Argus,* May 14, 1840; Thorp, *Early Days in the West,* 94.
5. Pessen, *Jacksonian America,* 221.
6. Shalhope, "Thomas Hart Benton."

the enormously popular Jackson, who by 1840 had served two terms as president and then had placed his hand-picked successor in the White House. The state machine was led by a powerful group of Democrats under the strong-arm domination of Senator Thomas Hart Benton, and though the party was divided among itself into pro- and anti-Benton factions it seemed to unite whenever the Whigs mounted a serious threat. For example, when Whig stalwart George Sibley pressed Benton hard for his Senate seat in 1844, the Democracy pulled together to ensure "Old Bullion Benton's" reelection. For their part, some Whig leaders regarded Sibley as a "foolish idealist" for running against him. They advanced a strategy that if the Whigs did not run a candidate the Democratic party might exhibit its persistent fracturing and enable the Whigs to support the most acceptable of the Democratic candidates to enter the race. As a result, Whig leaders essentially considered their efforts in Missouri a losing proposition. It is difficult to get excited about political prospects, or to make a hard run for office, if defeat seems likely. That was the situation Doniphan and his Whig associates faced with every election.[7]

Within the confines of these beliefs, the Whigs ran a surprisingly effective political campaign in 1840. The national party nominated William Henry Harrison, a military hero from the War of 1812 and numerous fights with Indian tribes, for president. Doniphan and his fellow Missouri Whigs sniffed victory in the air, as the nation was reeling from the Panic of 1837 and the Democratic incumbent in the White House, Martin Van Buren, was becoming increasingly viewed as an aristocratic political manipulator without the qualities of a statesman. The Whigs pulled out all stops to win, and when the election ended Harrison had 234 electoral votes to 60 for Van Buren.[8]

Doniphan worked hard for Harrison in Clay County. In May 1840 he participated in a rally in Liberty that kicked off his own campaign for the state legislature, pressing hard for the re-creation of a national bank to regulate the economy and inflated currency to provide venture capital. Both centrifugal and centripetal force, in Doniphan's view, would hold an intelligently designed banking system together, and the republic need not fear its power over the economy. Doniphan also spoke eloquently about the "union of force and sword," as equal to the role of supply and demand for the welfare of the nation. He also took several hard shots at former president Andrew Jackson and his antibanking stance.[9]

Doniphan became a workhorse for the Whigs in western Missouri, persuading the high number of "floating ballots" to move into the Whig

---

7. Robert E. Shalhope, "Jacksonian Politics in Missouri: A Comment on the McCormick Thesis"; Herbert Ershkowitz and William G. Shade, "Consensus or Conflict? Political Behavior in the State Legislatures during the Jacksonian Era."

8. The best work on this remains Robert Gray Gunderson, *The Log Cabin Campaign.*

9. *Missouri Argus,* May 14, 1840; Thorp, *Early Days in the West,* 92–93.

column in the 1840 election. He helped to organize and spoke at innumerable rallies and parades, leading the electorate both in songs and to the hard cider keg. Judge Joseph Thorp remembered later that few elections generated more enthusiasm among the voters of Liberty than the election of 1840 when Harrison took the presidency and swept into office with him such men as Doniphan. Doniphan took Clay County by 104 votes. When Harrison won the election, Doniphan led the Whigs of Liberty in a wild celebration. Impromptu tar barrels appeared that they promptly fired to light up the autumn sky. Carrying torches they marched around town and into the city square singing campaign songs. Snow fell lightly on his head as Doniphan addressed the crowd; the rally did not end until the wee hours of the morning as chilled men, their grog beginning to wear off, slid home.[10]

During the days before the opening of the next session of the legislature on November 16, 1840, Doniphan tried to close out his affairs in Liberty and to ready himself for Jefferson City. The second of his three terms in the General Assembly, this was probably the most productive of Doniphan's experience in elected office. Recollecting the experience to longtime friend D. C. Allen in 1875, Doniphan said he had tried to be cautious during his first term in 1836 but that this time the Whigs looked to him for leadership.[11]

Doniphan appears everywhere in the *Journal of the House of Representatives* during the 1840 term, serving in both mundane and significant capacities. Not surprisingly because of his background and interests, he asserted his views in the areas of banking and commerce, the military, and criminal justice. For instance, he served on the Committee of the Judiciary, a joint select committee to deal with the dispute over the border between Missouri and Iowa, a select committee to investigate issues arising from the Heatherly war of 1836, several committees to ascertain the legitimacy of claims on the state treasury made by citizens, and the House Committee on Criminal Jurisprudence. Those committee assignments represent the priorities and issues that Doniphan emphasized in the 1840 General Assembly.[12]

Doniphan pressed for economic reforms in the wake of the general depression of the latter 1830s. The Missouri state bank had suffered because of the Panic of 1837 and its practices constricted the money supply in the state. Because of this, St. Louis businessmen, many of whom were Whigs, turned to currency issued by Illinois and other state banks for the conduct of their trade, some of which was issued by non-specie-paying

10. Thorp, *Early Days in the West*, 136; *Liberty Weekly Tribune*, January 4, 1841; *History of Clay and Platte Counties, Missouri*, 136.

11. A. W. Doniphan to D. C. Allen, May 4, 1875, Doniphan Papers.

12. *Journal of the House of Representatives of the State of Missouri, 1840–1841*, 10–11, 26, 45–46, 48–50.

banks. Suspicious of this other currency, in November 1839 the Missouri state bank refused to accept it for either deposit or the repayment of loans. In response, some other St. Louis corporations entered the commercial banking business.[13]

By the time that Doniphan arrived in Jefferson City in November 1840 a full-fledged banking crisis loomed. The Democrats were in an ugly mood over the usurpation of banking in Missouri by corporations, pushed by the Whigs, that had not been chartered as banks. The Young Men's Democratic State Convention of October 1840 even resolved that "all charters obtained for an ostensible object and actually applied to a different object, [were] frauds upon the legislative authority, and [were] proper subjects for the exercise of repealing power." William Gilpin, editor of the powerful Democratic newspaper, the *Missouri Argus,* attacked Whig policies as instruments of the state's ruin and denounced their "corporations, banks, insurance companies and monopolies of every kind and quality" as the "embryo of the reduction of the government into the hands of a few."[14]

With the seating of the Eleventh General Assembly, the newly elected governor, Democrat Thomas Reynolds, called for a rolling back of whiggish corporate elitism. He expressed concern at the "dangerous tendency of that partial and unequal legislation unhappily too prevalent of late, which by grants . . . of privileges and immunities of an exclusive nature, with the ostensible design of aiding and stimulating industry," had now wrested authority from the people and placed it in the hands of a "privileged order," the Whig aristocracy, whose members wantonly spurned those "very laws to which they owed their being." He urged the repeal of those violating corporations and the return of the state's economic system back to its honest citizens.[15]

Doniphan and other Whigs counterattacked Reynolds's anticorporate stance, arguing its antagonism to the economic welfare of the state. The Whigs' *Missouri Republican* charged the Democrats with a general failure to take positive action enhancing "the wealth and prosperity of several counties in this State to an incalculable extent."[16] Most important, Doniphan aided in the ultimate defeat of Democratic-proposed legislation that would have severely limited the circulation of currency within the state by penalizing any person or organization that traded with denominations smaller than twenty dollars. Sponsored by Representative Joshua W.

13. *Missouri Argus,* March 22, 1839, January 31, 1839, February 22, 1839; Cable, *Bank of the State of Missouri,* 179; Brown, ed., *Corporations Chartered or Organized,* passim; Primm, *Economic Policy,* 40–42.

14. *Missouri Argus,* April 21, 1840, October 16, 1840.

15. Buel Leopard and Floyd C. Shoemaker, eds., *The Messages and Proclamations of the Governors of the States of Missouri,* 1:454–56.

16. *Missouri Republican,* April 12, 1841.

Redman of Howard County, this bill barely passed the lower house on a fairly split vote along party lines, but was defeated in the Senate. Doniphan helped to turn back the cause of Democratic currency restriction in the short term, but in the Twelfth General Assembly, where Doniphan did not serve, the Democrats passed legislation that the Whigs referred to as "bills of pains and penalties." This legislation significantly restricted, at least in the view of Doniphan and the Whigs, the ability of commerce and industry to finance economic development in the state.[17]

While Doniphan involved himself in Whig politics during the early 1840s, he also continued to build his law practice in the western part of the state. While in the House, on January 29, 1841, Doniphan introduced legislation to create the Twelfth Judicial Circuit, which consisted of the counties made from the Platte country plus Clinton County, and he was delighted when the governor nominated his old friend and sometime rival, David R. Atchison, as judge for this circuit on February 5, 1841. Although Atchison was a die-hard Democrat and Doniphan just as die-hard a Whig, the two men remained close friends throughout their lives despite their sometimes heated discussions over political issues. Atchison then moved from Liberty to Platte City, the headquarters of the new circuit, to begin his duties, living there until 1857. The circuit opened in March, and Doniphan, with Atchison, often traveled around it to conduct business.[18]

The circuit remained a rustic environment for Doniphan and Atchison throughout much of the 1840s. Doniphan worked in Atchison's circuit, as well as courts in five additional towns served by other circuits. Traveling between these different locations to hold court created hardship and turmoil both for Doniphan and his family, but he was still a hardy young man who enjoyed the arduous schedule. As an example of the nature of court that Doniphan attended, Napoleon B. Giddings described one gathering of Atchison's bar in Andrew County:

> When the weather would permit, the courts were held out of doors under a large elm tree. . . . The Hon. "Dave," as he was familiarly called, seated in his large chair, elevated on a huge pine box, presided with the dignity of a Jay, a Livingstone or a Marshall, the attorneys and jurors occupying humbler positions. The attorneys, when engaged in the trial of a cause, used the crowns of their hats as substitutes for tables. The places for the deliberations of the grand and petit jurors were spaces cut out of a hazel patch sufficiently capacious to comfortably hold the occupants. Each of these jury

17. Clarence H. McClure, *Opposition in Missouri to Thomas Hart Benton*, 19; *Missouri Statesman*, January 20, 1843; *Missouri Register*, October 3, 1843; *Missouri Reporter*, September 15, 1843; Primm, *Economic Policy*, 47.

18. *Journal of the House of Representatives . . . 1840–1841*, 328; Parrish, *David Rice Atchison*, 30.

spaces was entered by a narrow path, at the entrance of which were placed sentinels to protect, unmolested[,] the deliberations of these honorable bodies.[19]

For his part, Doniphan appreciated pleading cases before "Judge Dave." "As a judge," Doniphan recalled, "he was quick, expeditious and industrious; seemed to arrive at his conclusions almost intuitively, and his high sense of justice always enabled him to decide equitably."[20]

Perhaps the most spectacular case for Doniphan during this period involved a continuation of Doniphan's service to the Mormons in the 1830s. The Mormons intensely hated Lilburn W. Boggs, by 1842 no longer governor of Missouri and retired to his home in Independence, as the major culprit in the earlier Mormon War. On the evening of May 6, 1842, he adjourned to his favorite chair in the study of his house to read the newspaper, as was his wont. A torrential rainstorm so common in the Midwest during the springtime beat against the roof, and Boggs positioned his chair with its back to a window to allow what light available during the downpour to illumine his reading. Without warning someone discharged seventeen small balls through the window into the back of the chair. Four slugs entered his neck and head; two penetrated his skull, one passed through the hollow of his neck and into his mouth, and the last embedded itself into Boggs' neck muscle. The rest of the shots missed their mark and the family spent days digging them out of the study's plaster and woodwork.[21]

Boggs's six-year-old daughter, Minnie, had been in the study hunched beside a cradle rocking her tiny sister to sleep when the shots rang out. Although unhurt she screamed when she saw her slumped, bloody father unconscious in his chair. The air in the study hung thick with smoke and the smell of gunpowder as Boggs's wife ran to Minnie and, after checking to see that she was unhurt, attempted to stop the flow of blood from her husband. A son, William, ran to the shattered window to see if he could see the shooter but the storm blew rain in his face and fog floated thick over the crime scene. He could see nothing, but sprinted for help to the neighbors. He brought back a doctor and Jackson County Sheriff J. H. Reynolds. The doctor worked on Boggs, but he had lost a lot of blood and the head injuries made prospects for recovery bleak. Most believed he would die within a day or two.[22]

19. Quoted in Parrish, *David Rice Atchison,* 31.
20. *History of Clinton County,* 441–42.
21. *Jeffersonian Republican,* May 14, 1842; William M. Boggs, "Sketch of Lilburn W. Boggs."
22. Monte B. McLaws, "The Attempted Assassination of Missouri's Ex-Governor, Lilburn W. Boggs"; Harold Schindler, *Orrin Porter Rockwell: Man of God, Son of Thunder,* 74–80.

Reynolds conducted a search of the crime scene, hampered in his efforts by curiosity seekers who trampled the ground around the window and disturbed the evidence. They did find, however, a firearm in a mud puddle, which Reynolds described as a "large German holster pistol, chambered for four shots." Three of the chambers were loaded with buckshot, like that later recovered in the Boggs home, and the sheriff concluded that the assailant had fired once through the window with a heavier charge than normal and the recoil had sent the seventeen shots forward and the pistol backward. Rather than try to retrieve the weapon and fire again, the perpetrator had fled the scene. Philip Uhlinger, a merchant in Independence, quickly identified the weapon as one that had come up missing from his store about a week earlier. Then he offered the first lead to the sheriff about who might have committed the crime. "I thought the niggers had taken it," Uhlinger said, "but that hired man of Ward's—the one who used to work with the stallion—he came in to look at it just before it turned up missing!"[23]

Cyrus Ward, a prosperous farmer in Jackson County, had hired in the spring of 1842 a young man named Brown to train and care for a stallion he hoped to race. Brown's real name was Orrin Porter Rockwell, a shirttail relation of Joseph Smith, and a man who would later become known for his enforcement of Mormon will upon those reluctant to accept it. In February 1842 Rockwell had taken his family to Independence to visit his wife's family. His wife was pregnant with their fourth child and they planned to stay with her family until the baby was born. Since Jackson Countians had expelled Mormons from the area in 1833, Rockwell traveled incognito and hired out under an assumed name.[24]

Rockwell disappeared immediately after the shooting; Reynolds could find him nowhere and no one seemed to know where he had gone or when he would return. The sheriff issued a reward of $3,000 for Rockwell's capture, and developed an elaborate conspiracy theory about Boggs's shooting. Since Rockwell was a Mormon and the Mormons hated Boggs, it seemed likely that Joseph Smith had ordered the assassination as vengeance for their treatment during the ex-governor's administration. Rockwell, he surmised, had been Smith's chosen instrument to carry out this assassination and had slipped into Independence under an assumed name. The visit to the family of Rockwell's wife was merely a convenient pretext for the sinister mission. Once in Independence Rockwell spent some months learning Boggs's routine, and when the time was ripe he struck. The irony of the attempt to avenge Mormon suffering in Missouri was that Boggs refused to die; he eventually recovered and went overland to California in 1846 where he grew wealthy as a supplier of gold

23. Boggs, "Sketch of Lilburn W. Boggs," 108; *Jeffersonian Republican*, May 14, 1842.
24. Schindler, *Orrin Porter Rockwell*, 73.

seekers before passing away of natural causes in the Napa Valley region in 1861.[25]

The invalid Boggs, recovering enough to sign his name to an affidavit, made a complaint against Rockwell for the attempted murder. Thereafter, Sheriff Reynolds tried to arrest Rockwell for the crime, and Missouri officials finally captured him in St. Louis on March 4, 1843. Transported across the state in irons, Rockwell, after a seemingly interminable wait in prison and one attempted jailbreak, appeared before Judge John F. Ryland's circuit court on August 3, 1843. At this point Doniphan reentered the story. "I was taken into court," Rockwell said in an affidavit,

> and was asked by the judge if I had any counsel. I told him I had not. He asked if I had any means to employ a counsel. I answered that I had none with me that I could control.
>
> He then said, here are a number of counselors: if I was acquainted with any of them, I could take my choice. I told him I would make choice of Mr. Doniphan, who arose and made a speech, saying he was crowded with business, but that here are plenty of young lawyers who could plead for me as well as he could. The judge heard his plea, and then told me he did not consider that a sufficient excuse, and I could consider Mr. Doniphan my counsel.

Ryland then ordered Rockwell back to jail while Doniphan prepared a defense. Doniphan asked for a change of venue, and Ryland ordered the case transferred to the circuit court serving Clay County. Doniphan was an unwilling counsel in this case, but a few days before the trial, according to Rockwell, his "mother found where I was, and she came to see me and brought me $100, whereby I was enabled to fee Mr. Doniphan for his services as counsel."[26]

Sheriff Reynolds took Rockwell to Clay County on the night of August 21. For technical reasons Rockwell remained in Clay County only ten days before the court returned him to Independence without bringing him to trial. Judge Austin A. King, however, heard Rockwell's case on December 11, 1843, not for the attempted murder but for the thwarted jailbreak. Doniphan represented Rockwell, contending that he had not so much escaped as just walked out of an unlocked door. Missouri law read that, "in order to break jail, a man must break a lock, a door, or a wall," and Doniphan made the claim that Rockwell had not violated that law. In the end the jury brought in a verdict of guilty and assessed the penalty

25. *Missouri Republican*, June 30, 1842; Boggs, "Sketch of Lilburn W. Boggs," 107–8; Joseph F. Gordon, "The Political Career of Lilburn W. Boggs."

26. Orrin Porter Rockwell affidavit, quoted in Smith, *History of the Church*, 6:138, 140. See also Court Record E, 170, 196–98, Jackson County Courthouse, Independence, Mo.; and *Niles National Register*, September 30, 1843.

of "five minutes imprisonment in the county jail." At about eight o'clock in the evening of December 13, Doniphan came to see Rockwell and told him he was free to leave, but that he should get out of the state as quickly as possible before he could be rearrested by the Missourians. He arrived at the Mormon stronghold of Nauvoo on Christmas Day and was greeted with a hero's welcome. No one ever stood trial for the attempted murder of Lilburn Boggs.[27]

As Doniphan practiced law, he continued his political career. In October 1843 he supported the appointment of his old friend, David Atchison, to fill the vacancy in the U.S. Senate left by the sudden death of Lewis F. Linn. When Atchison asked his advice about the appointment, Doniphan told him: "Judge, fortune does not shower her favors on us very often, and a man should not turn his plate bottom upwards when it does happen, but should turn the right side up and catch all he can. Your refusal will mortify Governor Reynolds, and as you have some political ambition, you ought to accept. It is your duty to do it. We have never had any senator from the western half of the state." He accepted the offer and Atchison served until 1855, when he failed to gain reelection during a grueling senatorial campaign in which his principal opponent was Doniphan.[28]

During the 1844 presidential campaign Doniphan also ran as elector for the Whig party. He wanted to win, for it would have given him an opportunity to cast a ballot in the electoral college for his idol Henry Clay, again running for the presidency. Unfortunately, Clay did not take the state of Missouri and Doniphan's Democratic opponent, Willard Preble Hall, received the nod as elector. Instead, Democrat James K. Polk entered the presidency on an expansionist platform, and this set the stage for the centerpiece experience of Doniphan's life, his command of the First Missouri Mounted Volunteers in the United States' war with Mexico in 1846–1847.[29]

With Polk's election, the question of the United States' annexation of Texas ignited into a full-fledged fire from the smoulder underway since Texas's uneasy independence from Mexico in 1836. The leadership of the Whig Party opposed Texas annexation, largely because it upset the long-standing balance of power between free and slave states. Henry Clay, himself a southerner and a slaveholder, tried to lead his party away from the troublesome issue of Texas annexation during the presidential campaign

27. *State of Missouri v Orrin Porter Rockwell*, 236, Clay County Courthouse, Liberty, Mo.; McLaws, "Attempted Assassination," 58; Schindler, *Orrin Porter Rockwell*, 100–108.

28. Quoted in Parrish, *David Rice Atchison*, 36–37.

29. *Columbia Statesman*, March 22, 1844; Connelley, ed., *Doniphan's Expedition*, 239–40; Stewart, ed., *History of the Bench and Bar*, 410; Ralph Emerson Twitchell, *The History of the Military Occupation of the Territory of New Mexico from 1846 to 1851 by the Government of the United States*, 230–37.

of 1844, but ultimately the Whigs could not escape the controversy. This stand on principal may well have cost Clay the election.[30]

Regardless of an overall Whiggish reticence to annex Texas, Doniphan and other Missouri Whigs embraced the move. Fur trade entrepreneurs William H. Ashley and Auguste and Pierre Chouteau were St. Louis Whigs who also believed annexation the right decision. All were Whigs, but they were also men of their time and place—and in that time and place, the state swelled with war hawks. When the governor called for volunteers Doniphan answered, like a lot of other Missourians of all political stripes. He led the First Regiment of Missouri Mounted Volunteers in the Army of the West on an epic trek throughout the Southwest with skill and daring. His campaign has been compared to Xenophon's and Cyrus's march, but it was more for him personally. It was a campaign of liberation.[31]

Doniphan believed he was part of a great army of manifest destiny sent from a republican Anglo-Saxon nation to free a people under the domination of a dictator, Santa Anna. The war was the singular event of his life, and Doniphan appropriately talked about his role in it as an act of conquest. However, he contended that it more appropriately represented an act of kindness, done out of a sense of duty to help his fellow man in the Southwest. His army of occupation at Chihuahua in the spring of 1847 published a little-known, bilingual newspaper, *The Anglo Saxon,* that described some of this mentality. Only two issues survive, but in the first one the editor wrote—and Doniphan certainly agreed with the perspective—that he wanted to explain to the Mexican people about what had been "done to *them* and to *us,* by the gross abuse of power and influence, of which *ci derant,* distinguished office-holders in this State have made themselves guilty." In answer to charges of conquest, he responded by saying that Mexican "functionaries have trampled upon and outraged the rights and the nationality of the Mexican people with more impunity and more flagrantly, then even the 'cruel invader' and the 'perfidious Yankee' himself."[32]

In the second issue the editor published a special message that asked the citizens of Chihuahua's neutrality. It commented that North Americans did not intend to occupy the province indefinitely, but while there the people should behave or go freely to some other place his troops did not control:

> Instead of bringing ruin with them they introduced *wealth* into a state, which was devoid of means even for sustaining a small army during a short period for its support. They proclaimed to the

30. See Frederick Merk, *Slavery and the Annexation of Texas;* and Frederick Merk, *Manifest Destiny and Mission in American History: A Reinterpretation,* 182–210.
31. Kimball Clark, "The Epic March of Doniphan's Missourians."
32. *The Anglo Saxon,* March 18, 1847.

citizens that they should be secure in their persons, their property and their industry. Instead of levying a tax upon the inhabitants to furnish the means to support the conquering army, they purchased with money, at *high prices* every article which the army wanted for its subsistence; the property of no individual was touched, no citizens molested—and apart from the fact, that the American flag waves now, where formerly waved the banner of the Mexican republic—no change had occurred in the state of Chihuahua since its conquest by the Americans, which Mexican citizens would have a right to deplore. . . . [33]

Far from international bullying, Doniphan accepted the manifest destiny argument of the war as a merciful act to free a people controlled by a tyrannical usurper.

The question must be asked, was this mere rhetoric and rationalization or a genuine perception of the war? In Doniphan's case it was a good war, necessary to free an enslaved people from tyranny. That made him like many Whigs, especially those in the South and West, and represented a major current of whiggery in the nation. Indeed, in 1848, when war hero and career soldier Zachary Taylor ran for the presidency as a Whig, Doniphan enthusiastically supported his candidacy. When Taylor was elected, indicative that many in the United States shared a view that the war had been a good cause, Doniphan was pleased.[34]

Doniphan was not yet thirty-eight years old when he heard the bugle calls of the war with Mexico and enlisted in the Missouri volunteer forces called up for service. On May 13, 1846, Congress authorized President Polk to enlist 50,000 volunteers from throughout the Ohio Valley. Scheduled to serve for twelve months, these volunteers would form their own regiments and serve under the regular army. According to plans developed in the War Department, the army's strategy called for movements of troops against three objectives. First, brevet Brigadier General Zachary Taylor, the regular army officer whose force deployed to Matamoros on the Rio Grande in early 1846, would ford the river and move south to occupy Monterrey. Second, Brigadier General John E. Wool would concentrate a combined regular army and volunteer force at San Antonio, Texas, for an invasion of the Mexican province of Chihuahua. Finally, Colonel Stephen Watts Kearny, commander of the army's First Dragoons at Fort Leavenworth, would lead his troops into New Mexico, occupy Santa Fe, and then conquer California. Kearny built the grandiloquently styled "Army of the West" around his crack dragoon regulars, eventually, by

33. Ibid., April 3, 1847.
34. Thomas Hart Benton, *Return of the Missouri Volunteers . . . ; Address Delivered in the Chapel at West Point . . . by the Hon. Ashbel Smith, of Texas, and Col. A. W. Doniphan, June 16, 1848,* appendix A; Duchateau, "Missouri Colossus," 279–89; Doniphan to Allen, "Sketch of Life," 4–8, Doniphan Papers.

late 1847, obtaining a force of 446 regulars and 3,546 volunteers (including Doniphan and the Missouri regiments) to swell his ranks.[35]

Doniphan was attending court in Richmond in the middle of May 1846 when he received word from Governor John C. Edwards that the president had called for volunteers to fight the Mexicans. The governor specifically asked Doniphan to raise mounted troops to meet the presidential levy. Doniphan immediately sent calls to several outlying counties, informing his friends that the state would raise both infantry and cavalry units, and that the mounted force—which he planned also to join—would provide their own horses, accoutrements, and uniforms.[36]

The young lawyer followed up on this call to arms with a series of public appearances to recruit troops throughout the western counties. The Liberty newspaper reported:

> By the last mail *Gen. A. W. Doniphan*, received a communication from Mr. Parsons the Adjutant General of Missouri Militia, authorizing him to raise *two companies of volunteers* of not less then 50, nor more than 100 men each. We understand that there will be a meeting held in his place on Saturday the 30th for the purpose of raising the requisite number of men. Volunteers are to expect no pay unless called into actual service. They are to hold themselves in readiness to march at a moment's warning to any part of our frontier that may be in danger.[37]

The same newspaper caught something of the spirit of the May 30 recruitment rally in the square in the Clay County seat.

> Last Saturday being the day appointed for raising 114 men to accompany Col. Kearney [*sic*] to Santa Fe, and 200 to protect our frontier, Liberty was crowded; there being something like 3,000 persons in attendance. The 114 men were raised in a short time, and twice that number could have been raised had they been needed.
>
> After the above company was raised Gen. A. W. Doniphan delivered a short, but eloquent address to the assembled multitude, and then proceeded to raise the number required to protect the frontier, and in a few minutes hundreds presented themselves as volunteers. The number of men wanted were raised without difficulty. The people generally appeared to sacrifice every interest for the good of their country. The Santa Fe company left yesterday for Ft. Leavenworth.[38]

35. Report of the Secretary of War, Doc. No. 4, *Executive Documents*, 29th Cong., 2d Sess., 47, 64.

36. Doniphan to Allen, "Sketch of Life," 4–6, Doniphan Papers; Frank S. Edwards, *A Campaign in New Mexico with Colonel Doniphan*, 21.

37. *Liberty Weekly Tribune*, May 23, 1846.

38. Ibid., June 6, 1846.

Doniphan confirmed the newspaper's report of the ease of recruitment by commenting later that, "Patriotism was at fever heat."[39]

The unit raised at the rally in Liberty on May 30 formed up on the morning of June 4, 1846, for the march to Fort Leavenworth. It would be mustered into Kearny's Army of the West, given some basic instruction in the art of war, and sent westward toward New Mexico. Initially commanded by Doniphan's brother-in-law, Oliver P. Moss, the company boasted a strength of 120 men, and they had to turn some volunteers away even as they prepared to leave Liberty. It was a ragtag collection of Clay men that showed up for the war. Although they had been instructed on what to wear and what to bring along, most of the costumes bore little relationship to any nation's uniform. Neither did Doniphan, who had enlisted as a private, wear a uniform. His slouchy, homespun clothes did not set him apart from the other Missouri volunteers, but Doniphan's broad-rimmed white hat was distinctive enough to get him noticed by officers and troops alike.[40]

When the Clay company reached Fort Leavenworth on the evening of June 6, they found a military post on the verge of overload. Established in a natural amphitheater overlooking the Missouri River two decades earlier, the post had one of the most beautiful settings in the West. Now it teamed with men who bore little resemblance to soldiers; a sea of canvas tents surrounded the permanent structures as if to rise up and overpower them, with horses and wagons stashed in every conceivable place. It had transformed into a launching pad for one of the country's first military expeditions into a foreign enemy's territory; preparations were excitedly carried out. The bugaboo of every commander in every war, logistics, dictated the activities of Fort Leavenworth in the summer of 1846. Throughout the month of June riverboats arrived at the Leavenworth docks with supplies brought from St. Louis and points eastward. Wagons pulled by oxen or mules and driven by gristled teamsters arrived from Independence and Westport. The tiny quadrangle of wooden barracks, offices, and outbuildings, flanked by the fort's corner blockhouses that had been built to handle some 300 troops, now became the headquarters of a great force charged with extending the American empire into Mexico-America.[41]

At the center of the maelstrom stood Colonel Stephen Watts Kearny, seasoned from years of experience on the western frontier. A career army

39. Doniphan to Allen, "Sketch of Life," 5–6, Doniphan Papers.

40. Rollin J. Britton, "General Alexander W. Doniphan," February 20, 1914, address available in LDS Archives, Salt Lake City, Utah; Gregory P. Maynard, "Alexander William Doniphan, the Forgotten Man from Missouri," 47–48.

41. On Fort Leavenworth, see Lt. William H. Emory, *Notes of a Military Reconnaissance from Ft. Leavenworth in Missouri . . .* , 7–8; and George R. Gibson, *Journal of a Soldier under Kearny and Doniphan, 1846–1847,* 22–24, 29–31, 36–40, 119–20, 125–26.

"The Volunteer," frontispiece of John Taylor Hughes, *Doniphan's Expedition.*

officer who had served in the War of 1812, the fifty-two-year-old Kearny personified the best attributes of professionalism prized by the military. His fellow officers characterized him with not a little envy as "efficient, effective, courteous, quiet, and tough." Tall and slender, alluring and aloof, Kearny was as thoroughgoing a Whig in politics as he was a professional army officer in bearing. In an irony of the first proportion, Kearny owed his command of the First Dragoons to Democratic Senator Thomas Hart Benton of St. Louis—with whom he would part company over the actions and insubordination of Benton's son-in-law, the ambitious John Charles Frémont, in California later in the year.[42]

When Kearny received his orders to mobilize and undertake an expedition into New Mexico in early June, he set in motion the whirlwind of activity at the fort witnessed by Doniphan and his fellow Missourians. He sent his commissary throughout the Ohio Valley in search of supplies, livestock, wagons, and arms. Santa Fe trader Edward J. Glasgow remarked in late May 1846 that Independence was abuzz with war preparations. "In this good town everything is now alive with excitement," he wrote. "All the traders are busy, hurrying to get off, and the balance of the lords of creation are drumming up their courage and enlisting to go west and carry destruction and all sorts of balls and bowie knives into the humble village of Santa Fe."[43] With considerable expediency, Kearny dispatched wagon trains southwestward throughout the month of June to position supplies for the troops to follow. By the middle of the month he had more than 100 wagons and 800 cattle on the Santa Fe Trail, escorted by parties of trail-hardened hunters stockpiling game for the army. Records from the quartermaster general in 1846–1847 show that the nascent Army of the West obtained 1,556 wagons, 14,904 oxen, 3,658 mules, 459 horses, and 516 pack saddles. By the time the Army of the West hit the trail, Kearny supposed that he had enough provisions on the plains to sustain 1,300 men for three months. But he was wrong; while his preparations were adequate, the troops on the trail suffered from short rations throughout the march to Santa Fe.[44]

On the morning of June 7 Kearny officially mustered the Clay County volunteers into the Army of the West as Company C, First Missouri

42. On Kearny, see Dwight L. Clark, *Stephen Watts Kearny: Soldier of the West*; K. Jack Bauer, *The Mexican War, 1846–1848*, 127–41; and John S. D. Eisenhower, *So Far from God: The U.S. War with Mexico, 1846–1848*, 205–6.

43. Edward J. Glasgow to Susan Glasgow, May 27, 1846, in Mark L. Gardner, ed., *Brothers on the Santa Fe and Chihuahua Trails: Edward James Glasgow and William Henry Glasgow, 1846–1848*, 79; *Niles National Register*, June 6, 1846.

44. John Taylor Hughes, *Doniphan's Expedition*, 29–30, 43–44; Robert Selph Henry, *The Story of the Mexican War*, 124; Louise Barry, *The Beginning of the West: Annals of the Kansas Gateway to the American West, 1540–1854*, 618; Leo E. Oliva, *Soldiers on the Santa Fe Trail*, 60–61; Walker D. Wyman, "The Military Phase of Santa Fe Freighting, 1846–1865," 415–16.

Mounted Volunteers Regiment.[45] The regular officers serving under Kearny handled the task of whipping the Missouri volunteers into shape prior to departure for the Southwest. They set up impromptu military instruction on a field called "Campus Martius" to teach linear warfare, marching by sections of four, proper methods of firing, sword usage, and the like. More important for their immediate welfare, however, Kearny had his officers instruct the volunteers on such mundane things as making camp, finding combustibles for their fires on the prairies, standing guard, cooking, and other skills necessary for survival on the harsh prairie. Wrestling with obstinate mules proved a necessary but difficult part of the training. "It is difficult to muster these stubborn animals into service," wrote one of the men in the volunteer regiment. "I, with a fellow soldier, was detailed from the fort until a late hour. We were employed in the novel pursuit of pulling two of the mules by main force through the hazel bushes two miles. Only think of it! Two of Uncle Sam's worthies pulling a jackass two miles through the bushes."[46] Such training, conducted each morning and afternoon in the hot June sun, did not sit well with the Missourians, who claimed that they had volunteered to fight Mexicans, not to play soldier. They could do that in the state militia where the infrequent drills usually preceded a trip to the local tavern to cool off.

Kearny told his officers to deal with the Missourians on as friendly terms as possible, but many of the regular officers displayed the arrogance and rigidity drilled into them as plebes at West Point. That, coupled with the long-standing disdain felt by professionals for the dilettante volunteers, made tempers flare. Kearny tried to control affairs in what in mid-June quickly became a contentious situation. On one occasion Kearny went onto a riverboat at the fort's docks to inspect the cargo, followed by some lounging volunteers despite his telling them to remain behind. "One of them apologized, slapping his commander on the back: 'You don't git off from us old hoss! for by Injun corn we'll go plum through fire and thunder with you. What'll you drink, General?'" Most regular officers would have disciplined these men, perhaps hours of full-pack parading in the summer sun, but after a brief scowl Kearny let it pass and had a drink with his recruits.[47]

These actions helped win the adoration of the Missouri volunteers, including Doniphan, and numerous soldiers remarked on the fine leadership qualities of Kearny. They applauded the War Department's decision to promote him to brigadier general just as the Army of the West prepared to march. Doniphan commented, "I did not fear the Genls

45. D. C. Allen, "Colonel Alexander W. Doniphan—His Life and Character," in Connelley, ed., *Doniphan's Expedition,* 19–20, 542–45.
46. William H. Richardson, *Journal of Doniphan's Expedition,* 28.
47. Quoted in Bernard DeVoto, *The Year of Decision: 1846,* 232.

criticism—for they would be kind if not complimentary—and he would have courteously corrected my blunders—but I did fear the host of Lieuts & Subs fresh from West Point—always envious, jealous & disrespectfully contemptuous of Volunteers." As for Doniphan's troops, they gained renown for their fighting ability, despite their notable lack of military bearing.[48]

As the drilling continued, military units trickled into Fort Leavenworth. Before the end of June 1846 the Army of the West had grown from the initial cadre of the First Dragoons. The largest segment was the First Missouri Volunteer Regiment, consisting of 856 men divided into eight companies, A through H. A St. Louis company known as the Laclede Rangers, a short battalion of two companies of infantry, and two companies of artillery from St. Louis, also entered the Army of the West. The artillery eventually came under the command of Major Meriwether Lewis Clark, son of William Clark and a West Point graduate who had none of the pomposity of many of his classmates. Two additional companies of regulars from the First Dragoons, stationed at Forts Crawford and Atkinson in the upper Midwest, returned to Kearny's headquarters to join the main force. Kearny also employed fifty Indian scouts of the Delaware and Shawnee nations and attached a party from the U.S. Topographical Engineers, headed by Lieutenant William H. Emory (later of Civil War fame).[49]

On June 18 the First Missouri Mounted Volunteer Regiment held an election for its field- and company-grade officers. A practice that went back to the volunteer units of the Revolutionary War, this right to elect officers usually ensured that members of the elite in civilian society entered the officer corps. Among the elites, however, competition was often keen. Sometimes the elections were hard-won contests, in which the candidates tried to woo the support of the rank and file with gratuities and promises. This certainly applied among the Missourians, but no evidence exists of widespread vote-buying or unreasonable guarantees.[50]

Doniphan had enlisted as a private with Company C, but virtually everyone assumed that because of his impressive physique, celebrity status, previous military service, political activity, and homespun manner he would become an officer. As one historian put it, "Doniphan mingled with his youngsters, draping an avuncular arm around the shoulders of the homesick farm boys, guiding them in the rudiments of soldiering, and altogether playing the role of the chum rather than a colonel." Additionally, "The self-possessed Doniphan gave confidence to the untested

48. A. W. Doniphan to D. C. Allen, September 19, 1883, Doniphan Papers.
49. Henry, *Story of the Mexican War,* 123.
50. *Liberty Weekly Tribune,* June 20, 1846; Doniphan to Allen, "Sketch of Life," 5, Doniphan Papers; Dudley H. Cooper, "A Sketch," n.d., Dudley H. Cooper Papers, Harold B. Lee Library.

band of men who gathered at Fort Leavenworth, and many of the soldiers no doubt needed Doniphan's pat on the back."[51] Doniphan mocked military formality and discipline, and though not truly of them, he mingled with the foulest of privates and spoke "with strong expressions which many eastern men would call something like swearing."[52] In such circumstances, many troops liked Doniphan more than some proper military gentleman.

When the election for regimental commander came, Doniphan ran against John W. Price, a state militia general from Howard County who had served in the Seminole War in Florida but had not acquitted himself well there. Both men gave speeches to the troops from the top of ammunition cases, Doniphan stressing his resistance to the already apparent tyranny of West Pointers. Some of his Liberty comrades also provided liquor to the troops as a means of backing Doniphan. With the speeches done, the troops lined up behind the man they supported for the colonelcy. Late in life Doniphan wrote to a friend that he had an almost unanimous vote, but his election in reality came "by a majority of some 500."[53] It turned out that Doniphan possessed what his soldiers wanted most, common sense, leadership skills, a willingness to stand up for his men, and freedom from the polish of West Point regular officers.

Elections for the other officers progressed quickly. They elected as lieutenant colonel Charles F. Ruff, and as major, William Gilpin. The West Pointers observing the proceedings probably preferred either of these two men to Doniphan for command of the regiment. Ruff had graduated from West Point and had served five years in the First Dragoons. Gilpin had attended West Point as Ruff's classmate and had served with distinction in the Seminole War before settling in Independence to practice law. "He vibrated with the premonition of empire," Bernard DeVoto wrote of Gilpin, and "saw the great central valley as the focus of all future civilization, predicted and charted the future of Kansas City, and so competently understood the westward currents that he had insisted on accompanying the second Frémont expedition."[54]

Doniphan backed Gilpin for the lieutenant colonelcy, the second in command of the regiment. Kearny and most of the regular officers, however, supported Ruff. This probably resulted from nothing more than the fact that Ruff had served with the First Dragoons. Ruff won the election by a mere two votes and became second in command. With such a close

---

51. Clark, "Epic March," 135.
52. Edwards, *Campaign in New Mexico,* 76.
53. *Liberty Weekly Tribune,* June 20, 1846; Doniphan to Allen, "Sketch of Life," 5, Doniphan Papers; H. S. Turner, Adjutant General, "Orders No. 1," June 19, 1846, Records of the Adjutant General, Vol. 42 1/2, National Archives; Dudley H. Cooper to Parents, June 19, 1846, Cooper Papers.
54. DeVoto, *Year of Decision,* 234.

election, Gilpin relatively easily won the regiment's third rank of major.[55] The election of company commanders followed thereafter.

After this election, Kearny took Doniphan aside and explained to him his responsibilities, wartime strategic considerations, tactical requirements of the mission, and how the Army of the West's expedition meshed with efforts by other military and diplomatic organizations. Kearny told Doniphan the details of the march to Santa Fe, for while the young western Missourian had a wealth of experience dealing with frontiersmen and Santa Fe traders, he had never taken the trip himself and did not appreciate fully the aridity of the climate and the harshness of the landscape, not to mention the hostility of the Indian tribes in the Cimarron area. Because of his lack of experience as a military officer, despite years of senior rank in the state militia, Kearny gave to Doniphan a book on French dragoon tactics written for an American audience. Doniphan also studied on his own the military tactics available in the works of William Duane and Winfield Scott. Doniphan began to study these books with understandable intensity while at Fort Leavenworth, and as he later wrote, "at every leisure moment on our hard march."[56] In his conversations with Kearny, Doniphan realized the enormity of the task he had ahead of him. Late in life Doniphan recalled to D. C. Allen Kearny's almost mentoring approach toward him as a junior officer, concluding that "a more gallant and accomplished officer never drew a sword. . . . He was and still is Doniphan's beau ideal of a military commander."[57]

Before leaving to engage the Mexicans, Doniphan set a number of personal affairs in order. The most important involved taking care of his family in the event of his death, but he also arranged for someone to handle his business affairs while gone. Not long before leaving he executed a power of attorney appointing John Thornton, his father-in-law and a fellow resident of Clay County, to manage all of his undertakings. It said that Thornton was "to sell all my personal property & slaves and also to sell & dispose of all & any lands I own in Clay, Lafayette, Jackson, Ray, Anderson, and all other places—and to make deeds in any named therefrom to which deeds my wife will assent" in the event of calamity.[58]

55. Thomas L. Karnes, *William Gilpin: Western Nationalist*, 140–41.

56. Doniphan to Allen, September 19, 1883, Doniphan Papers. William Duane wrote *The American Military Library* in two volumes published in Philadelphia in 1807 and 1809. He also wrote the *Military Dictionary*, published in Philadelphia in 1810. Winfield Scott published *Infantry Tactics* in 1835, the basic manual of the U.S. Army throughout this period.

57. Doniphan to Allen, "Sketch of Life," 5, Doniphan Papers.

58. Alexander W. Doniphan, Power of Attorney, June 20, 1846, MS 3045, LDS Archives. The original of this is located in the Jackson County Courthouse, Independence, Mo. See also John Thornton's statement to this effect in the *Liberty Weekly Tribune*, July 18, 1846.

As time approached for the departure of the First Missouri Volunteers, excitement mounted. A seemingly constant round of parties, ceremonies, and public speeches, all with the most patriotic sentiments, took place in preparation for the departure. At one ceremony on June 23, several ladies from Liberty came to Fort Leavenworth to present to the local Clay County contingent, now Company C of Doniphan's First Missouri, a flag to symbolize their support for the troops in the field. The ladies announced to the assembled unit that "We trust then that your conduct, in all circumstances, will be worthy of the noble" war heroes that have gone before. Pointing to the inscription on the flag, she added, "let your motto be 'Death before Dishonor.' " Captain Oliver Moss, commanding the company, accepted the flag and assured those present that the Clay men would acquit themselves in a way bringing honor upon the county.[59]

It did not take Kearny long after the formation of the First Missouri Mounted Volunteers to get his forces on the trail to Santa Fe. He would have liked to complete more training, but merchant trains had already begun heading for Santa Fe, as they had every spring since 1821, and Kearny's orders said he should escort traders and ensure their safety in selling to the New Mexicans without paying the usual tariffs on goods. This requirement grew more complicated by the fact that a Prussian emigrant, Albert Speyer, left Independence with a caravan of goods bound for Santa Fe in late May 1846. The fact that Speyer had not waited for military escort did not bother Kearny, but in talking to Captain David Waldo, commander of Company A of Doniphan's regiment and an Independence businessman who knew most of the Santa Fe traders, Kearny learned that Speyer carried not only seventy thousand dollars' worth of merchandise but also two wagonloads of Mississippi Jager rifles with ammunition. Chihuahua provincial governor Angel Trias had contracted with him to secure these weapons the previous year but Kearny knew they could now be used against his army. Accordingly, on June 5 Kearny dispatched two companies of his dragoons to interdict Speyer before he reached Santa Fe. On the twelfth he sent a third company to reinforce the dragoons already en route, in all an impressive 180 troops. Although not intended as such, these troops represented the formal invasion of the American Southwest controlled by Mexico.[60]

Kearny sent his troops out piecemeal over the next several weeks so that advance units could prepare for those to follow and to preserve the meager resources needed to support the army, such as forage for the

59. *Liberty Weekly Tribune,* June 27, 1846.
60. Letter of Benjamin D. Moore written at Pawnee Fork, July 10, 1846, in *Weekly Reveille,* August 17, 1846; *Missouri Republican,* August 3, 1846. Max L. Moorhead, *New Mexico's Royal Road: Trade and Travel on the Chihuahua Trail,* 153–54, sorts out the details of this strange episode. See also William J. Parish, "The German Jew and the Commercial Revolution in Territorial New Mexico, 1850–1900."

livestock. While some Missourians marched in these advance units, the First Missouri Mounted Volunteers officially departed Fort Leavenworth on June 22, 1846, when two mounted companies, A and D, left. Within two days, four more companies of the regiment left for Santa Fe under the command of Lieutenant Colonel Charles Ruff. And on the twenty-eighth the remaining two companies set out under Gilpin's command. Doniphan and his headquarters traveled with Gilpin. As written in the First Missouri's orders, "Col. D. will then proceed to overtake the companies now in advance and concentrate his Regiment near the 'crossing' of the Arkansas."[61] That "crossing" had long been one of the most important locations on the plains, for Bent's Fort located there served as a replenishment point.

Some 565 miles stood between Fort Leavenworth and Bent's Fort, and every inch proved a trial for the Missourians. On one of the most cluttered trails in America during the summer of 1846, by July 8 the first two companies of Doniphan's command, A and D, had linked up with dragoons sent in search of the elusive Speyer and encamped at Pawnee Fork, near the present-day town of Larned, Kansas. There the forage, game, and water proved plentiful. Three days later these forces headed on for Bent's Fort, arriving there without difficulty on July 21 and 22. Doniphan's remaining forces scattered out along the trail for several miles. Because of the crowdedness of the trail, however, forage for livestock and combustibles for fires, in addition to wild game, quickly became scarce. This set Doniphan's men up for an arduous time on the trail.[62]

Few of Doniphan's men, despite living in western Missouri, had experienced the prairies of the Santa Fe trail and they expressed surprise at what they encountered. "How discouraging the first sight of these immense plains is to one who has read the numerous glowing accounts of them!" exclaimed trooper Frank Edwards. They complained of the terrain, of the flora, of the aridity, of the monotony. They also complained of the unrelenting sun and heat on the plains, as it sapped the Missourians' strength, burned their skin, and cracked their lips.[63]

The First Missouri Volunteers struggled on, averaging between twenty and twenty-five miles a day. Even if he had intended to prevent it—and there is little reason to believe that he did—as they became a hardened group, Doniphan's already unkempt Missourians grew even more so on

61. H. S. Turner, Adjutant General, "Orders No. 4," June 27, 1846, Records of the Adjutant General, Vol. 42 1/2.

62. Frederick Adolphus Wislizenus, *Memoir of a Tour to Northern Mexico, Connected with Col. Doniphan's Expedition*, Senate Miscellaneous Document No. 26, 30th Cong., 1st Sess., 10; Hughes, *Doniphan's Expedition*, 29; Oliva, *Soldiers on the Santa Fe Trail*, 63; Jacob S. Robinson, *A Journal of the Santa Fe Expedition under Colonel Doniphan*, 13; Barry, *Beginning of the West*, 590–91, 596, 626.

63. Edwards, *Campaign in New Mexico*, 25–26.

the trail. Within two weeks, regulars complained that the men of the First Missouri were "unwashed and unshaven, were ragged and dirty, without uniforms, and dressed as, and how, they pleased." They noticed that Doniphan's men set a new standard for slovenliness in camp, loafing whenever not on the march, "listless and sickly-looking, or were sitting in groups playing at cards, and swearing and cursing, even at the officers." The only officer free from such treatment was Doniphan himself, who as likely as not was one of the card players raising a ruckus.[64]

Despite Kearny's detailed planning for the rough trip into the American Southwest, the inexperience of many of his teamsters and the inadequacies of government procurement regulations even in the young and bureaucratically small United States of the 1840s showed up on the march to Bent's Fort. To meet the wartime demand, Kearny's commissary had purchased large numbers of wagons and hauling animals from all over the Midwest regardless of condition. Many of them soon broke down on the trail and livestock seemingly did the same. The teamsters did not help matters, for many of them were inexperienced and compounded normal trail hardships. Kearny's command keenly felt these inadequacies during July 1846, and the trail became littered with "about $5,000,000.00 worth of U.S. government supplies, the bones of cattle, and in many places the drivers, lie side by side—a melancholy result, brought about alone by inexperience."[65]

Doniphan's troops also had inadequate provisions with them and the route between Fort Leavenworth and Bent's Fort held numerous episodes of near starvation. The situation grew so averse a week into the march that on July 9 Doniphan sent a message to Ruff, commanding a portion of the regiment a day's march ahead, that the rear echelon suffered from near famine. Doniphan asked Ruff to leave some provisions from his own meager stores for those trailing. Ruff cut his men's rations and cached two barrels of flour, two barrels of pork, and one of salt by the side of the trail for Doniphan. Ruff also sent a courier ahead to find a supply convoy and secure additional provisions for the entire column strewn out across Kansas.[66]

By July 11 Doniphan's vanguard had caught up with Ruff's troopers at a place called Cow Creek, but Doniphan scowled that between them they had no more than enough food for about five days at half rations. Then they learned that they had insufficient water on hand to sustain the troops for more than a couple of days. These supply problems grew doubly

---

64. George Frederick Augustus Ruxton, *Adventures in Mexico and the Rocky Mountains,* 178.

65. Wyman, "Military Phase of Santa Fe Freighting," 418.

66. William H. Glasgow to Susan Glasgow, July 9, 1846, in Gardner, ed., *Brothers on the Santa Fe,* 84–85; *Missouri Republican,* August 3, 1846.

nettlesome when Doniphan learned that even Kearny's foodstuffs did not meet his unit's needs and he could not spare any for the First Missouri.[67]

Fortuitously, Doniphan's men reached the Arkansas River on July 12, ensuring that sufficient water would be available—even if muddy and impure—for the rest of the march to Bent's Fort. At the same time, perhaps partly because of the river, buffalo roamed in large enough numbers to ensure a good supply of meat for the regiment's cooking pots. Hunters from the regiment spent the thirteenth taking down buffalo to resupply the regimental larder while most of the men lounged, washed, and swam in the shallow river. Others fished. That night Doniphan presided over a feast of buffalo steaks and fried fish. Some of the men also gathered plums and berries from thickets near the river. All they needed was a little alcohol to lubricate the revelry, and a few troopers produced that as well.[68]

By July 20 Doniphan's troops had crossed the Arkansas River and began traveling on the west bank toward Bent's Fort. Throughout the latter part of July, at Kearny's behest, Doniphan pushed his men to move more quickly, and between twenty-five and twenty-eight miles per day routinely passed without much incident. These forced marches broke down both animals and men and led to near mutiny on one occasion. It came when Ruff's battalion, four or five miles ahead of Doniphan's troops, stopped on the twenty-seventh to await Doniphan's force and spent the afternoon drilling in the more than 100-degree weather. Ruff's men blamed the lieutenant colonel for what they considered mistreatment. When the remainder of the regiment arrived almost to a man the volunteers rebelled. Doniphan tried to soothe emotions, but while he managed to quell the immediate disturbance the relationship of Ruff to the volunteers never improved.[69]

Because of the way in which Kearny pushed his army, and Doniphan's dislike of that approach, he had something of a falling-out with the general. As Doniphan recalled:

> The weather was intensely hot men & horses unused to service & permitted them to travel easily not confined to double file or strict military movement. The Genl said your men can never be soldiers, you indulge them too much & they will be utterly demoralised and unreliable unless you adopt more strict and soldier like discipline. I

67. Wyman, "Military Phase of Santa Fe Freighting," 416; Hughes, *Doniphan's Expedition*, 43–44, 158–60; Barry, *Beginning of the West*, 618; Raymond W. Settle and Mary Lund Settle, *War Drums and Wagon Wheels*, 20–21.
68. Hughes, *Doniphan's Expedition*, 160–68; Connelley, ed., *Doniphan's Expedition*, 159–60; Henry Smith Turner, *The Original Journals of Henry Smith Turner: With Stephen Watts Kearny to New Mexico and California, 1846–1847*, 59–60.
69. Connelley, ed., *Doniphan's Expedition*, 175; Abraham Robinson Johnston, Marcellus Ball Edwards, and Philip Gooch Ferguson, *Marching with the Army of the West, 1846–1848*, 87.

replied Genl, we are 600 miles from any enemy—I fear a more strict discipline would break down the men & horses—when the time comes for efficient action, you will find these men unflinching. He replied rather testily "well you will be held responsible for their efficiency." I said certainly, I would not have accepted the command of men for whom I would not be responsible in any emergency.

Kearny decided not to intervene and accepted Doniphan's explanation. Later, Doniphan chuckled, Kearny commended him for his good judgment. The First Missouri Mounted Volunteers became the model by which Kearny measured all the other non-regular army units he dealt with during the Mexican War.[70]

Day by sweltering day Doniphan's forces edged closer to Bent's Fort. The nearer the troops got, the more excited they grew for something that would break the tedium and rigors of the trail. Consequently, they pushed all the harder to achieve the goal. Then, not long before the end of July, the volunteers sighted the Rocky Mountains, still more than seventy-five miles to the west. A collective cheer ascended from the ranks and the companies raced to reach Bent's Fort. In just about one month the First Missouri Volunteers had traveled more than five hundred miles and were positioning themselves for a thrust into New Mexico.

Meanwhile, an advance party of dragoons reached Bent's Fort on July 22. Six days later Kearny's infantry arrived at the fort, beating Doniphan's mounted Missourians despite leaving Fort Leavenworth a day later. Dispensing with the care and feeding of livestock had given them more time each day to march, and their passing the First Missouri Mounted Volunteers caused them great pride. During the next three days the rest of the army arrived at Bent's Fort. For the first time since leaving Fort Leavenworth Kearny concentrated his army into a single area, bivouacking in a grassy meadow by the Arkansas River. Near the camp a group of more than 150 wagons owned by Santa Fe traders waited for the army to provide it protection as it headed south into Mexican territory. As they camped on the evening of July 31, the residents of Bent's Fort prepared for the inevitable celebration that would take place as the army regrouped prior to marching southward into Santa Fe.[71]

70. Doniphan to Allen, September 20, 1883, Doniphan Papers.
71. Henry, *Story of the Mexican War*, 127–28; Gardner, ed., *Brothers on the Santa Fe*, 29.

5

Conquering New Mexico

BENT'S FORT rose from the prairie like an adobe castle reminiscent of feudal Europe. It had stood as a guardian of American expansionism since 1832, above the present site of Pueblo, Colorado, where Fountain Creek empties into the Arkansas River. Built by the brothers Bent—William, Charles, and George—and their partners, Ceran and Marceline St. Vrain, by 1846 the fort had for more than a decade held undisputed sway over the economic and social institutions of the vast northern territory then under the nominal suzerainty of the republic of Mexico. More than a frontier trading post, Bent's Fort—Fort William as some called it—served as a crossroads of the West where travelers met to trade news and goods, replenish stores, recuperate from their experiences on the trail, and prepare mentally for the ardors of what followed.

Brigadier General Stephen Watts Kearny planned for his Army of the West in the summer of 1846 to use the facilities of the fort to the fullest extent possible, and Colonel Alexander William Doniphan, commanding the First Missouri Mounted Volunteer Regiment under Kearny, agreed. His men feasted, drank, washed, gambled, recreated, and lounged with the best that had ever visited Bent's Fort.

Doniphan saw immediately that the legendary Bent's Fort was beautiful as much for what it represented as for the facilities it offered. Historian Francis Parkman, who ranged throughout the West in the summer of 1846 on a nonmilitary lark, described it as being "visible from a considerable distance, standing with its high clay walls in the midst of the scorching plains."[1] A 137-by-178-foot rectangle constructed of adobe four feet thick and standing fifteen feet high, the fort was a bastion built to withstand

---

1. Francis Parkman, *The Oregon Trail*, 264. David Lavender, *Bent's Fort*, is the classic history of the fort and its place in the Santa Fe trade.

any siege that might come. Two turretlike towers at opposite corners of the stockade stood thirty feet high and ranged ten feet wide, loopholed for gunners and topped by artillery, ensuring that any enemy had a disadvantage. Inside, the fort's owner, the trading firm of Bent and St. Vrain, had attempted to make it entirely self-sufficient. It had living quarters, storerooms, warehouses, a smithy and wainwright shop, an ice house, and recreation facilities that included a billiards room. The owners kept as many as 150 men employed there much of the year, and Indians and trappers often wintered within easy distance of the comforts the fort provided.[2]

Susan Magoffin, the eighteen-year-old wife of longtime Santa Fe trader Samuel Magoffin, arrived at Bent's Fort while Doniphan's regiment camped nearby and recorded a puissant description of the fort: "the outside exactly fills my idea of an ancient castle. It is built of adobes, unburnt brick, and Mexican style so far. The walls are very high and very thick with rounding corners. Inside is a larger space some ninety or an hundred feet *square,* all around this and next to the wall are rooms, some twenty-five in number." The fort proved to be nearly indestructible, as the Bent and St. Vrain brothers had intended—in 1852, when the Federal government tried to purchase it, William Bent's efforts to destroy rather than to accept Washington's terms necessitated that he blow it up with gunpowder.[3]

Bent's Fort attracted a disparate congregation of people, groups, and perspectives at the end of July 1846. Kearny had sent Captain Benjamin D. Moore ahead with a troop of dragoons to detain traders along the trail, and he had rounded up and forced into encampment at the fort several companies of Santa Fe traders—more than 500 men and 414 wagons. These merchants were to follow the army into New Mexico. The conquest had a mercantile as well as an ideological dimension, for waiting until after the United States took possession ensured that the traders would not have to pay tariffs on the goods brought into the new American dependency.[4]

Near Bent's Fort, Kearny's scouts captured three New Mexicans presumably sent by the colorful and opportunistic Mexican governor in Santa Fe, Don Manuel Armijo, to ascertain the strength of the American army. After a brief interrogation Kearny sent them on their way to report to Armijo that the Army of the West was bent on neither destroying property nor killing people.[5] As Missouri Senator Thomas Hart Benton put the

2. Connelley, ed., *Doniphan's Expedition,* 178–81; Edwards, *Campaign in New Mexico,* 40–43, 134–38, 179–80.

3. Susan Shelby Magoffin, *Down the Santa Fe Trail and into Mexico: The Diary of Susan Shelby Magoffin, 1846–1847,* 60–61.

4. Moorhead, *New Mexico's Royal Road,* 152–83.

5. These representatives of Armijo may not have been sent explicitly to spy on the Americans. One of Armijo's nephews was involved in the Santa Fe trade and he and his friends may have been accompanying traders en route to New Mexico. When Kearny rounded them up at Bent's Fort, these Mexicans were among the other traders.

matter, so Kearny and Doniphan agreed: "Our first care in this sudden change in our relations with that country (Mexico) was to try and take care of our Santa Fe trade. For this purpose it will be proposed to the people of New Mexico, Chihuahua, and other internal provinces, that they remain quiet and continue trading with us as usual, upon which conditions they shall be protected in all their rights and treated as friends."[6] They carried with them a copy of the proclamation "to the citizens of New Mexico" Kearny formally issued on July 31, 1846. It advised that the Army of the West was entering the province of New Mexico "with a large military force for the purpose of seeking union with and ameliorating the conditions of its inhabitants," and it promised protection to those who cooperated and punishment for those who opposed the army.[7] To one of the Mexicans he promised that not "an onion or a pepper would be taken from them without a full equivalent in cash." Besides releasing the Mexicans, Kearny sent a Santa Fe trader with strong ties to the Indians of the pueblos, Eugene Leitensdorfer, to Taos—the first major town to be "liberated"—with this same proclamation.[8]

On August 2, Kearny dispatched to Santa Fe his trusted dragoon captain, Philip St. George Cooke, and a detachment of dragoons, to escort James Wiley Magoffin—Susan Magoffin's brother-in-law—a beefy, oafish-looking but exceptionally savvy man who knew the hoi polloi of Santa Fe like no other Anglo. They carried this same proclamation and a personal letter from Kearny to Armijo. Magoffin was to meet with Armijo, the cousin of his wife, and to arrange a peaceful capitulation of the province to the Americans. Interestingly enough, Magoffin's mission began under the direction of Thomas Hart Benton 2,500 miles to the east during the middle part of June 1846. While in Washington on business, Magoffin had met twice with Benton and President James K. Polk about the possibility of a bloodless capture of Mexico's northern provinces. Because of his close ties to New Mexico, Secretary of War William L. Marcy commissioned Magoffin a colonel of cavalry and dispatched him to the Southwest to aid in its capture.[9]

For ten days Magoffin and his entourage rode toward Santa Fe, during which time, according to Max Moorhead, "Magoffin's seemingly inexhaustible supply of Irish wit and red claret kept the entire party in high spirits." When they arrived in Santa Fe, leaving Magoffin to attend to

---

According to Santa Fe trader William H. Glasgow, they were "frightened to death & thinking the army is going to eat Mexico & the Mexicans" (William H. Glasgow to Susan Glasgow, July 9, 1846, in Gardner, ed., *Brothers on the Santa Fe*, 83–84).

6. Quoted in Gibson, *Journal of a Soldier*, 61–62.

7. Brig. Gen. Stephen Watts Kearny, "Proclamation," July 31, 1846, in *House Executive Document 60*, 30th Cong., 1st Sess., 168.

8. James Madison Cutts, *The Conquest of California and New Mexico*, 44.

9. Milo Milton Quaife, ed., *The Diary of James K. Polk during His Presidency, 1845–1849*, 1:472, 474–75.

his personal business, Cooke met privately with Armijo and presented Kearny's letter. Kearny told Armijo that the United States had annexed New Mexico and would be taking possession of the territory to the east of the Rio Grande; that the Army of the West preferred to occupy the territory peacefully and to develop a friendly relationship with those already present; that the inhabitants would be guaranteed freedom of property, person, and religion; and that resistance would be futile and that Armijo would be held personally accountable for opposition. The two men discussed the situation for some time that day without resolution. In the evening, however, Magoffin returned to the conference and he and Cooke convinced Armijo to capitulate without a fight. A bribe of property and money might have greased the conquest, but whatever the arrangements Armijo found them compelling.[10]

Meanwhile, on August 2, Kearny began to send his troops down the road to Santa Fe. Doniphan's Missourians, rested from nearly a week of lounging at Bent's Fort, quickly learned why they had been given the time off. The terrain from Bent's Fort to the New Mexican capital was the most rugged of the trip. Southbound from the fort, the First Missouri Volunteers encountered what they called the "Great American Desert." According to Isaac George of Doniphan's regiment:

> The American desert, is, perhaps, no less sterile, sandy, parched and destitute of water and every green herb and living thing than the African Sahara. In the course of a long day's march we could scarcely find a pool of water to quench the thirst, a patch of grass to prevent our animals from perishing, or an oasis to relieve the weary mind. Dreary, sultry, desolate, boundless solitude reigned the distant horizon. We suffered much with the heat, and thirst, and the driven sand—which filled our eyes, and nostrils, and mouths, almost to suffocation.[11]

The march was grueling. Henry S. Turner, who served in St. Louis's Laclede Rangers, remarked on August 5 with not a little pride and probably a fair measure of overstatement that while his unit was bearing up well, Doniphan's regiment "to a man is sick & tired of the business. . . . But for the example set for the regulars, I verily believe the volunteers would not reach Santa Fe."[12]

10. Col. Stephen Watts Kearny to Gov. Manuel Armijo, Bent's Fort, August 1, 1846 (certified copy in Spanish), L-E-1085, Tomo 31, 175, Archivio de la Secretaria de Relaciones Exteriores, Mexico City, Mexico, cited in Moorhead, *New Mexico's Royal Road*, 158–59. James Magoffin to William L. Marcy, August 26, 1846; Capt. Philip St. George Cooke to James Magoffin, February 21, 1849, both in *The Magoffin Papers*, 43–44, 60–62. Philip St. George Cooke, *The Conquest of New Mexico and California: An Historical and Personal Narrative*, 6–31.

11. Isaac George, *Heroes and Incidents of the Mexican War, Containing Doniphan's Expedition*, 39.

12. Henry S. Turner to Julia Turner, August 5, 1846, Henry S. Turner Collection, Missouri Historical Society.

After crossing this arid wasteland, Doniphan's men reached the clear waters of the Purgatoire River, where they recouped their strength before tackling the Raton Mountains. Not long thereafter Kearny gave the army a day off. It was a Sunday and Kearny was trying to be a humane commander, but he still did not think the Missourians should be let off from "soldiering" altogether. They needed all the practice they could get in marching and infantry tactics. Kearny asked Doniphan, in a leading question dripping with sarcasm about his troops' skills: "Colonel, would you rather have me present or not when you drill your regiment?" Doniphan replied, "I do not suppose you can learn anything new. But I may learn much from your kindly criticism." Kearny watched the short drill that Doniphan conducted, and thought the results acceptable.[13]

Raton Pass, the "Mouse" as the Mexicans called it, was one of the steepest and most difficult crossings of a mountain chain in North America. This crossing—over mountains separating the valleys formed by the Arkansas and Canadian Rivers—required days of dogged determination. There was no road, nor even a decent trail, for much of the trip. By the time Doniphan reached the foot of the pass he had to place his men on half rations, and later had to cut even that to a third. Although his men were supposedly "Mounted Volunteers" their horses were dying rapidly and wolves and turkey vultures trailed the column to feast on the remains. Nearly half of his command was on foot by the time they reached the summit of the pass. From the top of Raton Pass, 7,754 feet above sea level, Doniphan had a vista of New Mexico that was as spectacular as it was forbidding. Brilliant shades of color and panoramic valleys greeted the Missourians.

Within a week of departing Bent's Fort, the Army of the West, with Doniphan's regiment in a central position in the march, reached the first Mexican settlements. The Missourians were wonderfully impressed; most of them had never beheld such villages. One of Doniphan's men wrote: "The first object I saw, was a pretty Mexican woman, with clean white stockings, who very cordially shook hands with us and asked for tobacco."[14]

In the evening of August 14, the night before the planned entrance into the first village in New Mexico, Doniphan met with Kearny. The commander had received dispatches from the War Department and needed legal help to carry out some of the president's wishes. Doniphan recalled in 1883 that Kearny

> handed me some orders & said these will explain themselves—
> it is fortunate you are a lawyer—for it is more the province of a

13. A. W. Doniphan to D. C. Allen, September 19, 1883, Doniphan Papers.
14. Hughes, *Doniphan's Expedition*, 61–70. See also Gibson, *Journal of a Soldier*, 173–91; and Johnston, Edwards, and Ferguson, *Marching with the Army of the West*, 92–98, 143–51.

lawyer than a military officer. The first informed him that the Govt designed holding at least New Mexico & California, besides Texas at the conclusion of the War. That to that end he must take military occupation of this State[,] administer the government as a military Ty—*naturalize all* the male citizens as we reached their respective localities—appoint officers &c.

They debated what naturalization meant, but in the end Doniphan recommended that Kearny swear the Mexicans "to obey our Constitution & laws & be true & faithful citizens & this you should do here—make the Alcaldes assemble them all in the morning early, men women, children & dogs & swear them from the house top of the chief Alcaldes, flat adobe roof." That was exactly what Kearny did throughout New Mexico.[15]

On August 14 the army peacefully occupied Las Vegas, the first town of any size encountered in northern New Mexico, before continuing southward toward Santa Fe. As Doniphan had suggested, Kearny climbed to the top of one of the adobe houses and, with a translator, announced that the locals were now under the protection of the president of the United States and were subject to both the rights and the laws of that nation. He told them the army of occupation would respect their rights and their property, protect them from Indians and any other marauders that might arise, and allow them full rights of citizenship. He then presided over the giving of an oath of allegiance to the United States. Doniphan remembered that Kearny assembled the "men, women, children and Donkeys. At his request I had written the substance of the oath proper to be administered & without his request of my own notion the points of a brief address touching their change of allegiance &c."[16]

Kearny told the Las Vegans that he "came by order of the Government of the United States, to take possession of New Mexico, and to extend the laws of the United States over them." He promised to protect them but that they had to swear allegiance to the United States of America. He then administered a hastily written oath of allegiance: "You do swear to hold faithful allegiance to the United States, and to defend its government and laws against all its enemies, in the name of the Father, Son and Holy Ghost."

Leaving Las Vegas in the charge of the local alcalde, and therefore changing immediately very little of substance, Kearny's force, with Doniphan now in the vanguard, headed southward. At each village encountered, Kearny repeated this scene.[17]

15. Doniphan to Allen, September 19, 1883, Doniphan Papers.
16. A. W. Doniphan to D. C. Allen, September 20, 1883, Doniphan Papers; Karnes, *William Gilpin*, 149–50; Henry S. Turner to Julia Turner, August 14, 1846, Turner Collection.
17. *New York Herald*, October 3, 1846.

General Stephen W. Kearny delivering a proclamation at the Plaza, Las Vegas, New
Mexico, August 15, 1846; Mexican War. Neg. no. 163233, courtesy of the Museum of
New Mexico.

As they advanced southward, rumors abounded that the New Mexicans, under the leadership of Manuel Armijo, planned to defend the province and were organizing a resistance force of as many as two thousand
men. Three officers toward the tail of the army galloped south on their
own to join Kearny's vanguard, having heard that a battle was developing
and wanting to get into it. So did trader William H. Glasgow, who left his
wagon train in the rear and "rode on as fast as my mule could bring
me" because he wanted to "get up in time to see the fun."[18] Not long
thereafter an American from Santa Fe rode north to inform Kearny that
a sizable contingent of New Mexicans was gathering at Apache Canyon,
about fifteen miles north of Santa Fe, and planned to make a defense of
the province there. Charles Bent and a scout confirmed this possibility,
prompting Kearny to discuss the matter with Doniphan. The Missourian
recalled:

> He came to my tent & desired me to come out—in a short walk,
> he said "the scouts have just come to report that Gov Armiho,
> with quite a number of troops & several pieces of artillery[,] is
> fortifying the Can[y]on a few miles from here through which the
> road to Santa Fe passes. The Canon is about half a mile long, very

18. William H. Glasgow to Susan Glasgow, August 22, 1846, in Gardner, ed., *Brothers
on the Santa Fe*, 86–87.

narrow & perpendicular walls 1000 feet high with timber & stone fortifications or impediments are being rapidly constructed—to flank it by another route will be ten miles or more out of a direct route—what you say?" I modestly but firmly replied "to produce a proper sense of fear an invading army should not flank or avoid any difficulty that can be swept away by a forward & prompt movement." He gave me a bright cheery smile & said I am glad to have this opinion—it only confirms my own, for I had determined to advance without hesitancy or delay.

Kearny then asked Doniphan how he thought his regiment should be deployed during the approach to the canyon. Doniphan recalled that he told Kearny, "my regiment constitutes more than half your force—there is but one position for them—the *front* & if we fail which I do not fear—we can fall back and rally behind the veteran Dragoons." Kearny agreed.

The next morning Doniphan took up the line of march to Santa Fe. The rest of Kearny's force fell in behind. Doniphan recollected:

after we had passed a half mile or more I galloped back & asked the Genl if he had any new light that would cause a change of programme—was still gazing intently on the men in line, double file—as they had been halted—instead of replying to my questions —he said in an exultant or rather approving tone "I have done your regiment some injustice in my private estimate of their fighting qualities—of course I have not given shape to these doubts to any one but yourself—but this morning I marked their deportment & bearing as they marched along and I congratulate you, for there is no discount on them they will fight like devils without doubt."

Doniphan added that "After that morning the Genl placed the most implicit confidence in the regiment."

In marching toward Apache Canyon Doniphan used some old trappers in his regiment as guides to send some of his men on either flank over the mountain on foot and to approach the canyon from the back. He noted that "this was promptly effected in good order—as we advanced as Cavalry sustained by Capt Weightman's Artillery, through the can[y]on in column." Doniphan recalled:

The enemy on learning from their spies our movement retreated— the retreat became a rout & we captured (I think) four new pieces— six pounders English made—some ten miles south. Although there was no engagement, the regiment made a lasting & favorable reputation by their cheerful Gallantry & soldierly conduct. It was all the better we did not have to storm their breastwork under such disadvantages, for many good lives must have been lost to no purpose as the same purpose was achieved by common sense or good luck.[19]

19. Doniphan to Allen, September 20, 1883, Doniphan Papers.

While the potential for a massacre obviously existed and everyone in Doniphan's command seemingly knew it, Armijo had decided to leave the door open for the Army of the West to enter Santa Fe. He ordered home what small numbers of defenders he had roused on August 16, 1846.[20] William Glasgow reported that when the presumed attack did not take place, he decided to ride on to Santa Fe. When he arrived he "found every body frightened out of their wits, Gen. Armijo with his troops run away, the citizens leaving town with their families and all in confusion."[21]

Kearny may have been fully aware of this situation when he sent Doniphan into Apache Canyon. If so, it had been merely a cautious battlefield stance. Kearny felt confident that Armijo did not intend to mount a defense. If the negotiations failed and combat occurred, however, Kearny was at a disadvantage and letting Doniphan's volunteers get cut to pieces in the pass rather than the regulars would have been the lesser of two very bad outcomes. In reality Kearny's Army of the West was operating outside the parameters of acceptable military judgment. It had a thousand-mile supply line, was small and ill-prepared, and was in the heart of a foreign and unknown territory. The feat was not lost on Philip St. George Cooke, who noted that

> A colonel's command called an army, marches eight hundred miles beyond its base, its communication liable to be cut off by the slightest effort of the enemy . . . the whole distance almost totally destitute of resources, to conquer a territory of 250,000 square miles; . . . the people of this territory are declared citizens of the United States, and the invaders are thus debarred the rights of war to seize needful supplies; they arrive without food before the capital—a city two hundred and forty years old, habitually garrisoned by regular troops! . . . This is the art of war as practised in America.[22]

20. Any reasonably led force could have chopped Kearny's command to pieces in the mountain passes above Santa Fe. It is probably a testament to both the long-standing ties of the region to the United States and to the skill of James Magoffin and other Anglo negotiators that the New Mexicans acquiesced so readily to American conquest in August 1846. The story of the aborted defense of New Mexico is told in detail in Paul Horgan, *Great River: The Rio Grande in North American History*, 716–28; and William Y. Chalfant, *Dangerous Passage: The Santa Fe Trail and the Mexican War*, 18–19. Estimates of the number of New Mexican defenders vary. John Taylor Hughes, in Connelley, ed., *Doniphan's Expedition*, 195–98, thought there were about seven thousand troops, an outrageously high number. Lieutenant William H. Emory, *Notes of a Military Reconnaissance . . .*, 6, estimated more conservatively that four thousand were on the scene, "tolerably well armed." More likely it was a few hundred, but they had been ordered to withdraw by the time the Anglos arrived.

21. William H. Glasgow to Susan Glasgow, August 22, 1846, in Gardner, ed., *Brothers on the Santa Fe*, 86–87.

22. Cooke, *Conquest of New Mexico and California*, 21; A. W. Doniphan to William A. Morton, September 4, 1846, Doniphan Papers; *Liberty Weekly Tribune*, October 10, 1846.

The success of the Army of the West brought glory to Kearny, Doniphan, and the other members of the army. Had it failed it would just as surely have brought censure and disgrace. A pitched battle in the canyon might have thrown back the Americans, and conquest—while it would undoubtedly have taken place later—might have had to await reinforcements. Even without committing to a full-fledged battle, Armijo could have established guerrillas in the mountains to harass the columns and destroy supply trains. The results would have been confusion and a delay in conquest. But there is good reason to believe, as Doniphan and Kearny probably understood, that New Mexico increasingly allied with American trade and many residents did not object to the replacement of a weak and corrupt provincial government that had little economic hold on the region with another government that was exceedingly far away, might be less corrupt, and whose economic policies were in concert with those of many of the wealthiest people of the region.[23]

On the night of August 17 Doniphan's regiment encamped a few miles from Santa Fe. That evening an American living in the town rode up to relay information about what to expect when the Army of the West arrived the next day. He told Kearny that Armijo had abdicated the day before and, with a force of about one hundred dragoons, was heading south into the Mexican province of Chihuahua. After his departure the alcaldes had met to discuss the affair, even considering the possibility of "tearing down the churches, to prevent their being converted into barracks, and that the American citizens interfered and assured them, that they had nothing to fear on that subject, and thereby saved the churches." The American told Kearny that he had tried, successfully he believed, to calm fears and to explain that no real danger existed. He also informed the general that he could expect no opposition when he arrived in Santa Fe. This was certainly welcome news to the officers of the Army of the West, if not to the men of the First Missouri Volunteers who were spoiling for a fight.[24]

The rain had been pouring down most of the day on Tuesday, August 18, and the road to Santa Fe was muddy but not impassible. Doniphan got his men onto it early, with orders to reach Santa Fe before dark. By midafternoon the first troops had arrived at the outskirts of the provincial capital, the prize Kearny had sought for more than two months and over more than a thousand miles. Most New Mexicans were by then more curious than afraid; for days, they had been hearing about the great Anglo army bound for them, and the local officials in Santa Fe had assured them that it would be a bloodless capture if they did not resist. They did not. About five o'clock in the afternoon, flanked by dragoons with drawn sabers more for show than for use, Kearny rode into the central plaza. As

23. DeVoto, *Year of Decision,* 267–71.
24. *New York Herald,* October 3, 1846.

General Stephen W. Kearny raising the American flag over the Palace of the Governors, Santa Fe, New Mexico, August 18, 1846, drawing by Kenneth Chapman. Neg. no. 6725, courtesy of the Museum of New Mexico.

he did so, in a dramatic gesture that could not be believably scripted, the sun pierced the clouds for the first time that day and shown brilliantly down on the slender American and his troops. Kearny dismounted and greeted Lieutenant Governor Juan Bautista Vigil y Alarid, now the ranking Mexican official, at the stately named but unimpressively constructed Palace of the Governors on the north side of the plaza. Vigil formally surrendered in the face of the Army of the West and while American cannon rang out from a northern hill overlooking the town, Kearny's dragoons replaced the Mexican national flag at the palace with the "stars and stripes" of the United States.[25]

The formal ceremony concluded, Kearny and his officers, including Doniphan, entered the palace and enjoyed what they all concluded was excellent "El Paso wine." They then gorged themselves on a feast prepared in their honor. After hours of revelry they retired to the palace for the night, Kearny and his officers sleeping on the floor using their saddles for

25. Ibid; Henry S. Turner to Julia Turner, August 17, 1846, Turner Collection; Doniphan to Morton, September 4, 1846, Doniphan Papers; *Liberty Weekly Tribune*, October 10, 1846; Connelley, ed., *Doniphan's Expedition*, 198–200.

Santa Fe, New Mexico, ca. 1846; Abert Report, 1848. Neg. no. 10118, courtesy of the Museum of New Mexico.

pillows. Their troops, encamped outside the town, were less fortunate, and the volunteers never let their officers hear the end of it.[26]

While Doniphan's troops made camp on a gravelly hill a mile east of Santa Fe proper, the Missourian gave them the freedom of the city whenever they were off duty. His volunteers made the most of it. Their immediate impression was shock and confusion at the architecture, society, and customs of a culture located on the same continent as their own but so strikingly different. Doniphan's men commented on the city of Santa Fe, a community of some five thousand people depending on how one defined its borders. Daniel Hastings, a private in Doniphan's regiment, recorded the standard reaction to their first sight of the city: "Great indeed was the contrast between the beautiful and magnificent city which my imagination had pictured, and the low dirty and inferior place which I then beheld. . . . Perfect contempt was my predominant impression while beholding Santa Fe for the first time."[27] Private M. E. Edwards wrote a description to his brother that gave more particulars. He remarked that Santa Fe was

> a city known all over the world and what sort of a city do you suppose it is? Well it is a dirty filthy place built entirely of mud

26. Cook, *Conquest of New Mexico and California*, 39–46.
27. Daniel H. Hastings, "With Doniphan in Mexico," August 20, 1846, Justin Harvey Smith Papers, Vol. 15, Latin American Collection, University of Texas Library, Austin.

and flat roofed houses it covers a considerable extent of ground but chiefly with corn fields. The city of course has a filthy appearance from the width of the streets which are very narrow and walled in with mud fences the houses of mud and not whitewashed and the women wetting right in the street in plain view no difference who is present. . . . No people in the world have been more overrated than this.[28]

Doniphan's Missourians, who themselves had received severe criticism for their lifestyles from Yankee visitors, quickly learned to look down on the Santa Feans for their supposedly inferior culture.

The day after his arrival in Santa Fe, Kearny assembled the local leadership and administered Doniphan's oath of allegiance to the government of the United States. Kearny used a Missourian, Antoine Robidoux of St. Louis, as his interpreter. The assembled crowd, along with the troops, turned the occasion into quite a party. They passed the time with food and drink and dancing and assorted carousing. Throughout the day small groups came and went between the Palace of the Governors and the hinterlands meeting with Kearny and his officers about the new circumstances. Some of these delegations were Indians from nearby pueblos visiting to ascertain the meaning of the change of government and pledging their fealty to the United States. Outside, Doniphan had built at Kearny's request a hundred-foot-tall flagpole in the central plaza from which they flew a fifteen-by-thirty-foot silk United States flag. There would be no uncertainty in Santa Fe about who controlled the territory.[29]

Throughout his regiment's stay in Santa Fe, Doniphan had to contend with a large variety of institutional and personnel problems almost completely unknown on the trail. For instance, Doniphan had to handle a perceived sense of superiority that the regulars had over his volunteers. This had been a persistent source of friction since the beginning of the march, but it became more pronounced when everyone was together in Santa Fe and had free time on their hands. A member of the Laclede Rangers from St. Louis, himself a volunteer, commented derogatorily on Doniphan's lack of attention to military discipline. He remarked how his own company had fooled the locals into thinking that it was a regular unit because it was so well appointed. The rift between the regulars and the volunteers expanded because of the problem with supplies that had plagued the Army of the West since it left Fort Leavenworth. As far as the volunteers believed, the meager supplies coming to the army were reserved for the use of the regulars. The choicest of the rations, virtually

28. M. B. Edwards to Joseph Edwards, August 23, 1846, Mexican War Files, Missouri Historical Society.
29. Connelley, ed., *Doniphan's Expedition*, 201–3; A. W. Doniphan to D. C. Allen, "Sketch of Life," 6, Doniphan Papers.

all the uniforms and accoutrements, and much of the other necessary matériel to maintain an army in the field apparently went to the dragoons. Missourian George Gibson noted that when the Americans first entered Santa Fe he learned that there was no remedy in sight for the lack of supplies; "we have a fair prospect of going without supper and of having no blankets."[30]

Inevitably, the general lack of discipline that Doniphan allowed his men, fueled by the difficulty of supply, led to problems. One might suspect that the men would steal food and other items from the New Mexicans, but there was surprisingly little theft. Instead, the issue came to a head when Doniphan's regimental lieutenant colonel, Charles F. Ruff, had one of his officers refuse to obey his orders. Ruff, himself a West Pointer and therefore suspect in the eyes of many members of the regiment, had led a detachment to oversee the grazing of the regiment's livestock twenty-seven miles to the southeast at Galisteo Creek. Ruff's unit had been in the hinterlands for only a short time when their requests for food and other supplies made to the military government in Santa Fe seemingly went unanswered. Finally, Second Lieutenant James S. Oldham told Ruff he was going to Santa Fe to obtain food for his men. Ruff, with typical West Point rigidity, ordered him to remain, but Oldham refused and Ruff arrested him and pressed charges in a court-martial for "disobedience to orders." His court-martial on August 26 dismissed Oldham from the military and sent him home, a decision that neither side endorsed (the defense, supported by most of the men, demanded acquittal, and the prosecution wanted to punish Oldham as an example to others).[31]

Oldham's court-martial widened the rift between regulars and volunteers in Santa Fe. Within Doniphan's regiment the men took increasingly oppositional attitudes toward regulars, and with Ruff as a specific representative of the professionals. "Who is a scoundrel?" came a bellow from one end of the camp almost every night after the men went to bed. From the other end came the reply, "Ruff; he's a damned scoundrel." From that exchange the bellows grew more obscene with comments on Ruff's parentage and personal habits. Although some officers tried to ferret out the troublemakers, by the time they arrived at the location from which the hollering had come, the troops appeared to be asleep in their bedrolls. Ruff's men also seriously considered dunking (or perhaps drowning) him in a stagnant pool and on one occasion fouled his bed with sheep entrails.

---

30. Gibson, *Journal of a Soldier,* 205–6. See also Connelley, ed., *Doniphan's Expedition,* 200–204; Doniphan to Allen, "Sketch of Life," 6, Doniphan Papers; and Thomas B. Hudson to James Clemens, August 24, 1846, James Clemens Collection, Missouri Historical Society.

31. Connelley, ed., *Doniphan's Expedition,* 207–17; Johnston, Edwards, and Ferguson, *Marching with the Army of the West,* 160–62; H. S. Turner, Adjutant General, Army of the West, Orders 14, August 19, 1846, Records of the Adjutant General, Vol. 42 1/2.

More seriously, some sought to vote Ruff out of office and to replace him with someone less "spit and polish."

Doniphan apparently agreed with much of the derision that the volunteers felt for his second-in-command and did little to curtail their harassment. For his part, Ruff resented the treatment he received, the lack of support he got from Doniphan, and the general problems of the army in Santa Fe. It was not a sad farewell when Ruff decided to resign his lieutenant colonelcy of volunteers in Santa Fe on September 17 to return east and accept a captaincy in the regular army. Never a military leader of exceptional skill, Ruff eventually served through the Civil War and was finally breveted to brigadier general in 1865 after several years as a recruiting officer.[32]

The next day Doniphan presided over the election of Ruff's successor as second-in-command of the First Missouri Mounted Volunteers. Three candidates emerged: William Gilpin, the West Point dropout, who was then third-in-command of the regiment, and Captains John W. Reid and Congreve Jackson, both of whom served as company commanders. When Reid withdrew from the competition after no clear majority emerged from the voting, his supporters moved over to Jackson's camp and he became lieutenant colonel. In the end the election was a vote of no-confidence to professional soldiers. Jackson had never been anything other than a Missouri militiaman, but Gilpin had attended West Point, however briefly. Jackson was apparently even less of a disciplinarian than Doniphan, and much of the onus for maintaining anything resembling a military organization then fell to Gilpin, who assumed the duties of regimental staff officer.[33]

While the men of Doniphan's command were invariably deprecating toward the New Mexican culture and people, they seemed to enjoy themselves in Santa Fe. The city was famous for its "Fandangos," and the Missourians had heard stories about them from traders for years. Often undertaken for the profit of the host, these huge "come-as-you-are" parties allowed the Americans an opportunity to purchase food and drink and to gamble and dance and sing until they slumped into a Bacchanalian stupor. While, as one American observer noted matter-of-factly, in the fall of 1846 "Saloons, gambling dens, and dance halls remained open day and night, seven days in the week," the fandangos were especially stupendous opportunities for debauchery.[34] There they also met senoritas as nowhere else. "The volunteers cut a wide row among the Spanish girls," wrote one Missourian to his brother, adding that "most of them are dark and homely but I have seen some as pretty girls here as in any country."[35]

32. Connelley, ed., *Doniphan's Expedition*, 235, 247–49.
33. Ibid., 249–50; Karnes, *William Gilpin*, 154–55.
34. Quoted in John P. Bloom, "New Mexico Viewed by Anglo-Americans, 1846–1849," 171–72.
35. T. J. Edwards to Joseph Edwards, September 15, 1846, Mexican War File, Missouri Historical Society. See also M. L. Baker to sister, September 13, 1846, Mexican War File.

Doniphan greatly enjoyed the fandangos and attended them as time and energy permitted. At one of them he met the stately Susan Magoffin, whose travels on the trail from Bent's Fort had paralleled his own. Magoffin expressed her impression of both his eminence and his bearing. "There was Col. Donathan," she wrote, "a native of Ky. 'as you will see by my *stature* Madam,' leaving unknowing listeners to believe that state the mother of a giant tribe."[36] Doniphan had, of course, left Kentucky in 1830 and there is no evidence that he had returned there since.

During this period of August and September 1846, Doniphan had two major responsibilities in Santa Fe other than overseeing his regiment during occupation. The first was the construction of Fort Marcy, a U.S. military installation built on a hill overlooking Santa Fe from the north. It was a sturdy facility; Doniphan's regiment built it of adobe bricks to an irregular pattern of thirty sides. The classic crenelated field fortification of dried mud made an imposing impression of Anglo imperial might compared to the previously weak government of the province of New Mexico. Designed to hold a garrison of a thousand men and several batteries, this installation would serve as a fortress that could withstand either lengthy siege or massive assault. Lieutenant Jeremy Gilmer of the U.S. Topographical Engineers had designed the fort with the help of several Missouri volunteers, especially Lachlin A. MacLean of Company D from Saline County, and some of Doniphan's men worked on its construction every day for several months.[37]

More important, Kearny put Doniphan in charge of establishing a new Anglo civil government in the conquered province. On August 22 Kearny announced via proclamation that the province of New Mexico would be incorporated into the United States as a territory and that all loyal residents would be granted citizenship in their new country. While the old Mexican provincial laws would remain in effect for the time being, Kearny added, a new law code would be written in the coming weeks.[38]

Kearny, knowing Doniphan's background as one of the finest attorneys in Missouri, placed him in charge of writing a law code for the territory of New Mexico. Doniphan assembled a committee to merge the best attributes of the Spanish colonial and Mexican legal tradition with the American system based as it was on English common law. He especially relied upon Captain David Waldo, of Independence, Missouri, who commanded the Jackson County company. Waldo was something of a scholar of Spain and its colonies, so Doniphan put him to work translating Spanish-language documents into English and preparing background

36. Magoffin, *Down the Santa Fe Trail*, 121.
37. Ibid., 244–45; Connelley, ed., *Doniphan's Expedition*, 548.
38. Brig. Gen. Stephen Watts Kearny, "Proclamacion a Los Habitants de la Nuevo Mexico por et General de Brigadar Esteven Guilleme Kearny mandaned las fro par de Las Estados Unidas an dicho Deparsamente," August 22, 1846, Gov. Stephen Watts Kearny Papers, State of New Mexico Records Center and Archives, Santa Fe.

analyses of the Mexican legal system. Charles Bent, who handled the New Mexican part of the Santa Fe trade from his home in Taos for the firm of Bent and St. Vrain, was as close to a local as one could get, and Doniphan enlisted him to advise on how the old Mexican government had been run. Bent especially proved helpful in assessing the Mexican laws and determining what should be kept in the new code. Based on his extensive knowledge of the region, Bent also helped Doniphan understand which American laws were practical for transferral to Spanish culture and which should be rejected or revised. Francis Preston Blair Jr., a St. Louisan who had come west for his health and had been traveling with the Army of the West since Bent's Fort, also served on the committee writing the new legal code. Although Blair's role on the committee was less well-defined than the others, as an attorney, politician, and newspaper editor it seems likely that he helped prepare appropriate language for the legal code. Several other men worked on the committee, notably John Taylor Hughes, who was keeping the Missouri press informed of the march of the First Missouri Mounted Volunteers and who would soon publish a book about the Mexican adventure, transcribing documents.[39]

The critical member of Doniphan's code-makers committee, however, was Willard Preble Hall, a private in the First Missouri Volunteers. Although a lawyer from Buchanan County who had been running a spirited campaign for the House of Representatives in the United States Congress as a Democrat, when the war began Hall had enlisted in Clay County's company of the First Volunteers. Doniphan had known and respected Hall for several years, even though they were political rivals who had run against each other as electors in the presidential campaign of 1844. Hall, who apparently had exceptional recall of whatever he read, served as the "library" for the committee drafting the new legal code. They had only a few law books with them, but Hall partially made up for that problem. He also became the principal author of the code, drafting a version for Doniphan's revision and approval. The congressional election bid continued after Hall's departure for Santa Fe, and Doniphan learned by dispatches from Missouri that Hall's friends had secured his victory. Doniphan walked from his office in the Palace of the Governors to where Hall and John Hughes were transcribing laws. He told Hall about his victory when word first arrived of it on September 20. After he had completed his work on the legal code Hall resigned from the First Missouri Volunteers and returned to the East to take his seat in the House of Representatives, where he served for many years.[40]

39. John Taylor Hughes, "Diary of John T. Hughes," 65–72, Missouri Historical Society; Twitchell, *History of the Military Occupation*, 84–86; Lavender, *Bent's Fort*, 283.

40. Doniphan to Morton, September 4, 1846, Doniphan Papers; *Liberty Weekly Tribune*, October 10, 1846; Connelley, ed., *Doniphan's Expedition*, 240–41, 250–52; Twitchell, *History of the Military Occupation*, 233–36.

Working from his office in the Palace of the Governors, Doniphan commented on the challenges his committee faced in drafting a new legal code. "It is a very arduous matter," he told his brother-in-law, Dr. William A. Morton of Liberty. "The laws are all in Spanish and every thing is done through an interpreter, and there is so much in their laws conflicting with our constitution to be altered."[41] After a month of taxing effort Doniphan and his associates had finished their work. The Kearny Code consisted of 115 double-columned printed pages, written in both English and Spanish. Doniphan formally presented the code for approval to Kearny on September 21, 1846, and the general sanctioned its adoption for the territory with only limited revision. It officially went into effect on September 22 and was first published on October 7, 1846. An amalgam of the Mexican, Texan, and Coahuilan statutes, the Livingston Code of Louisiana, and the organic acts of Missouri, it succeeded in establishing a practicable governmental structure for New Mexico that upheld the objectives of the Northwest Ordinance of 1787 that prescribed the creation of new territories in the United States.[42]

In the Kearny Code, as drafted by Doniphan and his assistants, the executive branch of New Mexico government would consist of a governor and a secretary, a decision that corresponded to the Mexican offices of *jefe politico* and assistant that had been in place. It also met the basic requirement of the Northwest Ordinance for executive leadership. A legislative branch charged with making laws, which included a territorial legislature elected by the citizens of New Mexico, was something unique in Spanish colonial and Mexican tradition, but it also was a requirement of the Northwest Ordinance. The code also provided for the appointment of three justices, who would form a supreme court, another innovation responding to the guidelines of the Northwest Ordinance that had no true parallel in Spanish or Mexican law. In addition, the Kearny Code established a basic set of organic laws for the new territory, created counties for local government, named the alcaldes as justices of the peace, and established sheriffs and tax assessors.[43]

Later, critics in Congress chose to censure Kearny for exceeding his authority in New Mexico by establishing a civil government. The Kearny Code was only part of the problem, however. In implementing the legal system, Kearny also designated the territorial officials, probably

41. Doniphan to Morton, September 4, 1846, Doniphan Papers; *Liberty Weekly Tribune,* October 10, 1846.
42. Stephen Watts Kearny to Adjutant General, U.S. Army, September 22, 1846, Stephen Watts Kearny Diary and Letter Book, 1846–1847, Missouri Historical Society; *Leyes del Territorio de Nuevo Mejico: Santa Fe, a 7 de octobre 1846;* Cutts, *Conquest of California and New Mexico,* 64; Connelley, ed., *Doniphan's Expedition,* 240–43.
43. *Leyes del Territorio de Nuevo Mejico;* Howard Roberts Lamar, *The Far Southwest, 1846–1912: A Territorial History,* 64.

overstepping his legal power. He appointed the American Charles Bent, a resident of Taos, as governor; Donaciano Vigil as secretary; Francis P. Blair, the transplanted St. Louisan, as U.S. district attorney; Charles Blumner, treasurer; Eugene Leitensdorfer, a St. Louis German and a Santa Fe trader, auditor of public accounts; and Joab Houghton, Antonio José Otero, and Charles Beaubien justices in the court system.[44] These of his appointments were either Anglo-Americans or Mexican poltroons closely allied to the Santa Fe trade. All these appointees had much to gain from the American conquest of New Mexico, and their appointments set off the ire of both Mexicans and Indians alike. Historian Howard Roberts Lamar concluded that Kearny had "violated both the spirit of the Code and Polk's orders to retain, so far as possible, the existing native government. Instead Kearny delivered the new creation into the hands of the 'American Party' of Taos and the Santa Fe merchants." It also set the stage for a January 1847 uprising and years of difficult relations between the Anglo-Americans and the Hispanic peoples in the territory.[45]

On the other hand, many people, mostly since 1846, have praised the Kearny Code as a model of organic law. It brought an American-style democratic government to the Spanish-heritage Southwest that benefited both conqueror and conquered. Observers have rightly noted that the code's promulgation symbolized a constitutional revolution for the region. Reflecting on the code, and his role in writing it, many years later, Doniphan commented: "It is astonishing, considering the short time we had been there and our limited means of information, there we should have written a code that Congress after the annexation of the territory, re-enacted and which, after thirty-five years[,] I found still in vogue in 1881." With the ratification of the Kearny Code, there could be no doubt to the native New Mexicans that the Americans had arrived and change was the order of the day, perhaps change for the better, but change nonetheless.[46]

While involved in writing what became the Kearny Code, Doniphan also received word that his commander would soon be leaving New Mexico and that in Kearny's stead he should act as territorial military commander until reinforcements from Fort Leavenworth arrived. Kearny, anxious to move on to the conquest of California for the United States,

44. Stephen Watts Kearny to Adj. Genl. R. Jones, September 22, 1846, Records of the Adjutant General Office, Letters Received, microcopy 567, roll 319, National Archives.

45. Lamar, *Far Southwest*, 65. On January 19, 1847, a conspiracy hatched among several groups led to the so-called Taos Revolt in which a mob composed mostly of Pueblo Indians stormed the home of Charles Bent and killed him and five others. In other parts of the territory other Americans, about fifteen altogether, were killed by anti-American mobs. The American military in New Mexico responded promptly and in some cases ruthlessly to quash the uprising. On the Taos Revolt, see Lavender, *Bent's Fort*, 304–17; and Horgan, *Great River*, 764–68, 770–73.

46. Quoted in *History of Clinton County*, 444.

left Santa Fe on September 25, 1846. He left Doniphan in charge of the military remaining in New Mexico. Doniphan would be relieved by the Second Missouri Mounted Volunteers, a unit en route to Santa Fe under the command of Sterling Price of Chariton County, and "On the arrival of Col Prices Regt here, Col Doniphan with his Regt will proceed to Chihuahua & report to Brig Gen [John E.] Wool (as will other troops, if any more should come here from Missouri)."[47]

Doniphan saluted Kearny as he rode out of the plaza of Santa Fe, past the large American flag that now flew above the Palace of the Governors, and westward toward California and the Pacific Ocean. It was the afternoon of September 25, 1846, and a certain crispness in the air signaled an early winter. Kearny's column of dragoons appeared a little silly sitting atop Missouri mules, the best mounts that could be found in large supply, but Kearny could not wait. The lure of conquering California, perhaps in the same bloodless manner as New Mexico, beckoned him. He did not anticipate that California had already fallen to a renegade group of Americans led by the ambitious John Charles Frémont of the United States Topographical Engineers and the equally ambitious Navy Commodore Robert F. Stockton, and he did not understand the nature of the Navajo Indian troubles in New Mexico that he would later ask Doniphan to handle.

47. Stephen Watts Kearny to Brig. Gen. R. Jones, September 24, 1846, in Connelley, ed., *Doniphan's Expedition*, 253–54.

6

Indian Campaigner

NO SOONER HAD Brigadier General Stephen Watts Kearny, commander of the Army of the West, departed for California with his regular dragoons than Alexander William Doniphan swirled into a problem he could not handle. That made him not unlike a lot of other government officials in New Mexico both before and since, for Navajos had fought European descendants for centuries without defeat. Neither the war-fighting spirit of his First Missouri Mounted Volunteers nor, perhaps, even the far greater power of the U.S. Army, could have subdued the Navajo nation in New Mexico in the fall of 1846. Doniphan, however, received orders to bring the local Indian tribes under control before he departed south. He tried, but failed, to provide a "quick fix" to this historic problem before pushing into Mexico.

Although the challenge had legendary implications, Doniphan wanted to handle it quickly so he could invade Mexico proper. The Utes, Apaches, and especially the Navajos had roamed the region for thousands of years and for much of that period their culture and lifestyle had reigned supreme. As late as the Mexican national era in New Mexico these tribal warriors had taunted isolated settlers and small villages with impunity. Some Indians apparently boasted that if it were not for the service the Mexican settlers provided in raising livestock for them, they would purge them entirely from the land. Even at the time of Kearny's invasion, according to Susan Magoffin, Navajos had mounted a raid "and carried off some twenty families."[1]

Kearny had organized a campaign beginning on September 2, 1846, to secure the release of these people, now American citizens (after all he

---

1. Magoffin, *Down the Santa Fe Trail*, 110–11. See also Johnston, Edwards, and Ferguson, *Marching with the Army of the West*, 176; and Cooke, *Conquest of New Mexico and California*, 47–48.

had promised the New Mexicans protection from the Indians and had to deliver here to ensure credibility). This eventually led to an uneasy truce. He spent a week in the field with seven hundred troops in early September 1846, but to little avail. Then, because of his requirement to move on to California and to fight the "real enemy," Kearny had Doniphan send three companies of his regiment to garrison the area around the villages of Cebolleta and Moquino about 120 miles west of Albuquerque. He also dispatched two companies of Doniphan's men to protect Abiquiu and the upper part of the Rio Grande Valley some one hundred miles northwest of Santa Fe. Kearny himself also moved several other troops toward the homeland of the Utes, Apaches, and Navajos, offering peace treaties with only limited success.[2]

Each of these units met chieftains from the various tribes and invited them to Santa Fe to meet with Kearny and see the might of the United States Army. Delegations of Utes and Apaches did treat with Kearny in the capital, promising "good conduct in the future." Some Navajos were also seen in the community, but they neither met with Kearny nor agreed to amicable behavior toward the New Mexicans. Instead, as the Americans gradually realized, they were on an intelligence gathering mission. They sought to learn, in the words of Frank McNitt, a scholar of the Navajo/American relations, "everything—everything, no doubt, from . . . the number of volunteer troops quartered about the town to the nature and possible quality of their muskets, and the number and sorry condition of their gaunt horses. Conclusions were thereby formed that had direct bearing a few weeks later, on Navajo raids in perilous proximity to Kearny's marching columns."[3]

Doniphan continued Kearny's efforts to bring the Navajos under control and to secure the release of their captives after the departure of the general and his Army of the West for California in mid-September. Doniphan's efforts on this score were aided by the arrival in Santa Fe of Sterling Price's Missourians three days after the departure of Kearny. For two weeks after Price's advance elements on September 28, companies straggled into Santa Fe, beaten by the trail. Now Price's regiment could garrison Santa Fe and other outlying presidios, while Doniphan could take to the trail and round up the Navajo chieftains for a treaty. Doniphan began calling his men from garrison duty about the settlements of New Mexico, substituting Price's units. He also stockpiled supplies and repaired wagons and other

2. H. S. Turner, Adjutant General, Army of the West, Orders 23, September 15, 1846, Records of the Adjutant General, Vol. 42 1/2; Stephen Watts Kearny to Adj. Gen. Roger Jones, September 16, 1846; Stephen Watts Kearny to Adj. Gen. Roger Jones, Order No. 30, September 23, 1846, both in Records of the Adjutant General Office, Letters Received, microcopy 567, roll 319, National Archives; Lieutenant William H. Emory, *Notes of a Military Reconnaissance from Ft. Leavenworth in Missouri . . .*, 80.

3. Frank McNitt, *The Navajo Wars: Military Campaigns, Slave Raids, and Reprisals*, 96.

equipment needed first for the Navajo campaign and later for the invasion of the Mexican province of Chihuahua.[4]

While Doniphan began deliberate preparations to take the field, Kearny, leading his dragoons to California, perceived the craftiness of the Navajos endured by the New Mexicans for centuries. On September 28, Kearny's command, now on its way to California and in the western part of the province, learned that a few days before, the Navajos had stolen about two thousand sheep and killed several New Mexican shepherds in a raid. Three days later Kearny heard that a party of forty Navajo warriors were on a raiding party within a few miles of his line of march. Kearny's course was clear: he had promised protection to the New Mexicans loyal to the government of the United States, and he must deliver.

On October 2 Kearny sent an order to Doniphan to take the field to force the Navajos to give up their prisoners and stolen property. Kearny wrote to Doniphan that he should "require from them such security for their future good conduct as he may think ample or sufficient by taking hostages or otherwise." He also should negotiate a treaty of future peace with the Navajo.[5]

Within a few days, even as Kearny made his way westward away from the New Mexican settlements, Navajo relations degenerated. Raids seemingly took place in defiance of the new American government. Tribal warriors attacked the village of Polvadera on the morning of October 3, 1846, for example, chasing the inhabitants from their homes and stealing their cattle and horses. It was the last straw. Kearny issued a proclamation that called for the Navajo's defeat, and asked the locals to get involved: "Now be it known to all, that I, Brigadier General S. W. Kearny, Commanding the Troops in the Territory of New Mexico, hereby authorize all the Inhabitants (Mexican & Pueblos) living in the said District of Country, viz the Rio Abajo, to form War Parties, to march into the Country of their enemies, the Navajoes, to recover their Property, to make reprisals and obtain redress for the many insults received from them." This order bore a striking similarity to many predecessors given by Spanish colonial and then Mexican provincial leaders about subduing the Navajo raiding parties. It also had similarly inconclusive results.[6]

When the orders from Kearny arrived by express rider in Santa Fe, Doniphan received them with his typical sense of duty. He immediately

4. *Liberty Weekly Tribune*, November 14, 1846; Hughes, *Doniphan's Expedition*, 253, 263–64; James Austin to brother, October 23, 1846, Box 4, James Austin Letters, M72–5/1, Museum of New Mexico, Archives, Santa Fe.

5. H. S. Turner, Adjutant General, Army of the West, Orders 32, October 3, 1846, Records of the Adjutant General, Vol. 42 1/2; Cooke, *Conquest of New Mexico and California*, 75; Emory, *Notes of a Military Reconnaissance*, 81.

6. Stephen Watts Kearny, Proclamation, October 5, 1846, Records of the Adjutant General Office, Letters Received, K-196–1846, filed with K209–10, microcopy 567, roll 319, National Archives; Turner, *Original Journals*, 78–79.

issued orders to his subordinate commanders to break camp. He sent Lieutenant George P. Gordon, attached to Lieutenant Colonel Congreve Jackson's detachment on the frontier of the Navajo lands near the villages of Moquino and Cebolleta, with an order for Jackson to find the Navajo chieftains and invite them to a peace council.[7]

One of the quartermaster officers in Santa Fe, helping Doniphan acquire sufficient resources for the invasion of Chihuahua, remarked on the incident with the cynicism and disdain one might expect from a regular officer commenting upon the activities of the volunteers. Captain William M. D. McKissack informed his superior:

> Col. Doniphan has received orders to proceed against the Nava-hoe Indians, who have been at war with the Mexicans for years & refuse to make peace. . . . Since our arrival in the country they have committed many depredations & will require severe punishment before they cease to molest the Inhabitants; but I fear another Florida War if the Indians desire to protract it; as they live in the mountains impracticable for roads & can only be pursued slowly with pack mules for transporting stores, etc.[8]

Volunteer forces, some of whom had been Missouri units, had received thorough criticism in the Seminole wars in Florida and McKissack foresaw a replay of that unhappy episode in New Mexico, with mountains replacing swamps and Doniphan's volunteers replacing those who had made a poor showing in Florida.

McKissack must have expressed surprise a week later, therefore, when Major William Gilpin and the detachment from Jackson escorted into Santa Fe a delegation of about sixty Ute leaders who wanted to make peace with the Americans. Doniphan treated with them on October 13, and within two days had a signed treaty that effectively ended problems with the Utes, at least for the short term. While this was not a solution to the Navajo raids, it at least secured one part of the New Mexican frontier so that Doniphan could concentrate on another.[9]

Meanwhile, Doniphan planned a three-pronged thrust into Indian territory with forces led by Major William Gilpin on the left and Lieutenant Colonel Congreve Jackson on the right, with Doniphan hounding the Navajo chieftains and their people in the middle until they were willing to meet at a treaty table. Jackson was the first to move out. He directed Captain John W. Reid to take a party of thirty troops, ten volunteers

7. Hughes, *Doniphan's Expedition,* 262, 264–66.

8. Capt. William M. D. McKissack to Maj. Gen. Thomas S. Jesup, October 6, 1846, Records of Army Commands, Office of the Quartermaster General, Consolidated Correspondence, file 1794–1915, Box 987, RG 92, National Archives.

9. A. W. Doniphan to Secretary of War, William L. Marcy, October 20, 1846, Records of Army Commands, Office of the Adjutant General, Letters Received, file 294-D-1846, RG 94, National Archives.

each from the three companies under his command, westward from the Moquino/Cebolleta camp into the Chusca Mountains in search of the Navajo. They were to travel with four days' rations only, moving swiftly to locate Navajo headmen and to set with them a meeting place and location for a discussion with Doniphan. Jackson and the main force would follow Reid's detail about one day behind, sufficient not to threaten the Navajos but close enough to be within striking distance if trouble erupted.[10]

Reid was to have as his guide the colorful and controversial Dine Ana'aii Navajo chieftain known by many names but called by the Americans "Sandoval." Historian Frank McNitt described Sandoval as

> a plotter, a man who played any three sides against a shifting middle. He was an informer for the whites but occasionally, with a surprising loyalty—unless again, the information was paid for— for the Navajos. Wherever trouble occurred, Sandoval was likely to be found. He would buy and sell slaves among his own people. He became a wealthy man whose services, for almost any murky or evil purpose, were for hire. He was a dealer, at a price, in Navajo scalps.[11]

Doniphan or his men apparently paid well in the fall of 1846. Sandoval agreed to take Reid to the main Navajo enclaves and there to help him obtain agreement on a meeting date with the Missourians' commander.

Reid and his detail took off on the morning of October 11, with Sandoval leading the way, bound for the far western Chusca Mountains and the stronghold of the Navajo kingdom. Jackson followed the next day with the main part of his three companies. His initial destination was near the steamy, defanged village of Cubero on the Rio San Jose. The site of their camp was near some abandoned Dine Ana'aii Navajo hogans that Jackson's men took great delight in destroying and burning for their cooking fires. This led to Navajo retaliation about ten days later, and nearly destroyed the possibility of obtaining anything approaching a reasonable peace.[12]

With Sandoval guiding them, Reid's party traveled through Cebolleta Canyon and ascended to the high tableland to the west. At 8,500 feet they gasped for air and viewed some of the most exquisite country in the American Southwest. By October 13 Reid had reached what one of the men in the expedition described as a plateau near present-day Mount Taylor, some twenty-five miles northwest of Cebolleta, where Sandoval had his ranch, a stunning spread of thousands of acres with more than five thousand sheep and one hundred horses—the men speculating that most were probably stolen from New Mexicans. Reid continued northwestward

10. Robinson, *Journal of the Santa Fe Expedition,* 39–40.
11. McNitt, *Navajo Wars,* 71–72.
12. Hughes, *Doniphan's Expedition,* 287–97, 302–3.

for another ninety miles during the two following days, viewing the remnants of Navajo hogans and fortresses periodically but seeing no Indians. Finally, on the evening of October 15, Reid met an aged Navajo chieftain who assured him that the tribe would talk with Doniphan and negotiate a truce. The next morning they set out together and had not gone far when they ran across a group of about thirty warriors and a much smaller number of women, representatives sent to meet and escort the Americans to a preliminary meeting with the headmen.[13]

Reid and his soldiers set out with the Navajos for the camp of Narbona, one of the most important leaders of the tribe and the major spokesman for its peace faction. They were soon met by an estimated eight hundred Navajo warriors and almost that many women for the two-day trip to visit Narbona. The scene was impressive and colorful, the Indians decked out in their elaborate headgear and finely crafted blankets, and the Missourians in their less ornate uniforms rendered near rags by the months on the trail. As they rode to Narbona's village, at no time did Reid fail to understand that he and his thirty-troop detail were prisoners of the Navajos and at their chieftain's whim could be either rewarded or reviled.

But the large crowd of Navajo had neither larceny nor murder on their minds. Instead, when they arrived at Narbona's, Reid realized that they wanted to enjoy trade and games. The mood was festive, and even if Reid worried, most of his men enjoyed the bartering. They obtained beautifully crafted buckskin hunting shirts for dirty shirts and blue wool army cloaks, braided rawhide lassos and striking woven blankets for tin cups or battered coffee pots. In all the trading that occurred, the Missourians thought they got the better of the Navajo. The party continued with games, gambling, and a steeplechase of sorts as the Navajo warriors displayed their horsemanship. Then there were the women, which the Missouri volunteers noticed were surprisingly beautiful in comparison to the women of other Indian tribes they were familiar with from Santa Fe. They were decidedly friendly, something the Missourians appreciated.[14]

John Reid met with Narbona and other Navajo chieftains in council while his men enjoyed the party in the village. Everyone agreed that the Navajos and the Americans should make peace. A few of the chiefs, however, questioned the propriety of making peace with New Mexicans as well, since they were traditional enemies and a people whom they considered as being without honor. In the end, however, and probably because of Narbona's stance on the issue, the chiefs agreed to meet with Doniphan at Ojo del Oso (Bear Spring, near the present-day town of

13. Robinson, *Journal of the Santa Fe Expedition*, 41, 56.
14. Most of the information that follows on the Reid party's encounter with the Navajos is taken from John W. Reid to John T. Hughes, letter appearing in Hughes, *Doniphan's Expedition*, 170–72.

Gallup) toward the end of November and there to conclude a general peace treaty that would presumably end the bloodshed in New Mexico. The rest of the night went quickly in celebration, and by all accounts it was a wild night. The next morning, however, Reid got his troops on the trail again, traveling through Wingate Valley back to the camp of Lieutenant Colonel Jackson near Cubero.

While Reid was away, Jackson had busied himself with little more than allowing his men to participate in fandangos in the nearby New Mexican villages and in losing forty horses to a Navajo raid that had been staged in retaliation for the burning of the Navajo village on October 13. Jackson had sent a detail of sixty troops out in search of the horses, and more important, the Indians who stole them, with orders to scalp any Indian in possession of his horses. The detail recovered twenty-seven horses, punished no Navajos, and returned to Jackson's camp on November 2. In the end, the two details and the overall campaign by Jackson had been arduous for the First Missouri Mounted Volunteers. The men were sick and emaciated and constantly complaining. Their livestock were lame and exhausted. Marcellus Edwards, a volunteer in Doniphan's regiment, insightfully commented that Doniphan's unit, or any volunteer unit for that matter, did not have adequate preparation and equipment for that type of military activity. "If the government has to bring them [the Navajos] to terms of peace by force," he wrote in his journal, "she must employ men for that purpose who must come prepared to undergo the greatest hardships before they can dislodge them from their mountain retreats."[15]

Major William Gilpin also moved out on October 22, 1846, under Doniphan's orders with 180 Missourians, heading northwest from his main camp at Abiquiu. With a guide, Santiago Conklin, at the head of the column, Gilpin traveled through the Chama River valley. Mostly his men suffered from a strong wind that brought at first freezing rain and then near blizzard conditions. They trekked in search of Navajos for the next three weeks, mostly in snowy conditions. The Chama is a region of biting canyons carved into sharp peaks and interspersed with grassy meadows where the Indians had made their homes for thousands of years. Then they reached the Chuscas, which are no less difficult to negotiate than the Chama. Diarist John T. Hughes, in an overstatement, compared Gilpin's march in this mountainous region with Hannibal's crossing of the Alps. In the process of this journey, Gilpin lost two soldiers, and several others became sick from exposure and poor dietary and sanitary conditions.[16]

On November 9 Gilpin made contact with Navajo leaders, who informed him of the council Narbona had held with Captain Reid and of

15. Johnston, Edwards, and Ferguson, *Marching with the Army of the West*, 186–88.
16. Connelley, ed., *Doniphan's Expedition*, 298–300, 593–94; Hughes, *Doniphan's Expedition*, 175–83; McNitt, *Navajo Wars*, 112–14.

a supposed final peace treaty between the United States and the Navajo nation. The major sent word back to Doniphan about this contact and his (mistaken) belief that it had resulted in a final agreement, as if Jackson had not already done so. Gilpin also decided to push further westward, traveling another forty miles into the Chusca Mountain range where he met additional Navajos, who corrected his mistake and informed him that a major council would take place between Narbona and Doniphan in the latter part of November 1846. When Doniphan received the dispatch from Gilpin on November 12, he also corrected the major's misunderstanding and told him to rendezvous with the main part of the regiment on November 20 at Ojo del Oso, bringing with him as many Navajo leaders as he could.[17]

For his part, in late October Doniphan wrote to the secretary of war, William L. Marcy, that he was taking the field in opposition to the Navajo and that he would compel them to make peace. He boasted that his Missourians would "bring the war to a close in 30 days—We deem this a very important duty as the Government owes the New Mexicans protection."[18] He then ordered the remainder of the regiment, scattered up and down the Rio Grande, to gather at the pueblo of Santo Domingo, on the same river about halfway between Santa Fe and Albuquerque. Doniphan permanently departed Santa Fe on October 26, with his immediate staff and the few troops of the First Missouri remaining in the city, leaving the military district in the care of Colonel Sterling Price and the Second Missouri. Confirming the need for the expedition, on the day of Doniphan's departure, the Navajos raided the Rio Grande villages of Tome, Valencia, and Valverde, killing several New Mexicans and stealing some five thousand sheep. By the first of November the rest of the First Missouri had rendezvoused and Doniphan had moved on to Albuquerque. From there he directed Jackson in the south and Gilpin in the north to converge with him at Ojo del Oso by November 20. He also told the remainder of his troops to gather at Albuquerque before the expected thrust into Chihuahua; he was not going to return to Santa Fe.[19]

For Doniphan, and probably for the remainder of the First Missouri, the Navajo campaign was a sidelight to the major reason for volunteering to fight in the Mexican War. Only by getting out of New Mexico and into Mexico proper could the rambunctious Missourians beat up on the Mexicans, what they had all signed up to do in the first place. Fighting Indians had been something many had done before and it did not have the glamour

17. Hughes, *Doniphan's Expedition*, 298–303; Emory, *Notes of a Military Reconnaissance*, 47; Karnes, *William Gilpin*, 159–61.
18. Doniphan to Marcy, October 20, 1846, Records of Army Commands, Office of the Adjutant General, Letters Received, RG 94.
19. Horgan, *Great River*, 743.

of great armies on the battlefield. The Navajo campaign was something they simply had to get over with to get on to the major task at hand.[20]

Not surprisingly because of this, Doniphan's men bellyached throughout their march to Ojo del Oso. Why couldn't Price's Second Missouri Volunteers, fresh and rested and without the task of invasion before them, deal with the Navajo? They had other reasons to complain as well. The delay in invading Chihuahua, some of the more thoughtful reasoned, would only give the Mexicans time to prepare their defenses and thereby make their campaign all the more difficult. More important, however, the troops were improperly equipped for the expedition because of problems with the army's Quartermaster Corps. The regiment had not received any pay since leaving Fort Leavenworth nearly six months earlier. The paymaster had brought checks to Santa Fe to deliver to the troops, but the New Mexicans wanted to deal only in hard currency and the American merchants in town often discounted the checks as much as 25 percent. As a result, Doniphan held up dispersal of the checks and ordered the paymaster to obtain specie. The army sent some, but it did not arrive in Santa Fe until January 1847, after Doniphan's men had already invaded the province of Chihuahua. Thus, they did not receive any of it.

Without pay, much of which was a clothing allowance, Doniphan's men were both ill-clad and ill-equipped by the time of the Navajo campaign. Few had complete uniforms, and they looked like a motley crew of Santa Fe traders mixing army-issue blue wool jackets with buckskins and military boots with Indian blankets. Later they would largely discard the tattered remains of their original uniforms and boots for the more practical and obtainable buckskin hunting togs and moccasins of the mountain men and Indians that served as their guides and interpreters. By the end of the Navajo campaign only Doniphan and his senior officers would have clothing that bore any resemblance to a military uniform and they too looked trail worn.[21]

Notwithstanding the poor condition of his unit, Doniphan moved down the Rio Grande from Santo Domingo during the first week of November 1846. He soon came to Valverde, on the river some one hundred miles south of Albuquerque and a central point on the Chihuahua trail into deep Mexico. There he met a merchant caravan cooling its heels awaiting his force's invasion of Chihuahua so that it could follow safely in the wake of the Missourians. Valverde would become Doniphan's staging base for launching into Chihuahua after the Navajo campaign. Quickly the area became an army outpost on the southern New Mexican frontier

20. Hughes, *Doniphan's Expedition*, 267, 299–304; Isaac Vaughn to T. W. W. De Courcey, December 13, 1846, published in *Liberty Weekly Tribune*, December 19, 1846.

21. Col. A. W. Doniphan to Brig. Gen. R. Jones, March 4, 1847, *Senate Documents*, 30th Cong., 1st Sess., Vol. 1, 1847, 495–96; Richardson, *Journal of Doniphan's Expedition*, 29, 39; Gibson, *Journal of a Soldier*, 245–50; Hughes, *Doniphan's Expedition*, 267–68.

with a population of some five hundred Missouri volunteers reinforced by three hundred teamsters and traders. From Valverde Doniphan and a smaller escort wheeled westward and headed for Congreve Jackson's encampment at Cubero on the Rio San Jose, a tributary of the Puerco River, arriving there on November 5.[22]

Doniphan spent the next week fidgeting in Jackson's base camp waiting for additional information or some Navajo to show up. They finally did, led by Sandoval, and met Doniphan only to tell him what he already knew about holding a council with Narbona and other chieftains at Ojo del Oso on November 20. After a brief meeting with the Navajos, Doniphan dismissed them "with a few presents." Doniphan hung around the Cubero camp until November 15, when he set out with Jackson and 150 troops westward toward Ojo del Oso. They followed the Puerco River to its source for the next two days, fighting snow that grew deeper and more treacherous as they went. On the night of November 16 it snowed thirteen inches in the valleys, where they tried to stay, for the mountain passes contained even deeper snow. They crossed the Sierra Madres beginning on November 17 through snow that was waist deep before reaching the rich grazing plains of the Navajo tribe that lay to the west of the mountain range.[23]

It was something of a triumphal arrival for Doniphan and his column at Ojo del Oso on the morning of November 21. "Fashionably late," he found Gilpin's small force already encamped by the springs. Gilpin was surrounded by more than 500 Navajos, according to John Hughes. Doniphan refused to place a numerical value on the gathering, reporting only that "large numbers of them, perhaps three-fourths of their tribe, collected at Ojo del Oso." More important for Doniphan than total numbers, Narbona and several of the other important Navajo chiefs were present. Doniphan learned that Gilpin had been present since November 20, as ordered, and that most of the Indians had already been in place when he arrived. Captain David Waldo also arrived on November 22 with 330 troopers, raising the total American presence to about 700 men.[24]

Doniphan and the Navajo chiefs immediately went into council on November 21, but only briefly before beginning the real work the next day. For the formal meeting with the Navajo chieftains on November 22, Doniphan wore his finest uniform—bluecoat, gold epaulets, and the jewelry of his station. His saber gleamed after a thorough polishing and he washed and pressed his sash to impress the Navajo leaders. A massive man, something he had always been able to use to his advantage, his

22. Hughes, *Doniphan's Expedition*, 268–74; Vaughn to De Courcy, December 13, 1846, in *Liberty Weekly Tribune*, December 19, 1846.

23. Johnston, Edwards, and Ferguson, *Marching with the Army of the West*, 296; Hughes, *Doniphan's Expedition*, 303–5.

24. Col. A. W. Doniphan to Adj. Gen. Jones, March 4, 1847, in *Senate Executive Documents*, 30th Cong., 1st Sess., no. 1, pt. 1, 496.

six-foot-four-inch frame seemingly towered over the Navajos he met. His reddish hair, said to stick out "like porcupine quills," was especially troublesome in the autumn wind, so he kept his wide-brimmed hat on through most of the negotiations. As his men were wont to note, Doniphan was "not afraid of the Devil or the God that made him." He appeared to the Navajo every bit as regal and omnipotent as the far-off United States seemed to be to the tribal leaders. The personification of the new conquering nation, the Navajos called Doniphan "Bilagaana," a term of respect meant to symbolize both Doniphan as a man and the United States as a great power.[25]

At the council of November 22, Doniphan through an interpreter explained his purpose for the meeting and his nation's intentions. As Hughes recorded the meeting, Doniphan noted that

> the United States had taken military possession of New Mexico, that her laws were now extended over that territory; that the New Mexicans would be protected against violence and invasion; and that their rights would be amply preserved to them; that the United States was also anxious to enter into a treaty of peace and lasting friendship with her red children, the Navajos; that the same protection would be given them against encroachments, and usurpation of their rights, as had been guaranteed the New Mexicans; that the United States claimed all the country by the right of conquest and both they and the New Mexicans were now to become equally her children; that he had come with ample powers to negotiate a permanent peace between the Navajos, the Americans, and New Mexicans; and that if they refused to treat on terms honorable to both parties, he was instructed to prosecute a war against them.

Doniphan also told the Navajo chieftains that he intended to leave Ojo del Oso with a treaty of mutual peace that the Indians must strictly abide by. He commented that the United States "first offered the olive branch, and if that was rejected, then powder, bullet, and steel" would follow.[26]

The Navajo chief Zarcillos Largos was the leading spokesman for his tribe during this early part of the council, apparently occupying center stage in the negotiations for Narbona. He began eloquently to speak of the Navajo admiration of the spirit and enterprise of the Americans, and of the long-standing manner in which his people had "detested the Mexicans." He added:

> Americans! You have a strange cause of war against the Navahos. We have waged war against the New Mexicans for several years.

25. Nelson McClanahan to John McClanahan, June 19, 1847, McClanahan-Taylor Papers, Southern Historical Collection, University of North Carolina, Chapel Hill.
26. Hughes, *Doniphan's Expedition*, 305–6.

We have plundered their villages and killed many of their people, and made many prisoners. We have just cause for this. *You* have lately commenced a war against the same people. You are powerful. You have great guns and many brave soldiers. You have therefore conquered them, the very thing we have been attempting to do for so many years. You now turn upon us for attempting to do what you have done yourselves. We cannot see why you have cause to quarrel with us for fighting the New Mexicans on the west, while you do the same thing on the east. Look how matters stand. This is *our war.* We have more right to complain of you for interfering in our war, than you have to quarrel with us for continuing a war we had begun long before you got here. If you will act justly, you will allow us to settle our own differences.

It was a powerful argument, and rational men such as Doniphan might have had reason to nod their heads upon hearing it, but it opposed the Missourian's purpose representing the United States. He would turn away from achieving that purpose, if for no other reason than Mexican armies— and perhaps glory—awaited in Chihuahua.[27]

Doniphan phrased his answer carefully, seeking the kind of eloquence he had so often shown in the courtrooms of frontier Missouri. He told Zarcillos Largos and the other Navajo chiefs

that the New Mexicans had surrendered; that they desired no more fighting; that it was custom with the Americans when a people gave up, to treat them as friends thenceforward; that we now had full possession of New Mexico, and had attached it to our government; that the whole country and everything in it had become ours by conquest; and that when they *now* stole property from the New Mexicans, they were stealing from us; and when they killed them, they were killing our people, for they had now become ours; that this could not be suffered any longer; and it would be greatly to their advantage for the Americans to settle in New Mexico, and that they then could open a valuable trade with us, by which means they could obtain everything they needed to eat and wear in exchange for their furs and peltries.

Doniphan then addressed the younger warriors, asking for peace and threatening the alternative of relentless war. He also invited them to the United States to see firsthand the power of a young, technologically advanced, and populous nation.

Doniphan's reasoning might not have convinced the hardened warriors of the Navajo nation, but they could not understand his position. They had been at war with the New Mexicans for generations. Few had not suffered grief from the death of a loved one in combat with the Spanish colonials. More than that, the New Mexicans were the enemies of the Navajos from

27. Ibid., 306.

birth. The Navajos had no understanding of the idea of surrender—it was either kill or be killed—and that had been the nature of their struggle with the New Mexicans for years. How could they stop now? Also, how could the Americans call off their war with the New Mexicans until they had exterminated them? What could Doniphan mean when he said the New Mexicans had been conquered and were now under the protection of the United States, something unprecedented in Navajo tradition? Doniphan may personally have impressed the Navajo headmen, or more likely the obvious power and energy of the United States did so, but Zarcillos Largos took a conciliatory position and agreed that hostilities should cease. The Navajos, he said, had no quarrel with the United States and no desire to begin a war with such a powerful nation.[28]

The council then adopted a five-part treaty:

> Art. 1. Firm and lasting peace and amity shall henceforth exist between the American people and the Navajo tribe of Indians.
> Art. 2. The people of New Mexico and the Pueblo tribe of Indians are included in the term American people.
> Art. 3. A mutual trade, as between people of the same nation, shall be carried on between these several parties; the Americans, Mexican and Pueblos being free to visit all portions of the Navajo country, and the Navajos all portions of the American country without molestation, and full protection shall be *mutually* given.
> Art. 4. There shall be a mutual restoration of all prisoners, the several parties being pledged to redeem by purchase such as may not be exchanged each for each.
> Art. 5. All property taken by either party from the other, since the 18th day of August last, shall be restored.

Doniphan, Jackson, and Gilpin signed the Treaty of Ojo del Oso for the United States, while Zarcillos Largos, Narbona, Sandoval, and eleven other chiefs all affixed their marks to the treaty instrument. Thereafter, Doniphan presented gifts to the Navajo chiefs and received blankets in return, souvenirs he prized the rest of his life.[29]

When the council broke up on November 23, Doniphan sent most of his command back to the staging area near Valverde. He, however, took a detachment south to the land of the Zuni Indians with the intention of making a treaty with them as well. Accompanied by three Navajo chiefs who acted at guides, Doniphan arrived at a sedate Zuni pueblo on November 25. Since the Navajos and the Zunis were at war, the presence of the Navajo chiefs caused no small controversy, but Doniphan forcefully stepped into an argument on the evening of their arrival and secured a truce. The next day he negotiated the semblance of a treaty that he believed would be lasting and that would secure the peace of the southwestern

28. Ibid., 306–7.
29. *Santa Fe Republican,* October 2, 1847; George, *Heroes and Incidents,* 60–61.

frontier for years. He then hurried back to the main force at Valverde, looking forward to the glory of the battlefields of Chihuahua.[30]

Doniphan ended his Navajo campaign, with the Zuni expedition tacked on for good measure, with a sense of accomplishment and not a little pride. As he told Brigadier General Roger Jones, Adjutant General of the U.S. Army, he had secured "a permanent treaty" of peace with the Navajo.[31] John Hughes summed up the perspective of the First Missouri Mounted Volunteers on the Navajo campaign. Doniphan and his officers used

> every energy to collect the entire Tribe of the Navahoes in to one Council for the purpose of forming a Treaty. He penetrated still farther [into Navajo territory]. He & his troops secured the whole Navajo country. They overcame every opposition. They ascended into the heights, & gorges of that Range of mountains, almost inaccessible to human beings, which divided the waters of the river Gila, the Colorado, & the Rio Del Norte & are covered with perpetual snow. I have not room now, but will give you an account of the Navajo Expedition in future. It suffices, that the Colonel succeeded in collecting the whole Navajo nation into a Grand Council, & formed a Treaty with Narbona, the Grand Sachem, which he believes will be observed faithfully by that powerful Tribe, numbering not less than 2,000 warriors.[32]

Hughes mistakenly believed, as did Doniphan, that the Treaty of Ojo del Oso was a success. It did not take long to learn otherwise.

In reality, the treaty was hardly worth the paper it was written upon, and it squandered both the time and effort Doniphan had expended to obtain it. Much of that was Doniphan's fault, for both errors of omission and commission had queered the agreement from almost the time of the council. First, there were the outright errors of commission. Neither Doniphan nor anyone else in the New Mexican government made any real attempt to carry out the treaty. In his desire to get into the "real war" against the Mexicans, Doniphan neglected to take any action to see that the terms of the treaty received implementation. He did not make arrangements for the exchange of prisoners, for the return of property, or for the interaction of New Mexicans and Navajos in trade or any other discourse. Such omissions are inexcusable. The only possible explanation might be that Doniphan was anxious to get on to the war in Chihuahua and that he thought Sterling Price would carry out the treaty's terms. If so, he placed his trust in a military commander whose career in New Mexico

30. Hughes, *Doniphan's Expedition*, 312–14; Connelley, ed., *Doniphan's Expedition*, 303, 594.

31. Col. A. W. Doniphan to Brig. Gen. Roger Jones, March 4, 1847, *Senate Documents*, 30th Cong., 495–96; A. W. Doniphan to D. C. Allen, "Sketch of Life," 8, Doniphan Papers.

32. John T. Hughes to Editor, *Liberty Weekly Tribune*, January 4, 1847, Robert H. Miller Papers, Missouri Historical Society.

was one of the least effective in the history of the territory. Price's regiment caused no end of problems in New Mexico during its occupation, inspiring hostility contributing to anti-American riots in Santa Fe and Taos and the death of the territorial governor in early January 1847.[33]

Doniphan also did not bother to inform Charles Bent, the civilian governor of New Mexico Territory, that he had signed a treaty with the Navajo before heading on toward Chihuahua. That may not have mattered much, because when Bent learned of the treaty it impressed him not at all. "I have been informed indirectly," Bent wrote to U.S. Secretary of State James Buchanan matter of factly, "that Col. A. W. Doniphan who in October last marched with his regiment against the Navajo Indians has made a treaty of peace with them. Not having been officially notified of this treaty, I am not able to state the terms, upon which it has been concluded, but so far as I have been able to learn, I have but little grounds to hope it will be permanent." Although he perhaps lacked the ability to do so, Bent certainly had no interest in carrying out the terms of the Treaty of Ojo del Oso.[34]

In addition, Doniphan's failure was directly related to omissions in the treaty process. Although he obtained the marks of several Navajo chieftains representing the peace faction of the tribe, a sizable number of warriors and headmen did not view the United States as any more of a threat than they had the Mexican government and did not participate in the council. Based upon what they had seen in Santa Fe in September and observations made while Doniphan was in the field, many Navajo were notably unimpressed with the numbers and power of the American soldiers. They saw no advantage to making peace with the United States and thereby having to desist from their raids on New Mexican rancheros. Notably, three belligerent Navajo chieftains—Cayetano, Armijo, and Aguila Negra—did not sign the treaty and did not abide, even for a brief honeymoon period, with its provisions.[35]

What was, then, the value of Doniphan's Navajo campaign? Probably almost nothing of a lasting nature and very little that was of even short-term consequence. There was no cessation of hostilities between the Navajo and the New Mexicans, and only after nearly a generation more of warfare and hard-fought and bitter campaigns would the United States Army finally defeat the Navajo tribe.

33. *New-York Herald,* March 3, 1847; *New York Daily Tribune,* June 12, 1847; Albert Castel, *General Sterling Price and the Civil War in the West,* 4–5; Lamar, *Far Southwest,* 69–71.

34. Charles Bent to James Buchanan, December 26, 1846, Department of New Mexico, Adjutant General's Office, Old Letter Book No. 1, RG 94, quoted in McNitt, *Navajo Wars,* 122–23.

35. Hubert Howe Bancroft, *History of Arizona and New Mexico, 1530–1888,* 437, 463; McNitt, *Navajo Wars,* 119–20.

The final irony of Doniphan's career as an Indian campaigner came upon his return to his staging camp on the Rio Grande near Valverde. On the morning of November 26, only four days after signing the treaty, one of his units near Socorro discovered that seventeen government mules and eight hundred head of sheep purchased to feed the regiment had been abducted. The New Mexicans hired to guard them were also missing. Suspecting that the sheep had wandered off on their own, despite the nation's wartime status and the possibility of danger being just around the next rock, the First Missouri's local officer sent Privates James Stewart and Robert Spears, volunteers from Lafayette County, in search of the livestock. It was a foolhardy order, for the task required at least a detail. It became all the more careless since neither Stewart nor Spears bothered to carry their weapons with them as they left the camp. Comrades found their bodies six miles west of the camp perforated with a large number of Navajo arrows. Their heads had also been smashed into a gooey mess by boulders. The local commander immediately sent Lieutenant Linnaeus B. Sublette and a detail of thirty troops westward in search of the Navajo raiding party with orders to take revenge on the Indians. Sublette failed to catch up to a single Navajo, and returned to the main camp the next day after a merry chase in which his troops nearly rode their mounts into the dust and ended up as infantrymen. The incident, probably carried out by a small band of Navajos not aligned with any of the headmen agreeing to the terms of the Treaty of Ojo del Oso, was a clear sign that Indian conflict in New Mexico was not at an end. The two Missouri volunteers were the first Americans killed by the Navajos in the New Mexico territory. They would not be the last.[36]

Inexplicably, Doniphan took no action. When he returned to Valverde on December 12, 1846, he instead busied himself with preparations for the invasion of Chihuahua. Movement into Mexico proper had always been his major objective and Stewart and Spears—indeed the entire Navajo campaign—had been sacrifices for that overarching goal. Now he would finally pursue his long-standing dream of liberating Mexico. He had a piece of paper that said the Navajos would behave themselves; he had fulfilled the letter of the order Kearny had given him to quell the Indian disturbances. Now it was time to move on to the Mexican province of Chihuahua and the "real war." One of Doniphan's officers blatantly commented that the Missourians willingly "laboured in the trench, suffered fatigue, privation and thirst, upon long marches, and fought the unequal combat, *and gained nothing for it,* BUT OUR OWN IMPERISHABLE GLORY!"[37] And move on the Missourians did.

---

36. Ralph Emerson Twitchell, *The Leading Facts of New Mexican History,* 2:219; Robinson, *Journal of the Santa Fe Expedition,* 63; Magoffin, *Down the Santa Fe Trail,* 109.
37. Captain of Volunteers, *Conquest of Santa Fe and the Subjugation of New Mexico,* 40.

7

Combat on the Camino Real

IN LATE NOVEMBER 1846 Alexander William Doniphan expressed excitement about his prospects for the next several months. With the completion of the Navajo campaign, as inconclusive as it turned out in reality, he looked forward to entering the "real" war against Mexico. Colonel Sterling Price and the Second Missouri Mounted Volunteers had been in Santa Fe since the early part of October with orders to relieve Doniphan's regiment, but the vexing Navajos had forced him to push back his departure for more than two months. Now it was time to go. As far as Doniphan thought, the curtain was down and the postlude was over for his unit in New Mexico. Gleefully, with almost childlike excitement upon Christmas Eve, he prepared to march on old Mexico. This campaign, not the one against the Navajos, would make Doniphan a household name in the United States. Almost universally praised for the skill of its execution, Doniphan's slashing movement into Chihuahua became for the rest of his eventful life the Missourian's principal claim to national fame.[1]

While a fair thirst for glory probably motivated the men of the regiment to turn their attention southward as soon as possible, ideals also motivated the volunteers. Doniphan believed he headed a heroic army of manifest destiny sent from a great republic to free a people under dictatorship. John T. Hughes, the most important chronicler of the expedition, captured this "missionary" intensity when he wrote: "Our bosoms swelled with the same quenchless love of freedom which animated the breasts of our ancestors in '76 and caught inspiration from the memory of their

1. See Robert W. Johannsen, *To the Halls of the Montezumas: The Mexican War in the American Imagination*, 43, 51–55, 84–86, 123, 141, 158, 170; and Jim Dan Hill, *The Minute Man in Peace and War: A History of the National Guard*, 19–25.

achievements."[2] Another volunteer described the general invasion of Chihuahua as "at times almost disheartening to any mortal of sensation," but that he and his companions recognized the importance of what they were doing "when we looked upon our colours of Freedom."[3] Such idealism, besides less lofty goals, motivated Doniphan and his one thousand.

Valverde was the starting point for the campaign. Located on the east bank of the Rio Grande, not far below Socorro, it became the marshaling yard for the strike to the south to link with the regular army under the command of Brigadier General John E. Wool in central Mexico. Long considered the southernmost settlement in the province, Valverde was a traditional transit point between Old and New Mexico. By 1846, however, Valverde had been abandoned for years because of frequent and indefensible attacks by Indians who raided livestock and took slaves. Valverde, moreover, would be the site of the first battle in New Mexico between Union and secessionist forces in 1861.

At Valverde Doniphan assembled his nearly eight hundred men of the First Missouri Mounted Volunteers. As the disparate troops met up by the banks of the Rio Grande they held impromptu reunions after months of not seeing each other. Doniphan wanted greater artillery support for the invasion of Chihuahua, so he sent a request to Sterling Price at Santa Fe for Meriwether Lewis Clark's artillery unit to join him for the thrust into the province of Chihuahua. The battery caught up with him only after the first battle in late December, because Price thought he needed the ten cannon and their 125 attendants to ensure peace against the Indians in the territory. Price did send, however, without Doniphan's requesting them, Lieutenant Colonel David D. Mitchell, to help on the commander's staff, and the "Chihuahua Rangers," one hundred men who had been a part of the Second Missouri regiment under the command of a Captain Hudson. With their addition Doniphan's command numbered 856 men who could, according to popular belief, "whip anything in or this side of Chihuahua."[4] Doniphan's force received support by several of the Quartermaster Corps' supply wagons.

More than this, three to four hundred Santa Fe traders with 315 wagons were holed up in a cottonwood grove nearby awaiting the march of the Missouri regiment so that they could follow their way into the provincial capital, Chihuahua City, a major trading center for the Americans. They were even more anxious to leave than Doniphan, but their reasoning had

2. Quoted in DeVoto, *Year of Decision,* 254.

3. William R. Franklin to Editor, *Liberty Weekly Tribune,* January 27, 1847, Miller Papers.

4. *Executive Documents,* House Reports No. 458, 30th Cong., 1st Sess. (1847), 499–501. See also Johnston, Edwards, and Ferguson, *Marching with the Army of the West,* 216; Hughes, *Doniphan's Expedition,* 255–56; and Connelley, ed., *Doniphan's Expedition,* 360–65.

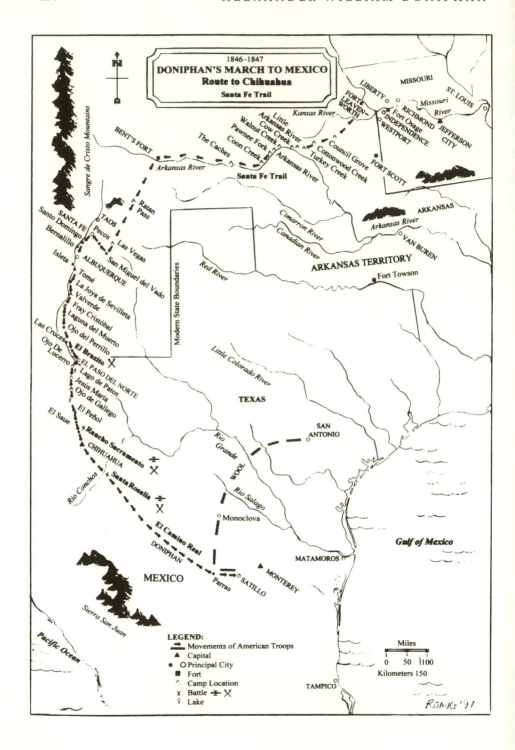

nothing to do either with high-minded ideals or with military glory; every day they waited meant they cut into their profit margin for goods brought for sale in the Mexican province. Some got tired of waiting and lit out on their own for the city of Chihuahua, only to be fetched back by Doniphan's troops. They were to wait for the army, and wait they would! This stiff-arm tactic brought political retribution upon Doniphan by the Democratic press back in Missouri. Some of the most powerful of the traders, including Doniphan's old friends James Aull and Samuel C. Owens, sympathized with Doniphan and defended the decision as being in the best interest of the traders.[5]

Doniphan intended to move out smartly, so on December 14, 1846, he dispatched Major William Gilpin and three hundred troops southward. They would lead the way to the first major objective, the taking of El Paso del Norte, another Rio Grande town of some ten thousand inhabitants, two hundred miles to the south. (Not to be confused with the present U.S. city, El Paso del Norte rested across the river on the present site of Ciudad Juárez in the province of Chihuahua.) Two days later Doniphan sent two hundred men under Lieutenant Colonel Congreve Jackson down the same path. Doniphan left Valverde with the remainder of the regiment, and the baggage and supply wagons, on the nineteenth. The epic march was on, and it would not end until the First Missouri had returned to their homes near the Missouri River more than six months later.

The Missouri Volunteers knew they were in for a tough time when they started crossing the ninety-mile Jornada del Muerto (Journey of the Dead), an exceptionally tough stretch of arid real estate between Fray Cristóbal and Robledo. Beginning nine miles south of Valverde, the Jornada del Muerto went south when the Rio Grande ambled westward like a bow, with the Jornada as the string. Doniphan considered, as had many travelers before, following the river rather than crossing the Jornada, but the Rio Grande's flow through steep mountain passes and the threat of Indian attack prompted him, as it had so many others, to take the desert route. It was a notoriously waterless stretch, with only one watering hole, but there was virtually no other means of moving into Chihuahua from New Mexico and it had been for good reason the traditional means of traveling from the colonial province into the more lush Mexican regions to the south. Crossing the Jornada would have been difficult under any circumstances, but because it was December and winter had set in, the wind whipped against the column and snow stung their faces. It was

---

5. Owens & Aull et al., to Commander of the Troops Stationed at Valverde, December 9, 1846, *Senate Documents,* 30th Cong., 486–87; Hughes, *Doniphan's Expedition,* 276–82; *Liberty Weekly Tribune,* December 26, 1846; Isaac Vaughn to T. W. W. De Courcey, December 13, 1846, published in *Liberty Weekly Tribune,* December 19, 1846; *New York Tribune,* March 3, 1847; Lewis E. Atherton, *The Frontier Merchant in Mid-America,* 109–10.

The march of Doniphan's First Missouri Mounted Volunteers across the Jornada del Muerto in December 1846, the grueling desert at the doorstep of the Mexican province of Chihuahua. First published in 1847, this facsimile is from the *Centennial History of Missouri*, p. 274. Photo courtesy of the State Historical Society of Missouri, Columbia.

also a fireless crossing, mostly because there was nothing to burn on the Jornada but also because of the rumors that Mexican spies were tracking the column and planning to attack. Dispensing with campfires would make the Missourians harder to find. It usually took three days to cross the Jornada del Muerto, but by December 22, 1846, the last of the column had reached Doña Ana, ten miles below the Jornada (some forty miles north of El Paso del Norte) and a location where water, forage, and food were available. Even though his regiment had made the trek without incident, Doniphan still halted his men for a day at Doña Ana to reform the column.[6]

From Doña Ana the First Missouri Mounted Volunteers made their way slowly southward down the historic Camino Real (King's Highway) that had been the route between Santa Fe, New Mexico, and the main part of the country since the sixteenth century. The march symbolized the general style of the Missourians in their famous trek. Their column stretched out for days from end to end, as much as one hundred miles separating the vanguard from the last wagon. The regiment sweated down the trail in their own free style, some companies marching to the beat of a drum but most just slouching toward the halls of the Montezumas. Interspersed between individual companies, parties of traders maintained a smart pace that at times outstripped the military unit nearby. So intermixed were the two groups, and so unmilitary in appearance was Doniphan's regiment, that it was almost impossible to tell who was the soldier and who the civilian. Perhaps that was fitting, for the Mexican War and Doniphan's place as one of its heroes can best be understood through recognizing that Americans carried it out as a firm statement of popular national will that reached from the grassroots all the way to the White House.[7]

The lack of an impressive appearance and the noticeable inefficiency of the regiment immediately gained the attention of observers watching the strange gaggle of Missourians and merchants on the road to Mexico. An English traveler, the urbane and condescending and elitist George F. A. Ruxton, encountered Doniphan's men and had little good to say about them either as human beings or as soldiers. He wrote of Doniphan's camp:

> From appearances no one would have imagined this to be a military encampment. The tents were in line, but there all uniformity ceased. There were no regulations in force concerning cleanliness. The camp was strewed with the bones and offal of the cattle slaughtered for its supply, and not the slightest attention was paid to keeping it clear from other accumulations of filth. The

6. Hughes, *Doniphan's Expedition*, 257–58; Connelley, ed., *Doniphan's Expedition*, 86, 367–69; Johnston, Edwards, and Ferguson, *Marching with the Army of the West*, 215–26; Robinson, *Journal of the Santa Fe Expedition*, 65.
7. Horgan, *Great River*, 743.

men, unwashed and unshaven, were ragged and dirty, without uniforms, and dressed as, and how, they pleased. They wandered about, listless and sickly looking, or were sitting in groups playing at cards, and swearing and cursing, even at the officers if they interfered to stop it (as I witnessed). The greatest irregularities constantly took place.

For all his derision, Ruxton conceded that Doniphan's Missourians "were as full of fight as game cocks." They would have the opportunity to prove how observant Ruxton was on Christmas Day in 1846.[8]

Doniphan had been only a day into his crossing of the Jornada del Muerto when Gilpin and Jackson sent a messenger back with a dispatch containing intelligence gathered from around Doña Ana concerning an immediate attack from a Mexican army gathering in the hills to the south. This information came from a scouting party under Captain John W. Reid, the company commander who had led the detail providing yeoman service for the regiment in the Navajo campaign. He had ranged a dozen miles ahead of the column in search of signs of any Mexican opposition. On the evening of December 23 Reid ran into a small party of Mexicans, presumed to be scouts for a Mexican army, who rode away in haste when they saw the Americans. A private, Frank Smith of Saline County, was quite a sharpshooter and he put bullets into two of the Mexicans as they galloped away, killing them outright, much to the chagrin of Reid who wanted to question them. Reid learned some intelligence from other informants, however. A large force of Mexicans, supported by artillery, was assembling at El Paso del Norte, Doniphan's immediate objective on the Rio Grande. More than this, Reid sent word to Doniphan that James Magoffin, who had done such a fine job making way for the bloodless conquest of New Mexico in August and who had recently journeyed on to Chihuahua for the same purpose, had been arrested for treason and taken in irons to Chihuahua City. There would be for Doniphan no easy conquest, such as Kearny had enjoyed at Santa Fe; any victory over the Mexicans would have to be won on the battlefield. The Missourians would have to stay on guard from then on.[9]

That many people questioned the competence of the First Missouri and its commander was a matter of public record. Stephen Watts Kearny had wondered whether the regiment would hold up on the march to New Mexico, much less under fire from a trained military unit. Even back in Missouri Democrats took bets that Doniphan's unit would be defeated. As one St. Louisan speculated upon the invasion of Chihuahua by the First Missouri, "I would not be at all surprised to learn of Doniphan's capture as they seem to be entirely ignorant of passing events in the

---

8. George A. F. Ruxton, *Ruxton of the Rockies,* 174–75.
9. Hughes, *Doniphan's Expedition,* 257–58; *Senate Documents,* 30th Cong., 497.

other parts of Mexico." And others predicted an even more complete fiasco. "I have some forebodings that when he [Doniphan] meets with an opportunity to have [a battle]," wrote Missouri politician and artist George Caleb Bingham, "he will be out numbered and whip[p]ed."[10]

With the danger of assault obviously present, Doniphan brought his men into a tighter column and imposed more strict discipline. At least he posted sentries in the night and ensured that his troops had their weapons handy if attacked. The men did not complain about it for once, not this time. They understood. On December 24 Doniphan started his column early toward El Paso del Norte, some fifty miles to the south. Even without uniforms, and not nearly as well mounted as they had once been, on that day the First Missouri Mounted Volunteers looked every inch a fighting force. Some sang as they marched. By the end of the day the column had made fifteen miles, but no attack had come. Doniphan, in a fit of concern about the future, went that evening to the nearby encampment of the Santa Fe traders that traveled with the regiment to discuss the prospect of combat. He mentioned the reports of a Mexican army forming to engage the First Missouri and asked that the leading traders organize a battalion from among their teamsters to help in any battle that might come. Since he could promise no pay or other booty, the traders declined to volunteer but they promised, they said, to defend themselves and their goods if attacked while accompanying the regiment.[11]

Christmas Day 1846 became the moment of truth for Doniphan; his performance that day would determine whether his leadership would be vindicated or vilified. Private Isaac George described the progress of the unit:

> On the morning of the 25th of December, a brilliant sun rising above Organic mountains to the eastward burst forth upon the world in all its effulgence. The little army, now not exceeding 800 strong, was comfortably encamped on the east bank of the Del Norte. The men felt frolicsome indeed. They sang the cheering song of Yankee Doodle, and Hail Columbia. Many guns were fired in honor of Christmas day. But there was no need of all this had they known the sequel.

Doniphan pushed on, despite the Christmas holiday, camping only in the early afternoon with his regiment on the east bank of the river at a place called Los Temascalitos by the locals and popularly called El Brazito (Little Arm)—where the Rio Grande splits into two channels with an island

10. James Glasgow to William Glasgow Jr., March 18, 1847, William Carr Lane Collection, Missouri Historical Society; George Caleb Bingham, "Letters of George Caleb Bingham."

11. Johnston, Edwards, and Ferguson, *Marching with the Army of the West,* 238; Connelley, ed., *Doniphan's Expedition,* 87; Hughes, *Doniphan's Expedition,* 369–70.

between—so that his men could have something akin to a Christmas supper.[12]

Notwithstanding efforts to keep the regiment together, on Christmas Eve some of the livestock had wandered off and some of his men, especially those involved in handling the baggage wagons, had to spend a lot of time in the morning rounding them up. This ensured that the column strung out along the Camino Real once again, with men straggling into the Christmas Day camp hours after Doniphan had given the order to bivouac. This contributed to a laxness of order among the members of the regiment throughout the afternoon of December 25th. George Rutledge Gibson noted that "men and wagons were scattered along the road for many miles, but a few marching in the ranks, as it was not expected to meet the enemy this [east] side of the crossing nine miles above El Paso."[13]

Throughout the Christmas Day march, a Mexican cavalry officer had observed Doniphan's regiment from the dry hills overlooking the Camino Real valley. He marveled at the apparent unconcern the troops had for the possibility of a fight, and recalled that he "reconnoit[e]re[d] them to his satisfaction, and unobserved." When he returned to his commander, the cavalryman reported that the American unit was "without a single piece of artillery," but more than this it had encamped without taking any serious precautions.[14] Private George Robinson later expressed surprise that although "some spies were seen, . . . no suspicions of a battle were excited."[15]

Doniphan bedded his men down in an encampment in a valley near the Rio Grande's El Brazito arm. John Hughes reported at the time that it was "an open, level bottom, excepting the bunches of mesquite which grew thick adjacent to the mountains, some half mile or more east & southeast."[16] Although the location of this encampment has been in some question, with sites suggested along a stretch of more than eighteen miles down the Camino Real, the best evidence suggests that the bivouac took place about two miles south of the principal landmark in the area, Vado Hill, just east of the present town of Vado. Upon halting for the day, Doniphan set out rather unenthusiastic pickets to guard the encampment while most of the men scattered about the valley in search of wood for their cooking fires

12. George, *Heroes and Incidents*, 67. The "little arm" by which Doniphan identified the area of the encampment no longer exists. The river's course was moved into the valley in the floods of 1862 and 1865, and now runs about three miles farther west (P. M. Baldwin, "A Short History of the Mesilla Valley," 319).

13. Gibson, *Journal of a Soldier*, 300; Hughes, *Doniphan's Expedition*, 369–70.

14. Ramón Alcaraz, *The Other Side: Notes for the History of the War between Mexico and the United States*, 169.

15. Robinson, *Journal of the Santa Fe Expedition*, 65.

16. John T. Hughes to Editor, *Liberty Weekly Tribune*, January 4, 1847, Miller Papers.

and forage for their livestock. They left their stacked rifles attesting to their lack of readiness for battle. The camp appeared to Marcellus Edwards a little like the lackadaisical militia drills of his native Boone's Lick country in the middle of Missouri.[17]

Doniphan's advance scouts had not been completely inactive, however, for they had captured a superb Mexican horse, a white stallion, in the brush, and Doniphan sat down with some of his officers to engage in a card game of three-trick-loo to decide who should have it for a mount. As Doniphan played cards and his men went about mundane camp chores, a few spied a cloud of dust to the southeast. At first they thought nothing of it. Doniphan gazed up from his cards toward the horizon and lazily opined that the dust cloud probably resulted from the wind.[18]

Advance scouts who galloped back to Doniphan's headquarters soon brought word that the enemy now moved toward them in an orderly column and that this force was responsible for the cloud of dust. This turned out to be an army raised by the Chihuahua provincial governor, Angel Trias, who had been trying to mount a defense since mid-December. To help do so he had fostered rumors about the Americans, claiming that they were wild frontiersmen who plundered and pillaged everything within reach. "Besides abusing the women," the Mexican leader noted, "these ruffians would brand them on the cheek as mules were branded."[19] Little bands of militia began to congregate in El Paso del Norte in response to Trias's pleas to help repulse the "pirates." He appealed to them to "reestablish the Charter of the Mexicans & to chastize the enemy if he should have the audacity to set foot upon the soil of this state."[20]

Trias assembled nearly 1,200 men in El Paso del Norte to oppose Doniphan's regiment. These consisted of 514 regulars from the local presidio, lancers who had been veterans of the fall of Vera Cruz and were as tough and as hateful of Americans as hard-bitten victims of defeat could be, and local militia who had spent years in an involuntary toughening program by fighting Apaches in the mountains. They had also scrounged up four pieces of artillery. Lieutenant Colonel Luis Vidal, an experienced battlefield commander, led this unit. Vidal gave his advance unit unequivocal orders: "The enemy shall be engaged until put to flight, or until the greatest possible advantage over it has been achieved, provided its numbers do not exceed, according to assurances, from three to

17. Marcellus Ball Edwards to Father, January 5, 1847, Mexican War File, Missouri Historical Society; Andrew Armstrong, "The Brazito Battlefield."

18. George, *Heroes and Incidents,* 68.

19. C. L. Sonnichsen, *Pass of the North: Four Centuries on the Rio Grande* (El Paso, 1968), 112, as quoted in Phillip Thomas Tucker, "The Missourians and the Battle of Brazito, Christmas Day, 1846," 162.

20. Angel Trias, Proclamation, November 9, 1846, Miller Papers.

four hundred men."[21] If anything, Vidal underestimated the quality of the Missourians he opposed, bragging that he would soon send Doniphan and his amateurs packing after some had been "lanced like rabbits" by the Vera Cruz dragoons.[22]

When a messenger finally arrived with firm intelligence about the large Mexican force approaching, Doniphan took it nonchalantly. The commander threw down his cards with a statement about having an "invincible hand, but I'll be damned if I don't have to play it in steel now."[23] He, Major William Gilpin, and Lieutenant Colonel David Mitchell, the principal officers involved in the card game, decided to leave the hands as they were and to organize a defense. Doniphan told everyone to "remember that I am ahead" as he ordered the bugler to sound assembly.[24] "The men came running from all quarters," wrote John Hughes, "& fell into line under whatever flag was most convenient. The officers dashed from post to post & in an incredibly short time the Regiment was marshaled on the field of fight."[25]

Doniphan adopted a defensive position because of the substantial difference in size of the two armies; he had only about five hundred men in camp, with the rest spread out along the road, while the Mexican force numbered as many as twelve hundred, many of them veteran dragoons. Doniphan formed his force into a rough line running north and south. Gilpin commanded three companies—B (from Lafayette County under the command of Captain William P. Walton), C (a scattering of Captain O. P. Moss's men, most of whom still dragged into camp), and E (a Franklin County unit under Captain John D. Stephenson)—on the right or southern wing, nearest El Paso del Norte. Mitchell took charge of two companies—A (Captain David Waldo's men from Jackson County) and F (Captain Mosby Monroe Parson's unit from Cole County)—and a unit called the Chihuahua Rangers on the left or northern end of the line. Doniphan commanded the center with companies D (Captain John Reid's troopers), G (a Howard County unit under the command of Captain Horatio Hughes), and H (the Callaway County volunteers under Captain Charles B. Rodgers). As a sidelight to the battle, several black slaves in the bivouac—one of whom belonged to Doniphan—grabbed weapons, took up positions in the lines, and acquitted themselves well during the

21. Luis Vidal to General Commanding the Advance Guard, December 25, 1846, Battle of Brazitos, Typescript of Documents Relating to Battle, 1846, Museum of New Mexico, Library, Santa Fe.

22. Sonnichsen, *Pass of the North,* 113, quoted in Tucker, "Missourians and the Battle of Brazito," 162–63.

23. John Taylor Hughes, in Connelley, ed., *Doniphan's Expedition,* 370.

24. Quoted in Sonnichsen, *Pass of the North,* 114, in Tucker, "Missourians and the Battle of Brazito," 165.

25. Hughes to Editor, *Liberty Weekly Tribune,* January 4, 1847.

fighting that followed. Doniphan positioned the baggage wagons that had arrived directly behind the center of the line for protection, placing his headquarters there as well. He established two main lines so that they could alternate firing and reloading. He also directed Gilpin and Mitchell to place their flanks on the river so that the regiment could not be enfiladed. Doniphan then fixed some skirmishers before the main battle line.

As the troops formed, their officers made little speeches about their purpose on this battlefield and the glory that they had before them. Not a few referred to the American Revolution and the forebears of the American republic. Some recalled the exploits of the Missourians at the Battle of Okeechobee against the Seminoles in Florida on Christmas Day nine years earlier. Doniphan's efforts appeared very textbookish; he established a strong line with good position and easy logistical support to the rear. The textbooks he had borrowed from Kearny, and what he had learned from others, paid off here despite the apparent surprise of the Mexican attack.[26]

Inexplicably, the Mexican commander on the field sent by Vidal, a young squadron commander named Antonio Ponce de León, squandered his advantage of surprise; in seemingly slow motion he formed his lines about one-half-mile to the east of the Americans. The Mexican commander wrote in his after-action report:

> My advance guard now arriving at the point which I considered necessary, I commanded a halt and left-face, and the line of attack was formed, placing the howitzer in the center; and the seventy-five infantry forming two sections on the firing line, so that one occupied the right of the howitzer and the other section the left. The right wing of the cavalry and of the line of battle was formed by the 2nd. and 3rd. regiments, and three sections of the North and the garrison *principe*, and the entire left by the remainder of the cavalry and the National Guard.[27]

John Hughes noted that "Their strength was about 1,100 men, of which 514 were Regulars from Vera Cruz & Chihuahua; the rest were volunteers." He was surprised to learn that "The Dragoons were dressed in *Red uniforms*," making them excellent targets.[28] Color Sergeant Thomas I. Edwards observed those red uniforms as well, writing that "pretty soon we saw their red coats shining. They came up with a great deal of pomp and show, as

26. George, *Heroes and Incidents*, 68; Connelley, ed., *Doniphan's Expedition*, 371, 373–74, 377; A. W. Doniphan to R. Jones, March 4, 1847, *Senate Documents*, 30th Cong., 497–98; "Report of Secretary Marcy," *Senate Documents*, 30th Cong., 54–55.

27. Antonio Ponce de León to General Commanding Forces of the Detachment of the Vanguard, December 26, 1846, Battle of Brazitos, Typescript of Documents Relating to Battle, 1846.

28. Hughes to Editor, *Liberty Weekly Tribune*, January 4, 1847.

they generally do."[29] Indeed, the dragoons' opulent uniforms of scarlet and green and their tall hats with brass-plated fronts and horsehair or buffalo-tail plumes presented an imposing sight. Whatever its fighting abilities, to the homespun and buckskin clothed Missourians, the Mexican army was indeed stunningly costumed.

Once in position, de León sent one of his officers forward to request Doniphan's surrender. He rode to within sixty yards of the American line and saluted Doniphan by dipping a black "no-quarter" banner. The flag was a source of great interest to the Missourians, most diarists commenting on its two skulls and crossbones and the motto *Libertad ó Muerte* (Liberty or Death). Doniphan sent Mitchell and an interpreter to meet the Mexican officer. The Mexican demanded that Doniphan accompany him back to his commander for a conference. The interpreter replied, "If your general wants to see our commander, let him come here." The Mexican military officer then promised to send troops to break the American lines and to take Doniphan forcibly to meet de León. "Come and take him," said the American interpreter, before suggesting that the Mexicans could "Go to Hell."[30] Waving the black flag as he went, the Mexican officer then returned to his own lines and the battle was on.[31] As he rode away the solitary thought in the heads of Doniphan's regiment was to shoot him down as a lesson to the Mexicans. Even Doniphan considered it. "With my permission a hundred balls would have pierced the insolent bearer of the pirate flag," Doniphan reported, "but I deemed it most proper for the honor of our country to restrain them."[32]

Upon hearing the American response, de León gave a rousing speech to his troops. As he wrote in his after-action report:

> I shouted victory to the glorious General Santa Anna and to my country; and finding that all my troops responded with enthusiasm . . . [and] desire for combat, I was led to predict a certain victory, therefore I ordered my line of attack to move forward in regular time; and perceiving that the entire column of cavalry on the left, had ceased to move, I repeated my orders to my adjutants, so that they might move with uniformity; and commanded to sound the charge.[33]

On the right of the Mexican line a military band began to play, and bugles sounded the charge. A sea of red tunics began to move forward

29. Edwards to Father, January 5, 1847, Mexican War Files.

30. 1st. Lt. C. H. Kribben, "Semi-Official Report of the Battle of Bracito," in Edwards, *Campaign in New Mexico,* 169–71.

31. Doniphan to Jones, March 4, 1847, *Senate Documents,* 30th Cong., 497–98; *Liberty Weekly Tribune,* February 20, 1847, February 27, 1847, March 13, 1847; Hughes, *Doniphan's Expedition,* 371–73.

32. Doniphan to Jones, March 4, 1847, *Senate Documents,* 30th Cong., 497.

33. De León to General Commanding Forces, December 26, 1846.

in an orderly fashion on the right, and on the left the dragoons started to advance. The four Mexican cannon, by this time unlimbered and ready for action, began to fire on the American center, but with little effect.

What went through Doniphan's mind as he watched the advancing Mexican army is impossible to discern. Almost certainly he was aware that his regiment was seriously outnumbered and that if the Mexicans fought as finely as they looked he was in for a rough Christmas Day. Or perhaps he knew something about his unruly Missourians that only years in the backcountry of the state among the frontiersmen and rivermen could provide. Whatever the case, Doniphan ordered his men to hold their fire until the enemy came in quite close. "Our forces were ordered to receive their fire, without returning it, until it could prove effective," he wrote in his after-action report to Brigadier General Roger Jones. "Three rounds were fired by the whole [Mexican] line, also from a 2-pound howitzer, before they had advanced within rifle shot."[34] This tried-and-true infantry tactic of the American Revolution—"Don't fire until you see the whites of their eyes"—was only one instance of the Missourians' remarkable discipline in waiting for the order to fire.

Most of the soldiers' accounts of the battle agree on the basic details of how it unfolded. The Mexican regulars, especially the dragoons on the American left, charged Lieutenant Colonel Mitchell's men as ordered. Doniphan directed his line to take their fire, issuing the unusual order of "Prepare to Squat" as a means of keeping their heads down while the dragoons fired on them. Most of the dragoons' shots were wild and fell on the hill behind Mitchell's men, the hill from which Doniphan happened to be directing the battle at the time. When the Mexican dragoons were within sixty yards, Mitchell allowed his men to return fire. Doniphan later reported: "Their shot were falling thick around me. I put spurs to my horse, charged to the front, hollered 'Come on boys.' . . . The boys thought I was brave as hell but they did not know what drove me there."[35] He really wanted to get away from the fire on the hill. The volleys from Mitchell's men broke the dragoons' charge. With their main charge broken, some of the dragoons sheered off to the American left and tried to get around the flank. As they did, teamsters from the wagons in the American center went out to meet them and had a jolly time firing into a (by then) confused Mexican assault. Captain John Reid quickly put an end to the dragoons' attack by leading eighteen horsemen at their flank and cutting them to pieces in a saber charge.[36]

34. Doniphan to Jones, March 4, 7, 1847, *Senate Documents,* 30th Cong., 497.
35. Quoted in Clark, "Epic March," 147–49; Paul I. Wellman, *The House Divides,* 252.
36. Gibson, *Journal of a Soldier,* 300–309; Johnston, Edwards, and Ferguson, *Marching with the Army of the West,* 227–37; Karnes, *William Gilpin,* 168–69; Hughes to Editor, *Liberty Weekly Tribune,* January 4, 1847.

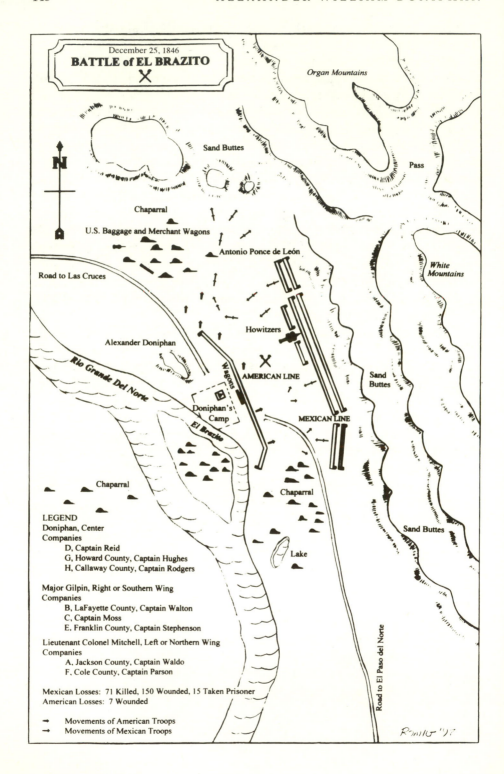

December 25, 1846
BATTLE of EL BRAZITO

Organ Mountains

Sand Buttes

Pass

Chaparral

U.S. Baggage and Merchant Wagons

Antonio Ponce de León

White Mountains

Road to Las Cruces

Howitzers

Alexander Doniphan

Rio Grande Del Norte

Wagons

AMERICAN LINE

Sand Buttes

Doniphan's Camp

MEXICAN LINE

El Brazito

Chaparral

Chaparral

Sand Buttes

Lake

LEGEND
Doniphan, Center
Companies
  D, Captain Reid
  G, Howard County, Captain Hughes
  H, Callaway County, Captain Rodgers

Major Gilpin, Right or Southern Wing
Companies
  B, LaFayette County, Captain Walton
  C, Captain Moss
  E, Franklin County, Captain Stephenson

Lieutenant Colonel Mitchell, Left or Northern Wing
Companies
  A, Jackson County, Captain Waldo
  F, Cole County, Captain Parson

Mexican Losses: 71 Killed, 150 Wounded, 15 Taken Prisoner
American Losses: 7 Wounded

→   Movements of American Troops
→   Movements of Mexican Troops

Road to El Paso del Norte

Romito '9?

The Mexican attacks against Doniphan's right and center were even less successful. Mexican regulars attacked the American right in an acceptable manner, but the militia supporting them were less enthusiastic and the attack crumbled after the first volley fired by the companies under Major Gilpin. Once again, Doniphan had his men hold their fire and lie flat in the grass as the Mexicans fired successive volleys. The Missourians then jumped up at sixty yards and mowed down the attackers as they tried to reload. This was all the Mexican infantry could stand, and they turned and fled, pursued by the Americans who were spurred to charge by the words of Doniphan, "every man for his turkey." The Howard Countians of Company G even stormed and captured a field piece, turned it on the retreating enemy, and fired a couple of rounds before the Mexicans were out of range. The infantry pursued the enemy for about a mile before giving in to the need for celebration. John Hughes wrote with not a little pride, "The consternation now became general among the ranks of the enemy, & they commenced a retreat which perhaps has not yet ended."[37]

In the end the Mexican losses included 43 killed and 150 wounded, according to the estimates of the Americans. Several of those wounded eventually died, bringing the total of Mexicans killed to 71. Squadron Commander Antonio Ponce de León received a wound, although he eventually recovered. The Missourians also captured about 15 of the enemy, holding them for a time as hostages. Doniphan's casualties were impressively low, with only 7 wounded. A victory as lopsided as nearly any in American history, El Brazito signaled the rise of Doniphan as a military hero. Except for the half-hearted and disorderly pursuit of the Mexicans, the Battle of El Brazito (Los Temascalitos to the Mexicans) took only slightly more than half an hour. By four o'clock in the afternoon many of the men were celebrating or preparing for their Yule evening festivities. Doniphan wrote in his official report of the battle an understatement of the first magnitude concerning the quality of the force he commanded on that Christmas Day. "I cannot speak too highly of the coolness and intrepid bravery of the officers and men under my command during this whole engagement," especially since they had a reputation as being poor soldiers averse to discipline and since "few of them had ever been in battle before."[38]

37. Hughes to Editor, *Liberty Weekly Tribune*, January 4, 1847; Doniphan to Jones, March 4, 1847, *Senate Documents*, 30th Cong., 497–98; Hughes, *Doniphan's Expedition*, 374–75; *Liberty Weekly Tribune*, February 20, 27, March 13, 1847; Tucker, "Missourians at the Battle of Brazito," 167–68.

38. Doniphan to Jones, March 4, 1847, *Senate Documents*, 30th Cong., 497–98; Hughes, *Doniphan's Expedition*, 375–77; *Liberty Weekly Tribune*, February 20, 1847, February 27, 1847, March 13, 1847. Incidentally, the Mexican commander gave different casualty figures, 11 killed and 17 wounded, but these were offered before all of his troops had regathered and he had final counts. See de León to General Commanding Forces, December 26, 1846, Battle of Brazitos, Typescript of Documents Relating to Battle, 1846.

Doniphan sent details about the battlefield to tend to the wounded, bury the dead, and collect the large quantities of ammunition, baggage, provisions, military accoutrements, unit flags and banners, weapons, and, happily, a wonderful stock of wine left by the Mexicans. Regrettably, the black flag was not among the implements captured on the battlefield. Doniphan, concerned that the Mexicans might regroup and try something more, posted a strong guard that evening at his bivouac and for once his men took the guard duty seriously. He and his men enjoyed the food and especially the wine left by the Mexicans at their Christmas dinner. Doniphan even finished his game of three-trick-loo, with a scout winning the game, but the equine prize had been lost in the confusion of the battle.[39]

As the First Missouri Mounted Volunteers were celebrating their victory two events took place that affected the rest of the Chihuahua invasion. First, the blacks who had fought in the battle asked for permission to form their own company as part of the regiment. Having just won a victory with their help and hundreds of miles from the nearest American army and expecting to fight additional engagements, Doniphan agreed to accept the slaves as comrades-in-arms. Like their white counterparts, the slaves elected their own commander. Joe, the servant of Company H's Lieutenant John B. Duncan, received the nod to head the company. "He was the blackest of the crowd," wrote Private Frank Edwards, "and sported a large black feather with a small black hat—also, a large sabre, with an intensely bright brass hilt—which same sabre was eternally getting involved with the intricate windings of his bow legs."[40]

More significant for the outcome of the rest of Doniphan's expedition into Chihuahua was the arrival in camp of James Kirker—also known to the Mexicans as Santiago Querque—an unprincipled opportunist of legendary proportions. Dressed in buckskin hunting shirt and breeches with a wide Mexican sombrero atop his head, Kirker carried a Hawken plains rifle and two pistols. He looked to Doniphan every bit the frontiersman that he claimed to be as he offered to help them with the conquest of provincial Chihuahua. As Doniphan listened to Kirker's story, he was amazed and not a little troubled by the prospects of enlisting the support of this unknown quantity. Kirker had been born in Belfast, Ireland, in 1793, but in 1810 had come to the United States and made his way to the frontier. Eventually settling in El Paso del Norte, Kirker alternated between trapping and trading throughout the Southwest and engaging

39. Hughes, *Doniphan's Expedition*, 377–78; *Liberty Weekly Tribune*, February 27, 1847; Horgan, *Great River*, 749–50.

40. Edwards, *Campaign in New Mexico*, 126–27. See also Phillip Thomas Tucker, "Above and Beyond . . . : African-American Missourians of Colonel Alexander Doniphan's Expedition," 135–36.

in the sporty game of Mexican provincial politics. In this last category he had traded sides between local Mexican leaders, powers in Mexico City, the Indian chieftains of various tribes, and American traders whenever it benefited the cause he happened to champion at the time. The more unsavory of his various exploits involved his work, for whomsoever would pay, as a scalp hunter. He had sold in his lifetime Indian scalps to Mexican authorities and Mexican scalps to the Indians, and Doniphan knew that unless he was careful, Kirker might try to sell Missourian scalps to either one or even both of those parties.[41]

In 1906, Edward J. Glasgow, a Santa Fe trader of long-standing tradition and good repute, commented on Kirker's career for William E. Connelley, who was compiling a history of the Doniphan Expedition. Glasgow recollected of Kirker:

> He was employed by the State of Chihuahua to drive out the Apaches and for that purpose employed a number of Delaware and Shawnee Indians. I was told that he received a stipulated sum, $40.00 each, I think, for the scalps of the men and half price for those of the squaws and children and succeeded in ridding the State of Apache annoyance. He met Doniphan above El Paso and offered his services as scout and guide against the Mexicans. Doniphan accepted the services but regarded him with suspicion as he had been living with his family in Chihuahua and employed as above stated, and although he led the scouting parties in advance, men were watching him, ready to put a bullet in him in case of treachery.

Glasgow concluded that "He proved faithful however to the end."[42]

Kirker had offered Doniphan his services and those of his Indian associates because he wanted to get revenge on Chihuahua governor Angel Trias, who had reneged on an agreement to pay thirty thousand dollars for scalps delivered by Kirker following a massacre of several Indian camps. Notwithstanding some reservations, Doniphan recognized the asset that Kirker might be for his little army and enlisted him and his men as scouts for the regiment. However, he indeed told the company commander to whom he assigned Kirker and his men, Captain Thomas Forsythe, that he should shoot Kirker at the first sign of betrayal. In the end, Kirker provided Doniphan valuable intelligence about the region that lay to the south and helped the Missourians stay out of trouble through his intimate knowledge of both the terrain and the Mexican military capability

41. On the strange career of James Kirker, see "Don Santiago Kirker," *Santa Fe Republican*, November 20, 1847; Ralph A. Smith, "The 'King of New Mexico' and the Doniphan Expedition"; and William Cochran McGaw, *Savage Scene: The Life and Times of James Kirker, Frontier King.*

42. Edward J. Glasgow to William E. Connelley, November 27, 1906, William E. Connelley Collection, Kansas State Historical Society, Topeka.

in Chihuahua. He eventually returned with the Missourians to St. Louis at the conclusion of their campaign in Mexico.[43]

The day after the Battle of El Brazito, Doniphan began a cautious march to El Paso del Norte. He ensured that the Missourians maintained a strong front and rear guard, not knowing that the Mexican force routed on Christmas Day had headed for the hills never to fight him again, and kept a tight column in between. On December 27 the regiment went through the "Great Pass," the traditional entrance from the north into El Paso del Norte. When within six miles of the city Doniphan's scouts encountered a number of leading citizens from the town who ventured out under a white flag to arrange a surrender. Doniphan sealed the surrender over a bottle of wine brought as a present to the American commander, and then moved into the city. Once in control of the town Doniphan released three American prisoners who had been arrested by the Mexican officials.[44]

Doniphan also gave the assembled El Pasoans a speech about what he intended for them. Doniphan said that he bore them no ill-will and offered them liberty from the tyranny of the Mexican dictatorship. If the residents "remained peaceable and neutral, during the existence of the war, [they] would be fully and amply protected," he told them. But if they took "up arms against the Americans, [they] would be punished as they deserved."[45] He also seized arms and ammunition in El Paso del Norte. John Hughes noted that he took "possession of about 20,000 pounds of powder, lead, musket cartridge, canon cartridge & grape & canister shot; 500 stand of arms, 400 lances, 4 pieces of canon, & some of their colors." On December 30 Doniphan also sent a detachment under Major Gilpin and Captain Reid to Presidio de San Elizeario twenty-two miles down the Rio Grande to recover a haul of armaments left there by the still-fleeing Mexican army.[46]

The congeniality of the El Pasoans surprised the Missourians, but they enormously enjoyed their stay. The town and its people captured Doniphan's regiment as much as the other way around. Food became plentiful, as did liquor, and the local residents were hospitable. On his own, Private John Hughes even sent a dispatch to Secretary of War William L. Marcy about the city and its ebullient resources. He described the rich agricultural products of the region and suggested that it should be annexed:

> If this valley were cultivated by an energetic American population it would yield, perhaps, ten times the quantity of wine & fruits, at

43. *The Picayune*, June 26, 1847; *Weekly Reveille*, July 3, 1847, July 5, 1847; *Santa Fe Republican*, October 24, 1847, November 20, 1847.
44. Richardson, *Journal of Doniphan's Expedition*, 48–49.
45. Hughes, *Doniphan's Expedition*, 378–82.
46. Hughes to Editor, *Liberty Weekly Tribune*, January 4, 1847; Hughes, *Doniphan's Expedition*, 383–85.

present, produced. Were the wholesome influences & protection of our Republican Institutions extended to the Rio Del Norte, an American population possessing American feelings & speaking the American language would soon spring up here. To facilitate the peopling of this valley by the Anglo-American race nothing would contribute so much as the opening of a communication between this rich valley & the western states of our Union by a turnpike, Railroad, or some other thoroughfare which would afford a market for the fruits & wines of this River Country.

In addition to the countryside and its bounties, many of Doniphan's men took a shine to the El Paso del Norte women, three even marrying senoritas during their stay in the town.[47]

While ensconced in the relative safety of El Paso del Norte, Doniphan had to make the most significant decision of his entire expedition. He had enjoyed almost no communication with the United States Army since leaving Santa Fe, and repeated stories of large Mexican armies massing in the south and lack of intelligence about the locations of friendly forces made him wary of venturing farther into the province of Chihuahua. His original orders had been to march to Chihuahua City where he would link up with Brigadier General John Wool's force. Without informing him to the contrary, though Doniphan suspected it, the War Department had diverted Wool's army to Saltillo to help General Zachary Taylor capture the city. If he pushed on into Mexico, Doniphan surmised that he might be on his own without even a secure supply line from New Mexico. After considering the options carefully, Doniphan decided he would move on to Chihuahua City, with or without relief from Wool. Besides, staying at this present location set him up for a Mexican counterattack that might prove devastating, or de León's dragoons might cut off his lines from New Mexico, or a version of the Taos Rebellion could occur in El Paso del Norte with his troops being massacred by the much larger Mexican population. If he returned to Santa Fe, that would be tantamount to admitting defeat. If he advanced, however, Doniphan reasoned that he could eventually link with Wool. And if he had to, judging from the bounty of the region around El Paso del Norte, he could live off the land rather than rely on a tenuous supply line from Santa Fe. That seemed to be the only course he had and, lacking other orders, the colonel decided to continue with those originally given to him by Kearny before he left for California. Doniphan called his officers together and announced that he intended to march farther south into Mexico and to capture Chihuahua City.[48]

47. John T. Hughes to Secretary of War William L. Marcy, January 25, 1847, Alvord Collection, no. 970, f80, Western Historical Manuscript Collection.

48. John T. Hughes to Editor, *Liberty Weekly Tribune*, January 26, 1847; James Glasgow to William Glasgow Jr., March 18, 1847, Lane Collection; George, *Heroes and Incidents*, 75–77; Bauer, *Mexican War*, 153.

Before moving on, however, Doniphan resolved to wait in El Paso del Norte for Sterling Price to send the long-promised artillery unit of Meriwether Lewis Clark. Doniphan sent a messenger back to Santa Fe with the request for Clark's artillery, but because of the Taos Rebellion against the Americans (in which Charles Bent lost his life in early January 1847), Sterling Price informed Doniphan that he had to keep the artillery in anticipation of further violence. Only after the rebellion had been put down and order restored did Price finally release it in late January 1847. Clark finally arrived in El Paso del Norte with 6 field pieces and 117 men on February 1, 1847.[49]

Doniphan also met with the Santa Fe traders, seeking to enlist their support for the further incursion into Mexico. He explained to them the tactical situation and told them of his decision to take Chihuahua City. He made it clear in word and deed that he would not allow the traders to go ahead to the lucrative market without his regiment and demanded, rather than asking as he had done at Doña Ana, that they form a battalion subject to his orders. The traders agreed to form two companies of infantry containing seventy-five men each. They elected Doniphan's old Jackson County friend, Samuel C. Owens, as their major. Doniphan directed that this unit remain with its wagons during the march but to stand in readiness for battle.[50]

With the arrival of Clark's artillery unit Doniphan delayed no longer. On February 3, 1847, some of the traders took off for Chihuahua City on their own, and Doniphan sent a detachment to catch and detain them until his regiment marched. By the eighth he had his entire regiment, by then over eleven hundred men, on the trail again. They lived off the land as they went, a march unlike that of Sherman's during the Civil War only in the lack of general destruction inflicted on the local populace. Doniphan also kept with him as hostages a few local residents whom he knew to be hotheads who might foment the kind of rebellion that had erupted in New Mexico and had led to the death of Charles Bent. The 250-mile trek to Chihuahua City did not yield many incidents of importance. The men complained about the march, the food, the officers, the weather, and anything else that they could think of, but they kept up the brisk pace that Doniphan demanded. More alert to signs of the enemy now, Doniphan wanted to reach Chihuahua City before the end of February. He hoped to find Wool there, but if not, at least he thought

49. Hughes to Editor, *Liberty Weekly Tribune*, January 4, 1847; Connelley, ed., *Doniphan's Expedition*, 93; Henry, *Story of the Mexican War*, 228–31.

50. Doniphan to the Merchants, Presidio, February 9, 1847, and Harmony claim, in *Executive Documents*, House Reports No. 458, 30th Cong., 1st Sess. (1847), 15–16; Johnston, Edwards, and Ferguson, *Marching with the Army of the West*, 244, 248; Moorhead, *New Mexico's Royal Road*, 170–71.

he would be closer to friendly forces than he had been since the first of the year.[51]

As the First Missouri Mounted Volunteers made their relentless march down the Camino Real toward Chihuahua City, Doniphan sent scouts ahead for any sign of resistance. James Kirker, who knew the territory and many of the people, provided invaluable service in this reconnoitering effort. On February 24 he brought word to Doniphan at Gallegos Spring, about fifty miles north of their destination, that the Chihuahua provincial authorities were massing seven hundred cavalry troops, several artillery, and a sizable infantry at Laguna de Encenillas, a portal to Chihuahua City. Early the next morning Doniphan sent Kirker and other scouts out to gather additional intelligence about the enemy force. They learned that the Mexicans were preparing to meet them at the Sacramento River about fifteen miles north of the provincial capital. In this area the Camino Real passed through a series of low but steep hills that bordered the river. The Mexican field commander, Major General José A. Heredia, scattered about three thousand troops in those hills and placed a strong force on a plain straddling the Arroyo Seco (a dry river bed) on one side and the Sacramento River on the other. The Camino Real passed through this plain and represented the only practical approach Doniphan had to the city. The Mexicans also set up several artillery batteries to bombard the Missourians as they reached the battlefield. There the Mexicans waited for Doniphan's troops to arrive, ready with ropes and handcuffs for the expected American prisoners.[52] It proved a sound location for battle, made all the more formidable by the efforts of the Mexicans to dig in and build redoubts. The Mexicans also had a well-developed order of battle; the only problem was that it required the Americans to stay on the Camino Real. They did not.

By February 27 Doniphan's regiment had marched to within fourteen miles of the enemy's lines at the Sacramento River. That evening he sent scouts to reconnoiter the area: a six-man detail under Lieutenant Colonel Congreve Jackson that provided superb intelligence. They occupied a mountaintop within five miles of the Mexican lines and used powerful field glasses to map the enemy positions. When they brought this information to Doniphan he assembled his staff, went over the intelligence, and developed a strategy for meeting the threat. At the conclusion of the conference, Doniphan told his officers, "Cheer up boys, tomorrow evening I intend to have supper with the Mexicans on the banks of a beautiful spring." That evening, Doniphan had supper with one of his El Paso del Norte hostages, a hotheaded priest named Ortiz, and explained

51. Hughes, *Doniphan's Expedition*, 396–403; Edwards, *Campaign in New Mexico*, 102–10.

52. Smith, " 'King of New Mexico,' " 41–45; Karnes, *William Gilpin*, 174.

exactly how he planned for his Missourians to carry the next day's battle. When Ortiz suggested that the Mexicans would rout Doniphan's men, the colonel offered that perhaps he would place Ortiz at the head of the column as a means of blunting the vigor of the Mexican attack. Ortiz quipped that he would prefer to be in the Mexican front line since it would definitely be a safer place. Doniphan laughed aloud as he walked away to attend to preparations for the impending battle.[53]

Doniphan's battlefield tactic at Sacramento was quite well developed, and it certainly stood in marked contrast to the "shake and bake" style of El Brazito. He had obviously been thinking about how to handle the Mexicans for some time and that consideration, coupled with the excellent intelligence he received from his scouts, went a long way toward victory. On the morning of February 28, Doniphan formed the wagons he had at his disposal into four parallel columns about thirty feet apart, nearly one hundred wagons to a file. In the center space between these four columns of wagons he placed Clark's artillery, and on the two spaces on the interior of the outer wagon columns he divided his regiment as equally as possible. Three companies of cavalry masked this formation in the front, with Captain Reid's horsemen again occupying a critical place in this cavalry ruse.[54]

About three miles from the Mexican lines Doniphan sent Clark to take one last look at the enemy positions before the Missourians moved in to engage the enemy. Approaching to within six hundred yards of the Mexicans, Clark noted:

> The entrenchments consisted of a line with intervals composed of circular redoubts, from three to five hundred yards interval, with entrenchments between each, covering batteries partly masked by cavalry. The redoubt nearest to my position, contained two pieces of cannon, supported by several hundred infantry.
>
> The enemy's right and left were strong positions—the *Cerro Frijoles* on his right, and having high precipitous sides, with a redoubt commanding the surrounding country, and the pass leading towards Chihuahua, through the Arroyo Seco. The Cerro Sacramento on his left, consisting of a pile of immense volcanic rocks, surmounted by a battery, commanded the main road to Chihuahuas, leading directly in front of the enemy's entrenchments; crossing the Rio Sacramento at the rancho, directly under its fire, and also commanding the road from Terreon, immediately on its rear; the crossing of the main road over the Arroyo Seco, at the point from which my reconnaissance was made, laid directly under the fire of the batteries on the enemy's right, which rendered it necessary to ascertain the practicality of a route more distant from the enemy's entrenchments.

53. Quote from Bauer, *Mexican War,* 153; Hughes, *Doniphan's Expedition,* 406.
54. Doniphan to Jones, March 4, 1847, *Senate Documents,* 30th Cong., 498–502.

Clark confirmed what Kirker and other scouts had already reported, that there was a passage to the left of the Mexican line that would allow the Missourians to maneuver around the main entrenchments and engage the Mexican left.[55]

At about two thirty in the afternoon and some two miles from the Mexican entrenchments at the Sacramento, Doniphan swung his column forty-five degrees to the right. They marched parallel to the Arroyo Seco until within sight of the Mexican entrenchments, and then moved onto an elevated plateau. This maneuver kept the Missourians out from under the Mexican guns and bypassed some of the forward Mexican positions. In so doing, Doniphan also partially flanked the Mexican left, using the cavalry as a feint to occupy the enemy until the maneuver had been successfully executed. When he realized what had happened, the Mexican commander had to shift his position so that his troops faced east on a north/south line rather than northward on an east/west axis as their battle plan had intended. No matter; the Mexicans made the first move with an all-out cavalry charge into the American center. John Hughes recorded that one thousand Mexican "cavalry, dashed down from the fortified heights to bring on the attack." Meriwether Clark's battery of six field pieces drove back this charge using canister shot, as his earlier reconnaissance had ensured that his batteries knew from whence the attack was coming and heightened the accuracy of their fire. Hughes commented that the cavalry retreated with "great confusion in their ranks."[56] The wagons had concealed the artillery and Heredia had been unaware of its presence until Clark began his barrage.

An artillery duel took place beginning at about three o'clock, which the Americans used to advantage. The cannonading continued for some fifty minutes, and while the Mexicans concentrated their fire on Clark's artillery, it had little effect. "Lieutenant Dorn had his horse shot out from under him by a nine pound ball, at this stage of the action," Clark recorded, "and several mules and oxen in the merchant wagons, in our rear, were wounded or killed, which, however, was the only damage done."[57] The Mexicans were apparently using an inferior gunpowder that heaved projectiles at exceptionally slow velocities. It also left an easily discernible blue streak through the clear mountain air. The Americans made sport of jeering at Mexican marksmanship and dodging the cannonballs hurled toward them. Not everyone was lucky in this activity, however, for one sergeant in Company F had both of his legs broken by a cannonball

55. Maj. M. Lewis Clark to Col. A. W. Doniphan, "Official Report of the Battle of Sacramento," March 2, 1847, in Edwards, *Campaign in New Mexico*, 173–74.

56. Hughes to Editor, *Liberty Weekly Tribune*, March 4, 1847.

57. Clark to Doniphan, "Official Report of the Battle of Sacramento," March 2, 1847, in Edwards, *Campaign in New Mexico*, 174.

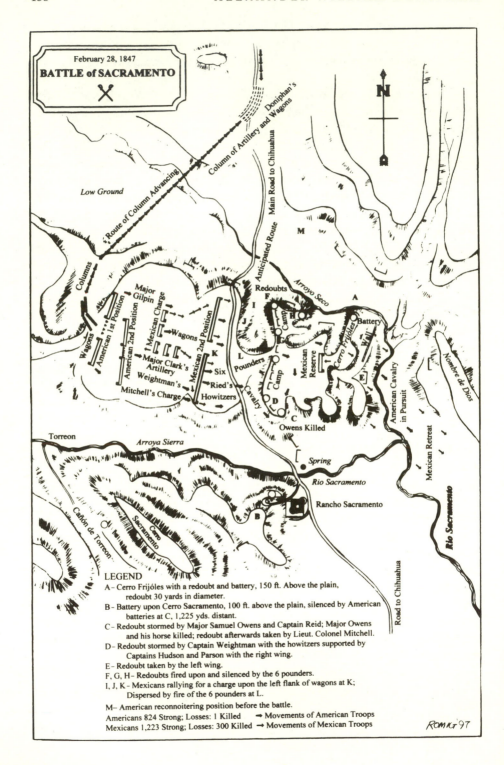

February 28, 1847

BATTLE of SACRAMENTO

LEGEND

A – Cerro Frijóles with a redoubt and battery, 150 ft. Above the plain,
        redoubt 30 yards in diameter.
B – Battery upon Cerro Sacramento, 100 ft. above the plain, silenced by American
        batteries at C, 1,225 yds. distant.
C – Redoubt stormed by Major Samuel Owens and Captain Reid; Major Owens
        and his horse killed; redoubt afterwards taken by Lieut. Colonel Mitchell.
D – Redoubt stormed by Captain Weightman with the howitzers supported by
        Captains Hudson and Parson with the right wing.
E – Redoubt taken by the left wing.
F, G, H – Redoubts fired upon and silenced by the 6 pounders.
I, J, K – Mexicans rallying for a charge upon the left flank of wagons at K;
        Dispersed by fire of the 6 pounders at L.
M – American reconnoitering position before the battle.

Americans 824 Strong; Losses: 1 Killed   → Movements of American Troops
Mexicans 1,223 Strong; Losses: 300 Killed → Movements of Mexican Troops

ROMKT '97

that did not miss him. In contrast, American artillery proved deadly during the duel. Hughes noted that "the enemy suffered great loss—our battery discharged 24 rounds to the minute."[58] At first Clark concentrated his fire on the rear corner of the Mexican left. Once he had reduced it, he methodically shifted his fire to the other entrenchments northward along the line. The American cannon killed at least fifteen Mexicans, kept the rest of the enemy's heads down, and destroyed one of the batteries. Throughout this artillery duel Doniphan sat serenely on his horse and at one point remarked sarcastically, "Well, they're giving us hell now boys."[59]

As Clark's cannon held off the superior numbers of Mexicans for nearly an hour, Doniphan's troops reformed into an attack formation. As he whittled on a stick with one leg hooked around his saddle horn in full view of the enemy—perhaps a pose to reassure his men and frustrate his enemy—Doniphan ordered a charge. A battalion under Lieutenant Colonels Jackson and Mitchell moved forward on the American right, while Gilpin commanded a battalion that advanced on the far left. The artillery, in an unconventional move, went forward in the center supported by three companies of cavalry. This was a maneuver that would have spelled doom in most engagements, but it worked here. The merchant battalion led by Major Samuel Owens kept close behind. Coordination among the various units was ragged, and the fighting was fierce.

John Hughes described this part of the battle, an attack on the Mexican center:

> As we neared the enemy's redoubts a heavy fire was opened upon us from the different Batteries consisting of 18 guns in all. At this moment Capt Reid's company of select horsemen, of which I had the honor to be a member, was ordered to charge the Battery that had annoyed us so much. Nobly & gallantly did Capt. Reid & his little handful of men dash into the midst of the enemy's ranks, they carried the battery & silenced the guns for a moment; but owing to some mistake, a portion of Capt. Reid's men were halted by an order that did not come from the Colonel, & the small squad that had charged the Battery could not hold possession of it. We were beat back & many of us wounded.

As they withdrew, Major Owens, who in the heat of moment had decided to charge on his own, was hit by a cannonball and instantly killed. Reid's horse was also shot out from under him, but one of his troopers dismounted and gave him his horse. By this time the cavalry had regrouped, the erroneous order had been countermanded, and the cavalry advanced

58. Hughes to Editor, *Liberty Weekly Tribune*, March 4, 1847.

59. Cutts, *Conquest of California and New Mexico*, 81–86; Ray Allen Billington, *The Far Western Frontier, 1830–1860*, 187.

again with strong support from the artillery. This time they captured the battery for good.[60]

The infantry to the north and the south had something of an easier time. Jackson's and Mitchell's men in the south captured three batteries and after a brief hand-to-hand confrontation put the Mexicans to rout. Gilpin, as always a methodical commander, first charged the Mexican cavalry then trying to reform in the north and then drove the infantry from their redoubts. He moved around their flank, causing them to turn and run. Many of the remaining Mexicans rallied around their artillery on the Sacramento hills to the rear of the battlefield and prepared to make a stand. Clark's battery shelled the redoubt from 1,225 yards; at the same time he sent howitzers forward to hit the Mexican position from a different angle. Those efforts, coupled with a final American cavalry charge from a unit that had sneaked around behind them, forced the Mexicans to abandon their final redoubt. By five thirty that afternoon it was all over and Doniphan's regiment had scored a second military victory. Although estimates vary, the Mexicans lost about seven hundred, either killed, wounded, or captured. The Americans lost Samuel Owens, probably because he had rashly left his assigned position and was the first American to reach the Mexican redoubt in the center. A half-dozen Americans were wounded, with one of them dying a few days later. The Mexicans inflicted the most "humorous" wound on Lieutenant Colonel Mitchell, who had his "whiskers shaved by a cannon ball." The battle, as Doniphan believed it would, secured the province of Chihuahua for the United States.[61] As in their previous engagement, Doniphan had his men scavenge the battlefield for useful items. They obtained some equipment and provisions in this way, notably ten artillery pieces, but the real prize was the black flag with the slogan *Libertad ó Muerte* on it from their previous battle. Meriwether Clark received this souvenir because of his excellent work in the battle, and he treasured it for many years.[62]

When news of the victory at Sacramento reached the United States, William Cullen Bryant compared Doniphan to the ancient Xenophon and the epic march of his army. The starched-shirt of a president James K. Polk, a man not given to praise in general and to Whig commanders

60. Hughes to Editor, *Liberty Weekly Tribune*, March 4, 1847; W. W. H. Gist to George W. Gist, March 23, 1847, Gist Family Letters, Western Historical Manuscript Collection.

61. Hughes to Editor, *Liberty Weekly Tribune*, March 4, 1847. Doniphan to Jones, March 4, 1847, 498–502; Maj. William Gilpin to Col. A. W. Doniphan, 506–7; Lt. Col. D. D. Mitchell to Col. A. W. Doniphan, 502–3, all in *Senate Documents*, 30th Cong.; *Liberty Weekly Tribune*, July 17, 1847; Clark to Doniphan, "Official Report of the Battle of Sacramento," March 2, 1847, in Edwards, *Campaign in New Mexico*, 172–78.

62. "Battle of Sacramento," *The Anglo Saxon*, March 19, 1847; Connelley, ed., *Doniphan's Expedition*, 541–54. This flag became a part of the Clark collection at the Missouri Historical Society.

in particular, also recognized in his diary the success of Doniphan's Missourians. "The number of troops engaged was comparatively small," he noted, "but I consider this victory one of the most signal which has been gained during the war. . . . The truth is our troops, regulars and volunteers, will obtain victories wherever they meet the enemy."[63]

The battles of El Brazito and Sacramento were the stuff of which legends are made. Because of the victories of the First Missouri Mounted Volunteers in the hinterlands of the Southwest, Alexander William Doniphan became the hero of a nation. No one, other than Zachary Taylor, captured the American imagination more effectively than Doniphan, mostly because of what he had done in these two engagements. Beckoned from his law practice to take up arms for his nation, like Cincinnatus at the plow, Doniphan epitomized the citizen-soldier. Unschooled in the art of war, he fought two battles against larger, better trained, and presumably superior Mexican forces. In both cases he won resounding victories. "When the deeds of the citizen soldiery shall be appreciated," wrote one of his volunteers, "then will the deeds of Doniphan and his gallant men shine forth with a brilliancy not to be surpassed." Doniphan demonstrated personally, as did his regiment, that the nation's leaders could entrust the defense of the United States to its ordinary citizens. With his victories at El Brazito and Sacramento, Doniphan proved to many in the country that its "heroic age had not passed."[64]

63. James K. Polk, quoted in Horgan, *Great River*, 769.
64. Quote from Johannsen, *To the Halls of the Montezumas*, 123.

8

The Occupation of Chihuahua City

ON MARCH 1, 1847, Colonel Alexander William Doniphan learned from James Kirker and his other scouts that the Battle of Sacramento had broken the back of Mexico resistance in the province of Chihuahua. The governor had apparently fled southward, leaving the capital for the taking, so Doniphan moved forward. He sent Lieutenant Colonel David D. Mitchell with 150 mounted troopers into the city on that day to establish an American military presence. The next day he made a triumphal entry, complete with formal parade and martial music. He did not plan, however, to stay long. As Private John T. Hughes wrote at the time: "It is Col. Doniphan's intention to continue his march still further down the country. He will perhaps return home by the Southern route. We hear that Wool & Taylor have joined their forces. This is a proud moment for us! The Battle of Sacramento gave us the capital & the Flag of our country, the 'Stars & Stripes,' are proudly & triumphantly streaming over the city. As the colonel entered the capital he fired a National Salute of 28 guns." Some of those guns had come from the Mexicans at the Battle of Sacramento so Doniphan especially enjoyed the irony of that moment.[1]

As the Americans advanced into the city, Dr. Frederick Adolphus Wislizenus recorded the scene. Wislizenus, a German traveler studying the botany and geology of the Spanish borderlands at the time of the outbreak of the war, was captured by the Mexicans and spent six months in Chihuahua City before the arrival of Doniphan and his men. Despite their triumphal entry into the provincial capital, he commented: "But, really, what a ragged set of men these brave Missouri boys were! There was not one among them in complete uniform, and not two in the whole regiment dressed alike. Some of the resident Americans in Chihuahua

1. John T. Hughes to Editor, *Liberty Weekly Tribune*, March 4, 1847, Miller Papers.

were so thunderstruck by the savage exterior of their own countrymen that they ran back to their homes to ascertain to just what tribe or nation they belonged."[2] Marcellus Ball Edwards, a nineteen-year-old private, remarked that "We rode through the principal streets and public square, and on a rocky hill on the south side of the city fired a national salute in honor of the conquest, stole wood enough to get supper, and went to bed as usual among the rocks."[3] One Santa Fe trader, who had been under Mexican guard in the city, recalled how quickly "Our flag floated in triumph at the head of the army (or regiment) and was raised upon the flagstaff of the plaza, and we felt grateful assurance that we were again free."[4]

Chihuahua City had about twenty-five thousand inhabitants at the time that Doniphan entered it in 1847. Its larger size caused it to be an order of magnitude more difficult to occupy than the earlier towns the First Missouri Mounted Volunteers had conquered, such as El Paso del Norte. Founded by Spanish colonials in 1690, Chihuahua had become rich in gold and silver, with several lucrative mines in the nearby mountains. Although most of the precious metals had been removed by the time of the American occupation, the vestiges of wealth abounded. The streets were neatly paved and curbed. The central plaza included a well-designed public park and speaker's arena. It also had a large, square stone fountain some ten feet high with four jets that sprayed upward another thirty feet. A large monument to Miguel Hidalgo y Costilla, the father of the first Mexican revolt in 1811, stood at the place where Spanish authorities had executed him, showing the allegiances of the local population. The city also boasted several public baths, complete with running water brought from the mountains via a complex aqueduct and pipe system. Many of the homes were elegant in comparison to Santa Fe standards, and several members of the expedition commented on their stone construction and attractive style.[5]

The Missourians loved the magnificent cathedral that graced the south side of the city plaza. It had taken more than thirty years to build during the latter eighteenth century and had cost an estimated one million dollars. "The exterior is covered with fine carving and statues," Frank S. Edwards wrote. "The front has three tiers of pillars, one above another, with figures of Christ and the twelve Apostles in different niches the size of life. Its two steeples, which are square and composed of pillars fancifully carved, were, a short time before, hung with bells; but the inhabitants cleared one of the steeples, in order to use the metal in making cannon."[6] Near the

2. Wislizenus, *Memoir of a Tour,* 54.
3. Quoted in DeVoto, *The Year of Decision,* 400.
4. James Josiah Webb, *Adventures in the Santa Fe Trade, 1844–1847,* 273.
5. Hughes, *Doniphan's Expedition,* 447–49; Edwards, *Campaign in New Mexico,* 121–22.
6. Edwards, *Campaign in New Mexico,* 123.

cathedral Doniphan spied some of Kirker's handiwork, nearly 150 scalps taken the previous June from the heads of Chief Reyes and his Apache followers. They swung in the breeze from the cathedral gate and fence within a few feet of some of his men's quarters. They served as a reminder of the brutality that could befall the Chihuahuans if Doniphan had reason to unleash Kirker on them. It was to this cathedral that the merchants of the Santa Fe Trail brought the body of one of their own, Samuel C. Owens, the only American killed outright at the Battle of Sacramento. He was a Catholic, and the local priest presided over his funeral at the cathedral on March 3, 1847.[7]

Although the Chihuahua provincial government under the control of Don Angel Trias had fled further south, Doniphan quickly recognized—from the monument to Miguel Hidalgo y Costilla and other not-so-subtle clues—that the inhabitants of Chihuahua City had an altogether different perspective on Anglo-American conquest than had the Hispanic settlers of New Mexico. While the New Mexicans had never been anything more than stepchildren of Spanish America, with their overseers in Mexico City viewing them as residents of a far-off, minor outpost, something of a buffer state on the frontier, Chihuahua City had fully identified with the Mexican republic. While the New Mexicans had enjoyed close ties to the United States for more than a generation, mostly through the lucrative Santa Fe trade, the province of Chihuahua had strong economic, social, and political relations to the south. Chihuahua City inhabitants were much less willing to accept the American conquest than the New Mexicans. Doniphan had to take precautions to ensure that the city remained firmly under his control and that his presence did not spawn guerrilla warfare.[8]

Because of an ever present fear of rebellion by the Chihuahuans, Doniphan limited contact between his troops and the citizens of Chihuahua City. He also mounted his artillery to command the streets and alleys leading into the Mexican central plaza. He then quartered his nearly one thousand troops as a unit in the public buildings and a few abandoned

7. Hughes, *Doniphan's Expedition,* 446; Smith, " 'King of New Mexico,' " 50.

8. Because of these reasons, as well as some of a more subtle nature, the United States government rejected the minority opinion of some in the nation, including President James K. Polk, to annex all of Mexico. In a political intrigue every bit as complex and manipulative as any envisioned by Shakespeare, the president's envoy, Nicholas Trist, refused to be recalled when he would not negotiate a peace treaty that gave to the United States all of Mexico north of the Sierra Madre, lower California, and the territory of the Isthmus of Tehuantepec. Trist's rationale was that Mexico should not be reduced to an unruly American colony. Instead, he argued, if the United States gave it a chance to obtain peace with honor, Mexico "would someday enter the temple of freedom" (quoted in Merk, *Manifest Destiny,* 181). He preferred a democratic, independent Mexico to a colonial one kept in line by the force of American arms. See J. D. F. Fuller, *The Movement for the Acquisition of All Mexico, 1846–1848;* and Thomas G. Paterson, J. Garry Clifford, and Kenneth J. Hagan, *American Foreign Policy: A History,* 111–12.

buildings around the plaza. Later he placed some of them at the Plaza de Toros (the bull ring), a huge amphitheater more than one hundred yards in diameter. Strong pickets patrolled the area and ensured that in an uprising the Missourians would receive warning before an opposing force reached their main living area. Very much a fortress by the time Doniphan finished with his preparations, this became an outpost of American might in the center of a wilderness of Mexican antipathy. One member of the regiment remembered that Doniphan's troops "held full and undisturbed possession of the city, keeping up strict discipline with a constant guard, and a patrol during the whole night, visiting every part of the city."[9]

During March 3 and 4, 1847, Doniphan conducted an exhaustive search of the public buildings of Chihuahua City in search of plans, orders, and any other information that gave him a sense of what Governor Trias might have in mind for the future. They found nothing of significance, but encountered an obstacle when the English consul to Chihuahua, John Potts, refused to allow Doniphan to search the home of Angel Trias, since he had the keys to the mansion. Potts had been belligerent ever since the Americans arrived, threatening them with the "displeasure of his government," and Lieutenant Colonel Mitchell especially did not much care for this obstinacy. "On being assured that the door would be broken open, he [Potts] said that being a British subject he considered the house under the protection of the British flag," commented the trooper Frank Edwards, "and that any violence to it would be resented by his government." Mitchell did not impress easily, and ordered two howitzers unslung facing the main entrance of the governor's palace. He lit slow matches to their charges, sparking Potts to propose a compromise. Mitchell searched the mansion, wrote Edwards, but "Pedrigo Potts was *not* a happy man!"[10]

Susan Magoffin, arriving with her husband's wagon train on April 4, 1847, after the First Missouri had been occupying Chihuahua City for a little more than a month, expressed horror at the treatment afforded the Mexicans and their elegant city. She recorded:

> Instead of seeing it [the city] in its original beauty as I thought to have done twelve months since, I saw it filled with Missouri volunteers who though good to fight are not careful at all how much they soil the property of a friend much less an enemy. The good citizens of Chi. had never dreamed I dare say that their loved homes would be turned into the quarters for common soldiers, their fine houses many of them turned into stables, the rooves made kitchens of, their public *pila* [drinking fountain] used as a bathing trough, the fine trees of their beautiful *alamador* [*alameda*— public walk] barked and forever spoiled, and a hundred other

9. Quoted in George, *Heroes and Incidents*, 115; Hughes, *Doniphan's Expedition*, 444; Robinson, *Journal of the Santa Fe Expedition*, 122–23.
10. Edwards, *Campaign in New Mexico*, 129–30.

deprivations equal to any of these, but yet all has been done;
Chihuahua was quite an indifferent looking place when I saw it.[11]

At least one of the Missourians, John Hughes, defended the regiment
against such criticism, concluding that upon the departure of Doniphan's
Missourians they left the city "untouched, & its magnificent architecture
unimpaired."[12]

Doniphan also contemplated Angel Trias perhaps rallying the Mexican
army defeated at Sacramento and returning to Chihuahua City. Such a possibility held disastrous consequences for Doniphan's one thousand, since
it would probably be a superior force even without the help of the citizens
of Chihuahua City, and he had every reason to believe that those residents
would join in helping any Mexican force that might march on the city. To
provide advance warning Doniphan sent a detachment of seventy troops
under the command of Captain Richard H. Weightman to reconnoiter the
region surrounding the city. Leaving on March 3, Weightman ranged as
far as Parral, on the border between the provinces of Chihuahua and Durango, nearly two hundred miles away. He reported back periodically by
express couriers. He brought word that Doniphan did not have to worry
about opposition mounting in the hinterlands. Doniphan also sent James
Kirker and his Shawnee and Delaware retainers about the area to ferret
out possible guerrillas. He especially wanted Kirker to search for any trace
of Angel Trias and an organized resistance to the American occupation.[13]

One of Doniphan's immediate concerns after reaching Chihuahua City
was to ascertain what he should do after securing the province. In his
after-action report on Sacramento sent to Brigadier General Roger Jones
on March 4, 1847, Doniphan included two options for what to do next:
"On the 1st day of March we took formal possession of the capital of
Chihuahua in the name of our government. We were ordered by General
Kearny to report to General Wool at this place. Since our arrival, we hear
he is at Saltillo [some 600 miles to the east], surrounded by the enemy. Our
present purpose is either to force our way to him, or return by Texas, as our
term of service expires on the last day of May next." Doniphan had fully
expected to find Brigadier General John E. Wool in command of the Army
of the Center at Chihuahua City, where he anticipated linking with Wool's
forces; he had only learned otherwise just before the Battle of Sacramento.[14]

11. Magoffin, *Down the Santa Fe Trail*, 228–29. Interestingly, Susan Magoffin and
her husband had no qualms about occupying one of the elegant homes of the city
abandoned by its well-to-do owners when they fled in advance of the American army.

12. Hughes to Editor, *Liberty Weekly Tribune*, May 28, 1847, Miller Papers.

13. Hughes, "Diary of John T. Hughes," 106; Duchateau, "Missouri Colossus," 223;
Smith, " 'King of New Mexico,' " 50–51.

14. A. W. Doniphan to R. Jones, March 4, 1847, in *Senate Documents*, 30th Cong., 502;
Liberty Weekly Tribune, July 17, 1847.

Doniphan also wrote to John F. Ryland in a fit of pique on March 7 about this problem:

> My orders are to report to Gen. Wool; but I now learn, that instead of taking the city of Chihuahua, he is shut up at Saltillo, by Santa Anna. Our position will be ticklish, if Santa Anna should compel Taylor and Wool ever to fall back. All Durango, Zacatecas and Chihuahua will be down upon my little army. We are out of the reach of help, and it would be as unsafe to go backward as forward. High spirits and a bold front, is perhaps the best and safest policy.[15]

Assuredly upset with the lack of movement by Wool and concerned for the welfare of his command, Doniphan acted decisively to ensure against capture.

Doniphan knew that the Mexican government under Don Angel Trias had also been holding, in what amounted to an internment, in Chihuahua City about thirty American merchants who had entered the territory before the military. He immediately gave these men their freedom, and from these released Americans Doniphan learned that even though there was antipathy for the conquerors, the city's dwellers had little fight left in them. He found that most of the inhabitants worried that the victorious American force would sack the city. One former prisoner, James Josiah Webb, confirmed that because of this fear most Mexicans "kept themselves in their houses for several days, and it was seldom they appeared on the streets for a week or so." Such a reaction set well with Doniphan early in his efforts to control the city and region surrounding it. It helped to ensure that the Mexicans did not revolt.[16]

After assuring the safety of his command deep in captured enemy territory, Doniphan set about several other tasks. First, he moved to reassure the Mexican populace of the beneficence of his Missourians. James Webb noted that the morning after the Battle of Sacramento he had gone into Chihuahua City's central plaza,

> and such excitement and wailing I never before witnessed and never hope to see again. The plaza was filled with women and children (but few men) with bundles of clothes, blankets, etc., upon their backs, and those who could raise a donkey or any other animal capable of bearing the least burden, had them packed. And all were excitedly discussing what they should do or where they should go to escape violence, which the priests had told them they must expect from our soldiers.

Webb spoke with several people, assuring them that they had nothing to fear from Doniphan's regiment. "A good many returned to their homes,"

15. Quoted in Hughes, *Doniphan's Expedition*, 450.
16. Webb, *Adventures in the Santa Fe Trade*, 273; George, *Heroes and Incidents*, 111.

he commented, "not in confidence I think, but not knowing how they could do better." Not all took Webb's advice, however, and some suffered exposure in winter weather in the mountains surrounding Chihuahua City when they took to the hills before the American force arrived.[17]

To help reassure them, on March 6, 1847, Doniphan issued his first decree to the residents of Chihuahua. He stated that the United States had taken charge of Chihuahua and asked that the residents of the town go about their business peacefully. The proclamation also declared "that the American troops will punish with promptitude any excess that may be committed, whether it be by the barbarous Indians or any other individual." Finally, Doniphan demanded "not that any Mexican shall assist us against his country, but that in the present war he remain neutral; for it cannot be expected, in the contrary event, that we shall respect the rights of those who take up arms against our lives." The decree was also issued in Spanish; Doniphan signed his first name as *Alejandro* on this decree.[18]

Doniphan's early actions toward the Chihuahuans may have been fair but they were not benevolent. Unlike Kearny on entering New Mexico, Doniphan had no orders directing him to incorporate the region and its populace into the United States. He had no requirement to swear them to allegiance to the Constitution and no desire to write for them a legal code that reflected the values of the American republic. Instead, he declared martial law and ruled with a stern hand. He had little sympathy for the people of Chihuahua and he treated the territory as a conquered province. As he wrote to John Ryland soon after entering Chihuahua City on March 7, 1847: "How often have I again and again determined to send you hearty curses of everything Mexican? But, then I knew that you had seen the sterile and miserable country, and its description would be, of course, no novelty to you."[19]

In reality, theft became the most serious problem in Chihuahua City, and Doniphan dealt with it both calmly and harshly. He never intended to rehabilitate those who committed crimes; instead he punished them as a deterrent to others. His standard punishment for theft was whipping, carried out either publicly or privately depending on the seriousness of the offense, and several Mexicans felt the teamster's bullwhip when caught stealing American goods.[20] The unsavory Kirker loved this kind of work, and Doniphan put him to punishing supposed thieves. Gabe Allen and James Hobbs, two of Kirker's most trusted men, led this effort. Mexican jailers had opened the cells of the local prison as they fled the

17. Webb, *Adventures in the Santa Fe Trade,* 272–73.

18. Hughes, *Doniphan's Expedition,* 444–45; *Liberty Weekly Tribune,* May 22, 1847. A copy of a Spanish-language version of this proclamation is at the Missouri Historical Society.

19. Quoted in George, *Heroes and Incidents,* 109.

20. Hughes, *Doniphan's Expedition,* 446–47.

town before the American army and those incarcerated were loose on the streets of Chihuahua City when Doniphan arrived. It did not take long to notice their presence and one after another Allen and Hobbs hunted down and gave these criminals numerous lashes for crimes both real and imagined. One died during a punishment of four hundred lashes while tied to a tree, and a second died two days thereafter in a similar manner. John T. Hughes, writing to the editor of the newspaper in Liberty, Missouri, downplayed this restitution, commenting that during the stay of the regiment in Chihuahua City, "Only a few thieves were scourged."[21]

The most important demonstration of this type occurred soon after the American occupation of Chihuahua City, when a large number of the Missourians' horses turned up missing and Doniphan sent Kirker and his men in search of the thieves. They tracked the herd into the mountains and in a confrontation shot one of the thieves dead. They brought back eight more Mexicans, along with the horses, for punishment. Doniphan turned James Hobbs loose to enjoy some sadistic punishment and he dragged the thieves through the street behind a wagon pulled at breakneck speed. Doniphan used the episode as an object lesson, demonstrating what would befall lawbreakers.[22]

The effort to maintain military order in the city involved forming the First Missouri Mounted Volunteers for regular drills in the city plaza. Doniphan used these daily four-hour drills as both a means of keeping his regiment functioning as a military unit while on garrison duty and as a way of demonstrating the unit's fighting ability. These actions stood in contrast to those of the lackadaisical and good-humored commander that the Missourians had known in Fort Leavenworth and on the trail to El Paso del Norte. Now, miles inside the interior of Mexico and surrounded by people who, if not openly hostile, were at least contemptuous of the "Gringo" army, he was much more of a disciplinarian who kept his men alert to any danger and ready to fight any invading force.[23]

By the middle of March 1847 Doniphan's command had settled into the routine of occupation. He kept the troops busy with drills and patrols and also made preparations for fights that might be forthcoming. He fortified the approaches to the city and set to work on battle plans. Private Frank Edwards described how his company made cartridges for the regiment's captured cannon, "and it certainly would have frightened any nervous man to have seen the quantity of gunpowder strewed through our building day after day." He added that some five hundred pounds of gunpowder suffered in the elements, "and subject, at any moment, to a chance spark of fire—several of our men occasionally passing over it with

21. John T. Hughes to Editor, *Liberty Weekly Tribune,* May 28, 1847.
22. Smith, " 'King of New Mexico,' " 51.
23. Hughes, "Diary of John T. Hughes," 107; Duchateau, "Missouri Colossus," 226.

lighted cigars." It made Edwards shudder at the possible consequences, but most of the troops seemed oblivious to the danger.[24]

There were also cultural and other activities that occupied the time of the First Missouri's troops while in Chihuahua City. A theater troupe from Santa Fe put on nightly plays, including "She Stoops to Conquer" and "Pizarro," all big hits among the Missourians. A minstrel show drew large audiences among both the Americans and the Mexicans, if not among the slaves that had organized their own company and fought at Sacramento. There was also the same possibility of liquor, exotic foods, balls or fandangos, women, and gambling in Chihuahua City as before. On March 18, 1847, the Americans began issuing a bilingual newspaper, *The Anglo Saxon*, to inform the members of the occupying army of news and as a means of communicating the ideas of the Americans to the conquered people of the city. Published by John S. Webb and edited by Lieutenant Christian Kribben, this periodical offered equal parts information and propaganda to its readers. The most unusual amusement involved Major Meriwether Lewis Clark, who found the books in the governor's palace's library improperly classified, so he set a detail to work reorganizing them.[25]

Doniphan also had to deal with American traders in the city, his most difficult issue as military governor. He moved without much success to punish violations of trade restrictions with the enemy soon after reaching Chihuahua City. For all intents and purposes this boiled down to bringing to trial the Prussian emigrant, Albert Speyer, who had raced the Army of the West to Santa Fe and had managed to stay one step ahead of Doniphan all the way to Chihuahua City. Speyer had carried contraband weapons and ammunition to Angel Trias, and as far as Doniphan knew he should be considered an enemy of the United States. Understandably, little was seen of Speyer after the arrival of the Americans, but soon Doniphan sent Lieutenant Colonel David Mitchell in search of him. Mitchell accosted James Webb about Speyer's whereabouts, learning that the arms Speyer carried had been ordered, along with other goods, more than a year before the declaration of war, and that Speyer was a loyal American who only sought to get into Mexico before the army so he could beat the other traders to market. Mitchell interrupted Webb, "Well, if you and his other friends can give any evidence to clear him of what he is accused, all right. If not, we shall hang him in a day or two."

Learning of this, Speyer sought to ingratiate himself with the Missourians and entertained them daily for more than week in his elegant home in Chihuahua City. As Webb recalled, "Whist parties with wine were held every night in his rooms, and many articles of bric-a-brac which

---

24. Edwards, *Campaign in New Mexico*, 130–31.
25. Karnes, *William Gilpin*, 178–79; "To Our Readers," *The Anglo Saxon*, March 18, 1847; "To the Mexican Public," *The Anglo Saxon*, April 3, 1847.

he had bought at the fair, such as silver bridle reins, silver fans, and other Mexican curiosities, disappeared from his shelves. And after a couple of weeks he was tried before a court-martial and honorably acquitted. Who was hung? And did the silver bridle reigns serve as the rope?" Webb concluded Speyer had pulled one over on Doniphan and the Missourians. He realized, however, that Speyer had "simply followed the course of an enterprising merchant" in the whole episode.[26] The report in the *Missouri Republican* in St. Louis also acquitted Speyer. "It turns out, that Speyer was innocent of any crime," noted the paper. "He had six kegs of powder when he left Independence, and sixty muskets, which the Mexicans took from him. Speyer knew he was pursued, but hastened forward to make some $80,000, by being the first in market with his goods."[27]

Doniphan also ran afoul of the Santa Fe traders when he stated that he did not intend to remain in Chihuahua City for long. At first it had been a free-for-all among the merchant princes of the Santa Fe Trail to set up shop. James Webb recollected that after Doniphan marched into Chihuahua City, "The banished Americans returned to town [and] opened their places of business. [Francis] Macmanus and Dr. [Henry] Connelly opened their stores and began distributing their goods for cash value instead of seeing them flouted on the streets '*de locos.*' "[28] Within three days of arriving in Chihuahua City, however, Doniphan announced to the traders that he intended to leave with the regiment of First Missouri Mounted Volunteers in one week. They should prepare to leave with the regiment, he said, or he would leave them to the whims of the Mexican inhabitants of Chihuahua. Santa Fe trader William H. Glasgow wrote about this to his father in Missouri. "As the amt of goods thus introduced amtd to *only* about 1.000.000 $ it may readily be supposed that they could not easily be disposed of," Glasgow groused, "particularly as the Congress of this State issued a decree (from Parral where they removed immediately after the battle of Sacramento) forbidding any one from purchasing any goods introduced by the army under penalty of confiscation." To leave with the army ensured that traders could not sell all their goods. To remain without the regiment's protection, however, meant running the risk of Mexican reprisals. The only answer was to persuade Doniphan to garrison the city for as long as possible.[29]

To keep Doniphan in the city, the merchants emphasized the potential of invasion by a reconstituted Mexican army under Angel Trias. When a rumor arose early in March that Trias had set up a government in exile

26. Webb, *Adventures in the Santa Fe Trade,* 275–76.
27. *Missouri Republican,* May 18, 1847.
28. Webb, *Adventures in the Santa Fe Trade,* 273.
29. William H. Glasgow to William Glasgow, May 6, 1847, in Gardner, ed., *Brothers on the Santa Fe,* 117.

at the town of Parral and was making preparations for an invasion of Chihuahua City, Doniphan sent James Kirker with Captain Weightman's detachment on a grueling two-day ride through Apache country to check out the report. They found nothing, but Doniphan still kept a close watch.[30]

Also, the traders talked Doniphan into remaining in Chihuahua City until some treaty could be negotiated with Trias. On March 8, 1847, Doniphan sent a military escort with Henry Connelly, one of the American merchants who knew Trias well, to meet with him at Parral. The Missourian made simple propositions. According to Private Marcellus Edwards, Doniphan offered to reinstate Governor Trias "in his office and evacuate the city with American forces, and the traders should pay the rates of duty as heretofore, if he [Trias] would ensure them protection." He may also have asked for the release of James Magoffin, very nearly the only American left in Trias's custody. Because of Magoffin's service for the United States Doniphan deemed his loss unacceptable. Trias knew this and refused to release Magoffin until the Americans withdrew, using him as an insurance policy against further American encroachments into Chihuahua and Durango.[31]

Ten days later Connelly returned to Chihuahua City without an agreement with the Mexican governor. Trias did, however, send three commissioners to meet with Doniphan and offer a counterproposal. According to an account published in the Missouri press, Trias "would pledge protection for the traders upon condition that the American forces would immediately evacuate the city, leaving the artillery and everything captured at Sacramento and pay liberally for all damages done Chihuahua since our possession of it. These propositions were of course rejected." Doniphan then offered another proposal, "if the people of Chihuahua will guaranty the safety of the American residents and traders in Chihuahua, and will hold themselves aloof from any participation in the war, he will evacuate the town and proceed on his course." At first, it appeared that "the Mexicans were favorably inclined to the terms proposed."[32] They apparently later thought better of it, however, and the negotiations broke down on March 20, 1847, when Trias refused to promise future neutrality.[33]

30. Smith, " 'King of New Mexico,' " 50–51; William H. Glasgow to Mary Susan Glasgow, March 23, 1847, in Gardner, ed., Brothers on the Santa Fe, 113.

31. Johnston, Edwards, and Ferguson, Marching with the Army of the West, 275; Hughes, Doniphan's Expedition, pp. 450–51. Magoffin was finally released in July 1847 and found his way back to Chihuahua City.

32. Missouri Republican, May 12, 1847.

33. William H. Glasgow to Mary Susan Glasgow, March 23, 1847, in Gardner, ed., Brothers on the Santa Fe, 113–14. A Mexican version of these negotiations later appeared in the Weekly Reveille, May 10, 1847. In this account, which seems far-fetched in the extreme, Doniphan demanded not only Chihuahua's neutrality but also that its residents pay an indemnity of fifty thousand dollars to the Americans and allow the traders to sell their goods duty free. The report commented, "It is not to be believed

When Connelly returned from Parral on March 18 he also brought reliable information about the decisive Battle of Buena Vista, fought on February 23, 1847, before Doniphan's regiment had reached either Sacramento or Chihuahua City. Not long thereafter Doniphan learned of the successful amphibious landing of General Winfield Scott's army at Vera Cruz and the march on Mexico City. With these developments, *The Anglo Saxon* announced that "Mexico therefore is fairly subdued; without a Government, without means, without an army, her citizens in revolt and rebellion—she will in all probability now assent to such terms of peace as our government will dictate." The editor overstated his case, but these reports not only increased the morale of Doniphan and his Missourians in Chihuahua City but also gave the First Missouri's commander hard intelligence about the whereabouts of Brigadier Wool. He ordered a victory salute fired from the captured cannon and assembled his officers for a council to discuss a march to link with Wool at his headquarters near Saltillo.[34]

On the nineteenth his senior officers assembled in Doniphan's office at the governor's palace in what everyone called a council of war. Doniphan explained that his orders had been to help Wool take Chihuahua. That done, however, Wool was nowhere to be found, and the occupation of Chihuahua City might grow more precarious as time passed. Since the original orders had also directed Doniphan to link with Wool, the colonel proposed doing so now that they knew his location. As Private Frank Edwards put it, "A few of the officers proposed staying in Chihuahua, others were for trying to join General Taylor, and some suggested a retrograde march to Santa Fe; most, however, were in favor of pressing home by way of Monterey." Those officers that wished to remain in the provincial capital, Doniphan believed, had apparently been seduced either by the splendors of the city or by the entreaties of the traders. This represented a core of his officer contingent, Doniphan knew, and without winning over some of them he could obtain no consensus for any effort to leave the city. Unwilling at the time to issue a direct order beyond the purview of his initial instructions from the War Department, Doniphan believed he had to obtain a consensus from his officers about what to do next. Accordingly, he adjourned the council without any clear course of action agreed upon.[35]

A second council met a short time later but by then the traders had convinced most of the senior officers to remain in Chihuahua until the

---

that the sons of Chihuahua could consent to so disgraceful an agreement." In this version negotiations broke down because of Doniphan's unreasonable demands. This version is not corroborated elsewhere, however, and it seems highly unlikely that he would have made such outrageous proposals.

34. "News from the South," *The Anglo Saxon*, April 3, 1847; Hughes, *Doniphan's Expedition*, 452–53.

35. Edwards, *Campaign in New Mexico*, 131.

regiment's enlistment was up on June 1, 1847. Presumably, this enabled them to enjoy the privileges of the city and to avoid any further combat. It also pleased the traders and infuriated Doniphan. While he allowed that the Missourians "might possibly have found *fair* reasons for staying . . . *I'm for going home to Sarah and the children.*" He convinced several that they should push eastward to meet Taylor and Wool and then return to Missouri and their "Sarahs," or whatever their wives' names might be, via the Gulf of Mexico and the Mississippi. The only agreement they reached involved sending a messenger to Doniphan's nominal superior officer, John Wool, for further orders. If Wool directed them to join him, they would support the move.[36]

The next day Doniphan wrote to General Wool about his command and its predicament, sending along a copy of his official report of the Battle of Sacramento. In some respects the First Missouri was the Mexican War's lost battalion; no one in U.S. Army leadership knew exactly where it was and what had befallen it. More than that, most military officials had all but forgotten about it. Doniphan tried to explain this to Wool, a commander who knew of the First Missouri only tangentially even if aware of it all. He even had to identify who they were for Wool. "The forces under my command are a portion of the Missouri volunteers, called into service for the purpose of invading New Mexico," Doniphan wrote, "under the command of Brigadier-general (then colonel) Kearney [*sic*]." He narrated how the First Missouri Mounted Volunteers had occupied Chihuahua City, describing briefly the fights at El Brazito and Sacramento. He also commented that "On yesterday we received the first even tolerably reliable information, that a battle had been fought near Saltillo between the American and Mexican forces, and that Santa Anna had probably fallen back on San Louis de Potosí."

Doniphan then came to the crux of his problem:

> My position here is extremely embarrassing. In the first place, most of the men under my command have been in service since the 1st of June, have never received one cent of pay. Their marches have been hard, especially in the Navajo country, and no forage; so that they are literally without horses, clothes or money, having nothing but arms and disposition to use them. They are all volunteers, officers and men, and although ready for any hardship or danger, are wholly unfit to garrison a town or city. "It is confusion worse confounded." Having performed a march of more than two thousand miles, and their term of service rapidly expiring, they are restless to join the army under your command.

At this point Doniphan came directly to the problem of the American traders in the city:

36. Ibid., 131.

Still we cannot leave this point safely for some days—the American merchants here oppose it violently, and have several hundred thousand dollars at stake. They have sent me a memorial, and my determination has been made known to them. A copy of both they will send you. Of one thing it is necessary to inform you: the merchants admit that their goods could not be sold here in five years; if they go south they will be as near the markets of Durango and Zacatecas as they now are. I am anxious and willing to protect the merchants as far as practicable; but I protest against remaining here as a mere wagon-guard, to garrison a city with troops wholly unfit for it, and who will be soon ruined by improper indulgences. Having been originally ordered to this point, you know the wishes of the government in relation to it, and of course your orders will be promptly and cheerfully obeyed. I fear there is ample use for us with you, and we would greatly prefer joining you before our term of service expires.[37]

Doniphan then dispatched this message, and other letters, to Wool via James L. Collins, a Missouri trader serving as Doniphan's interpreter. On March 20 Collins left at the head of a thirteen-man expedition in search of Wool at Saltillo.

On the same day that he dispatched Collins to Wool, the negotiations between Doniphan and Trias broke down. The traders blamed Doniphan and the Missouri colonel blamed the traders for this failure. William H. Glasgow thought Doniphan obstinate, and "fearing to compromise himself, would not accept of their propositions nor would he make any himself."[38] For his part, Doniphan complained that some of the traders "objected to my making a treaty for them." Instead, they "by that time had come to the conclusion that a tremendous meeting & sundry resolutions would force me to stay there as long [as] there was a shirt-tail full of goods in the City."[39] Such a posture by the traders made sense only if they could get out of paying duties to the Chihuahuan government, something that Doniphan had specifically offered, and that might have motivated them to hobble the negotiations. By the end of March, after a month in Chihuahua City, James Webb summed up the deadlock in the provincial capital: "The merchants all were anxious to force sales, the troops were waiting anxiously for orders from General Taylor what to do, and all was anxiety and uncertainty for some time."[40]

37. Quoted in George, *Heroes and Incidents,* 113–14.

38. William H. Glasgow to William Glasgow, May 6, 1847, in Gardner, ed., *Brothers on the Santa Fe,* 117. See also Manuel Harmony to Col. A. W. Doniphan, March 23, 1847, and Manuel Harmony to Col. A. W. Doniphan, April 3, 1847, *House Report No. 458,* 30th Cong., 1st sess., 17–18.

39. A. W. Doniphan to David Waldo, January 10, 1848, Alexander William Doniphan Letter, State of New Mexico Records Center and Archives.

40. Webb, *Adventures in the Santa Fe Trade,* 277.

While this waiting game progressed, on April 2, 1847, the vice governor of Chihuahua, Laureano Muñoz, issued a decree from Parral that heightened the traders' apprehensions about their businesses. It declared that no goods brought into the region under the protection of Doniphan's army could be transported or sold in any of the unoccupied portions of the province, and that no Mexican merchants could stock or sell American goods obtained after the Battle of Sacramento. He would confiscate goods in this category. This effectively limited the market for all the Santa Fe Trail goods to Chihuahua City and its immediate environs, thereby making it impossible to sell the stock on the shelves in anything approaching a reasonable time. They would not be gone by the time that Doniphan's Missourians left, even if they stayed until their enlistments expired on June 1. It was now all the more important that Doniphan stay in Chihuahua City until the regiment's enlistment was up, and not only that but the traders wanted to obtain an additional garrison for the city. They sent dispatches to the American commanders at Saltillo importuning military protection and tried to keep the Missourians in place as long as possible.[41]

As this took place Doniphan faced perhaps the toughest crisis of his command, and inadvertently it aided the cause of the traders by keeping the First Missouri Mounted Volunteer Regiment in Chihuahua City longer. Both Lieutenant Colonel Mitchell and Major Gilpin had agitated since arriving in the city for the regiment to march on. As William H. Glasgow explained, Mitchell pressed "for the hasty departure of the U.S. army as he never failed from the first day he entered this place to importune & harass Col Doniphan to leave the place and not allow the interest of a *few paltry speculators* to influence his movements." Because of this, Glasgow said that every trader held for Mitchell "a universal contempt for him as an officer & a most cordial hatred as a man."[42]

If Mitchell desired to vacate the city because he did not believe in fighting the war to aid merchants in their business, as he apparently genuinely believed should not be the case, Gilpin based his pressure to leave on the expansion of the United States through the conquest of all of Mexico. Gilpin's scheme proved both simple and insidious. The First Missouri had charged hell-bent into the heart of Mexico, lived off the land, survived the desert, neutralized the Indians, and fought two successful engagements against the Mexicans. Why not continue the sweep and march on Mexico City? The campaign, with or without orders, seemed predestined. Gilpin thought the door lay open for the Missourians to walk right into the Mexican capital. All the cosmic tumblers were in place; such

41. Vice Governor Laureano Muñoz, decree, Parral, April 2, 1847. A translation is contained in *House Report No. 458*, 30th Cong., 1st sess., 28–29.
42. William H. Glasgow to Mary Susan Glasgow, March 23, 1847, in Gardner, ed., *Brothers on the Santa Fe*, 120.

an opportunity might not present itself again for a century, and Doniphan had exactly the right instrument at exactly the right moment in exactly the right place to strike a decisive blow. It would mean unimaginable glory for all the members of the First Missouri and achieve the reality of manifest destiny, something Gilpin firmly believed a part of America's fate. Gilpin argued effectively for his half-baked plan, despite its problems, and got several of the junior officers to go along.

Doniphan appointed a tribunal to consider the matter, stacking the deck with officers he thought agreed with him. In a scene that must have been amazing to the frontier lawyer, used to swaying an audience with his oratory, Gilpin eloquently appealed to the tribunal about the opportunity that lay before them. He even suggested that the regiment finance the campaign with a reported eight hundred thousand dollars in the Chihuahua mint. Doniphan pointed out the problems with the plan: the nearly one thousand miles of desert between Chihuahua and Mexico City, the poor state of the troops, the lack of a logistical base, the uncertainty of Mexican opposition, the term of service expiring on June 1, and the regimental orders to link with General Wool. None of these seemed to matter. Gilpin's eloquence and passion for the cause of manifest destiny marveled even Doniphan, and in the end the group found in favor of pursuing Gilpin's scheme. It amounted to a form of mutiny, and Doniphan considered resigning, but that would only give Gilpin what he wanted. Instead, the colonel soon decided to scuttle the plan through subterfuge.[43]

Acting quickly to maintain a semblance of control over his regiment, Doniphan decided to get most of the troops out of the capital for a time. On April 5, 1847, he led a force of nearly six hundred men and fourteen cannon southward toward San Pablo where there had been reports of activity by a Mexican force. Gilpin, of course, thought Doniphan was leading the vanguard of the regiment toward Mexico City and glory. The march would do the bored Missourians good, Doniphan believed, but he wanted to make sure that the trip did not get out of control and allow Gilpin to push his foolhardy scheme of taking Mexico City. He kept the larger purpose of the march envisioned by Gilpin secret from anyone outside the confines of the regiment's senior leadership. The traders, for instance, thought he went in search of a supposed Mexican army. In a sentence dripping with sarcasm, William H. Glasgow wrote to his father that "Our Gallant Col then thought he would go down to Parral to root out the Mexican Congress &c he accordingly departed with one half of his force . . ."[44]

43. Wislizenus, *Memoir of a Tour*, 61; Hubert Howe Bancroft, *Chronicles of the Builders of the Commonwealth*, 537; Karnes, *William Gilpin*, 180.

44. William H. Glasgow to William Glasgow, May 6, 1847, in Gardner, ed., *Brothers on the Santa Fe*, 117–18; Wislizenus, *Memoir of a Tour*, 61.

As one means of subverting Gilpin's grand design, Doniphan left some three hundred troops under the command of Lieutenant Colonel Jackson at Chihuahua City as a garrison to pacify the traders. Without the whole regiment there was very little likelihood of successfully taking the Mexican capital and Jackson always proved himself notoriously slow to leave the comforts of any city in favor of the trail. Doniphan also took the fifty-mile trip at a leisurely pace, passing through Mapula and Bachimba, before reaching San Pablo three days later. At every opportunity he lobbied with the senior officers against Gilpin's plan, offering to resign his commission, but not doing so, if they insisted on pushing on. As it turned out, most of the officers were not interested in changing horses in the middle of the stream. Doniphan, the man that had brought them this far, could continue to command them until he himself quit. They would not overthrow him. Wisely Doniphan refrained from resigning, for to do so ensured Gilpin's success.[45]

On April 9, while encamped at San Pablo, Doniphan received a letter from an American named Hicks, possibly an American merchant by the name of Young E. Hicks, who did business in the region. Hicks claimed that a Mexican army of between five and six thousand men was on its way to Chihuahua City from Durango. Doniphan knew a fortuitous turn of events when he saw one, and he sent scouting parties in search of the enemy. It turned out to be a phantom army, never where reported. The possibility that Trias had raised a force allowed Doniphan to return to Chihuahua City for its protection. As William Glasgow incorrectly believed, although Doniphan did not mind him thinking so, he "toddled back in double quick time frightened out of his wits."[46]

The next morning after receiving the Hicks report, Major Gilpin lined up his battalion and waited for the order to march farther south. Instead, Doniphan and several of the other officers mounted their horses and rode northward toward Chihuahua City. Within only a few minutes, Doniphan had a courier deliver written orders to Gilpin. They said that because the province was full of hostile bands and because reports indicated the capital's danger, that he should march with the regiment back to Chihuahua City to ensure that Lieutenant Colonel Jackson's command, and American citizens under regimental protection, were not massacred. Gilpin faced an important decision. He could ignore the order and continued southward, in open mutiny against a superior officer. Or, he could obey the order and

45. Bancroft, *Chronicles of the Builders,* 537; Wislizenus, *Memoir of a Tour,* 61.

46. William H. Glasgow to William Glasgow, May 6, 1847, in Gardner, ed., *Brothers on the Santa Fe,* 118; Webb, *Adventures in the Santa Fe Trade,* 133; Wislizenus, *Memoir of a Tour,* 62; Benjamin Riddell to John Black, December 30, 1842, Box C.8.2, Correspondence Received, 1829–1841–1842 to 1844, U.S. Consulate General, Mexico City, Mexico, in RG 84, National Archives; Johnston, Edwards, and Ferguson, *Marching with the Army of the West,* 277.

return to the capital, dashing his dreams of glory and manifest destiny. Had Doniphan been present he might have argued with him, but in this instance Gilpin had little choice but to march the regiment back to the city. His troops returned on April 12, 1847. Doniphan's play near San Pablo was not unlike a similar one he had made in 1838 when he refused to execute the Mormon prophet and some of his followers. Like this time, in 1838 he had delivered a written ultimatum and departed the scene, leaving the commander in the field with the option of accepting or rejecting Doniphan's position. If he rejected it, however, in both cases dire consequences awaited the officer.[47]

As Dr. Wislizenus concluded, Doniphan's men returned to garrison duty and waited for two weeks "for the large army from the south, till we became convinced at last that it was but a hoax—invented, perhaps, in Chihuahua, by some persons whose interest it was to keep the troops there as long as possible."[48] The traders were not fooled by the Hicks ruse; it is probable that neither was Doniphan. William Glasgow suggested that Hicks made his claims because the Durango merchants "feared the competition of the Chia merchts" that would arise if the regiment occupied the territory to the south and the Chihuahua traders moved behind them.[49]

Doniphan never talked about this near mutiny in any of his correspondence or reflections, and few of his troops commented on it so they likely knew nothing of it. At most, Marcellus Edwards expressed an unwillingness to return to garrison duty at Chihuahua City. He commented in his journal that "this is the first retrograde movement we have made, and the Mexicans are already laughing us to scorn; and even the women throw it at us, forgetting the example set by their own troops." Most, however, took the return in stride. As for Doniphan and Gilpin, they never trusted each other and rarely agreed thereafter, but both decided for the good of the regiment to work together until their enlistments were up. They acceded to abandon plans either to invade Mexico City or to return home until they heard from Wool at Saltillo.[50]

Fortunately, Doniphan and Gilpin did not have to wait long for orders from Wool. Within two weeks, on April 23, 1847, the trusted Collins—along with a company of Arkansas Rangers under the command of Captain Albert Pike—returned from Saltillo with clear and direct orders from Brigadier General Taylor, who had met Wool in northeastern Mexico. He ordered the First Missouri Mounted Volunteers to join his command at

47. Bancroft, *Chronicles of the Builders*, 537.

48. Wislizenus, *Memoir of a Tour*, 62.

49. William H. Glasgow to William Glasgow, May 6, 1847, in Gardner, ed., *Brothers on the Santa Fe*, 118. See also E. V. Pomeroy to Robert Aull, May 29, 1847, E. V. Pomeroy Letters, Western Historical Manuscript Collection.

50. Johnston, Edwards, and Ferguson, *Marching with the Army of the West*, 277; Bancroft, *Chronicles of the Builders*, 537.

Saltillo. When they arrived, the volunteers would be offered the opportunity to reenlist for the duration or they could go home. "As for the traders," read Taylor's orders, "they may, at their option, remain in Chihuahua, or come under the protection of your column to Saltillo."[51] The traders declared surprise at this turn of events. Gilpin was heartsick but willing to accede to the direct orders of a superior officer. Doniphan, according to William Glasgow, "immediately issued his orders to evacuate the town upon the '*next day*' and sent each of us a copy of Gen Wools orders."[52]

The American merchants in Chihuahua City had already reopened negotiations with the Mexican officials of the region, on the off-chance something like this might happen, and when Doniphan issued his evacuation order they stepped up efforts to make a deal to remain in the city. They sent the Chihuahua City *prefecto* Felix Maceyra to Parral as their ambassador, instructing him to "state our willingness to pay duties &c to the govt and get from the vice govr an obligation to protect our persons & property after the army left in case we would guarantee the forces to leave the State within one month."[53]

For his part, Doniphan suggested the traders offer as a bargaining chip the "immediate withdrawal with our forces from the State of Chihuahua & the payment of New Mexican duties." In addition, Doniphan gave Connelly a written statement for the Mexican authorities at Parral stating "that if the treaty was made that I would leave with our forces in a few days—that I would use my influence to prevent Gen Wool or any detachment of his army from marching on Chihuahua—and the Mexicans having heard that some reinforcements were coming from New Mexico I was to leave written order with Dr. Conelly [*sic*] directing such force not to occupy Chihuahua but to pass through as speedily as convenient."[54] Doniphan also encouraged the traders to sell or pack up their goods and travel with his army. He made one last visit to the local Mexican leadership and threatened that if they mistreated Americans after the regiment's departure he would return to punish them.[55]

Before agreeing to a final plan, although virtually assured by then, Doniphan started moving out of the provincial capital. On the morning of April 25 Doniphan's second battalion, under the command of Congreve Jackson, along with the artillery, began to march the more than six hundred

51. Extract of orders from Gen. Zachary Taylor to A. W. Doniphan, *House Report No. 458*, 30th Cong., 1st sess., 38; Edwards, *Campaign in New Mexico*, 132.

52. William H. Glasgow to William Glasgow, May 6, 1847, in Gardner, ed., *Brothers on the Santa Fe*, 119.

53. Ibid., 118; *Missouri Republican*, June 22, 1847.

54. Doniphan to Waldo, January 10, 1848, Alexander William Doniphan Letter, State of New Mexico Records Center and Archives.

55. Wislizenus, *Memoir of a Tour*, 61; Josiah Gregg, *The Diary and Letters of Josiah Gregg*, 2:104–5.

miles east to Saltillo. With the salutes of the officers and the music of the fife and drum, Jackson led his troops slowly out of the city and onto the harsh trail to Saltillo. As they marched for the last time through the streets of Chihuahua City, private Frank Edwards noted that the bell ringing and catcalling by Mexicans drowned out the cadence of the drum. "Their principal shout was, 'The *gringoes* are gone, hurrah!' "[56] This reaction to the departure of the first part of Doniphan's regiment only heightened the anxiety of the American merchants in the city and most now prepared to leave with the last contingent, scheduled to depart on April 28. They hurriedly sold what goods they had left and packed whatever they could for the journey either to Saltillo or back up the Camino Real to Santa Fe. According to John Hughes, only about "ten *Mexicanized* Americans remained in Chihuahua" after the final element of the regiment withdrew.

At ten o'clock on the morning of April 28, as American traders scrambled to complete their withdrawal, Doniphan formed up the rest of his command in the city's central plaza. As he and Gilpin made their final inspections, a few Mexican ladies raced their horses through the Missourians' ranks. The troops held a short ceremony, took down the American flag, and assembled for the trek to Saltillo. The infantry then led the way out of the city, with their baggage wagons and the wagons of the merchants following along a short distance behind. Again the people of the city cheered the American departure; most were happy to see them leave. Even as Doniphan headed to the east, a merchant train left northward up the Camino Real for Santa Fe—some of the traders were testing their luck by returning the way they had come. The rumor circulated among Doniphan's troops that this train carried a large amount of gold bullion or specie, gained either legally or by sleight of hand the Missourians did not know. Doniphan believed that leaving was the right thing to do—and after fifty-nine days of garrison duty in the provincial capital, he led his men on to Saltillo and eventually home to Missouri.[57]

---

56. Edwards, *Campaign in New Mexico,* 132.
57. John T. Hughes to Robert H. Miller, May 28, 1847, Miller Papers; Webb, *Adventures in the Santa Fe Trade,* 277–78; Moorhead, *New Mexico's Royal Road,* 181–82; Gardner, ed. *Brothers on the Santa Fe,* 37–38.

9

Hail the Conquering Hero

IN LATE APRIL 1847 the First Missouri Mounted Volunteers began their long march of more than six hundred miles from Chihuahua City to Saltillo, where they finally rejoined other American forces. As they left Chihuahua City, no doubt, Doniphan's troops had mixed memories of their nearly two-month stay in the provincial capital. Dr. Frederick Adolphus Wislizenus, in a more reflective mode than most Missourians, undoubtedly spoke for others in the expedition. "When, in the distance of about four miles, in crossing a chain of hills that encompass Chihuahua on the south," Wislizenus wrote, "I looked for the last time over the interesting city in which I had seen . . . a whole drama performed, and had been forced myself to act a rather passive part in, I could not help admiring once more its romantic situation, and my first, favorable impressions returned."[1]

Colonel Alexander William Doniphan marched his troops over the next several days to the town of Santa Rosalia, located on the Durango road 120 miles east of Chihuahua City. There, on May Day, they rendezvoused with advance elements for the remainder of the march to Saltillo. Doniphan then sent the second battalion, the remaining cavalry, the artillery force, and Captain John Reid with a detachment of seventy men to Parras. They were to reach the town within four days, scout it, and then wait for the remainder of the regiment. The main part of the regiment and the baggage wagons followed. Private John T. Hughes editorialized about a "dreadful desert" march, adding:

> It was excessively hot. Every man prepared to take a canteen of water along with him, some filled the scabbard of their sabres with

1. Wislizenus, *Memoir of a Tour*, 62–63.

water, & let the naked sword hang jingling by their sides. . . . The
artillery & baggage train made harsh grating music on the rocks, &
fire sparkled beneath the wheels. In the march the greatest hilarity
prevailed. The banners streamed bravely before the puffing gales
of the Desert. Some would crack their jokes & pass the lively repar-
tee; while others would tell a Rocky mountain story or recount a
daring affray with Indians; & while a third would sing "Yankee
Doodle" or some other lively song for the amusement of a crowd a
fourth would sentimentally & in a half-suppressed tone hum "The
Girl I Left Behind Me."[2]

They were happy to be heading for home, however, and that, for the
moment, was enough.

On May 6 the column reached the province of Durango, and the next
day its advance scouts encountered about thirty armed Mexicans at the
small town of Pelayo. The scouting troop took away their arms, but returned them when the Mexicans said that leaving them without weapons
made them easy prey for the Comanche Indians raiding the area. Hughes
noted that "Since 1835 the Indians have encroached upon the frontiers of
Mexico & laid waste many flourishing settlements, waging a predatory
warfare, & leading women & children into captivity. In fact, the whole
of Mexico is a *frontier*." The scouts swore the Mexicans not to use their
weapons against the Americans and sent them on their way.[3]

Other than this incident, only two other events of note took place during
the march to Saltillo. The first occurred when the regiment encountered
a Mexican bandito named Canales. While marching for San Lorenzo on
May 11, Doniphan's regiment passed along a road hedged with a huge,
thick, almost impenetrable chaparral. Waiting for them in the chaparral
was Canales with almost a hundred outlaws who wanted to kill stragglers
and take provisions from the merchant train accompanying the regiment.
One trooper, Thornton A. Mount of Jackson County, wandered off the
road and disappeared. He apparently died at the hands of the robbers,
who also stripped his body of all possessions. When the Missourians
discovered him missing, Doniphan sent out a search party that found the
murdered soldier but nothing else, tightened the formation, and deployed
troops into defensive positions along the column. With that action Canales
could find no vulnerable place to attack and the rest of the day passed
without incident. When Doniphan bivouacked for the night, however,
a rider entered camp with news that Canales had attacked wagons from
the Magoffin brothers nearby. Doniphan dispatched a detachment of sixty
men to help Magoffin and its arrival prompted Canales to withdraw. He
did not bother the column again.[4]

2. John T. Hughes to Editor, *Liberty Weekly Tribune*, May 28, 1847, Miller Papers.
3. Ibid., June 8, 1847; Wislizenus, *Memoir of a Tour*, 67.
4. Hughes, *Doniphan's Expedition*, 474–75.

The second episode of importance during an otherwise strenuous but monotonous march took place when the people of Parras enlisted Doniphan's support to pursue an Indian raiding party on May 12–13, 1847. A war party, reportedly Comanche (but actually Lipan Apache), had attacked the town and captured nineteen of its children, three hundred mules, two hundred horses, and trade goods and money after murdering several villagers. Captain John W. Reid and a detachment of horsemen followed the tracks left by the Indians to the hacienda of El Pozo where he encountered another detachment of Doniphan's one thousand. Just as the two groups joined forces, between fifty and sixty Apache appeared on the horizon. Reid learned at the hacienda that the Indians were the same ones who had raided Parras and that they had their captives and booty with them. The Indians were intending to water their stock at the hacienda and perhaps take more prisoners and animals; Reid prepared to ambush them. As a participant described it:

> Capt. Reid concealed his men (about thirty-five in number) in the hacienda, and sent out Don Manuel Ybarro, a Mexican, and three or four of his servants to decoy the Indians into the hacienda. The feint succeeded. When the Indians came within half a mile, the order was given to charge upon them, which was gallantly and promptly done. Capt. Reid, Lieuts. Gordon, Winston and Sproule, were the officers present in this engagement, all of whom behaved gallantly. The Indians fought with desperation for their rich spoils. Many instances of individual prowess and daring were exhibited by Capt. Reid and his men, too numerous, indeed, to recount in detail; the captain himself, in a daring charge upon the savages, received two severe wounds, one in the face and the other in the shoulder. These wounds were both produced by steel pointed arrows. This engagement lasted not less than two hours, and was kept up hotly until the Indians made good their retreat to the mountains.[5]

Three times Reid led charges at the Apaches, who had taken positions behind cover. The Missourians could gain no decisive victory over the Apache raiders until Manuel Harmony, one of the Santa Fe traders traveling with the regiment, arrived with twenty-five men and combined with Reid to charge the Apache positions for a fourth time. This drove the Apaches into retreat. During the fighting no Missourians died, although several received wounds. The troops counted fifteen Indian dead and estimated that another twenty-five had been wounded. They also recovered thirteen of the captive Mexicans and most of the spoils.[6]

5. George, *Heroes and Incidents,* 126–27.
6. Capt. J. W. Reid to Brig. Gen. J. E. Wool, May 21, 1847, in *House Executive Documents,* no. 56, 30th Cong., 1st Sess., 334–35; Hughes, *Doniphan's Expedition,* 476–77; Wislizenus, *Memoir of a Tour,* 71.

After the engagement, the Mexicans at the hacienda dragged the Indian bodies to one location, stripped them of anything valuable, and left the corpses to rot in the desert. "The dead bodies were lying there all day; neither Americans nor Mexicans seemed to care about them, and their burial was no doubt left to the wolves," wrote Dr. Wislizenus. "I saw, therefore, no impropriety in taking another curiosity along for scientific purposes—to wit, the skull of the medicine man, which I have, since my return, presented to that distinguished craniologist, Professor Samuel G. Morton, of Philadelphia." Wislizenus hacked off the head, and displayed it on the wagon pole during the day and boiled it each evening to take the flesh off. This was a little too much even for the "rough as a cob" Missourians. They called him "Whistling Jesus," complained about both the grisly nature of the decapitation and of the stench, and kept their distance during the rest of the march.[7]

By May 21 Doniphan's ragged regiment had reached the American lines at Encantada, not far from Saltillo. That night they bivouacked with a unit of cavalry from Arkansas and the men from both groups traded war trophies, gossip, and lies until the wee hours of the morning. Doniphan gave his command full rations, drawing upon the hospitality of the Arkansans' commander, who had offered to share his troops' food. The commissary officer stopped short, however, of letting the Missourians have any soap. A wit replied: "Soap! Hell, what do we need with soap? We have no clothes to wash!"[8]

The next morning Doniphan marched his men to Brigadier General Wool's headquarters. Leaving his men to set up an encampment near the Buena Vista battlefield, Doniphan visited the general and his staff. Wool, perhaps a little curious by the appearance of this "lost battalion," asked to review the troops. Doniphan hurried back to his regiment to prepare for the review and had little trouble getting them excited about a visit from the "brass," but Wool and his staff arrived an hour later than agreed. The men snapped to as best they could, but their curiosity was every bit as great as Wool's and many leaned forward to get a better view of the fastidiously groomed Wool and his martinet-looking staff. Trooper Jacob Robinson commented that "They craned their necks and followed his progress down the line." When told to get back in line, one Missourian responded that he did not have as good a view from there. Periodically the Missourians cheered Wool, threw their hats in the air, and generally behaved like undisciplined volunteers. Doniphan followed along on his own somewhat haggard horse, his broad-brimmed

7. Wislizenus, *Memoir of a Tour,* 72; William Clark Kennerly, *Persimmon Hill: A Narrative of Old St. Louis and the Far West, as told to Elizabeth Russell,* 202–4; Karnes, *William Gilpin,* 182.

8. Connelley, ed., *Doniphan's Expedition,* 482.

white hat and makeshift uniform setting him far apart from Wool and his staff.[9]

Wool, as spit-and-polish as any officer in the Army, was repelled by the appearance of the men he inspected. At first he seemed to take exception to them, with their beards and hair unkempt, their uniforms nonexistent, and their lines far from perfectly aligned due to the "various protuberances fore and aft."[10] Then he perceived the full measure of what this unit had endured during the last year and he chuckled to himself. In the end, Wool complimented the accomplishments of the First Missouri Mounted Volunteers. As written in a commendation on May 22, 1847:

> The general commanding takes great pleasure in expressing the gratification he has received this afternoon in meeting the Missouri volunteers. They are about to close their present term of military service, after having rendered, in the course of the arduous duties they have been called upon to perform, a series of highly important services, crowned by decisive and glorious victories.
>
> No troops can point to a more brilliant career than those commanded by Colonel Doniphan; and no one will ever hear of the battle of Brazito or Sacramento, without a feeling of admiration for the men who gained them.
>
> The State of Missouri has just cause to be proud of the achievements of the men who have represented her in the army against Mexico, and she will without doubt, receive them on their return with all the joy and satisfaction to which a due appreciation of their merits and services so justly entitles.
>
> In bidding them adieu, the general wishes to Col. Doniphan, his officers and men, a happy return to their families.

Wool's favorable comments about Doniphan and his men were motivated as much by his desire to entice them to reenlist as it was by his respect for their battlefield prowess. He had almost no success, however, in persuading any to remain with the army for a second tour in Mexico.[11]

No matter what the reason, Wool was cordial toward the Missourians, and even took them on a battlefield tour of Buena Vista. Sitting on a camp chair overlooking the battle scene, still not entirely clear of the dead and debris, Wool pointed out the unique features of the terrain and narrated the important events of the hard-fought confrontation. Wool recalled:

> And while I was telling them this, a brawn[y] young Missourian, almost naked, dirty and bearded like a pirate, hair unkempt and

9. Robinson, *Journal of the Santa Fe Expedition,* x, 482; Rollin J. Britton, "General Alexander W. Doniphan," address at the eighth annual banquet of the Gallatin Commercial Club, February 20, 1914, 9, Missouri Historical Society.

10. Robinson, *Journal of the Santa Fe Expedition,* x.

11. Quoted in George, *Heroes and Incidents,* 131–32; Hughes, *Doniphan's Expedition,* 482–83.

falling over his shoulders, but of fine appearance and manly countenance, was squatting beside me, completely absorbed in the story. When I concluded he slapped me on the thigh and said: "Right there is where you made a mistake, General! When they retreated you ought to have pressed them and charged like we did at Sacramento! If you had done that you would have destroyed them, as we did! Yes, sir, there is where you made a damned big mistake."

Wool took the advice in stride; Doniphan said nothing. The outspoken trooper, Robert D. Walker of Company G from Howard County, may well have been right. Although Zachary Taylor and John Wool had good reason for consolidating their victory at Buena Vista, the opportunity to destroy all of Santa Anna's army presented itself there, and it might have opened the door for the capitulation of all of northern Mexico.[12]

The day after this episode, May 23, Doniphan marched his regiment to General Wool's camp to deliver the artillery, no longer needed by the men since they were returning to the United States. While there Wool noticed the cannon taken from the Mexicans at Sacramento and perhaps considered the possibility of acquiring it for his troops' use as well, but in the end he told Doniphan that his unit could keep all its war trophies, including the cannon and battle flags. When the First Missouri arrived home they presented the field pieces to the state government. One of the cannon, named "Old Kickapoo," was stolen and used in the fighting during the Kansas border war of the 1850s. Another, named "Old Sacramento," went to Lexington, where it was fired during Fourth of July celebrations. During the early years of the Civil War, Southern sympathizers brought it into service at the battles of Wilson's Creek, Elkhorn, and Pea Ridge.[13]

After finishing with Wool, Doniphan's regiment marched some seventy miles to the east to Zachary Taylor's headquarters near Monterrey. Arriving on May 26, Doniphan's troops met "Old Rough and Ready," and it was a high point for the unit. While Wool had been prim and a bit of a dandy, Taylor looked like one of the overweight, middle-aged loungers that sat around every Missouri courthouse square on Saturday afternoons. He wore a short brown coat and a straw hat, without any trace of rank about him or any sense of military attire or discipline. Even Doniphan looked more like an officer of the U.S. Army than Taylor. Soon after arrival and during some free time Lem White, a private from Jackson County, mistook Taylor for a camp loafer and asked him where he might find a tall drink of whiskey. Not in the least taken aback, Taylor gave him directions to the sutler's quarters and then cautioned, "But you had better not let General

12. Connelley, ed., *Doniphan's Expedition*, 484.
13. Young, *Young's History of Lafayette County*, 1:80; Hughes, *Doniphan's Expedition*, 483.

Taylor know you got any whiskey, for he might make trouble for you."
White found a jug without incident, and upon his return passed it around
to his friends. Then he decided to share it with Doniphan and went in
search of the colonel. After asking for him, White found him at Taylor's
quarters. He tried to walk into Taylor's tent but a guard barred the way.
White then tried to peep into the tent to get Doniphan's attention, so he
would come out for a drink. While trying to get the attention of Doniphan,
who never did see the private, White spied the same chap who had given
him directions to the sutler. He asked the sentry, "Who is that fat old fellow
sitting in there?" "That," replied the guard, "is General Taylor." "The hell
you say," was all White could gasp as he got out of officer country as fast
as possible.[14]

Taylor impressed most of the rest of the members of the regiment just
as he had Lem White. The general took his wide-brimmed straw hat
off as he reviewed them, fanning himself periodically, and they noticed
with favor that his uniform was nearly as rough as theirs. He seemed
to eschew formality and military discipline. He also showed the First
Missouri Volunteers that their efforts and their accomplishments during
the previous year had indeed been appreciated, something that most of
them at one time or another had wondered about during their march to
Mexico. Within a day after arriving at Taylor's headquarters, Doniphan
had orders for his regiment to return home via water from Brazos Island to
New Orleans and then up the river to St. Louis. The formal orders directing
these movements Taylor closed by commending the regiment. "In thus
announcing the arrangements which close the arduous and honorable
service of the Missouri volunteers," he wrote, "the commanding general
extends to them his earnest wishes for their prosperity and happiness,
and for a safe return to their families and homes."[15]

Doniphan spent the next several days shepherding his men from Taylor's headquarters to the coast of Mexico. By the first of June they had
reached the town of Reynosa, on the Rio Grande and still some sixty
miles from Brazos at the mouth of the river, where Doniphan arranged
transport for his troops. The Missourians did not much care for Reynosa,
as it was raining when they arrived and it was raining when they left.
While there was a large military presence at the port, it had no facilities
for these transient troops. Sleeping in the mud on maggot-laden blankets
and eating spoiled fly-filled food was not their idea of enjoyment. At this
point, not even the thought of returning home mitigated their ill will.
As they had done throughout the march, the Missourians complained
to anyone or anything that would listen. Their ire grew more expressive
when Doniphan loaded the sick, infirm, and maimed members of the

14. Hughes, *Doniphan's Expedition*, 484–85.
15. Quoted in ibid., 484–85.

regiment, a large percentage of the group by this time, into the first boat that stopped at Reynosa and set out with them for Matamoros on the Gulf of Mexico. He left Lieutenant Colonel Congreve Jackson in charge, with orders to follow as soon as boats came by, but the men griped at having been abandoned by their commander. They did not know, however, that Doniphan had gone ahead to arrange for ships to take the regiment from Mexico to New Orleans. In effect, Doniphan's action saved his men several days' wait on the hot beaches of the gulf with even worse conditions while he procured transport.[16]

As they waited by the river, Jackson and William Gilpin had the regiment dispose of their equipment, which they could not take home and had no desire to leave for the despised Mexicans. They built a huge pyre by the river and burned their saddles, harnesses, and extra equipment. Frank Edwards remarked: "All our extra blankets, buffalo robes, and everything we could spare, we cast upon the pile. I observed a Mexican knocked over by one of our men for offering him one dollar for his saddle, the latter declaring that a saddle which had carried a Missourian so many miles as his had, should not be sold to a Mexican for twenty dollars—and it was instantly committed to the flames."[17] Even as they were leaving, whether right or wrong, Doniphan's Missourians had little sympathy for their former enemies.

It did not take long to move the rest of the regiment to Matamoros, and on June 10 Doniphan arranged for transport to New Orleans. "Our embarkation for New Orleans was in two vessels," recalled Frank Edwards, "one of them a small bark, wherein myself and some three hundred and fifty companions were packed." Edwards traveled on the schooner *Murillo*, but not luxuriously.

> Her hold, containing one hundred double berths, was in such a filthy condition that we preferred the deck as a sleeping-place, and it was a struggle with us who should get his blanket first on deck, as those who were crowded out were compelled to go below. We ran short of water, and began to think ourselves on a worse *jornada* than ever.
>
> Oh! the relief felt after almost four thousand miles of rough travel, as we reached New Orleans, and placed our feet once more upon American soil! We were still in our tattered clothes, with unshorn beards and without a cent in our pockets; but "Sarah and the children" were now not far off!

Doniphan and nearly seven hundred men traveled to New Orleans on the *Republic*, an American ocean-going transport.[18]

16. Ibid., 488–91.
17. Edwards, *Campaign in New Mexico*, 164.
18. Ibid., 165; Hughes, *Doniphan's Expedition*, 491–92.

The entire regiment arrived in the Crescent City on June 15. A heroes' welcome greeted the regiment in New Orleans, but the locals who turned out disliked the Robinson Crusoe look of the First Missouri. One veteran had thrown away his deerskin hunting pants because he had nothing left to patch. Another wore nothing more than a tattered set of long underwear covered by an old overcoat. Nonetheless, the citizens saluted them from their rooftops and balconies in the French Quarter with flying flags, waving handkerchiefs, and hoarsely shouting "good show" and "bravo." Within twenty-four hours Missouri politicians, perhaps to capitalize on the popularity of the volunteers, showed up to welcome the regiment back to the United States. Claiborne F. Jackson, who would later become governor of Missouri, and Robert W. Donnell, Doniphan's brother-in-law, arrived with two local wholesale-clothing merchants in tow. With Doniphan they arranged clothing for the troops, and purchased on credit about sixty thousand dollars' worth. The regiment also officially mustered out of the army at New Orleans. Decked out in their new civilian duds, its remaining members stood formation one last time on June 28 and accepted honorable discharge from the military.[19]

Thereafter the men began finding ways back to Missouri, most of them hitching rides on Mississippi riverboats northbound for St. Louis. The first began arriving on June 27, almost a year to the day after the regiment had left Fort Leavenworth for its trek to Mexico. Some men headed straight for their homes and farms. Some stayed in St. Louis for a few days to carouse and participate in a huge formal celebration scheduled for July 2, 1847. Doniphan, of course, stayed. He had arrived in St. Louis on June 30 on the steamer *Old Hickory*, greeted by a cannon salute from Camp Lucas, located west of the city. He spent the intervening days in a series of meetings with political, military, and civic officials. It was all very much a blur but it sealed in the minds of those who met him that Doniphan's one thousand had been led by an impressive figure, one who in every respect matched the impressiveness of the expedition.

Three hundred of Doniphan's regiment paraded through the streets of St. Louis on July 2, joining uniformed volunteer fire companies and several Missouri militia units that had not been mobilized, including the Missouri Dragoons, two battalions of German-speaking dragoons and fusiliers, the St. Louis Grays, and the Montgomery Guards. The captured Mexican cannon, the prizes of the expedition, were garlanded with flowers and banners; these excited the several thousand residents who turned out to cheer the returning veterans. The Camp Lucas commandant roused his artillerymen for more fireworks from the hilltop overlooking the city, and while the cannon saluted Doniphan's accomplishments, the bells of

19. Doniphan, *Address;* Floyd C. Shoemaker, "Some Colorful Lawyers in the History of Missouri," 713; Connelley, ed., *Doniphan's Expedition,* 492–94, 499.

the local churches and fire companies rang long and loud. Local political leader Thornton T. Grimsley led the parade down St. Louis's Fourth Street to the front of Planter's House in the city center. There, Judge James B. Bowlin formally welcomed the regiment back to the state. Lieutenant Colonel David D. Mitchell, a citizen of the city, accepted the honors for Doniphan's volunteers.[20]

After these formalities, Doniphan and the other members of the regiment continued the parade to Camp Lucas, near the city. There, about seven thousand residents listened intently to Senator Thomas Hart Benton sing the praises of Doniphan and his one thousand. "Old Bullion," as staunch a political opposite as the whiggish Doniphan could ever want, spent more than an hour numbering the virtues of the colonel and his men. On such an occasion, despite their differences of philosophy and politics, Benton could be nothing but gracious.

When Benton had finished his speech Doniphan also addressed the crowd, summoning the best of his courtroom theatrics to create an emotional memory for those present on that day. He spoke of his reasons for volunteering, and of the meaning of the war for the course of the American republic. He explained what he knew of the military situation in Mexico and of the political relations of the two nations:

> It is not for me, fellow-citizens, to discuss the merits of this war. But, it is natural that I, for one, should say something in relation to it. It is a strange war: when first commenced, it was denounced by a large party of our country—the party to which I belong—as a war for political purposes. But, when soldiers were to be raised for its prosecution, you find that men of all parties—the opposers and the advocates, the accusers and the accused—were ready to engage in the war, to rally under the same standard, to fight in the same tented field. What a spectacle for the people of the old world to gaze upon!
>
> Men who were engrossed in the strife of political prejudice were willing, like Roderick Dhu and Fitz James, to lay aside those prejudices, for the time, when a common enemy was to be engaged—to renew their dissensions, if ever, when peace should be restored.

Doniphan realized that this was the appropriate response for all members of the nation in a time of crisis.

Doniphan then went on to denounce those who did not support the war, regardless of their party allegiances. For him, a soldier, it was not a rhetorical issue but a question of supporting the troops in the field. Not to do so represented, in essence, treason, if not to the flag at least to the men fighting in far-off lands. He said:

---

20. Connelley, ed., *Doniphan's Expedition,* 495–502; William F. Switzler, "Alexander W. Doniphan," in Conard, ed., *Encyclopedia,* 2:295.

Fellow-citizens—I wish that the same patriotic feeling had existed
in the councils of this nation: I wish that Mexico could have seen
the same unanimity in our people, in the prosecution of this war,
that they have seen in our forces, in the field. I recollect well, the
impression made on my mind, on one occasion, when an express
sent by me to Gen. Wool, brought me such stray papers as had
found their way to the General's camp—the latest dates were of
the 29th November—consequently, we had seen nothing of the
proceedings of the last session of Congress, or of the President's
message. The first thing I cast my eye upon was a speech of
Mr. Corwin, Senator from Ohio, denouncing the war, and those
engaged in it, as little better than a band of robbers. Gentlemen, a
winter shower bath would have been pleasant compared with my
sensations on reading it! Freezing—chilling! Such speeches might
have been deemed patriotic in the United States; but, place yourselves where we have been and endure what we have undergone,
and then imagine our sensations. We were in a city numbering
in population at least twenty times our force, and surrounded by
enemies on all sides. We had crossed the Sierra Madre, and found,
when we had arrived at Chihuahua, that we were looked upon as
little better than a band of robbers! Fellow-citizens, the speeches
which are made in opposition to this war, are said to emanate
from the peace party; but I say that they are made by those who
are postponing the peace eternally!

It was a stinging criticism of those who opposed the war, especially the
Whigs who refused to support it once the fighting was a fact. Doni-
phan urged the conflict's successful conclusion through victory over
Mexico.

Doniphan also eloquently characterized the conduct of his troops in
more than a year of hardship, conflict, occupation, and neglect by the
Army. He discussed various aspects of the march, now increasingly compared to that of Xenophon's army of the ancient era for its sheer extent.
As he concluded his ringing speech, Doniphan said, "I will not detain
you longer; may your destiny be onward, and as rapid as the great stream
that washes the border of your great city." That last comment showed
the Missouri colonel's essential belief in the idea of progress, and the
Whig goal of the positive liberal state.[21] The formal ceremonies concluded
with Doniphan's rousing speech, but everyone then went to the St. Louis
Park for a picnic. Those festivities lasted well into the night, and not a
few people awoke the next morning with hangovers and, at least on the
veterans' parts, a few swelled heads. As James Glasgow reported to his
brother, the activity in St. Louis was a "grand fete" in which everyone
overindulged their egos and their palates.[22]

21. Benton, *Return of the Missouri Volunteers; Liberty Weekly Tribune,* July 17, 1847.
22. James Glasgow to William Glasgow, July 4, 1847, Lane Collection.

More to the normal liking of most St. Louisans was the observation about the exploits of the First Missouri made by local resident Elizabeth Gowen Sargent. She wrote:

> Week ago last Friday, the volunteers were welcomed back from Mexico, Col. Doniphan's regiment, the poor fellows looked bright and happy though sunburnt and weary. His regiment has taken 80 guns from the Mexicans—10 of them I saw pass in procession, there were five Mexican flags taken from them which were displayed in the procession, one of them a black one two feet long and about as wide with a death head on it. Little pleasure would they have felt if they could have seen the guns and flags unfurled and waving in triumph through our streets. The bells ringing and all looking happy and greeting them on their return from the scene of their peril and privation.[23]

The formal welcome completed, during the next several days Doniphan and his boys took steamers, or coaches, or even walked back to their homes. Joyfully reunited with "Sarah and the children," most recalled the expedition in ever increasing heroic terms as time progressed.

Even as the festivities in St. Louis proceeded, Doniphan's hometown of Liberty prepared for the return of its first and greatest war hero. The editor of the *Liberty Weekly Tribune* reported in late June that

> Our community are anxiously looking for the Hero of Sacramento and his brave little army, and are prepared to give them a welcome as will convince them that, however much we may be divided upon some subjects, there is but one sentiment as to the manner in which they have discharged their duty. The glorious 4th of July is close at hand and we should be most happy to hear the shrill sound of Col. Doniphan's eloquent voice on that day. We are pleased to see the spirit manifested by our citizens in making arrangements for the Dinner contemplated . . .

Doniphan missed the Fourth of July celebration in Liberty, but he had returned and appeared on July 17 when the town held its own scaled down version of the St. Louis welcome. Doniphan's speech differed little from that given in St. Louis, and the local politicos—whether rivals or not—heaped praise on the Missourian and his troops.[24]

There followed a succession of ceremonies throughout western Missouri honoring the commander and troops of the First Missouri Mounted Volunteers for their service in the Mexican War. On July 29 Doniphan and several of his former troops participated in a formal dinner in Independence to which more than five thousand people turned out to honor

23. Elizabeth Gowen Sargent to Mother, July 10, 1847, St. Louis History Papers, Missouri Historical Society.
24. *Liberty Weekly Tribune,* June 26, 1847.

the veterans. In late August he also attended a dinner at Gallatin, in northwestern Missouri, and accepted the praises of local political and business leaders. As reported in the *Liberty Weekly Tribune:* "The towering stature, the majestic appearance and modest mien of the Col. satisfied every beholder that there stood a hero indeed. He proceeded to address the multitude and for two hours was listened to with the most rapt attention and satisfaction convincing all that he was as powerful in the forum as he had been overwhelming in the field. A more able, eloquent and entertaining speech, I never heard. His St. Louis speech was lame and lipless compared with this."[25] This was possibly the last of the major welcoming events, for the *Tribune* declared in its issue of August 28 that it represented the close of the "Campaign of 47."

Doniphan enjoyed enormous respect from the American public as a whole because of his leadership of the First Missouri in 1846 and 1847. Probably largely because he was a citizen-soldier, the public took heart that the nation's defense could be entrusted to its ordinary citizens and that the nation did not have to rely exclusively on a professional military. Moreover, Doniphan demonstrated in graphic terms that the nation's heroic age had not passed. So important was Doniphan in this process that the commandant of the U.S. Military Academy at West Point invited the Missourian to address the corps of cadets in 1848. While his appearance at West Point grated on the sensibilities of some officers in the regular army who still believed that volunteers were worth little in combat, it signaled the acceptance of their importance for the welfare of a democratic republic. For his part Doniphan acquitted himself well in this address, emphasizing the centrality of West Point's role in educating a small cadre of Americans in the art of war so that they might ensure the nation's preservation from opportunistic militaristic powers.[26]

Since Doniphan attained such an exceptionally positive image because of his success in the war, it is appropriate to analyze his combat skills. He followed quite rigorously the combat tactics shaped by the experience of the Napoleonic Wars and expounded by such tacticians as Antoine Jomini and Dennis Hart Mahan.[27] These called for lining up the troops in tight linear formations, usually two men deep, advancing elbow to elbow

25. Ibid., September 10, 1847. See also Meeting in Daviess County, n.d. [1847]; Letter to Editor of Liberty Tribune, August 7, 1847, both in Alvord Collection, collection 970; and Charles Henry Hardin, Speech, n.d. [1847], Charles H. Hardin Papers, collection 111, Western Historical Manuscript Collection.

26. *Address Delivered in the Chapel at West Point;* Johannsen, *To the Halls of the Montezumas,* 43, 123; Hill, *Minute Man in Peace and War,* 19–25.

27. On these tactics, see James W. Pohl, "The Influence of Antoine Henri de Jomini on Winfield Scott's Campaign in the Mexican War"; and T. Harry Williams, "The Military Leadership of North and South," in David Donald, ed., *Why the North Won the Civil War,* 33–54.

DONIPHAN'S

EXPEDITION.

BY JOHN T. HUGHES.
OF THE FIRST REGIMENT OF MISSOURI CAVALRY.

ILLUSTRATED.

CINCINNATI:
PUBLISHED BY U. P. JAMES,
No. 167 WALNUT STREET.

Title page to John Taylor Hughes's history, *Doniphan's Expedition*, published in 1847. This history, and others published during the same period, did much to lionize Doniphan for the American public.

against the enemy at a quick, measured pace. "Close-order line formations delivered the most effective musketry," concluded one recent historical analysis of the period, "and were the most common infantry formations of the Mexican War."[28] Linear warfare dominated every aspect of Mexican War tactics, and Doniphan employed it with great success at El Brazito. El Brazito demonstrated a classic linear warfare scenario as described in the tactical manuals written by U.S. Army general Winfield Scott. At El Brazito, Doniphan's Missourians deployed in a long double line facing the enemy. He chose not to advance on the enemy but instead to await the Mexican force's closure on the Americans. Using excellent musket tactics, Doniphan had his men fire volleys into the Mexican lines at close range and then to advance in a bayonet charge. All this came directly from the standard infantry manuals of the era.[29]

At Sacramento Doniphan employed the column formation, a tactic intended to deliver a decisive attack at a point or several key points in an enemy formation. These proved effective in dealing with the entrenched Mexicans on the highlands near the river. While linear warfare relied on a concentration of musketry and bayonets, column attacks emphasized shock tactics where localized mismatches of troop strength could carry the day, even if the force might be seriously outnumbered, the exact circumstance of Doniphan's Missourians at Sacramento. Also at Sacramento, Doniphan made effective use of his artillery, another aspect of the tactical understanding of the era. The *Instruction for Field Artillery, Horse and Foot,* first published in 1845, available to artilleryman Meriwether Lewis Clark, offered recommendations achieving excellent results at Sacramento. It described the process of maneuvering cannon and batteries on the march and in battle, and Clark and his troops efficiently demolished enemy artillery, strongholds, and redoubts. One of Taylor's staff reflected on the use of artillery at Palo Alto and Resaca de la Palma, but his comments appear relevant for Sacramento as well. "There was a great deal of personal gallantry shown and the most enthusiastic and determined spirit both in officers and men," he wrote. "But the light artillery was the back bone of our success."[30]

Doniphan's campaign in northern Mexico served to harass the Mexican government at all levels and perhaps ensured that thousands of enemy troops were unable to join Santa Anna at the Battle of Buena Vista, which began on February 27, 1847, the day before Doniphan's engagement with the Chihuahuans at Sacramento. Doniphan's excursion into Mexico also neutralized the invaded region during the remainder of the war. From

28. Grady McWhiney and Perry D. Jamieson, *Attack and Die: Civil War Military Tactics and the Southern Heritage,* 33.
29. Compare this to the discussion in *Abstract of Infantry Tactics; Including Exercises and Manoeuvres of Light-Infantry and Riflemen; for the use of the Militia of the United States.*
30. Quoted in McWhiney and Jamieson, *Attack and Die,* 37.

political and economic perspectives, the expedition opened northern Mexico to American influence as never before. Doniphan's conquest gave the United States claim to northern Mexico, even though its diplomats chose not to exercise it. Such a claim, however, played a role in the peace negotiations. Beforehand, Chihuahua had been only the domain of the U.S. Santa Fe traders, but after 1847 it became an ever more important trade and transportation region.

Despite the generally capable leadership that Doniphan provided his regiment, and the critical acclaim that he enjoyed as a result, he had been quite lucky in his military campaign. Doniphan's leadership had been less than effective in dealing with the Navajo Indians, and his departure from New Mexico without an effective treaty deserves criticism. That it received none at the time rests largely on its being overshadowed by his other exploits. Doniphan had also not dealt with the Santa Fe traders accompanying his command as effectively as he perhaps could have, although whatever else he may have tried would have caused censure by someone. As it was, disgruntled merchants complained to the Federal government upon the return of the regiment and an investigation into Doniphan's decisions resulted in claims of some traders supposedly economically hurt. However, despite their providing the traders restitution, the investigators exonerated Doniphan of any duplicity and noted that he was acting because of the exigencies of war.

Finally, Doniphan was fortunate that the Mexican troops encountered at El Brazito and Sacramento had not prepared better. This was especially true at El Brazito, where the Mexican commander might have defeated him with a more aggressive attack of the bivouacking Missourians rather than allowing them time to form their lines and prepare a defense. The Mexican army's failure to take advantage of this opportunity resulted from its demonstrably poor quality at a critical time in the nation's history. The political constraints and conditions surrounding the war are complex. To summarize Mexico's situation, since its independence in 1822, it had spiraled into a series of civil wars. These pitted the forces of centralism, conservatism, and Mexico City, against federalists, liberalism, and the new regional centers of commerce like Chihuahua City. Fierce regionalism, inherited from colonial times, also fueled the forces for independence and semi-independence. Foreign interests (especially in commerce) and fear of new attempts by Spain to reconquer the region, also helped complicate the politics of Mexico.

Generalissimo and sometime presidente Santa Anna, one of the most successful and reprehensible political figures in the early Mexican republic, followed the tide of political change like a weather vane—first conservative centralist then liberal federalist, once champion of individual rights and later advocate of rule by the most "qualified." There are few positions that Santa Anna did not take at one time or another during his long political career. As the war started, Santa Anna faced the challenge of bringing order from chaos so that the nation could oppose the Americans. Yet he feared that any military force created to meet the Americans not under his personal command might be used against him. He also feared other successful generals, who might threaten his rule in the post-war era. From the beginning, therefore, the Mexican military was not as effective as it might normally have been had he not distrusted his generals so thoroughly. Because of this, the Mexican army that Doniphan—as well as other American commanders—faced in the field was divided, poorly led, demoralized, and inadequately prepared to meet the enemy.

In addition, the quality of the officer corps in the Mexican army was suspect. The great bulk of the national army had not seen fighting on the Indian frontier, and the most common kind of service they were likely to have experienced was in the internal fighting between centralists and federalists. There were, of course, some excellent leaders who served in such a way, but they were outnumbered by men who had purchased their ranks and lacked proper training. The Apache and Comanche wars, along with related struggles in northern and southern Mexico, did produce some very effective officers. This result, to an extent, came in spite of rather than because of Mexico City's involvement in frontier defense.

Finally, a series of profound changes had transformed the army of New Spain—formerly a more professional fighting force—during the early independence period. First, national conscription began, but with the provision that the wealthier, better-educated people could purchase their way out of service. Second, officers viewed assignments to fight Indians as inferior (in terms of career and general social prestige) to those involved in the centralist/federalist fighting. Altogether too many officers sought opportunities for political prestige from command, emulating the rise of Napoleon. Proper military education existed through the national officer's school (the National Academy at Chapultepec), which offered an education along the lines of contemporary European programs (especially that of Spain). But these officers were too few. In 1846, Mexico had forty-four thousand men in arms and twenty-four thousand commissioned officers. Of the latter, the vast majority were politicos of one type or another, and they probably knew very little about soldiering. While lack of quality among the officers did not foreordain Mexican defeat—especially given all of Santa Anna's missed opportunities and ill-conceived moves—without doubt, the legions of incapable politicos who filled the ranks of its officer corps did not help.[31]

This boded well for Doniphan and the American army in Mexico. Because of his Mexican War experience, Doniphan increasingly played

31. Comments of Jack S. Williams, Center for Spanish Colonial Archaeology, Mesa, AZ, April 22, 1994.

a central political and business role in Missouri. The expedition made Doniphan's career; through it he demonstrated remarkable character and ensured his place in antebellum Missouri. William H. Richardson, who served as a soldier in the First Missouri, captured this public sense of character in his diary of the expedition:

> The man who can familiarize himself with the poorest private, by some kind word, or ride among the troops, and make us forget that we were hungry or thirsty, by some pleasant converse, in our long and toilsome march;—that man who can forget his own personal safety in the hour of danger, and rise superior to every embarrassment—who can be prepared for every emergency by superior skill in the tactics of war—as well as refined sense of honor, and an open suavity of manner not only leading captive the hearts of his entire command, but those of the hostile foe— such a man is a treasure to society, and to his country—and such a man is the brave Doniphan.[32]

What he did with this fame and positive perception in the latter 1840s and throughout the 1850s is a subject filled with mystery and enigma, not to mention surprise.

32. Richardson, *Journal of Doniphan's Expedition*, 86–87.

10

Fortune and Tragedy at Waltz Tempo

BECAUSE ALEXANDER William Doniphan enjoyed enormous popularity as a result of his Mexican War experience, he could have sought national office in the Congress or perhaps even the presidency. At least he might have served in elected office at the gubernatorial level in the 1850s. Men with lesser success in the war did so, notably Jefferson Davis, Franklin Pierce, and, in Doniphan's own state of Missouri, Sterling Price. In Zachary Taylor's case, the career soldier who emerged from the war with the highest profile of any American, a heroic image facilitated his election as president in 1848 in spite of him never before running for political office.

Why did Doniphan neither seek nor agree to serve in high political office in the post–Mexican War years? He had the stature, and if his earlier career had been any measure, he had the inclination. With the sectional conflict unraveling the threads of national union, a period when leadership might have made a critical difference, Doniphan remained outside the mainstream of politics. Doniphan's not seeking office rests on his personality, his ideology, his family's fortune and tragedy, and his repulsion for the labyrinth of Missouri party politics.

Doniphan did not engage in office-seeking because of the Whig Party's lack of interest in him. He had just returned from Mexico when Whig wheelhorses began talking about him as the party's standard bearer in the 1848 gubernatorial election.[1] John Wilson of Fayette wrote to fellow Whig George R. Smith: "There seems to be a general disposition amongst our friends to run Doniphan for Gov., what say you to that?" Seeing an

---

1. See the enthusiastic endorsements of Doniphan for governor in the *St. Louis New Era,* the *Paris Mercury,* and the *Fulton Telegraph,* as quoted in *Liberty Weekly Tribune,* June 12, 1847, June 19, 1847, June 26, 1847, August 21, 1847, August 28, 1847.

opportunity, Wilson suggested that the Whigs "shout for Taylor Buena Vista & Sacramento & Doniphan for governor & my word for it we shall carry this state."[2]

Delegations of Whig leaders visited Doniphan during the first few weeks after his return from Mexico and asked him to accept the party's candidacy for governor, but he turned down the offer. His explanations for refusing were logical, obvious, and completely consistent with his personality. Doniphan said he wanted to spend more time with his wife and family after having been gone for more than a year. Whig courtiers replied that the political campaign would take place several months later and Doniphan could rest in the interim. They reminded him that also, in the gentlemanly manner of campaigning (although Whigs did not always follow this pattern), the office sought the man and the candidate usually stayed home while friends stumped for him. Accordingly, Doniphan could remain home most of the time while party members campaigned on his behalf. Doniphan replied that he also needed to rebuild his law practice, as it had eroded during his yearlong absence and his family needed the income. He also complained of his health, and there is every reason to believe that the expeditionary year had taken its toll. He never was quite fully healthy again.[3] What Doniphan did not expressly mention, but must surely have affected his decision as well, was his firm understanding of the nearly insurmountable difficulties any Whig had in seeking statewide office in a thoroughly Democratic state.

None of this would have prevented a politically ambitious man from seeking high public office. But Doniphan appears not particularly ambitious for public office. In essence, he emerged from the Mexican War with his strongest desire to provide well for his family and not to work particularly hard at it. Although he dallied with the Whig Party and the political and moral issues of the sectional conflict in the latter 1840s and early 1850s, he never became the key player that his Mexican War fame allowed. While friends and rivals became central figures in the era, Doniphan remained aloof, dancing at waltz tempo while the rest of the nation moved into a frenzied jig. Not yet forty years old in 1847, Doniphan had achieved the greatest public success of his life and it apparently suited him just fine.

Doniphan officially let the Whigs know that he would not run for public office at a dinner given in his honor at Independence, Missouri, on July 29, 1847. Citing the reasons stated above, he declared he had not been a candidate for public office for the past seven years and that he did not expect to be for the next seventy-seven years. As an old man, Doniphan

2. John Wilson to George R. Smith, July 16, 1847, George R. Smith Papers, Missouri Historical Society.
3. *Liberty Weekly Tribune,* July 31, 1847; Connelley, ed., *Doniphan's Expedition,* 127.

regretted this decision, mentioning that he might have accomplished much more had he been willing to serve in the public interest more graciously. In 1847, however, nothing came further down on his list of priorities than the Missouri governorship.[4]

It had always been difficult for Missouri's Whig Party to persuade its most attractive members to seek public office, and it missed Doniphan in the gubernatorial campaign of 1848. Although a crowd darling, Doniphan adamantly refused to run for Missouri governor. As a result, when the Whigs met in their state convention in April 1848, they nominated James S. Rollins of Boone County for the state's top post. Nominated by acclamation, Rollins possessed the three attributes required of any Whig candidate: many people knew him, he had a reputation as an effective orator, and he publicly wore the label of Whig. Doniphan had those same attributes in abundance, but with his unavailability, Rollins proved a worthy substitute. Doniphan supported Rollins for this position, but to no avail. He and the other Whig candidates for state office received a sound thrashing at the polls by an ideologically divided but dominant Democratic Party.[5]

Without Doniphan as their candidate, the Whigs did not capitalize on their party's military service in the late war and the general sense of patriotism in the nation. Whig strategist John Wilson understood and outlined fully the road to victory, but unfortunately he had not foreseen that the Whigs' best hope would be unwilling to run for office. Ironically, the Democrats used that very fact to their own advantage by running a wedge between Doniphan and the Whigs. Democrat Austin A. King, the Richmond judge associated with Doniphan for more than a decade on the circuit court, suggested on the campaign stump that Doniphan had refused to run for the governorship as a Whig because his political opinions differed with his party's. Specifically, he suggested that Doniphan seethed at the Whig Party's opposition to the Mexican War.[6]

Some justification existed for this, as Doniphan, after returning from Mexico, had repeatedly denounced the lack of support of some politicians in the United States. For him the important war issue had not been a matter of rhetoric, but of supporting American troops in the field. As he had said at his St. Louis homecoming, he was distraught that some members of Congress denounced "the war, and those engaged in it, as little better than a band of robbers." He noted that "Such speeches might have been deemed patriotic in the United States; but, . . . the speeches

4. *Liberty Weekly Tribune,* July 31, 1847; A. W. Doniphan to D. C. Allen, July 9, 1883, Doniphan Papers; Mering, *Whig Party in Missouri,* 143–44.

5. *Liberty Weekly Tribune,* July 21, 1848; Mering, *Whig Party in Missouri,* 143–49; John V. Mering, "The Political Transition of James S. Rollins."

6. *Liberty Weekly Tribune,* July 21, 1848, August 4, 1848.

which are made in opposition to this war, . . . are postponing the peace eternally!"[7]

Other Whigs in the state rose to defend Doniphan in the summer of 1848. Doniphan conveniently absented himself from Missouri, making a tour of the East. The loyal John T. Hughes, self-proclaimed regimental historian, persuaded several other Whigs in Clay County to publish a letter saying that Doniphan had not turned his back on the Whig organization. "We have it from his own pen that he is a warm friend and supporter of Gen. Taylor," they wrote. "The efforts of Judge King and others to make political capital by such assertions will be properly rebuked, we have no doubt, by Col. Doniphan on his return home."[8] The *Missouri Republican*, the Whig organ in St. Louis, also got into the act, questioning the morals of King for using Doniphan's refusal to run for governor to discredit the Whig Party. As it noted: "Those who know the gallant Colonel—his frank, manly open manner—his entire independence of all extraneous influences—his high sense of honor—his candid and independent way of expressing himself on all occasions—his honesty and his courtesy—will have no difficulty in forming an opinion of how the Judge arrived at so incorrect a conclusion." The Whigs demanded that King apologize and retract his questioning of Doniphan's commitment to the Whig cause.[9]

They did not get one. They received instead an explanation in some detail of what King thought Doniphan believed about the Whig Party.

> Early last April last [1848], when first commencing the canvass, I met Col. Doniphan at Savannah, Andrew County. The Whig State Convention at Boonville had just placed him on its Electoral ticket; and I therefore, asked him, if I should expect him to be in the canvass this summer. He replied, "No!" and assigned as a reason therefore that the Whig party was making issues which he could never sustain; which issues I understood to relate to the course of that party with regard to the war with Mexico.

He ended by suggesting that he had long been a friend and associate of Doniphan and that he had no interest in sullying him in any way. Furthermore, King remained convinced that Doniphan took no exception to his description of their conversation.[10]

Doniphan did not directly attack King, but on July 29, 1848, he returned to Liberty from the East and gave an impromptu speech casting King's comments in a sour context. In it he showed "the difference between the Whig, and other parties, and by comparison must have convinced

7. Benton, *Return of the Missouri Volunteers*; *Liberty Weekly Tribune*, July 17, 1847.
8. *Liberty Weekly Tribune*, July 21, 1848.
9. *Missouri Republican*, quoted in ibid., August 4, 1848.
10. Austin A. King, "A Card," quoted in *Liberty Weekly Tribune*, August 4, 1848.

his hearers that the Whig party is the true, conservative, constitutional, American party; the party of multitude, as opposed to the party of a favored few." He also advocated the election of Zachary Taylor to the presidency over the democratic candidate, Lewis Cass. In the end, whether King or Doniphan convinced others matters not, for the Democrats again carried the state. Doniphan did, however, affirm his whiggery and help Taylor to win Clay County; the ex-general received 626 votes to 418 for Cass.[11]

Throughout this period Doniphan remained true to his vow not to accept public office. In October 1847, nearly a year before the big election, President James K. Polk had offered Doniphan command of a battalion returning to New Mexico to restore order on the frontier. The Navajos, never pacified by Doniphan's First Missouri Mounted Volunteers, had arisen with other tribes and the territory entered dire straits. The weekly *Santa Fe Republican* observed in September 1847 that since Doniphan's departure the previous December, the Navajos had enjoyed virtually ceaseless marauding in the territory, stealing livestock, killing New Mexicans but not usually Anglos, and generally making travel hazardous and life unpleasant in the new American territory. By October American authorities realized that the military force in New Mexico, a short battalion under the command of Major Robert Walker made up of enlistees without serious combat experience, could not ensure peace in the territory. They called for help from the president.[12] Although Polk, through the governor of Missouri, asked Doniphan for assistance, the Missourian politely declined for the same reasons he formerly chose not to run for public office. He recommended William Gilpin for the post, but Gilpin also suffered illness from his ordeal on the expedition and he at first refused. Later he thought better of it and soon raised a battalion, setting out for Santa Fe with a mixture of First Missouri veterans and new enlistees. During the next year Gilpin's "Battalion of the Plains" patrolled the Santa Fe Trail and fought nine engagements with various Indian tribes, and counted 253 enemy dead.[13]

During this same period Doniphan could not escape his fame resulting from the Mexican War expedition. A disgruntled Santa Fe trader sought damages from the Federal government for Doniphan's supposedly capricious behavior during his expedition. Manuel X. Harmony, one of the most

11. *Liberty Weekly Tribune*, August 11, 1848; Settle, "Doniphan Collection, Notes and Misc.," 1:59, William Jewell College, Special Collections; Mering, *Whig Party in Missouri*, 149–53.

12. *Liberty Weekly Tribune*, October 15, 1847; *Santa Fe Republican*, September 10, 1847. The story of Walker's expedition is contained in McNitt, *Navajo Wars*, 124–27.

13. *Jefferson City Inquirer*, September 25, 1847; Connelley, ed., *Doniphan's Expedition*, 148–51; Thomas L. Karnes, "Gilpin's Volunteers on the Santa Fe Trail," 1–14; Chalfant, *Dangerous Passage*, 165–271.

obstinate of the Santa Fe traders that Doniphan had dealt with during the march, petitioned the government for damages. Doniphan remembered that Harmony had been an irritation ever since first encountering him at Bent's Fort in the summer of 1846. Although a United States resident, Harmony had been born in Spain and carried a Spanish passport. Operating out of New York, Harmony served as an agent for Hispanic merchants and bankers and a freighter in the Santa Fe trade. This gave him a unique status during the expedition and in the subsequent controversy.[14]

As he did with all the Santa Fe traders during the first year of the Mexican-American War, Doniphan had limited Harmony's trade with Mexicans not under occupation as a war measure. In essence, he did not want traders to engage in commerce with the enemy. He also commandeered supplies and equipment from traders as necessary to meet logistical requirements for his troops, presumably issuing promissory notes redeemable through the U.S. government. Doniphan also forced the creation of a traders' battalion after the Battle of El Brazito. Harmony thought Doniphan had exceeded his authority for these and other actions, thereby damaging his ability to turn a profit. In 1848 Harmony petitioned Congress for the recovery of alleged losses amounting to $82,956.82, plus $20,000 in damages for loss of time—a grand total of $102.956.82—that he incurred in Mexico because of Doniphan. "By reason and consequence of the acts of the troops of the United States," Harmony's attorney concluded, "his trading expedition has been utterly broken up, his expenditures rendered useless, and his goods and merchandise wholly lost to him."[15]

Harmony claimed losses for wagons and livestock, indemnity for being kept with the Doniphan expedition for both himself and his men, truly exceptional levels of recompense for his goods, interest at 7 percent, and the additional $20,000 in punitive damages. Whether or not there had been any legitimacy to his claim, the government viewed it as an attempt to gouge the American public, and that perception considerably weakened his position.[16] Both Congress and the secretary of war, William L. Marcy,

14. *Weekly Reveille,* September 14, 1846; *The New York City Co-Partnership Directory, for 1844 & 1845,* 18; Gardner, ed., *Brothers on the Santa Fe,* 139.

15. U.S. House of Representatives, "Report and Petition of Manuel X. Harmony," *Executive Documents,* House Reports, 30th Cong., 1st Sess., Vol. 1 (1847), Report no. 458 (Serial 525), 6–12, 17–19, 24–28; Johnston, Edwards, and Ferguson, *Marching with the Army of the West,* 249–50; E. W. Pomeroy to Robert Aull, May 29, 1847, Collection #2042, Robert Aull Collection, Western Historical Manuscript Collection; Rockwell petition, *Senate Documents,* 30th Cong., Report no. 458, 5, 40–41; Hughes, *Doniphan's Expedition,* 468.

16. For example, Harmony listed as losses under Doniphan's command $600 for six mules that died in the Jornada Cantarrecio; $200 for one American horse that died in the desert; $400 for four mules that died on the El Camino Real; $500 for five mules that the regiment kept; $8,312 for damage to his wagon train (about 75 percent of its

resented Harmony's contention that an American military commander in a theater of war had no right to stop anyone trading with the enemy. This was the most important issue about reparations for Manuel Harmony stemming from Doniphan's expedition. Marcy contended that only a poor commander would permit merchandise, especially gunpowder and rifles, to fall into the hands of the enemy. The conclusion of the House of Representatives allied closely with Marcy's stance: "If an American citizen is in the anomalous position of prosecuting a trading expedition in an enemy's country, he must be subjected to the delays and inconveniences inseparable from a state of war and the prosecution of military enterprises, and the risk and loss must be his own. If, however, the property of a citizen, engaged in a lawful trade, is seized or used by the United States officers, the government will be in equity bound to pay the loss or damage sustained."[17] Accordingly, Congress agreed to pay Harmony for goods used by Doniphan for the support of his force. It also went out of its way to exonerate Doniphan of any taint from this episode.

Manuel Harmony refused to accept this decision and took the case to the U.S. Supreme Court. In *Harmony v. Lieutenant Colonel D. D. Mitchell* (one of Doniphan's key officers during the expedition), the court ruled that a military officer could not exercise greater authority over an American in a foreign nation than in the United States. The court ruled, "when the owner [of property] has done nothing to forfeit his rights [in a foreign nation] every public officer is bound to respect them whether he finds property in a foreign or hostile country or his own." The court noted that a military officer must not confiscate without compensation property from an American citizen, either in time of war or not. It also found that no confiscation had taken place in this instance and that the U.S. government had offered fair compensation for the goods used by Doniphan's regiment in 1847.[18]

In the midst of this debate, in October 1847 Doniphan decided to take his family and travel around the eastern part of the United States. He said that his wife's illness necessitated this trip, and that they looked forward to an opportunity to see new sights and enjoy a change of scenery. They planned to visit his old stomping grounds in Kentucky, relatives in Ohio, and New York, in that order. Doniphan probably also wanted to get away from the constant importunings from Whigs in Missouri for him to lead the state's ticket. He told Whig leaders that he did not plan to return to

total value); $5,000 in expenses for men and animals; six months indemnity at $6,000; and thirteen months' interest on $63,800 at 7 percent. See *House Report,* no. 458, 27–28.

17. *Executive Documents,* House Reports, 30th Cong., 1st sess., Vol. 1 (1848), no. 458, 3–4, 6, 48–49.

18. Charles C. Whittelsey to Maj. Gen. Henry W. Halleck, December 31, 1861, in *The War of the Rebellion: A Compilation of the Official Records of the Union and Confederate Armies,* Series 2, 1:246.

the state until his wife returned to health, even if he had to be gone a year. The time frame suggests that he wanted to avoid the upcoming political campaign.[19] Doniphan's rationale for traveling to the East received a boost from his presidential appointment as a member of the Board of Visitors to witness the examination of the cadets at the United States Military Academy at West Point.

After visits to relatives, Doniphan and his family arrived, on June 5, 1848, at the quaint community on the Hudson River that serves as home to the nation's military academy. He enjoyed more than a week of relaxation at the town, and on June 15 he addressed the graduating class. In this oration, reportedly as eloquent as any he had ever given, Doniphan drew on his military experience to raise questions about the conduct of the national security of the Union and to address many of the important issues of the era. He noted, positively, that

> The world is strangely and startlingly convulsed; thrones are crumbling; dynasties are tottering to their fall; the iron heel is robbed of the power of oppression. Who can tell, in this vast whirlpool of confused elements, what results may be produced? Who can tell in its wild career, but its vortex, widening and deepening, may yet reach our own shores? Who can tell when this threatening volcano may begin to spout forth its burning lava, or from what particular apex? This ignitable mass needs but the magic spark to again envelope the world in flames. How soon may some meteor, ah! more than meteor—some comet come and again arise, which shall roll the lurid cloud of war over the fairest portions of Europe, until the curtain may drop at some second Waterloo? We fondly hope that the murmurs of the threatening volcano may be stilled, and the bright rainbow of peace may span the world. But one truth is clear—we cannot hide it from ourselves. God has decreed that man shall be free—"the right divine" has heard its final knell. But whether this glorious consummation is to be attained by the slow and peaceful progression of learning, of civilization and of Christianity, or the dread ordeal of war and violence, He has wisely concealed from man's feeble vision.

Doniphan might have foreseen the coming storm in the United States and urged the men of West Point, the group that would be most caught up in the struggle over slavery, to offer affirmative leadership. The only just reason for war, he believed, involved furthering liberty and individual freedom. While he dreaded war, in some circumstances he recognized its necessity. Such action, in his mind, prompted him to serve during the Mexican War.[20]

19. *Liberty Weekly Tribune,* September 1, 1848; Connelley, ed., *Doniphan's Expedition,* 125.

20. *Address Delivered in the Chapel at West Point.*

Throughout the rest of the summer of 1848 Doniphan traveled slowly back to Missouri, stopping periodically to speak and to visit with friends and relatives. On July 15 he addressed the Brown County Whigs in Brookville, Kentucky, and on July 18 he spoke to the Rough and Ready Club of Maysville, Kentucky. He also addressed a group in St. Louis toward the end of July. Throughout this trip, Doniphan suffered from a noticeable hoarseness, brought on by a sore throat and bronchitis. These afflicted him throughout the remainder of his life, prompting him by the 1870s to give up courtroom law in favor of other types of work. It did not, however, keep him from making speeches for Zachary Taylor during the election of 1848. He touted Taylor as an exponent of the positive liberal state and an advocate of the liberty and peace that Doniphan prized so highly. When Taylor won the presidency in 1848, despite the poor showing the general received in Missouri, Doniphan expressed satisfaction.[21]

It seems that what Doniphan most wanted to do after the Mexican campaign was to rebuild his law practice. He did so in spectacular fashion, arguing in November 1847 one of his most famous cases, *Meredith v. Harper*.[22] At the November 1847 term of the Platte County Circuit Court Doniphan represented murder suspect John H. Harper. The case had originally been brought before the circuit court in Jackson County, where the crime took place, but Doniphan had it moved in a change of venue. Although taking place before the Mexican War, a series of legal turns—as well as a jail break—had delayed the case until 1847.

The Harper case had everything that would make it a cause célèbre in the state: murder, intrigue, and sex. The facts of the case are simple. Before the Mexican War, John H. Harper was a young attorney in Independence, Missouri, probably near the same age as Doniphan and known to him. Originally from Georgia, Harper was a bright, ambitious man smitten by the intelligent, vivacious, and attractive daughter of Santa Fe trader Samuel C. Owens, and he tried to persuade her to marry him. The daughter, Fannie Owens, toyed with him for a time, probably to anger her parents who did not approve of Harper, but eventually she cast him aside. When Fannie and her mother had a serious argument, however, the daughter sought the ultimate revenge on her parents by marrying Harper. She went to his law office and offered to marry him provided he acted immediately. Harper got his buggy and set out for the office of James Bean, a justice of the peace at Blue Springs, also sending a rider ahead to alert Bean that they were coming to be married. Bean rode out to

21. *Louisville Journal*, July 19, 1848; *Liberty Weekly Tribune*, July 14, 1848, July 28, 1848, September 1, 1848, November 17, 1848, January 19, 1849.

22. The information that follows relating to *Meredith v Harper* is taken from D. C. Allen, "Col. Alexander W. Doniphan—His Life and Character," in Connelley, ed., *Doniphan's Expedition*, 26–29; *History of Jackson County, Missouri*, 177–78; Settle, *Alexander William Doniphan*, 7.

meet Harper and performed the ceremony for them while they sat in their buggy. Irate and vengeful after learning what Fannie had done, Samuel Owens tried unsuccessfully to have the marriage annulled. He eventually resigned himself to his new son-in-law and he invited the couple to live in the Owens family home in Independence.

Then came the crime. A young man by the name of Meredith came west from Baltimore, Maryland, to improve his tuberculosis, and Samuel Owens took a liking to him. He invited Meredith to stay in his home during his recovery, and promised to take the young man with him on his next trip down the Santa Fe Trail. Also, Meredith and the now married Fannie Harper flirted incessantly while her husband grew increasingly jealous. Harper soon became convinced that Meredith and his wife were also having an affair, which they probably were, and he plotted revenge. Meredith had a habit of taking a constitutional every afternoon around the courthouse square in Independence, and Harper had a law office on the second floor of a building that fronted the square. On one particular afternoon Harper placed a deck of cards on a table in his office, loaded two pistols and left them on the same table, and then went down to the porch in front of his office to await Meredith. When he arrived, Harper invited Meredith up to his office and, a couple of minutes after they ascended the stairs, bystanders heard a shot fired from Harper's law office. Men rushed up the stairs to see what the trouble was. They found Meredith lying dead in a pool of blood on the floor with an unfired pistol by his side and the playing cards scattered about the room. A shocked Harper stood over the body with a smoking pistol in his hand.

Harper's defense proved paper thin. He said that he and Meredith had been enjoying a friendly game of cards when Meredith drew a pistol and Harper was forced to shoot him in self-defense. No one believed him since the shot had followed so closely after the two had gone into the office. Obviously, there had been no card game, and the liaison between Meredith and Fannie Harper had become common knowledge in the small town. Loafers in Independence speculated that Harper would be hanged for the murder, despite that it was a crime of passion. The county sheriff placed Harper in jail to await trial, but Fannie corroborated his story— even though few believed her. She also helped Harper to escape from the county jail, possibly by exchanging clothes with him during a visit, and he fled the state for New Mexico. More than a year passed before authorities caught up with Harper and returned him to Missouri for trial. In the meantime, Doniphan began and completed his famous expedition and Samuel Owens died at the Battle of Sacramento in February 1847. It may have been because Doniphan felt that he owed something to Owens that he took on the defense of Harper in the fall of 1847.

Doniphan worked with two other local attorneys on this case, Silas H. Woodson and John Wilson, both friends and sometime associates at the bar. They agreed that Harper's claim of self-defense had little merit and that it would succeed only in placing a hangman's noose around the young man's neck. Instead, they decided to establish legally in court what most of the people of the community already understood, that Harper was jealous of the possible adultery of Fannie Harper and Meredith. They did not have to establish the fact of an extramarital affair, only that Harper suspected it and that the murder had been a crime of passion. The technical fact they sought to establish was "criminal intimacy." With this proven, Doniphan believed he could gain an acquittal. When he brought up the matter in court, however, the judge ruled that only the prosecution could raise the matter and establish "criminal intimacy." Muzzled in this tactic, Doniphan protested the ruling with a frenzied response that Harper would surely hang without the establishment of "criminal intimacy." In the end they asked the court to adjourn until the next day so they could prepare another strategy.

That night John Wilson, in a planned move Doniphan and his colleagues hoped would help them gain an advantage over the prosecution, stayed up to the wee hours of the morning with the prosecuting attorney at a party that included large quantities of alcoholic beverages. The next morning both Wilson and the prosecuting attorney appeared at loose ends, and Doniphan realized that their plan had been successful in limiting the effectiveness of his opponent. When Doniphan called his key defense witness, the individual who could establish the possibility of extramarital sexual relations between Fannie Harper and Meredith, he had to tread carefully. The defense could not ask directly any question establishing the fact of "criminal intimacy," so they planned to trick the prosecution into doing so. Woodson took the lead in the examination and asked a variety of leading questions that danced around the issue of "criminal intimacy." In cross-examination, the sleepy and somewhat hungover prosecutor then popped the very question that the defense needed to establish this relationship. Realizing that he had made a mistake as soon as he asked the question, the prosecutor shouted, "Do not answer that question!" Before the witness could answer, the prosecutor asked the judge to strike the question, but Doniphan and Woodson acted quickly to object and demanded that the witness answer. The prosecution reasoned that since no answer had yet been given, the state had a right to withdraw the question, but Doniphan howled that the witness must answer. All the judge could do was excuse the jury while the two legal teams debated this matter before the bench. Finally, late in the day, the judge ruled that the witness must answer the prosecution's question since he had earlier ruled that only the prosecution could raise the issue of illicit sexual relations.

When the case reconvened the judge told the witness to describe fully any knowledge of sexual relations between Fannie Harper and Meredith.

With the issue opened, the defense asked several questions that firmly established the possibility of "criminal intimacy" in the minds of the audience and most importantly in the minds of the jury. When Doniphan delivered the closing argument for the case, he played deeply on the emotions of the all-male jury. His impassioned oratory—dealing with the covenant of marriage, the sanctity of the family unit, and the unrighteousness of sex outside of wedlock—so wrought up the hearers that they cheered at its conclusion. While Doniphan had been suffering from jaundice throughout the case and never felt his best, his summation had been remarkably effective. The jury acquitted Harper in short order, almost as a matter of acclamation, and the gallery members watching the proceedings hoisted Doniphan onto their shoulders and carried him around the town before depositing him at his hotel. Those who had experienced the episode reflected in later years that they had never seen anything remotely like it either before or since. It was an auspicious return to his old career for the war hero.

While most of his later cases did not unfold so dramatically, Doniphan returned to his career as an exceptionally successful lawyer in western Missouri during the remainder of the antebellum era. He became the attorney of choice for anyone with the wherewithal to retain his services, and those services proved more difficult to secure with every passing year. Doniphan's friend D. C. Allen recalled that, in the years immediately preceding the Civil War, virtually everyone in the state recognized that in a court case "a silent Doniphan in a cause would have meant defeat anticipated."[23] For instance, in 1849 Senator Thomas Hart Benton, Democratic nemesis of Missouri Whigs, asked Doniphan to represent him in a slander case brought against him by James Birch of Platte County. Possibly all the money in the state could not have enticed Doniphan to serve as counsel for the hated Benton, but Doniphan pled ill-health in declining the case and Benton found another lawyer.

Doniphan continued his career as a defense attorney for both criminal and civil proceedings. He gained a supportive ally and confidant in 1848 when his nephew John Doniphan immigrated to western Missouri. Since he later married one of the daughters of John Thornton, the younger Doniphan also became his brother-in-law. Also a native of Kentucky, John Doniphan had read law in Maysville. When he first arrived in the state, he stayed with his uncle several months before eventually setting up his own law practice in Weston, Platte County. The two relatives became close friends and confidants, and they periodically shared law offices and many business ventures during the remainder of the elder Doniphan's life. For example, the two served together as defense counsel in the *State of Missouri v. Floersch,* tried in Platte County in February

23. Allen, "Colonel Doniphan," in Connelley, ed., *Doniphan's Expedition,* 25.

1851. They did not gain the acquittal of Floersch from a murder charge—Doniphan was sure he was guilty anyway—but they blocked capital punishment and secured for their defendant only twenty-four years in the penitentiary.[24]

Doniphan expanded his business activities during this era. Always interested in earning a more substantial living than that provided by the practice of the law, he was constantly on the lookout for investments. Since his return from Mexico, Doniphan's severe bouts of bronchitis impaired his ability as an orator. Without that asset Doniphan lost his primary advantage, for it was his ability to move audiences and juries that made him especially attractive as a counselor. Doniphan also sometimes had difficulty collecting his fees from his law clients, which proved irksome to him, so he resolved to have other sources of income as well. In 1857 alone Doniphan had to take six clients to court to collect his legal fees, although they were not extraordinarily large amounts (varying from $172.50 to $632.35). He and his nephew purchased property, entered partnerships of various types, and took chances on several new industries. For example, in May 1853 he became president of the Liberty Insurance Company. A new type of business in the United States, this company was Doniphan's brainchild; he and thirty other investors started it to indemnify steamboats traveling on the Missouri River. Capitalized at $50,000, the company performed adequately during the latter antebellum period.[25]

Additionally, by 1856 Doniphan was ready to branch out into banking. In December he wrote a letter to his nephew John Doniphan proposing a bank to finance economic developments in northwestern Missouri and eastern Kansas. "Why are you not making some effort for a bank," he asked his nephew. He added: "A bushel could be made at it if a Liberal charter can be had. It is worth our going to Lecompton [the capital of Kansas Territory] to look after. . . . But still, two strings to a bow is best and as the state . . . banking institutions have a good credit, we ought to make a grand name for a bank in Weston. But if one cannot be had there, . . . go for St. Joseph and Donnell." While there is no evidence that Doniphan established a bank of his own, he remained interested in the business opportunities it afforded.[26]

Doniphan's insurance company, however, did engage in some banking transactions on its own. At least by 1856 it routinely purchased sight and time bills, sold exchange on all bank notes, received money on deposits, and paid interest of 3 percent on monies maintained for a minimum of

24. *Liberty Weekly Tribune*, February 27, 1851; Duchateau, "Missouri Colossus," 294.
25. Clay County Circuit Records, Ledger #22, March 31, 1857, numbers 71–76, Clay County Courthouse, Liberty, Mo.; *Liberty Weekly Tribune*, March 18, 1853, April 8, 1853, June 3, 1853; Platte County Index to Deeds, Books J–P, Missouri State Archives.
26. A. W. Doniphan to John Doniphan, December 15, 1856, Doniphan Collection.

thirty days and even higher interest rates on those deposited for longer periods. Always seeking expanded business opportunities, in March 1857 he moved briefly to Leavenworth City, Kansas Territory. Along with his brother-in-law Robert W. Donnell and Bela M. Hughes, the son of General Andrew S. Hughes, Doniphan formed a Kansas land development and banking firm.[27]

Doniphan also developed a keen interest in railroads and the investment opportunities they provided. In December 1853 he participated in an effort to build a railroad from Weston to the North Missouri Railroad head in Callaway County. He served on a three-member steering committee to oversee this effort, but after six months it remained unsuccessful and he went on to other activities. Two years later he reentered the railroad business as a member of the board of directors of the Platte Country Railroad. The line's route ran between St. Joseph and the major central transcontinental route at Kansas City, about seventy miles south. The directors also planned to build northward to Council Bluffs, Iowa, where they expected to link to the Chicago and Northwestern Railroad. This became a lucrative venture. The corporation had laid fifty-two miles of tracks by 1865, and further construction linked it with two major transcontinental lines. Known in later years as the Kansas City, St. Joseph, and Council Bluffs Railroad, it operated for years as the major north-south short-haul line in the region. Doniphan received a good return on his investment in this business, and his nephew John also invested and became the railroad's first president.[28]

Despite his interests in other directions, Doniphan constantly heard the siren call of politics between the time of his return from Mexico and the beginning of the Civil War. He usually protested and generally refused to participate, but the constant tugging affected him deeply. The tumult of the era came into graphic perspective in 1849 over the issue of liberty and peace, the central theme of his speech to the cadets at West Point in 1848 when Doniphan was dragged into a political debate over a set of resolutions passed by the Missouri General Assembly. Proposed by State Senator Claiborne Fox Jackson, these resolutions denied the authority of the United States Congress to legislate on slavery in the states, in the District of Columbia, and in the nation's territories. The sixth resolution directed Missouri's congressional delegation to "act in conformity with

27. A. W. Doniphan to John Doniphan, December 15, 1856, Doniphan Collection; A. W. Doniphan to John Doniphan, May 15, 1855, Doniphan Papers; *Liberty Weekly Tribune*, February 22, 1856, January 23, 1857. Stationery dating from this period, headed "Doniphan, Hughes & Donnell, Bankers and Land Agents, Leavenworth City, Kansas," indicates the business ties Doniphan developed in the new territory. See A. W. Doniphan to D. C. Allen, March 4, 1863, Doniphan Papers.

28. *Liberty Weekly Tribune*, December 9, 1853, March 3, 1854, April 14, 1854, February 2, 1855, March 2, 1855, January 11, 1856.

the foregoing resolutions," thereby raising the sensitive slavery issue as an explicit subject for debate. The Whigs as a party, including Doniphan, strongly opposed Jackson's Resolutions for two reasons. First, it took a "states' rights" stand that fundamentally weakened the power of the Federal government to govern for the greater good of the nation. As such, Doniphan believed, it violated the spirit of the Constitution, which was launched to protect the most liberty for the most people. Second, from a practical perspective, raising the debate over slavery ensured divisiveness and a probable fracturing of the Whig Party's unity. This made it impossible to secure majorities at the ballot box.[29]

The Jackson Resolutions had been proposed for the most Machiavellian of reasons: the anti-Benton Democrats wanted to defeat Senator Thomas Hart Benton in the next election. Benton had been an ardent Unionist since entering the Senate in 1821, and he believed that the Federal government had the authority to legislate slavery in the territories. Yet that issue had been a political "hot potato" ever since it had been placed on the national agenda with a proviso from Representative David Wilmot of Pennsylvania in 1846, which forbade slavery in all territory acquired by the United States in the war with Mexico. Benton had preferred to say nothing about it; Jackson's resolutions forced him to address it. In standing for the power of the Federal government to handle the slavery issue, as he had to do lest he overturn a lifetime position upholding the authority of the Constitution, Benton made many political enemies in proslavery Missouri. That probably led to his unseating in the senatorial campaign of 1850.[30]

In a rare instance in the personal history of Doniphan, he agreed fully with Thomas Hart Benton. He wrote in a letter to Benton on July 17, 1849:

> In relation to the sentiments of those present [at a recent political gathering in Clay County] touching the resolution of the last Legislature, I can give but an opinion—I have never doubted that the representative of this county very faithfully reflected the opinions of his constituency in voting against these resolutions—the Whigs almost unanimously oppose them in this county. At the conclusion of your speech, I feel assured that of the "whole people present," a majority were opposed to the Legislative resolutions.[31]

29. C. H. McClure, "A Century of Missouri Politics," 318–19; McCandless, *History of Missouri,* 2:247–48.

30. The best biographies of Thomas Hart Benton, although there is a crying need for a modern treatment that describes fully his position on slavery, is William N. Chambers, *Old Bullion Benton: Senator from the New West;* and Elbert B. Smith, *Magnificent Missourian: The Life of Thomas Hart Benton.* On the question of slavery in the territories that consumed national politics throughout the 1850s, see Michael F. Holt, *The Political Crisis of the 1850s.*

31. *Liberty Weekly Tribune,* July 27, 1849.

In taking this stand, Doniphan showed his commitment to the Union, and to the subverting of the proslavery prerogative to the larger question of national unity. It did not mean that he opposed slavery—that never seems to have been the case—only that he would stand with the Union. In so doing, he also rejected efforts by antislavery leaders to keep slavery from the territories. "We are in favor of the Union, under any, and all circumstances," he told a Liberty rally in June 1850, "yet [we] regard the Wilmot Proviso and all kindred measures, with the most perfect abhorrence." Using support of the resolutions as its main issue, anti-Benton Democrats won election of Henry S. Geyer, a sometime Whig, to the Senate in the place of Benton.[32]

Had Doniphan been willing to approve the Jackson Resolutions in 1849 he could probably have been elected to the Senate. Had Doniphan been willing to accept the proslavery argument that the Federal government had not the power to prohibit slavery anywhere in the United States at any time during the decade of the 1850s, he probably could have gained high political office. He never changed his political position on the sanctity and authority of the Union for the sake of office, however, even if he had been ambitious for the post. At the same time, Doniphan's devotion to principle also fit well with his overarching reticence to seek public office. There is little reason to believe he was interested in high office with his other priorities. His caginess and refusals to run despite being asked to do so with nearly every campaign can be explained at several levels ranging from personal inclination to high-minded principle. All seem to be valid. Whatever the case, Doniphan refused to get involved in seemingly every election. Often he pled bad health. On February 19, 1850, for example, he declined the Whig nomination for the Senate, writing:

> My health is an insuperable objection if I had no other—just re-covering from a painful and protracted attack of Bronchitis the exertions incident to an active and extended canvass at this time would insure a speedy and perhaps fatal return of the disease. I feel gratified that the Whigs have determined not to let the race go by default, and I feel entirely confident that with a proper nomination we will be successful. Knowing as I do that there are a number of able and eloquent Whigs in the District, any one of whom could make a successful race I feel that the public cannot suffer by my declining a position which has been kindly tendered me from personal friendship more than a sense of any superior claims on my part.[33]

32. Ibid., June 7, 1850; McClure, "Century of Missouri Politics," 318–19.
33. *Liberty Weekly Tribune*, February 22, 1850.

Photograph of Alexander William Doniphan about the time of the Civil War. Photo no. D-98, courtesy Library-Archives of the Reorganized Church of Jesus Christ of Latter Day Saints, Independence, Missouri.

He also declined the Whig nomination for governor in 1852, again for health reasons, although there was a misunderstanding about this and word did not get to some of the key party leaders that he would not join the canvass. This caused some excitement as Doniphan's name remained on the ballot but he failed to campaign.[34]

The one instance in which he stood for high public office took place in 1854, and it showed once again both the centrality of the slavery issue in the politics of the state and the devotion of Doniphan to the Union. By this time his health was better and personal tragedy had forced him to the brink of despair and back. On May 9, 1853, John Thornton Doniphan, his oldest son, died from accidental poisoning when he took a dose of what he thought was epsom salts but was actually corrosive sublimate (mercury chloride). Born during the height of the Mormon war in Missouri, on September 18, 1838, the fourteen-year-old John had been staying overnight at the home of his uncle, James Baldwin, when he had taken the poison. Apparently, he had gotten up in the middle of the night in search of something that would give him relief from a toothache, and he confused the poison for epsom salts. John lingered in pain for nearly a week before finally dying in his bed. Doniphan, his wife Elizabeth, and their second son, Alexander William Jr., born on September 10, 1840, took the death hard.[35]

Already ill at the time of their son's death, Elizabeth Doniphan suffered a stroke shortly after his burial. Perhaps induced by the stress of the tragedy, the stroke left her a semi-invalid the rest of her life. When she had recovered somewhat, Doniphan decided to take his family east to visit relatives and see the sights. He took Elizabeth to White Sulphur Springs in Virginia, where he hoped the natural healing qualities of the water would help her recover from her stroke.[36]

Relaxing in the soothing waters of the hot springs provided Doniphan with the time to read newspapers and correspond with friends. As he recuperated from his tragedies, as he sought to heal himself of his emotional wounds, as he tried to patch the hole left in his soul by the death of a dear son, Doniphan realized that he could no longer remain a bystander. Only leadership could mend the rift in the nation, preserve the precious liberties of the Union, and prepare the way for the next generation—his remaining son and others like him—so that they might have a better future than what loomed on the horizon. Doniphan believed that Henry Clay—

34. *Jefferson City Inquirer,* March 9, 1850; *Liberty Weekly Tribune,* May 7, 1852, May 28, 1852; Mering, *Whig Party in Missouri,* 182; Frederic A. Culmer, "A Snapshot of Alexander W. Doniphan, 1808–1887," 25; *Columbia Statesman,* May 21, 1852.

35. A. W. Doniphan to Cousin Emma Doniphan, [no day and month] 1875, Doniphan Papers; *Liberty Weekly Tribune,* May 13, 1853.

36. *The Conservator,* August 11, 1887; A. W. Doniphan to Emma Doniphan, May 3, 1876, Doniphan Papers.

with both his ideals and his flaws—had embodied a spirit of energy and enthusiasm for the uncharted future. Clay had foreseen a perseverance and even a greatness for the United States that most people failed to grasp. The "positive liberal state" that Clay and the Whigs had sought to further, Doniphan believed, could be rescued. He decided to reenter the public arena, despite his illnesses and his family tragedies, to help see that vision through to fruition. He had to return to Missouri and make a difference in the conduct of public affairs. Doniphan decided to pick up the tempo of the waltz—not quite to a jig, but he was willing at least to try a grand march.

11

A House Dividing

THE FAMILY OF Alexander William Doniphan stayed in the East until October 1853, returning to Liberty only after he and his wife had healed somewhat from the physical and emotional strain of their lives. Within days after taking up residence anew, Doniphan began speaking to Whig politicians about the fate of the Union and the issues that divided and separated the people. He expressed concern that the high principles of the founders of the United States and the heroic ideals of the succeeding generation seemed to be waning. He also anguished over a rampant self-interest destructive to the greater good. He told Whig leaders that he would reenter the political scene to do what he could to recapture the vision of an earlier age. He entered the sea of politics hesitantly, but he did wade in.[1]

The leadership of the Whig Party of the state, rapidly disintegrating as a national political force, happily embraced Doniphan's return. Some of his political friends, as a result, invited him a month after his return to Clay County to serve as commissioner of the public schools in the county. Education had interested Doniphan for many years. In 1849, when the Missouri General Assembly had granted a charter to the Baptist Church to build a new college, Doniphan had helped raise funds for what became William Jewell College and ensured that it was located in Liberty. He served periodically on the college's board and took quite a paternal interest in its welfare throughout the remainder of his life. These interests expanded in late 1853 when, as a means of satisfying his soul and perhaps to help him take his mind off his personal tragedies, Doniphan accepted leadership of the Clay County school system and served for

1. *Liberty Weekly Tribune,* October 14, 1853, December 9, 1853.

nearly a year before resigning to run for office in the Missouri General Assembly.[2]

While serving as Clay County education commissioner, the sectional conflict reemerged full-blown as *the* issue of the decade; ultimately, it was the only political dispute that could not be settled through the nation's constitutional political process. This, too, may have prompted Doniphan's reentry into the political sphere. The slavery issue, especially the rights of slaveholders to take their chattel property into territories, had been temporarily quieted with the Compromise of 1850, but the fix did not last.[3] By the time Doniphan returned to politics the compromise's provisions represented the most contentious issue in the nation's political process at all levels.

The issues of slavery extension especially recurred during the debate after May 1854, when Congress passed the Kansas-Nebraska Act. This legislation, masterminded by Illinois Democratic Senator Stephen A. Douglas, created the territories of Kansas and Nebraska and repealed the Missouri Compromise that prohibited slavery north of 36°30' in the Louisiana Purchase territory. The new law would allow settlers in these territories to decide for themselves if they wanted to allow slavery in their state constitutions, something that Douglas called "popular sovereignty." It was a completely rational idea in theory, but the slavery controversy's volatility ensured that each side would press hard for adoption of its beliefs. Accordingly, it set up a rush of immigration into the region, much of it sparked by sectional desire to stake out the land as either slave or free.[4]

Before passage of the act organizing Kansas and Nebraska, Missouri's senior senator, David R. Atchison, had insisted on the repeal of the Missouri Compromise. This ensured, he said, that slaveholders would be allowed to bring their chattel into the new land opened for colonization. Perhaps the noisiest senator from a pro-slavery state, Atchison was aggressive, explosive, and sometimes wild-eyed when handling issues that he held dear.[5] In the Senate, Atchison and the Missouri junior senator, Henry S. Geyer, enthusiastically supported the act. They especially

2. W. H. Goodson, *History of Clay County, Missouri,* 214–17; Settle, *Alexander William Doniphan,* 1; *Liberty Weekly Tribune,* November 11, 1853, November 18, 1853, May 28, 1858; *Jefferson City Inquirer,* December 10, 1853; McGroarty, ed., "Richardson's Journal," 200.

3. On the Compromise of 1850, see Hamilton Holman, *Prologue to Conflict: The Crisis and Compromise of 1850;* and William J. Cooper Jr., *The South and the Politics of Slavery, 1828–1856,* 284–301, 317–29.

4. The Kansas-Nebraska Act has been the subject of considerable historical investigation. Among the best work on the subject is James C. Malin, *The Nebraska Question, 1852–1854;* Roy F. Nichols, "The Kansas-Nebraska Act: A Century of Historiography"; Robert W. Johannsen, *The Frontier, the Union, and Stephen A. Douglas,* 19–32, 103–19.

5. *New York Tribune,* October 10, 1854.

embraced the abrogation of the Missouri Compromise to secure for slave-holders the right to move unimpeded into new lands. Atchison led the effort in favor of the bill, and it passed easily.

In the House, where large numbers of antislavery representatives from the rapidly growing industrial north opposed the measure, the legislation had a harder time. Eventually it passed, mostly with the near unanimous support of Southern members of Congress.[6] But Thomas Hart Benton, elected to the House of Representatives from Missouri in 1852 after his defeat in the 1850 senatorial election, vocally opposed the Kansas-Nebraska Act because it reopened the exceptionally difficult issue of the extension of slavery into the territories.[7] Moreover, he believed in the primacy of the Federal government to legislate on the welfare of the territories and argued that "popular sovereignty" represented a congressional shirking of its responsibilities.

Thomas Hart Benton carried his opposition to the Kansas-Nebraska Act into his home state, particularly criticizing the abrogation of the Missouri Compromise, and infusing every aspect of Missouri politics during the 1854 senatorial campaign with the dicey issue of slavery in the territories. Benton was increasingly characterized in later years by his commitment to the Federal Union and his breadth of vision that went beyond the perspective of his section to embrace what he considered a greater good. He denounced both Northern antislavery and Southern proslavery protagonists, crystallizing the schisms present in the Missouri Democratic Party. As he said in 1856, "I believe in the old doctrine, that the Territories are the property of the United States and under the guardianship of Congress, and subject to such laws as Congress chooses to provide for them (or to permit them to make for themselves) until they become States." None of this "popular sovereignty" mish-mash for Benton; he believed in the power of the Federal government. This threw the slavery issue back into the hands of the U.S. Congress, and there the larger numbers of antislavery representatives would probably deny it.[8] The slaveholding part of Missouri's population could very possibly be blocked off from movement into the nation's territories adjacent to the

6. *Congressional Globe*, 33d Cong., 1st sess., 532, 1254; Parrish, *David Rice Atchison*, 149–50; Parrish, Jones, and Christensen, *Missouri*, 133–34.

7. It is impossible to understand the depth of emotion of northern antislavery sentiment in this episode without recognizing that it derived from not only an aversion to slavery but also a fear of African Americans. See Eugene H. Berwanger, *The Frontier against Slavery: Western Anti-Negro Prejudice and the Slavery Extension Controversy*; Eric Foner, *Free Soil, Free Labor, Free Men: The Ideology of the Republican Party before the Civil War*; and Frederickson, *Black Image*.

8. This letter is quoted in the *St. Louis Democrat*, May 22, 1856. See also the astute observations on Benton by Allan Nevins, *Ordeal of the Union*, Vol. 2, *A House Dividing, 1852–1857*, 500–501.

Missouri River; there were few in the state who did not feel passionately about the act.

David Rice Atchison, likewise, used the 1854 senatorial campaign as a referendum on the opening of Kansas and Nebraska to slaveowners through the repeal of the Missouri Compromise. For the truculent Atchison, the opening of the territories to slaveholders on the same basis as freesoilers—people advocating the limitation of slavery to regions where it then existed—required the vigilance of a powerful champion. He perceived himself as that champion, and he expected the citizens of Missouri to hold the same view. Without his diligence, Atchison believed, the preservation of slavery in Missouri—to say nothing of its extension into the territories created out of the Louisiana Purchase—was direly threatened by the forces of abolitionism. In fact, Atchison came to believe that the outcome in Kansas would determine slavery's future elsewhere.[9]

Atchison's quest for opening Kansas to Missouri slaveholders rested in part on the richness of the land and a belief in its ability to support large-scale plantation agriculture along the river bottoms. In a state with a large population of southerners, such staple crop agriculture represented one of the important visions of economic prosperity and could not be dismissed lightly. Atchison considered the passage of the Kansas-Nebraska Act, with the repeal of the Missouri Compromise, as a step forward in the achievement of equal rights for slaveholders in Missouri and elsewhere. In opposing that legislation, Atchison believed, Benton had invalidated his responsibilities to the people of Missouri. Benton stood against the interests of his state, as Atchison argued to anyone who would listen.[10]

At first Doniphan sounded remarkably like Atchison on the question of slavery in Kansas. At a speech in Liberty on December 4, 1854, Doniphan declared the Kansas-Nebraska Act not only constitutional but also necessary to safeguard the liberties of those whose property the antislavery zealots would destroy. Like Atchison, Doniphan believed that the destiny of the United States would rise or fall on the development of its western lands through immigration and improvement from the settled East. Without permitting slaveholders to take their property into the new Kansas and Nebraska Territories, Southern interests, especially the rights of Missourians, would be impaired. If they got their way, antislavery supporters would bar slaveholders from those territories, perhaps forever. That must not happen, Doniphan argued.

Doniphan also accepted the prospect of "popular sovereignty" in Kansas and prodded Missourians to remove to the newly opened area where they could settle and then out-vote the antislavery forces also heading there. As editor of the Liberty newspaper summarized it:

9. Nevins, *Ordeal of the Union,* 2:89–90.
10. *Missouri Republican,* June 21, 1854.

Colonel Doniphan urged upon the people to take all legal and constitutional steps to prevent Kansas from becoming an abolition den, but persuaded them, in most eloquent and argumentative language, as they valued their peace, their lives, their homes, their property, and their all, to go to the scene of the contest—to Kansas—and there to identify themselves as citizens and prevent such an unfortunate result. He portrayed, in most glowing colors, the sad effect of throwing around us such a population as were willing to be "shipped from the East like cattle," in order to make Kansas a free state.[11]

The speech brought down the house at the December 1854 political rally in Clay County. Most Whigs and Democrats agreed with Doniphan, for this issue did not divide the parties in that part of the state. The enthusiasm that Doniphan engendered, however, worried leaders supportive of the vision of Thomas Hart Benton and of conservative Whigs who wanted to avoid the splits that came within the party when considering sectional differences.

It should not surprise anyone that Doniphan took the stand he made on slavery in the territories. He was himself a slaveowning southerner. He never questioned the legitimacy of the institution; slavery had been in existence in the American South for more than two hundred years before his birth and he had been raised within its ethos. Although never wedded to it as an economic institution the way southern planters were, Doniphan had an intellectual, social, political, and probably even racial attachment to the institution; he accepted it as the norm and not something that need be overturned. However, the most important point for Doniphan, respectful of the law as he was and reverent for the United States Constitution, was that slavery was a legal institution and slaves were property. To deny owners the right to their property simply because someone dubbed a region "free soil" seemed one of the worst violations of American liberty he could imagine. From a legal perspective this position appeared fully justifiable, and Doniphan and his fellow southern constitutionalists made the argument repeatedly. In doing so, however, they failed to understand the moral outrage brought by antislavery champions. Those opposed to slavery appealed to a higher law than the United States Constitution, the moral inequity of holding another human being in bondage. Such entreaties galled the southern politicos who believed, in a legal sense correctly, that they operated firmly within their rights as American citizens.[12]

11. *Liberty Weekly Tribune*, December 8, 1854.
12. The constitutional defense of slavery, and the rights of the slaveholders to carry their property anywhere, was tested in the courts in the 1850s. This led directly to the Dred Scott decision of 1857 in which the U.S. Supreme Court ruled that property was property, whether it be a human slave or something else, and could not be stripped from its owner without due process of law. The constitutionality of this decision no

In addition to a constitutional stand for the property rights of slaveholders, Doniphan had long embraced westward expansion—as did many people in western Missouri—and now that this new rich land opened for settlement he wanted to ensure its availability to all Americans (at least white citizens) on an equal basis. In the 1830s Doniphan had agitated for the removal of the Indian tribes from the Platte country and its settlement by Missourians. Its opening had provided him enormous investment opportunities and he had grown wealthy taking advantage of them.[13] He also constantly sought business possibilities across the Missouri River near Fort Leavenworth, even perceiving the possibility of establishing a bank there to support economic development in the territory and make a profit for himself in the process.[14] Without the new land available for settlement by Missourians, many of whom would be slaveholders, Doniphan's ability to capitalize on what most envisioned as an investment bonanza stood imperiled. For legal and public reasons, as well as for private ones, Doniphan supported the opening of the newly created territories to slaveholders.

This concern over the territories permeated the Missouri General Assembly's session that convened in Jefferson City on Christmas Day, 1854. For the first time since 1840 Doniphan played a leading role in this legislative session, but when he stood for election to the state house he probably did not conceive of his central role in the session. This episode began when Doniphan entered the Missouri General Assembly from Clay County in August 1854, an office he had held twice previously. When the legislature convened on Christmas Day, the Whigs held sixty seats in the state house. While this was more than at any time in the past though not an absolute majority, Whig leaders hoped to control the political process in the session.[15]

More important for state Whig leaders, however, they saw an opportunity to elect a Whig senator to Congress. Everyone knew the senatorial

---

one could question; the morality of the decision was another issue entirely. For a scintillating discussion of the moral and legal dimensions of this issue, see Don E. Fehrenbacher, *The Dred Scott Case: Its Significance in American Law and Politics.* See also Harold M. Hymen and William M. Wiecek, *Equal Justice under Law: Constitutional Development, 1835–1875,* 115–202.

13. In this regard, see Shortridge, "Expansion of the Settlement Frontier." See also Missouri Tax Lists, 1836–1839, Clay County, 59 (old numbering), 424–25 (new numbering); Missouri Tax Lists, 1840–1845, 938, 1028, 1074–75, 1172, 1212; Platte County Deed Book A, 147; and A. W. Doniphan to Capt. John Chauncey, June 11, 1836, Harold B. Lee Library.

14. A. W. Doniphan to John Doniphan, December 15, 1856, Doniphan Collection. See also Patrick E. McLear, "Economic Growth and the Panic of 1857 in Kansas City."

15. *Liberty Weekly Tribune,* August 11, 1854; *Journal of the House of Representatives of the State of Missouri, 1854–1855,* 18th General Assembly, Missouri State Archives; *Missouri Republican,* December 19, 1854; *Missouri Statesman,* October 13, 1854; Mering, *Whig Party in Missouri,* 202–3.

campaign would turn on the issue of slavery in the territories. Claiborne Fox Jackson, a lieutenant of David Atchison, wrote to his mentor early in the process to warn him. "We shall have warm times here next summer," he remarked. "Benton and his friends will make a desperate effort to elect him to the Senate again, and I think our friends are as fully determined to defeat him." Jackson opined in an overstatement, "The Whig party of the state is nearly all freesoil, and this makes the matter worse." The Democrats worried over the split in the party between the Benton and Atchison factions, with their acid test coming over slavery in Kansas, while the Missouri Whigs licked their chops.[16]

Disappointingly, even as one of the best opportunities to win elections in Missouri presented itself, the Whig Party disintegrated before the eyes of Doniphan and other party stalwarts during the campaign of 1854. St. Louisan James O. Broadhead accurately summarized the problem in March 1854. "I am very much disheartened about the future of the Whig party," he wrote to James S. Rollins, the available Whig candidate when no other would run. "This Nebraska question has split the Whigs wide open—upon this question the Whig party North and South are the very antipodes of each other—the Whigs of the North sincere in the position they assume, the Whigs of the South stifling their conscientious convictions are endeavoring to outrun the Democracy in the race of Demogguerism [sic]."[17] Even within the state of Missouri the Whigs divided over this question: Many of those from St. Louis lined up in favor of the position of Thomas Hart Benton. Most of the others, especially those such as Doniphan from the western and river-bottom areas, supported the Atchison position on slavery in the territories.

Another ingredient in this confused political situation also emerged in 1854, and Doniphan became an advocate of it. Many of the old Whigs could not stomach the apparent demise of the Whig Party and found a stopgap political home short of the Democracy of either Benton or Atchison. As a result, Doniphan and some of his fellow Whigs turned to the American Party, commonly called the Know-Nothings, which made a bald-faced appeal to patriotism toward the Federal Union. For Doniphan, who revered the Constitution and the nation as did his hero Henry Clay, this aspect of Know-Nothingism held the greatest prospect for uniting the country in the face of enormously divisive issues. The xenophobic and anti-Catholic aspects of Know-Nothingism, rampant on the East Coast, were somewhat less pronounced in Missouri, where men like Doniphan

16. Claiborne Fox Jackson to David R. Atchison, January 18, 1854, David Rice Atchison Papers, Western Historical Manuscript Collection; *Missouri Republican*, January 24, 1854; James Hughes to David R. Atchison, July 13, 1854, Atchison Papers.

17. James O. Broadhead to James S. Rollins, March 12, 1854, James S. Rollins Collection, Western Historical Manuscript Collection.

emphasized patriotism. Even so, Know-Nothing sympathizers provoked riots in St. Louis in the summer of 1854.[18] Also, since the Know-Nothing Party was essentially a lodge or fraternity at this point, the Missouri Whigs who affiliated with it could retain their old party allegiances. As a result, Doniphan and many of his old Whig colleagues kept the Whig name and plotted a revitalization of the national party organization. Even if they considered the American Party a pale reflection of the attributes the Whigs had earlier displayed under such inspiring national leaders as Henry Clay and Daniel Webster, it served a purpose they all understood.[19]

Know-Nothings of all political stripes abounded in Missouri by the summer of 1854. Benton and Atchison had their Know-Nothing supporters, as did various Whig politicos. In November 1854, Abram S. Mitchell, the editor of the *Intelligencer* in St. Louis, remarked to Abiel Leonard, "Before the coming legislature has been in session two weeks, two-thirds of them will belong to the mysterious order. I am not joking." He urged those Whigs with political ambitions to get on the bandwagon, "No man will be elected to the Senate who is not a Know-Nothing. Atchison is 'one of em' already—and I am not joking."[20] Whether Atchison was indeed a member is problematic, but Doniphan affiliated, and his dynamism—as well as others of like mind—pushed the organization toward a conservative constitutional position. J. J. Lindley, congressman from the Missouri Third District, commented in December that the Know-Nothings in the western part of the state devoted considerable attention to the constitutional rights of slaveholders, "banishing agitators on the Negro question from their midst."[21]

This situation existed when the Missouri General Assembly convened in December. The Whigs in the legislature who advocated the extension of slavery into the territories flirted with the Atchison men while those opposed to it met with Benton's lieutenants. To elect one of their own—if they could agree on a single candidate—the Whigs had to conciliate one or the other wing of the Democratic Party. Quickly and without much

18. There is no question that Doniphan harbored the nativistic prejudices of the Know-Nothings. As late as twenty years after the first appearance of the party, he expressed anti-Catholic sentiments. He wrote, "Then you say he is a Catholic & popular with his brethren all of whom are priest ridden & bigotted & Shields has a good grip of the priesthood, upon the whole the case is about equally balanced" (A. W. Doniphan to John Doniphan, March 14, 1873, Doniphan Collection). Even so, Doniphan's political rhetoric during this era did not emphasize these attributes, but played to a general patriotism.

19. So important was Doniphan to this party in Missouri that it was commonly called the "Doniphan Know-Nothings" in the 1850s. See S. M. Breckenridge to Abiel Leonard, October 25, 1854, Leonard Collection; *Liberty Weekly Tribune,* January 11, 1856; Duchateau, "Missouri Colossus," 313–14; and W. Darrell Overdyke, *The Know-Nothing Party in the South,* 111.

20. Abram S. Mitchell to Abiel Leonard, November 20, 1854, Leonard Collection.

21. J. J. Lindley to Abiel Leonard, December 7, 1854, Leonard Collection.

contention, both of these respective Democratic factions nominated their two long-standing party leaders for the Senate. The prospects for either of these candidates did not look too promising, however. Abram Mitchell soberly concluded a month before the legislature: "As to the Senate, I am sorry to say, I believe *we are sold.* . . . Bank and niggerism will put Atchison in, or I am greatly mistaken."[22]

When those calling themselves Whigs met in caucus at the opening of the Eighteenth General Assembly on December 25, 1854, they almost immediately split into two factions roughly parallelling the stands of Benton and Atchison on the extension of slavery in the territories. Those with Benton leanings put forward James S. Rollins for the Senate, while the proslavery wing, led by St. Louis stalwart George W. Goode, advocated the candidacy of Doniphan. In arguing for the nomination of Doniphan, Goode pointed out that Doniphan believed in the rights of slaveholders to take their property into the nation's territories. Goode also announced that those in his camp could never support any "so-called Whig" who entertained the possibility of nonextension of slavery into the western territories. The issue of Know-Nothingism apparently did not come up. After a long, involved, and sometimes heated debate, the Whigs adjourned their caucus without agreeing on a candidate for the Senate.

They did make some headway, however. In return for supporting a moderate Whig of the Rollins variety for Speaker of the House—William Newland of Ralls County—the rest of the party endorsed two resolutions that placated the proslavery wing. They first validated the position of Doniphan and others in favor of the Kansas-Nebraska Act, particularly its provision that slaveholders could bring their property into the region. The second declared the party's opposition to "the efforts of the Free-Soilers and Abolitionists" to enforce their will on other Americans through the destruction of slavery. This effort, the Whigs agreed, endangered the Union. This last position stood well with both moderates and proslavery advocates, for it harkened back to some of the cherished principles of the old Whig organization and raised patriotism in a time of crisis to an exceedingly high level.[23]

Whig leaders held several meetings over the next few days to hammer out an agreement on a candidate. Almost in desperation they eventually selected Doniphan as their senatorial nominee. He represented the best hope to hold what was left of the Whig Party together. He had vocally supported slavery extension, and that would prevent a defection of the proslavery element to Atchison. Yet Doniphan's striking nationalism and

22. Mitchell to Leonard, November 20, 1854, Leonard Collection.
23. William Carson to Hamilton R. Gamble, December 1854, Hamilton R. Gamble Papers, Missouri Historical Society; Paxton, *Annals of Platte County,* 189; William G. Cutler, *History of the State of Kansas,* 93.

patriotism, to say nothing of his Mexican War–hero status, attracted large numbers of moderate Whigs to his standard. Many of those agreeing with Benton on the Union would also be attracted to that aspect of Doniphan's persona. Doniphan had privately assured Whigs that while he approved of the repeal of the Missouri Compromise to allow slavery into the territories, he conceded along with Benton that Congress had the legal right to pass any legislation that it wished regarding those regions. This gave him something of a middle position. He was less "state's rights" and more pro-Union than Atchison and more proslavery than Benton.[24]

Whig leaders were most concerned about whether Doniphan could engage enough support from Atchison and Benton supporters to gain election. The Whigs had no absolute majority; they relied on a split Democratic Party and some defections from its factions for victory. In previewing the vote tallies anticipated in the legislature, Whig politicos knew that few among the Benton Democrats would throw their support to Doniphan, but Atchison was another story. Doniphan might attract some of his followers.

That became the political strategy, and on Thursday evening, January 4, 1855, the Missouri General Assembly met in joint session to begin what everyone recognized would be a grueling process to elect a United States Senator. David Rice Atchison and Thomas Hart Benton carried the nomination for their respective Democratic factions. When the Whigs put forward Doniphan's name, however, the room fell silent for a moment. The Democrats realized they had a serious contest on their hands, not only between Benton and Atchison but also with a third candidate of great charm and attraction. At no time in the past had the Whigs persuaded Doniphan to seek high office. This had suddenly changed, and, confirming his willingness, the balloting began.[25]

When the roll call sounded for the first ballot everyone involved was on edge. They had good reason, for the voting proved especially hard-fought. At the end of the first poll the contest stood at fifty-seven votes for Doniphan, fifty-six for Atchison, and forty-one for Benton. Ninety-one votes were required for anyone to be elected. In addition, Doniphan cast his vote for John Wilson of Andrew County. Since he refused to vote for himself but would not vote for one of his opponents, Doniphan had thrown his vote away. No one had received a simple majority and the only choice was to continue with a second ballot. The floor leadership for Atchison—Senators Robert M. Stewart of Buchanan County and

24. Joe Davis to Abiel Leonard, December 27, 1854, Leonard Collection; R. S. Thomas to James S. Rollins, November 9, 1854, Rollins Collection; *A Statement of Facts and a Few Suggestions in Review of Political Action in Missouri,* pamphlet in Western Historical Manuscript Collection.
25. *Journal of the House of Representatives . . . 1854–1855,* 63–64.

William C. Price of Greene County, and Representatives Lewis V. Bogy of Ste. Genevieve County and John W. Reid of Jackson County—took the time between the first and second votes to meet with Doniphan's supporters to try to sway them to the Atchison standard. The Benton men, led by Francis Preston Blair and B. Gratz Brown, also tried to win over support from other members of the legislature, but they failed. The Whigs concentrated on maintaining the coalition they had built. The second roll call ended the same as the first.[26]

Vote after vote followed, with essentially the same outcome. Doniphan never received more than fifty-nine nor less than fifty-seven votes during the first twelve polls. Atchison received within one or two votes of Doniphan in each of these ballots. Benton never came close to matching the support of Doniphan or Atchison, but his solid forty votes in every roll call ensured that the contest remained deadlocked. Doniphan's vote total shrank to fifty-four on the thirteenth ballot, while Atchison's rose proportionately, but all of the roll calls from the fourteenth through the twenty-first brought the totals back to the same numbers as in the first few polls. In each poll, Doniphan continued to waste his vote on a noncandidate.[27]

The senatorial campaign frazzled the members of the General Assembly. As the balloting dragged on for what seemed like an eternity over several leaden-footed days, the party wheelhorses scurried about seeking some way to break the deadlock. The obvious answer for the Whigs, everyone knew, necessitated dumping Doniphan as a candidate and seeking another that might be more attractive to voters pledged to other candidates. But the party as a whole could not agree. Moderate Whigs leaned toward James Rollins, whom the Bentonites liked. Those committed to a stand for slavery in the territories, nonetheless, vowed to support Atchison "before any Whig who admits the power" of the Federal government to prohibit slavery in the territories. Consequently, the Whigs stuck with Doniphan throughout the venture.[28]

Surprisingly, the Atchisonians tried to break the deadlock by replacing their champion with William Scott, an Atchison lieutenant, on the twenty-second and twenty-third ballots. But this proved useless as well. Sterling Price then replaced Scott on the twenty-fourth and twenty-fifth ballots, but this too failed to break the deadlock. Atchison returned to the ticket for the twenty-sixth through the forty-first ballots, but nothing could break the stalemate. Throughout the remainder of the voting, Doniphan received the same levels of support as earlier. On the thirtieth ballot he had a low

26. Ibid., 63–66, 70, 75, 89–92; Mering, *Whig Party in Missouri*, 203, 206–7; Norma L. Peterson, *Freedom and Franchise: The Political Career of B. Gratz Brown*, 36–39.
27. *Journal of the House of Representatives . . . 1854–1855*, 63–66, 70, 75, 89–92; Mering, *Whig Party in Missouri*, 203, 206–7.
28. James Davis to Abiel Leonard, January 1, 1855, Leonard Collection.

of fifty votes, but by the time of the forty-first and final tally his numbers had regained their earlier strength. That last vote, taken on February 1, 1855, remained a deadlock between the three candidates. The totals were Atchison fifty-eight, Doniphan fifty-six, and Benton thirty-eight votes.[29]

The Whigs, in tenaciously clinging to Doniphan as their nominee for the Senate, may have lost their chance to send another one of their own to Washington. Several of the moderate members of the party believed that had the party chosen a substitute candidate acceptable to the Bentonites, it might have achieved a majority. For instance, some members of the state house vocally argued for the nomination of either James Rollins or John G. Miller, a Whig then serving in the U.S. House of Representatives, as a substitute for Doniphan. As John C. McCoy wrote to George R. Smith, Whig representative to the state house from Pettis County:

> I like the course the Whigs have taken this far. But I believe that some other name would at this time gain some votes. I have been traveling through several counties since the first of Dec. I have heard the subject discussed numerous ways and within the 2 last days I have seen several democrats on their way home from Jefferson [City] and I hear but one opinion from them and that is that J. S. Rawlings [Rollins] of Boon[e County] or J. G. Miller of Cooper would receive enough Benton votes to elect. And if so I cannot see why Rollins is not as acceptable to the Whigs as Donophan [sic]. "I have seen him [Rollins] carry the Whig flagg [sic] as independently and do as good battle for the cause, yes and once when Donophan refused to carry it [in 1852].

McCoy added that "I think Whigs who doubt the Whig[g]ery of either of them is himself tainted with some foreign issue, and has affinities for abstractions[.] All the Whigs I have conversed with on the subject have a little more confidence in Rawlings or Miller than in Donophan." Then came the kicker. McCoy concluded by saying that the party owed "more to Mr. Rawlings than to any Whig in the state and believe him as true a Whig, yes just a little better and as competent [as Doniphan]."[30]

Benton political broker Edward Bates agreed, but his answer was a little different. Even though another candidate might have broken the deadlock, he believed that Doniphan might also have won if the party had pursued the election differently. "Pardon me for venturing the suggestion that all this trouble might have been avoided by a single effort of firmness at the beginning of the session; and might yet be cured by the same means," he told James Rollins in early February 1855. Even at that late date, Bates added, enforcing party discipline while nominating Rollins or

29. *Journal of the House of Representatives . . . 1854–1855*, 94–101.
30. John C. McCoy to J. T. Bradford and George R. Smith, January 17, 1855, George R. Smith Papers.

Abiel Leonard or some other candidate acceptable to Benton would have brought the unionist supporters into the Whig camp while only a few in the party would have defected to Atchison's queue.[31]

As it was, Doniphan's persistent candidacy stalemated the contest and eventually the members of the Missouri General Assembly gave up trying to reach a decision. On February 10, 1855, after days of debate and forty-one separate ballots, the state Senate adopted by an unrecorded vote a resolution—already passed in the House of Representatives—postponing the election of an individual from Missouri to fill the open seat in the United States Senate until November 1855.[32]

The Whigs may have made their strategic error by trying to deal with both factions of the Democratic party to elect Doniphan. While the Whigs might appropriately have moved to a different nominee at some point in the seemingly ceaseless polls for the three candidates, even with Doniphan as the standard-bearer for the Whigs throughout they still conceded Benton his forty or so votes at every turn and yet could dicker with the Atchisonians for issues that they wanted to assure. Doniphan and Atchison were old friends and associates, and they probably could have worked out some arrangement between them for one or the other to step aside and throw their support to the other. Both advocated similar positions on the slavery issue and might have joined forces rather than butted heads. Doniphan's record did not show that he was ever anxious for high political office so he might well have abdicated his candidacy in favor of Atchison had Whig leaders "cut a deal."

This never happened, nor did it ever seem to be a genuine possibility, and before the balloting had ended Whig tempers had grown volatile. They hurled epithets—"freesoiler" and "nullifier" were the most popular but more crass ones also wafted through the state house—at each other during floor debates. When the forty-one ballot marathon ended and plans to table the senatorial election emerged, Whig leaders breathed a sigh of relief. They had found holding their political coalition together increasingly difficult, and the stress shattered the tender relations between moderate and proslavery Whigs in the state. Never again would the Whigs possess anything approaching such an opportunity. When the legislature reconvened in November 1855, by this time without Doniphan as a member, only twenty-seven members called themselves Whigs. The next year, the party did not even hold a state convention and nominate anyone for office. Accordingly, Doniphan's senatorial candidacy in 1854 was both the high-water mark of whiggery in the state and the final curtain

---

31. Edward Bates to James S. Rollins, February 2, 1855, Rollins Collection; *Missouri Examiner*, January 18, 1855.

32. *Journal of the House of Representatives . . . 1854–1855*, 350; *Journal of the Senate of the State of Missouri, 1854–1855*, 189, 18th General Assembly, Missouri State Archives.

for the party. By the time of the 1856 presidential campaign most of its former members had joined the Democratic Party, many had affiliated (as had Doniphan) with the American Party, and a few of them (mostly from St. Louis) had become part of an emerging sectional party advocating antislavery, the Republicans. The ideal of the "positive liberal state" that had guided the Whigs ended up as just a memory for such men as Doniphan, who spent the remainder of the antebellum years seeking some return to it as well as soliciting a means to ensure both national unity and justice in the face of divisive centrifugal tendencies.[33]

If the fiasco of the 1854 senatorial election in the state house dampened Doniphan's resolve to participate in Missouri state politics there is no evidence of it. Throughout 1855 he facilitated the efforts of those who pressed for the extension of slavery into Kansas by participating in rallies and other political events.[34] With the formal adoption of "popular sovereignty" as the principle governing whether or not slavery would exist in Kansas, both sides began organizing efforts to send settlers representing their respective positions to the territory. Abolitionists organized associations to foster emigration to the territory; the most famous was the New England Emigrant Aid Company, established to finance a mass exodus from the Northeast into Kansas. Through 1854 these organizations had only managed to send about 450 people to the territory, but in 1855 the antislavery immigration into Kansas rose to about 1,240.[35] These people created the antislavery enclave of Lawrence and organized political opposition to the proslavery forces in the territory. Missourians determined that they had to fight fire with fire and organize their own proslavery political effort.

Doing so proved somewhat easier for the proslavery Missourians, since they lived nearer to Kansas than the organized antislavery forces. For instance, David Atchison presided over the creation of a series of "Blue Lodges" in western Missouri, secret fraternal organizations whose primary purpose quickly became the encouragement of proslavery settlement in Kansas. These lodges helped to found several proslavery towns

33. *Columbia Statesman,* December 14, 1855; Mering, *Whig Party in Missouri,* 207–9.

34. For example, on July 12, 1855, Doniphan served as a delegate from Clay County to the Proslavery State Convention held at Lexington, Missouri. It passed a series of resolutions that advocated the rule of law and the rights of slaveholders to take their slaves into the Federal territories. See *Liberty Weekly Tribune,* June 29, 1855, July 20, 1855; *Missouri Statesman,* August 10, 1855; Settle, *Alexander William Doniphan,* 5; and Samuel A. Johnson, *The Battle Cry of Freedom: The New England Emigrant Aid Company in the Kansas Crusade,* 154.

35. The activities of the New England Emigrant Aid Company have been described in James A. Rawley, *Race and Politics: "Bleeding Kansas" and the Coming of the Civil War,* 84–85; Horace Andrews Jr., "Kansas Crusade: Eli Thayer and the New England Emigrant Aid Company"; Samuel A. Johnson, "The Emigrant Aid Company in the Kansas Conflict"; Samuel A. Johnson, "The Genesis of the New England Emigrant Aid Company"; and Edgar Langsdorf, "S. C. Pomeroy and the New England Emigrant Aid Society, 1854–1858."

along the Missouri River ranging from Leavenworth City in the south to Atchison in the north. The lodges also served as focal points for organized forays of Missourians into Kansas to threaten antislavery settlers and to vote in local elections.[36]

Doniphan was not active in these lodges, but he sympathized with them. His personal antipathy to those with antislavery propensities also heightened during this period. Even among members of his own family he found fault with those opposed to the extension of slavery into Kansas. He wrote in disgust to his nephew John Doniphan about the fortunes of one of his relatives. "I fear from what sister writes that Will has married a yankee lady," he gasped. "That is a free soiler who will neither work herself nor have no group do it and that Will is doing about nothing."[37]

Such invective spilled over into his political activities. He cheered his fellow Missourians in the spring of 1855 when about five thousand of them crossed the border to vote in the election for a territorial legislature called for March 30, 1855, by Kansas territorial governor Andrew H. Reeder. In preparation for what could only be considered a referendum over the legality of slavery in Kansas, although no one officially billed it as such, the proslavery *Squatter Sovereign* newspaper published in Atchison called for immigrants from Missouri to vote: "The time is drawing near when you will be called upon to cast your suffrages for members of the Territorial Legislature, and though you may not have been numbered by the census taker, because you unfortunately emigrated from Missouri, remember that he cannot exclude you from the ballotbox. If any of you are visiting your friends in Missouri, and have your families with you, get back to your claims as soon as possible." The editor also said that as long as one had a claim on property in Kansas that he could and should vote, regardless of where his principal home might be. "Then come along with your claims," he concluded, "and don't be afraid to go to the polls; we can elect every member of both houses of the Territorial Legislature, friendly to our interests."[38]

The voting rules in Kansas Territory, as the editor of the *Squatter Sovereign* recognized and pointed out in his article, allowed entrance en masse from Missouri to participate in this election. Some of those who came in had claims—with many hastily established—and a good many did not. This set the election up for massive fraud, and led directly to the "Bleeding Kansas" of later years as the rule of muscle and gunpowder replaced the rule of law and equity. Because of these possibilities,

36. Parrish, *David Rice Atchison*, 162–65; James C. Malin, "The Proslavery Background of the Kansas Struggle"; Floyd C. Shoemaker, "Missouri's Proslavery Fight for Kansas, 1854–1855."

37. A. W. Doniphan to John Doniphan, December 15, 1856, Doniphan Collection.

38. *Squatter Sovereign*, February 13, 1855.

Doniphan's ideological and sometime legal colleague, David Atchison, led a group of "Filibusters" into Kansas for the double purpose of intimidating freesoil voters from coming to the polls and of voting themselves for friends of slavery. The congressional investigation that reviewed this election found that of the 6,178 ballots cast—overwhelmingly for proslavery candidates—4,968 were from nonresidents and therefore illegal. Also, this had not been the first instance of voting fraud; proslavery forces had likewise rigged an election in the fall of 1854. One such instance might have been happenstance, but Reeder quickly realized that this time it was enemy action and conferred with President Franklin Pierce over what to do. In the summer of 1855, with the Kansas question at an impasse, Pierce removed Reeder as governor.[39]

Atchison had entered Kansas Territory with armed men and went to the polls during the election to intimidate antislavery residents. No one denied this. Some also accused him of voting illegally, but according to the congressional investigation he apparently did not himself cast a ballot. Atchison's justification for going to Kansas during the election merely rested on the desire to prevent nonresident freesoilers from casting illegal ballots.[40]

While Doniphan had urged his fellow Missourians to take up residence in Kansas and to vote in this election, he does not seem to have gone into the territory himself. Some claimed that he had appeared at the polls, like Atchison, but Doniphan firmly denied this and there is no evidence that he voted in the election. Any story of Doniphan stealthily entering Kansas seems so utterly out of character for him that it probably represents more wishful thinking on the part of the antislavery leaders than reality. It would have been difficult for Doniphan to travel incognito under any circumstance—because of his tallness and celebrity status—and it makes little sense for him to have denied his presence when so many other Missouri political leaders were in the territory and admitted as much when questioned. He might just as easily have used the same excuse as Atchison, former Congressman Willard Preble Hall, and several others that went to the polls—that he desired to help oversee the election and to prevent nonresidents from casting illegal ballots.[41]

In other ways, moreover, Doniphan quickly became caught up in the Bleeding Kansas controversy. His proslavery position and his residence

39. *Squatter Sovereign*, August 7, 1855, August 14, 1855; *New York Tribune*, June 21, 1855, August 16, 1855; Rawley, *Race and Politics*, 87–92; Roy F. Nichols, *Franklin Pierce: Young Hickory of the Granite Hills*, 417–18.

40. *Report of the Special Committee Appointed to Investigate the Troubles in Kansas; with the Views of the Minority of Said Committee*, House Report no. 200, 34th Cong., 1st. sess., 9, 30–35, 283–85, 353–56, 435–36, 507–22, 865–66, 894–99, 927–30, 936. The story of Atchison's activities in Kansas in the 1850s has been ably pieced together in Parrish, *David Rice Atchison*, 161–74.

41. *Liberty Weekly Tribune*, June 22, 1855.

near the Kansas border in Clay County virtually assured his involvement even had he wished to divorce himself from it. Throughout the middle part of the decade he rallied proslavery forces and helped to organize Southern support for the confrontation. In the 1856 presidential campaign, for example, Doniphan beat the persistent drum of opposition to Republican candidate John Charles Frémont as someone inimical to the interests of the people of Missouri. He appealed to the patriotism of Missourians, arguing that the Union must be preserved against those who would tear it asunder. He appealed to anyone who would listen that the forces of "Black Republicanism," as Southerners called the followers of Frémont, required dispersal. He also explained that he thought the American Party had the greatest potential to do so. Its candidate, Millard Fillmore, had served before in the White House already, between 1850 and 1853. His election, Doniphan urged, provided the nation's best hope of saving the country from violent destruction.[42]

The outcome of the election, however, disappointed Doniphan. Throughout the nation Fillmore ran a distant third, with only 21.6 percent of the popular vote. The Democratic nominee, James Buchanan, received 45.3 percent of the popular vote and the Republican Frémont had 33.1 percent. Fillmore also ran poorly in Missouri, though he did win in Clay County in no small measure because of Doniphan's efforts. The strength of the Republican canvass especially terrified Doniphan, however, for he saw that party as entirely devoted to an antislavery agenda, and purely sectional in strength. It prompted him to redouble his efforts on behalf of the extension of slavery into the territories.[43]

In Kansas, events degenerated into a general border war and Doniphan found himself faced with the moral dilemma of continuing to appeal to law and national unity when neither of those attributes seemed plentiful to those on Missouri's western border. While Doniphan supported proslavery immigration to Kansas, he tried to keep the confrontation nonviolent. Never sanctioning the use of force to secure slavery in the territory, increasingly during the latter part of the decade of the 1850s that seemed to be the only way to ensure victory.[44] Moreover, Doniphan was a strong Union man and some Missourians increasingly talked about secession from the Federal Union unless they got their way in Kansas. He could not tolerate this position. In March 1856 Doniphan addressed a proslavery meeting where he stressed that those involved in the Kansas question must, despite

42. Ibid., May 2, 1856, May 23, 1856, May 30, 1856, July 18, 1856, July 25, 1856, August 1, 1856.

43. On the election of 1856, see Cooper, *Liberty and Slavery*, 246–47; Nevins, *Ordeal of the Union*, 2:487–514; and David M. Potter, *The Impending Crisis, 1848–1861*, 251–66.

44. Examples of Doniphan's rhetoric on behalf of proslavery forces can be found in *Liberty Weekly Tribune*, December 8, 1854, June 29, 1855, July 20, 1855, March 7, 1856, April 25, 1856, May 2, 1856, May 16, 1856, September 19, 1856; and *Columbia Statesman*, August 10, 1855.

seemingly desperate circumstances, abide by the Constitution and operate legally and trustworthily at all times. It especially troubled him, therefore, when antislavery advocates sometimes linked his name with violence in Kansas, for it went against everything he had said.[45]

Sometimes Doniphan failed to follow his own guiding principles, and such occasions indicate the desperate situation in western Missouri during the latter 1850s. As the Missouri-Kansas border erupted in violence, Doniphan found it easy to get caught up in the emotion of the moment. By the winter of 1855–1856 Kansas had held several elections and in every case considerable graft had taken place. Because of differences in the elections, pro- and antislavery state legislatures convened and passed legislation reflecting their positions. Enforcement of these measures created numerous confrontations between the two factions of government. Many of these disagreements happened at the hotbed of antislavery sentiment in Kansas, the town of Lawrence. A particularly bizarre and violent series of incidents involved a proslavery sheriff named Samuel J. Jones, who periodically showed up in Lawrence to arrest supposed criminals. In April 1856 someone in the town nicked him with a gunshot; in Missouri, however, early reports said that he died, the news setting the countryside ablaze with renewed violence. The freesoilers in the community disavowed any knowledge of who had committed the crime, but a proslavery grand jury in the territory handed down indictments without anything like real evidence against several of Lawrence's leading citizens. The same grand jury went on to denounce and demand the closing of the Free State Hotel and two newspapers in town, all bastions of antislavery politics. When United States Marshal Israel B. Donaldson attempted to arrest those indicted, he encountered the opposition of the antislavery settlers. Donaldson then sought assistance in apprehending the Lawrence fugitives, and Missourians up and down the Kansas border vowed to help their proslavery brothers in the territory achieve "justice." It was an invitation to violence.[46]

Along with a lot of other people involved in the controversy, Doniphan overreacted to the situation in Lawrence. He helped David Atchison, and his handpicked proslavery fireater Benjamin F. Stringfellow, raise a force of about eight hundred heavily armed men to march into Kansas and remove the accused from their Lawrence stronghold, by force if necessary. In addition to rowdies who had no formal organization, Doniphan and others enlisted the support of militia units, the Kickapoo Rangers and the

45. Shoemaker, "Missouri's Proslavery Fight," 335–36; Settle, *Alexander William Doniphan,* 5; *Liberty Weekly Tribune,* June 29, 1855, July 20, 1855, July 27, 1855, March 7, 1856.

46. This incident is related with not a little humor in Jay Monaghan, *Civil War on the Western Border, 1854–1865,* 51–52; McCandless, *History of Missouri,* 2:274–75.

Platte County Rifles, from Missouri. They also hauled over to Lawrence five cannon, notably the piece called "Old Sacramento" that Doniphan had brought back from the Mexican War and had placed on the court-house grounds in Lexington. A sizable force, apparently not including Doniphan, arrived at the antislavery stronghold on May 21, 1856. Seeing that they were outgunned, the Lawrence mayor invited them into the town. There the proslavery forces went wild, but apparently only after they had commandeered some whiskey from a local tavern. They threw the two freesoil presses into the river and trained the cannon on the Free State Hotel. They fired five volleys into the sturdy stone building, in the process demolishing the building while killing one of their own, who was squashed by a piece of the hotel wall thrown into the air. Soon they decided to set fire to the building and also burned Charles Robinson's and several other abolitionists' homes. They ransacked the town in fairly thorough fashion before retreating back across the Missouri River without achieving the intended arrest of those indicted for the Jones shooting. The "Sack of Lawrence," as appropriate a moniker as could be found and one that served well the purposes of the antislavery settlers in Kansas, excited furor in the North. It also led directly to retribution exacted three days later by abolitionist John Brown in the Pottawatomie Massacres and to the general escalation of the violence in Kansas.[47]

That Doniphan did not accompany this Missouri force to Lawrence is almost certain, although his whereabouts during the episode is un-known. Had he surfaced, like Atchison, eyewitnesses would have seen him. None did so, even though asked specifically about it. Doniphan approved of certain aspects of the action, however, even signing a petition after the fact backing the marshal's attempt to arrest those indicted for the Jones shooting. He stopped short of condoning violence, however, and denounced both that aspect of the operation and the butchery of John Brown's retribution. As if to make amends for what had started as a lawful action in Kansas and ended as the sack of Lawrence, Doniphan took to the stump to advocate law and order on the Missouri border.[48]

He did not give up, however, in peacefully advancing the cause of slav-ery in Kansas. Remaining active in political efforts aimed at securing the rights of slaveholders in the territories, by June 1858 he became a director of the Clay County Pro-Slavery Aid Association. This organization raised

47. Lester B. Baltimore, "Benjamin F. Stringfellow: The Fight for Slavery on the Missouri Border"; Monaghan, *Civil War on the Western Border,* 56–59; Potter, *Impending Crisis,* 208–9; Johnson, *Battle Cry of Freedom,* 155–60, 315; Nevins, *Ordeal of the Union,* 2:433–47; James C. Malin, "LeCompte and the 'Sack of Lawrence,' May 21, 1856"; Thomas Goodrich, *Black Flag: Guerrilla Warfare on the Western Border, 1861–1865,* 1–5.

48. *Liberty Weekly Tribune,* June 13, 1856; A. W. Doniphan to James S. Rollins, May 4, 1857, Rollins Collection; Paxton, *Annals of Platte County,* 213–17; William Frank Zornow, *Kansas: A History of the Jayhawk State,* 71–77.

funds and provided support for those from the South who wanted to migrate to Kansas. Of course, those receiving aid from the association understood that in any elections they should vote for candidates and issues that furthered the cause of slavery's extension in Federal territories.[49] Undeniably, Doniphan sought a peaceful solution to the problem of slavery in the lands of the Federal Union; he wanted a proslavery Kansas but if the price was too high in either destabilizing the Union or destroying lives he reluctantly accepted something less. His position in Kansas rested on a belief that true progress for the Union required peaceful accommodation. In the end he got neither.

Then personal tragedy struck again, and it prompted Doniphan's second political hibernation even as the controversy in Kansas reached a crescendo.[50] On May 11, 1858, Doniphan's second son, Alexander William Doniphan Jr., a lad of not yet eighteen years, drowned while swimming in a river swollen from spring rains. A student at Bethany College, in present-day West Virginia, young Doniphan and several of his friends decided to race across the stream. His roommate, James R. Rogers, made the crossing only with difficulty and arrived on the opposite side more than one hundred yards downstream. However, the current proved too much for young Doniphan, normally a strong swimmer, and he drowned before reaching the other side. Rogers recollected that

> we were foolish enough to brave the swollen waters of a stream nearby, for a bath, a perfect mill-race. . . . Doniphan, on the eve of leaping into the stream[,] used the familiar quotation, "Darest thou, Cassius, leap with me into this raging flood and swim to yonder point?" In the full current of the stream, a distance away, an exclamation of some words escaped him, which I failed to catch, but the turning-point of the quotation was applied by his friends who never entered the stream—"Help me, Cassius, or I sink." His remains were recovered a month later. When recovered, one foot was gone, and only by means of the other could I alone identify the body. It was distinctly a model foot, and was the only feature of the body unchanged.[51]

Doniphan received word of his son's death by telegram almost five years to the day after his other son had died of poison. After the authorities at the college sent the body home, Doniphan and his still near-invalid wife had him buried in the family plot in Liberty's Fairview Cemetery.[52]

This tragic loss grated on Doniphan even more deeply than had that of his first son. He now had no progeny, and Doniphan's direct family line

49. *Liberty Weekly Tribune*, June 13, 1858, August 13, 1858.

50. Ibid., May 21, 1858, June 25, 1858; *Columbia Statesman*, June 4, 1858.

51. James R. Rogers to William E. Connelley, March 27, 1907, in Connelley, ed., *Doniphan's Expedition*, vii–viii.

52. *Liberty Weekly Tribune*, May 21, 1858, June 25, 1858; *Columbia Statesman*, June 4, 1858, July 9, 1858, November 12, 1858.

would die out with his passing in 1887. Doniphan had been proud of his boys and sought to give them the best education and as much opportunity as anyone could hope for in western Missouri during the antebellum era. In addition, the larger questions of life and death and fortune and tragedy also affected Doniphan after the death of his remaining son. Indeed, those concerns prompted him to associate with the Christian Church in Liberty, becoming active in October 1858 and formally joining in November 1860. Something of his commitment to religion, as well as its role in helping him deal with his sons' losses, can be seen in a letter he wrote to a cousin in 1875. "But for my unchanging and undoubting faith," he wrote, "I should be the most miserable of men, but I have a most implicit confidence of again meeting my loved and lost ones in a brighter world."[53]

As Doniphan withdrew once more from the political arena because of his personal tragedy, the slavery controversy continued unabated. In many ways this controversy was more contentious and extreme than at any time during the previous five years. Abraham Lincoln, a candidate for the Senate from Illinois in the pivotal year of 1858, gave an important speech during the campaign that caught the essence of the debate; he noted matter-of-factly that a "house divided against itself cannot stand." A nation divided against itself, part slave and part free, he believed, could not continue. It must become all one or all the other. The simplicity and eloquence of Lincoln's speech expressed an important constitutional truth that five years of Doniphan's—or anyone else's—engagement had not defused.[54]

The ideological sides had crystallized during this period as exclusively antislavery freesoilism or radical proslavery and secessionism. There was essentially no place on the political landscape for other positions as serious contenders for public support. The house had divided into two, and the scope available for ambiguity and compromise had significantly constricted. Men of moderation like Doniphan, who struggled for a middle ground that recognized the value of the Union and sought its preservation while also arguing for the rights of slaveholders to their property, found it increasingly difficult to find a sympathetic ear. The nation followed a path to showdown—most people recognized that potential by 1858—and the sands left in the hourglass for temporizing appeared to be flowing out more rapidly than anyone could have imagined at the beginning of the debate over the Kansas-Nebraska Act five years before.

---

53. Ibid.; Settle, *Alexander William Doniphan*, 10; *Liberty Weekly Tribune*, October 15, 1858, October 22, 1858, November 30, 1860.

54. Lincoln's speech has received justified honor both for its supreme rhetoric and intense reality. See the discussion of it in Don E. Fehrenbacher, *Prelude to Greatness: Lincoln in the 1850s*, 70–95; and Albert J. Beveridge, *Abraham Lincoln, 1809–1858*, 4:181–225.

12

Preservation of the Union

THE AIR HUNG heavy, like wet and limp denim on the line, over the Missouri River bottoms in Clay County during August of 1860. It was the kind of summer that wits made cruel jokes about and old men singled out to remember. Before it was over it became a summer that no one ever forgot. And not only for its particularly hot and humid weather, but also for the momentous political events it portended. Most people realized that the political situation in the nation presaged a desperation for the future not felt since at least the crisis with Great Britain in the 1810s. "Men will be cutting one another's throats in a little while," predicted Alexander H. Stephens, an old Georgia Whig, in the summer of 1860. "In less than twelve months we shall be in a war, and that the bloodiest in history."[1] This proved an understatement as the violence of the Kansas border over slavery gained steam and spread elsewhere.

Alexander William Doniphan had busied himself with mostly private affairs during the previous two years, working to develop railroads, enhance his law practice, and advance banking activities. The census of 1860 reflected his success in business; he had forty thousand dollars in real property and six thousand in personal property. His stake in society was accordingly large and he felt connected to the political discourse taking place. He also held five slaves, and this too connected him to the larger political debate over the morality of slavery.[2]

1. Quoted in Richard Malcolm Johnston and William Hand Browns, *Life of Alexander H. Stephens*, 355–56.
2. His success is documented in *Liberty Weekly Tribune*, May 20, 1859, July 8, 1859, November 11, 1859, February 10, 1860, April 6, 1860, April 20, 1860, April 27, 1860, May 4, 1860, June 1, 1860, June 16, 1860; D. C. Allen, quoted in *Kansas City Star*, January 9, 1916. City of Liberty, Clay County, Mo., Population Schedules for the Eighth Federal

Positions had hardened on both sides of the slavery issue throughout the 1850s, and by the presidential election of 1860 they were clearly drawn. The northern political system, especially that dominant in the Old Northwest, had transformed itself into an ardent vehicle for the abolition of slavery. Every push from antislavery forces, of course, brought counteraction from proslavery southerners. Missouri's Alexander William Doniphan represented that perspective very well, but his experience also duplicated itself among those who resided in southern and border states within the Federal Union.

The showdown between these two positions was the presidential election of 1860. The recently established Republican Party, a powerful force in those states where slavery did not exist, ran on a platform that called for the non-extension of slavery into the territories and its eventual abolition where it presently existed. Its nominee for the presidency was Abraham Lincoln, himself born a Kentuckian like Doniphan, but an antislavery advocate of long-standing reputation.

In another time and place Doniphan and Lincoln might have become friends. Both were from Kentucky, both were successful attorneys, both were long-standing Whigs. Lincoln's conscience, like many other northern Whigs, made it impossible for him to endorse the Kansas-Nebraska Act and he split from the party to join the Republicans. While slavery had destroyed the Whig Party, the ideals of the "positive liberal state" still motivated Lincoln's actions. Doniphan, of course, embraced the constitutional rights of slaveholders to take their property into the territories. On that fundamental point, Doniphan and Lincoln parted company.[3]

The election split into a four-way race, Lincoln's "house divided" writ large. The Republicans ran Lincoln as their nominee and managed to make a campaign of it only in the non-slaveholding sections of the United States. The Democrats split over the question of slavery, just as the Whigs had more than a decade earlier, and states' rights southerners nominated John C. Breckinridge as their candidate. This wing of the party, finding success only in the South, made a stand on the rights of whites to own slaves and to take them wherever they wished. Abrogation of those rights necessitated secession from the Federal Union. The remaining Democrats nominated Stephen A. Douglas as their standard-bearer. Only

Census, 1860; City of Liberty, Clay County, Mo., Slave Schedules for the Eighth Federal Census, 1860, both in National Archives.

3. The election of 1860 is one of the most studied presidential campaigns in American history. Standard works on Lincoln and his party in the contest include Stephen B. Oates, *With Malice toward None: The Life of Abraham Lincoln;* Benjamin P. Thomas, *Abraham Lincoln: A Biography;* and Charles B. Strozier, *Lincoln's Quest for Union: Public and Private Meanings.* A basic discussion of the election in Missouri can be found in Doris Davis Wallace, "The Political Campaign of 1860 in Missouri."

this organization made any attempt to run a national campaign, using the popular sovereignty argument to skirt the slavery issue.[4]

Another political party, the Constitutional Unionists, nominated for president John Bell of Tennessee. Like most of the people identified with the Constitutional Union Party, Bell was an old Whig and Know-Nothing. This party represented very nearly the last gasp of moderation in an increasingly polarized political climate. Bell and his party's appeal to the Constitution and to law appeared absurd to many Americans then and now. The Constitution is meaningless without interpretation, and whose interpretation would the majority of Americans accept? Was it the strong national Union of Henry Clay or the weaker confederation of John C. Calhoun? Questions about the rule of law were akin to those of the Constitution. Whose law and who would enforce it? In the end, the Constitutional Unionists appealed only to those who could ignore both the desperation and the details of the situation in favor of abstraction and murkiness. Depending on the perspectives of individual Constitutional Unionists, the party moved in varying directions on the issues, and its equivocations upset even those embracing its lofty principles.[5]

The election troubled Doniphan, especially when extreme positions gained more and more adherents. Most of his fellow Missourians voted for the national Democratic Party candidate, Stephen A. Douglas. But he could not support extremists of either side and he had never before stooped to voting Democratic. Accordingly, he ended up with Bell. The two extreme candidates, antislavery Republican Abraham Lincoln and states' rights candidate John C. Breckinridge, split most of the rest of the vote and allowed Lincoln to capture the presidency. Lincoln became the first president in American history to receive a minority of the recorded popular vote. His total of 1,866,452 compared with a total of 2,815,617 for the other three opponents. In the end, as Doniphan and most other political observers understood, nearly 58 percent of the electorate had gone for an extreme position by voting for either Lincoln or Breckinridge, while only about 40 percent seemed in favor of compromise and supported a candidate committed to doing so. The election of Lincoln cinched the matter for many proslavery southerners, and they created a new confederated nation that would protect slavery.[6]

Try mightily though he did, Doniphan and his old Whig friends could not deliver Missouri to the Bell Constitutional Union camp during the

4. The classic account of the Democratic Party's efforts in 1860 is the Pulitzer Prize–winning study by Roy Franklin Nichols, *The Disruption of American Democracy.*

5. On the Constitutional Unionists, see Allan Nevins, *The Emergence of Lincoln,* Vol. 2, *Prologue to Civil War, 1859–1861,* 280–82; Cooper, *Liberty and Slavery,* 263–64; Daniel W. Crofts, "The Union Party of 1861 and the Secession Crisis"; and John V. Mering, "The Slave State Constitutional Unionists and the Politics of Consensus."

6. John C. Gardner, "Election of Lincoln to the Presidency in 1860," 2:935–40.

election of 1860. Early in August he addressed a pro-Bell rally in Kansas City, later speaking for two hours to a large assembly in Missouri City on behalf of the Constitutional Union program. In the latter discourse, which was universally praised as an eloquent plea for moderation and patriotism, Doniphan reviewed the history of the various political parties then in existence and demonstrated how they were on a collision course in which the Federal Union would be the chief victim. To preserve the Union, to ensure the viability of the United States of America, to continue the progress of the republican form of government, to enhance the development of a positive liberal state required adherence only to the Constitutional Union Party. No other party, and especially no candidate other than John Bell, held much hope for balancing the extreme ends of the political spectrum so that a more moderate position that preserved the rights of both sides could emerge.[7]

Despite fighting a bout of bronchitis, Doniphan kept up an aggressive speaking circuit for the Constitutional Unionists during the fall of 1860. He attended the Constitutional Union Party's state convention in late August, delivering a major address to the meeting. Doniphan also addressed large pro-Bell rallies in St. Louis, Independence, Barry, Lexington, Platte City, and Haynesville. The theme remained the same from first to last: John Bell was the only candidate who could avert the dissolution of the Union.[8]

Doniphan capped his stumping with an election eve address to a gathering in the upper courtroom in Liberty on November 5. In a rousing three-hour speech, Doniphan appealed to his fellow Clay Countians to work for national unity and patriotism. In this speech, Doniphan considered some of the key challenges to Bell and his party's abstract and seemingly naive appeal to the Constitution and the rule of law. The absurdity of the patriotism of the Constitutional Unionists, Doniphan explained, was really a moderateness and rationality not present elsewhere. He suggested that the real strength of Bell's Constitutionalism was a recognition that the nation's organic law was both broad and strong enough to meet the needs of all elements of society. It could both ensure majority rule and protect minority rights.

No doubt, Doniphan's impassioned cry for Bell played to the melodramatic and blatantly sentimental. He called the successful accomplishment of the American Revolution by the nation's founding fathers a divine miracle, and the writing and adoption of the Constitution just as great a miracle. But Doniphan also moved his crowd in ways no one could have

7. *Liberty Weekly Tribune,* August 3, 1860, August 24, 1860, August 31, 1860, September 14, 1860, September 28, 1860.

8. Ibid., August 31, 1860, September 28, 1860, October 5, 1860, October 19, 1860, October 26, 1860, November 2, 1860; B. B. Lightfoot, "Nobody's Nominee: Sample Orr and the Election of 1860."

predicted. As the local newspaper editorialized, the attorney's remarks were "replete with sound political wisdom and experience; with essentially conservative and patriotic sentiments; and with perfectly irresistible arguments and appeals in favor of the continued unity, and indivisibility, supremacy of our admirable form of government." Doniphan's speech had the desired effect. The next day Clay Countians went to the polls and voted for Bell two to one over Stephen A. Douglas. Lincoln came in a distant fourth in the county.

In his speech Doniphan also expressed great concern about the probable election of Abraham Lincoln. Doniphan, like many other political leaders and observers, could count the states in each column with some degree of certainty. He was convinced that Lincoln would run a very close race, and he knew that Bell almost certainly would fail. He warned his fellow citizens of repercussions from the election of extremists. Doniphan said he was "apprehensive of Mr. Lincoln's election" because of the "inevitable strife, the sanguinary feuds, and border warfare which must follow in a greater or lesser degree, the inauguration of Black Republicanism, with its sectional hate and oppressive policy." Catapulting Lincoln into the presidency would only exacerbate, according to Doniphan, the frenzy of "Bleeding Kansas," the previous "four years of incessant broils, and jealousies and bloody contests" of extremist positions.[9]

The next few days confirmed the worst fears of Doniphan and other moderates. Despite delivering Clay County into the Bell column, the Constitutional Union Party came in a poor fourth in the balloting overall. Almost certainly, he realized, pro-slavery zealots would campaign to take their states out of the Union. That would force a military confrontation and war could be the only result. Like a lot of other moderates—many of which lived in Missouri despite years at the flashpoint of antagonism over slavery—Doniphan refused to give up hope that the Union could be preserved and threw himself into the creation of a last-ditch compromise effort between extremists of both sides.[10]

Doniphan latched onto a proposal by Senator John J. Crittenden, Democrat of Kentucky, to resolve the issue. The Crittenden plan had emerged in Congress from the "Committee of Thirteen" that included an august body of senators who worked behind the scenes to effect a resolution to the crisis. Crittenden took ideas fleshed out in this committee and brought to Congress a plan for the ratification of a series of amendments to the Constitution. First and foremost for Doniphan and most other slaveowners who

9. *Liberty Weekly Tribune,* November 9, 1860.
10. The Missouri vote for Douglas was 58,801, for Bell 58,372, for Breckinridge 31,317, and for Lincoln 17,028. Consequently, Bell ran well in the state, but not sufficiently well to carry it. See Wallace, "Political Campaign of 1860," 183; William Roed, "Secessionist Strength in Missouri"; and Stephen Carroll, "Loyalty or Secession?"

promoted compromise, the plan guaranteed the permanence of slavery in the states where it then existed. Second, it reestablished the Missouri Compromise line of 36°30' as the demarkation point between slave and free states on all territories of the United States, either those "now held, or hereafter acquired." In addition, some sections also prohibited the abolition of slavery on Federal property and in the District of Columbia unless the states of Virginia and Maryland agreed. Provisions also dealt with the handling of fugitive slaves, regulated the internal slave trade, and guaranteed the rights of slaveowners. Finally, Crittenden demanded that once passed these proposals would not be amendable. When the Senate's Committee of Thirteen failed to reach agreement among themselves on the viability of this proposal, Crittenden took it directly to the Senate floor but he also lost there.[11]

With that decision (or lack thereof) taken, any leadership in favor of compromise fell to the states. One notable effort came from the state legislature of Virginia, inviting the other states to send representatives to Washington in February 1861 for a "Peace Conference." Doniphan was enthusiastic about this prospect, to say the least, and began campaigning on its behalf in early 1861. On the evening of January 28 he participated in a countywide meeting in Liberty where delegates to a state convention would consider the state's course in secession crisis. His every effort was aimed toward finding some compromise position. Although the ground was covered with new-fallen snow, Doniphan and his associates worked hard to attract those who would support a compromise position. "We had a tremendous meeting[,] the Court House would not hold one third of them and we had to adjourn out of doors," Doniphan told his nephew John Doniphan, "& I spoke from the Court House platform to a yard full— nearly or quite 2,000 people from Clay, Clinton & Ray." For ninety minutes Doniphan pleaded with the attendees to remain loyal to the Union, urged adoption of the Crittenden compromise plan, and advocated the election of delegates to the state convention who would accept a compromise to preserve the Union.[12]

His efforts were successful, and although he protested, the group nominated Doniphan, Elijah J. Norton, and James H. Moss to serve as delegates to the state convention. They did this by acclamation. While Doniphan appeared hesitant, telling his nephew, "the sacrifice is too great—it will not pay—much to risk & nothing gain[ed]," he agreed to serve. His bottom line was not monetary, as his comment to John Doniphan might have

11. *Congressional Globe,* 36th Cong., 2d Sess., 114, 409; Nevins, *Emergence of Lincoln,* 2:390–98.

12. A. W. Doniphan to John Doniphan, January 28, 1861, Doniphan Collection; *Liberty Weekly Tribune,* January 25, 1861, February 1, 1861. On the Peace Conference, see Robert G. Gunderson, *Old Gentleman's Convention: The Washington Peace Conference of 1861.*

suggested, but what he thought was best for the state. His persistent Whiggery showed through here. He told his nephew: "Let no man be nominated who is in principle radical—the Convention have to report & back any secession resolution—but we want none passed—for if they pass one & that or submission is the issue we give them a grand advantage— we must keep the issue secession or compromise—and hence we must have compromise union men so that no submission issue can be forced upon us." Perhaps better than most Doniphan realized that Missouri would never accept the radical antislavery agenda advanced by some Republicans, and he did not want to be forced into a position of having the state decide between it ("submission" as he called it) and secessionist extremism. He knew most Missourians would choose secession when faced with that choice. He worked to ensure that compromise would result from the meeting. Doniphan's views clearly mirrored majority sentiment in Missouri. Most Missourians, like Doniphan, believed in conditional Unionism at the same time that they embraced slavery.[13]

More than that, Doniphan believed that most other slaveowners would choose compromise rather than secession. In assigning to most southerners the same fundamental rationality and persistent whiggery that he held, always moving them to the center of the political spectrum, Doniphan proved disastrously incorrect. Had the South included even half of the Unionists that Doniphan believed present, some compromise might have resulted. A persistent but misplaced belief that southerners actually would not have the stomach to abolish the Union and that in the end patriotism would prevail motivated Doniphan to work for some compromise that preserved slavery and therefore the Union. But such a belief proved to be a gross misreading of the situation, for southern politicians elsewhere pressed for secession.

Doniphan, nonetheless, continued to work for compromise in Missouri. The state meeting nominated him—along with Waldo P. Johnson, John D. Coalter, Harrison Hough, and A. H. Buckner—to attend the last-minute conference in Washington beginning February 4, 1861. He caught the Hannibal and St. Joseph Railroad for Washington about the first of February, contemplating the serious nature of the work in which he had agreed to participate.[14]

On the way to Washington Doniphan's train stopped in Quincy, Illinois, and Orville H. Browning, an antislavery Republican from Illinois, boarded it for a trip to the state capital of Springfield. Doniphan and Browning

13. *Liberty Weekly Tribune*, February 1, 1861; Doniphan to John Doniphan, January 28, 1861, Doniphan Collection.
14. *Liberty Weekly Tribune*, February 8, 1861, February 22, 1861; *Columbia Statesman*, February 8, 1861; A. W. Doniphan to D. C. Allen, "Sketch of Life," 3, Doniphan Papers; Paxton, *Annals of Platte County*, 306–7; *Laws of the State of Missouri, Passed at the Regular Session of the 21st General Assembly, Begun and Held at the City of Jefferson, December 31, 1861,* 772.

struck up a conversation and inevitably the discussion turned to the seces-sion crisis. Browning, making a standard Republican argument, denied the right of secession to any state and suggested that any negotiations must accept that as a fundamental truth. Doniphan agreed that secession was unacceptable but concluded that "there were some grave difficulties to overcome in the settlement of our troubles." Browning did not accept this argument and insisted that the primary responsibility Lincoln had as president was to enforce the laws of the nation. Seeing a hole in the reasoning, Doniphan then asked Browning how Lincoln could possibly enforce laws in states that had seceded? Browning nodded, "If you use forces like the army you would be recognizing their right to secede and you'd have to bring them back as territories." Doniphan's knowledge of the law was impeccable, and his logic in this case faultless. It was also moot. While Browning could not answer his question, not so Lincoln, who would soon call on the states for troops to put down an insurrection in certain parts of the nation.[15]

It was a frustrating exchange for Doniphan, but nothing compared to what he encountered upon reaching Washington in early February 1861. Commissioners from twenty-one states assembled in Washington for this "Peace Conference." John Tyler of Virginia, a former president of the United States and an old Whig, presided over the gathering. Other illustri-ous participants included William Pitt Fessendon, David Wilmot, Reverdy Johnson, and Salmon P. Chase. But the conference came to nought. Histo-rians James G. Randall and David Donald concluded that "its voluminous journal gives more evidence of disagreement and footless speech-making than of a genuine spirit of accommodation."[16]

Doniphan expressed a rising frustration at the conference. As the de-bates continued, he wrote to his nephew John Doniphan, commenting that the Republicans stonewalled the proceedings almost from the beginning,

> they are determined to know Lincoln's wishes in regard to the adjustment—whether we are to have any or none & what guar-antees they will give—there are at least fifty open and avowed office seekers in our Convention who have availed themselves of the opportunity of visiting Washington at the expense of their respective states & haveing [*sic*] at the same time some decent pretext for being here, so as not to seem to be mere cormorants & birds of prey. Of course such as these only want to know Abraham's wishes in order to perform them.

Doniphan also had nothing good to say about Lincoln, whom he con-sidered the culprit in any failure to effect a compromise. Doniphan com-mented that

15. *Liberty Weekly Tribune*, February 15, 1861.
16. James G. Randall and David Donald, *The Civil War and Reconstruction*, 151.

it is very humiliating for an American to know that the present & future destiny of his country is wholly in the hands of one man, & that such a man as Lincoln—a man of no intelligence— no enlargement of views—as ridiculously [sic] vain and fantastic as a country boy with his first red Morocco hat—easily flattered into a belief that he is King Canute & can say to the waves of revolution, "Thus far shalt thou come and no farther." The consequence is that the most adroit flatterer and manager is, for the time being[,] the arbiter of the destinies of this mighty nation—if rash may at any time ruin all beyond redemption. . . .

Jesting aside Old Abe is simply an ignorant country buffoon who makes about as good stump speeches as Jim Craig, and will not be more fitted intellectually as President, but perhaps as *disinterested.*

Doniphan suggested that if his conference failed to achieve compromise, the Union would "be dissolved in a few days or months at most—Va leading all the rest following as they get ready." Doniphan's assessment of Lincoln's capabilities were certainly off the mark, but his assumption that the Republicans did not want compromise was on target.

In such an environment, with extremism on both sides, little room remained for the kind of middle-of-the-road compromise that Doniphan tried to hack out in Washington in February 1861. When the Washington Peace Conference finally drew to a close on February 27, it put forward four constitutional amendments much like those proposed by Crittenden and already shot down in the Congress. Presented to Congress, this plan met with a similar disapproval. Fed up with the process, Doniphan returned to Missouri closer to backing secession for his state than at any time before or since. He confided to his nephew in a letter from Washington that Missouri "must demand what the other slave states demand and accept what they accept—we cannot go out of the Union before them nor remain—as a unit—and by one act—and form a new GOV'T or go with the South—& this last is best[.] One respectable republic in numbers and power is better than twenty little rickety concerns." However, Doniphan soon thought better of this and returned his attention to keeping Missouri in the Union.[17]

While Doniphan was in Washington, on February 18 the Missouri General Assembly called for an election of delegates to a convention to consider the best course for the state. To attend this meeting, moderate candidates garnered a ten to one advantage in seats. Not a single avowed secessionist was elected, but four known Republicans—all from St. Louis—were chosen. Although he had not yet returned to Missouri by the time of the first session in Jefferson City on February 28, Doniphan was elected to this convention and attended its second meeting, which took

17. A. W. Doniphan to John Doniphan, February 22, 1861, Doniphan Collection.

place at the Mercantile Library Hall in St. Louis on March 4, 1861. The choice of St. Louis was important for this convention, for it removed the members from the secessionist sentiment of Jefferson City and plunked them down in the state's hub of Unionism. In this quieter environment, most agreed with Doniphan that Missouri should retain membership in the United States voluntarily, thereby retaining more stability to ensure the rights of its citizens.[18]

Nearly the first order of business at the convention was a report from Doniphan on the outcome of the Washington Peace Conference. He not only gave them a report on the ill-fated conference, but used the opportunity to lecture the convention on the reason for all the troubles, black slavery. As he said:

> It naturally occurs to every reflecting mind that in order to restore harmony and union, that question must be removed from the arena of politics—that there can be no restoration of harmony, peace and quiet unless that question is removed. That question has interposed between the North and the South and created a division, and you may plaster it together as you please; you may try Spalding's glue or anything else in the world but you cannot bring it together until this question is removed, and when this question is removed it will unite itself.

Because of this, Doniphan added, sectionalism had triumphed over nationalism.

He went on to blame the Republican Party for making this happen. "Sectionalism itself destroys, withers and crushes our nationality. If there is sectionalism at the South in the shape of slavery propagandism, or at the North in the shape of abolitionism, nationality cannot exist, and the vital element of the whole Union is crushed out." He added:

> There have been fiery spirits in one portion of the Union who have administered an ailment to discontented spirits in another portion of the Union, and this has gone on until a gulf has been created between the North and South which has broadened and deepened until a revolution has not separated one portion from the other. . . . It has now culminated in the election of two men to power, both of whom live in the North, and have been placed on a platform which is antagonistic to the South—entirely, in its whole aspect, antagonistic to one portion of the nation. And take out from that platform this antagonism to the South and the essence of that party is destroyed. I admit many imprudent things at the South, calculated to inflame the minds of men at the North. But we must

18. *History of Clay and Platte Counties*, 191–95; "Journal of the State Convention," February 28, 1861, in Settle, "Doniphan Collection, Notes and Misc.," Vol. 2, William Jewell College, Special Collections; Doniphan to Allen, "Sketch of Life," 5, Doniphan Papers.

> take matters as they are—we must take this revolution as it is—
> and we find that this revolution has grown out of the triumph of
> sectionalism, and that triumph had weakened the cords that bind
> us together, and disintegration is the natural consequence.

The Republican "revolution" had destroyed the nation, he said. "It is this
sectionalism that has stricken down the nationality of this Government,
it is this sectionalism that has . . . poisoned everything around it, which
has been the cause of the revolution that is now destroying the vitality of
this Government."

According to Doniphan, the central question inevitably revolved
around how to remove the slavery issue from the political sphere. The
only answer the Washington Peace Conference came to was a series of
proposed constitutional amendments that would protect both sides of
the dispute, both sections. "The Crittenden amendments were offered,
and I deemed those amendments as being the thing properly suited to
remove this question now and for all time to settle this question of the
Territories on the basis of 36. deg. 30 min. and to remove this whole subject
beyond the arena of politics." Doniphan thought that such a guarantee
might induce the remaining slave states to remain in the Union, "and to
induce the States that are now out eventually to come back." He added,
"I believe, if Congress had passed such an amendment, and the North
had acquiesced, the Southern States would come in not at the present
perhaps, but in the course of time." Unfortunately, Doniphan concluded,
the amendments were not adopted by the national government and the
compromise attempt had reached an impasse.[19]

The convention also explored Federal relations, and Doniphan found
himself appointed to serve on a committee for this purpose with six other
delegates. Along with Hamilton R. Gamble, soon to be governor of the
state, and longtime acquaintance and fellow veteran of the First Missouri
Mounted Volunteers, Willard Preble Hall, Doniphan went to work on a set
of resolutions for the convention. On March 9 this committee brought their
work to the full body. Among other resolutions, the committee advocated:

> 1. Containing the explicit declaration that there was no adequate
> cause to impel Missouri to dissolve her connection with the Federal
> union.
> 2. Taking unmistakable ground against the employment of mili-
> tary force by the Federal government to coerce the seceding States,
> or the employment of military force by the seceding States, to assail
> the government of the U.S.[20]

During consideration of these resolutions disagreements quickly surfaced between those wishing to remain in the Union and those with

19. *Liberty Weekly Tribune*, March 15, 1861.
20. *History of Clay and Platte Counties*, 193.

more strident proslavery positions. One group demanded that unless the northern states accepted amendments to the Constitution protecting slavery, Missouri should secede from the Union. The tenor of this stipulation made it appear that Missouri's secession would be the fault of antislavery forces. When the vote began on whether or not to include this stipulation, Doniphan rose to oppose it. "Missouri has no right to offer an ultimatum," Doniphan announced, "either to the Border Slave States, the Southern States, or the Northern States." The rider amounted to blackmail. Then Doniphan made a statement that summarized his entire political career:

> I AM A UNION MAN. I GO FOR THE WHOLE UNION—THE ENTIRE NATION. I Go for it North, South, East, and West. I do not intend to say how long I am going to uphold this Union which our fathers builded. They were seven years in building it, and two mighty miracles were wrought in its formation. For the revolution, which lasted seven years—seven years of blood and carnage and suffering, and finally crowned with victory. Second, the formation of this Constitution—which took seven years more—by men of the purest wisdom and unquestioned patriotism; and shall we talk of settling this question in a day, when we reap the fruition of their labors in ten thousand greater fold than was ever anticipated by them. Sir, I am willing to serve here seven years, and take every means for the preservation of this Union. I am willing to serve as long as Jacob served, before this Union shall be dissolved. I am not going to say when I shall stop; I am not going to say when Missouri shall stop. Never! Never, while hope is left. I live by hope, and as a Union man I shall only die when hope dies.

In the end the convention endorsed the spirit of the compromise framed by Doniphan and his colleagues, and adjourned with the stipulation that it would honor a call to return to session if the state legislature asked it to do so. Missouri would remain in the Union.[21]

Doniphan returned to western Missouri late in March, where he kept up his pro-Union rhetoric. He took his message of compromise and Union to anyone who would listen, speaking at a rally in Platte County set up for him by his nephew John Doniphan. He also filled the courthouse in Liberty for a pro-Union address. He spoke not of good and evil on that occasion, on opportunities missed, and prospects unknown. Rather he appealed to the patriotism of the audience to preserve the Constitution and the blessings of the democracy. Then he urged a middle ground that did justice to the Union and the rights of all its citizens.[22]

21. *Liberty Weekly Tribune*, March 29, 1861; Thomas L. Snead, *The Fight for Missouri, From the Election of Lincoln to the Death of Lyon*, 87; *History of Clay and Platte Counties*, 195.
22. *Liberty Weekly Tribune*, April 26, 1861.

Throughout the spring of 1861 Doniphan talked incessantly about the Union and the necessity of its preservation, but he privately harbored doubts about Missouri's fate. Although proud of his role in assuring moderation thus far, Doniphan did not presume that the convention and its aftermath sounded the death knell of secession. For one, Missouri Governor Claiborne Fox Jackson was an avowed secessionist. While he had remained cautious in expressing his viewpoint in the spring of 1861, after the attack on Fort Sumter on April 12, 1861, he urged taking the state out of the Union.

Under Jackson's direction the General Assembly created eight military divisions in Missouri in which the militia, now renamed the Missouri State Guard, would keep order. In early May Jackson offered Doniphan the rank of brigadier general and command of the Fifth Division in western Missouri, but Doniphan did not immediately respond. Jackson's offer was not merely a symbolic gesture, as some have concluded; Doniphan had demonstrated abilities in command and his skill would be valuable if conflict came. As a political figure Doniphan could also help Jackson, for as Doniphan went so would many others who advocated compromise. Doniphan had waffled on whether or not to support secession, especially after the beginning of hostilities, and his service on behalf of pro-southern sentiments might well sway those still on the fence. At several levels, therefore, Jackson's offer to Doniphan of command over a major part of the Missouri State Guard made sense.[23]

As Jackson maneuvered to enable Missouri to hold its own, Missouri's pro-secession movement was intensified by rash acts on the part of Federal officers in the state. Clearly Doniphan felt pressure to declare for secession because of these actions. Lincoln requested Missouri troops to put down the rebellion, and Republican Francis Preston Blair volunteered four thousand men from his Unionist St. Louis Home Guard to the United States government. Lincoln placed this force under the command of Nathaniel Lyon, a staunch antislavery regular army officer commanding Jefferson Barracks, near St. Louis. Rashly, Lyon used these forces to intimidate pro-southern sympathizers. Such actions infuriated Doniphan and galvanized many Missourians against Lincoln.[24]

People in western Missouri responded to news of these events with indignation. Many of those hesitant to cut ties with the Union before, such as David Rice Atchison and Sterling Price, now came out in favor of secession. Price, who had promptly accepted the rank of major general in the Missouri State Guard when tendered by Governor Jackson, responded

23. Castel, *General Sterling Price*, 14.
24. William E. Parrish, *A History of Missouri*, Vol. 3, *1860–1875*, 12–18; Arthur Roy Kirkpatrick, "Missouri in the Early Months of the Civil War," 235–66, esp. 235–39; William E. Parrish, *Turbulent Partnership: Missouri and the Union, 1861–1865*, 15–24.

by mobilizing forces to repel any invasion that might come from Lyon's troops. Doniphan very nearly declared for Jackson's stand against the Union at this time as well.[25]

That he did not do so probably came only because Brigadier General William S. Harney, commander of the U.S. Army's Department of the West, met with Sterling Price to restore the peace. They drew up an agreement that kept Federal troops in St. Louis while Price used the Missouri State Guard to maintain order everywhere else. This bought time at best, but it did ensure state sovereignty within the Federal system in the long run.[26]

Doniphan latched onto this agreement as something that could enable Missouri to remain at peace with the Union. On May 23, 1861, he finally responded to Claiborne Jackson's offer of command over the Fifth Division of the Missouri State Guard. Citing personal health, as well as the continued poor condition of his wife, Doniphan declined to serve. Then, almost as an afterthought, Doniphan added that "relations have been so adjusted as to promise entire peace in the future." He did not have to choose sides, apparently, because peace could be assured without doing so. It represented a convenient "out" for a conundrum keenly felt by the Unionist–Whig–military commander–proslavery Missourian.[27] He almost joyfully wrote to his nephew in Platte County that the compromise had taken the wind out of the secessionists' sails. "I hope we will get on quietly," he confided, "as the secessionists now swear that they can do nothing by themselves and as the union men are not willing to make or invite war that they will not do their fighting for the cowardly scoundrels although they are nearly spoiling *inwardly* for a fight with Lincoln[,] Blair[,] & Co."[28]

With the compromise in place, Doniphan believed that the next step in securing peace in the state involved getting both sides to disarm. He and several other moderate leaders went to St. Louis, the flashpoint for conflict in the state because of the Union troops stationed there and the Unionist German immigrants who had taken up arms on behalf of Lincoln, to meet with officials of both sides. They sought the removal of all Federal troops from the state, and in return offered to secure the disbanding of the Missouri State Guard. Meanwhile, the War Department removed Harney as commander in the West and replaced him with Lyon. A much more bellicose commander, Lyon was not interested in treating with moderates

25. *Liberty Weekly Tribune*, May 17, 1861, May 24, 1861; William Larkin Webb, *Battles and Biographies of Missouri*, 280; Parrish, *David Rice Atchison*, 215; Castel, *General Sterling Price*, 12–15.

26. Snead, *Fight for Missouri*, 185–88; *Missouri Republican*, May 25, 1861; Castel, *General Sterling Price*, 16–17; Kirkpatrick, "Missouri in the Early Months," 239–40.

27. A. W. Doniphan to C. F. Jackson, May 23, 1861, reprinted in *Journal of the Senate, Extra Session of the Rebel Legislature, Called Together by a Proclamation of C. F. Jackson*, 31.

28. A. W. Doniphan to John Doniphan, June 2, 1861, Doniphan Collection.

of any stripe. Thereafter Jackson headed a Missouri government committed to secession. Eventually, it became a government in exile in the South as a Federal army swept across the state in search of rebel forces. It fought several skirmishes at places such as Boonville and Carthage in central Missouri and a major battle at Wilson's Creek on August 10, 1861. At Wilson's Creek, Price's troops soundly defeated Lyon's Federals, in the process killing Lyon.[29]

Would Doniphan now set his course for the Confederacy? Would he follow many of those with similar antebellum perspectives into rebellion against the United States? Men that he respected, such as Sterling Price and David Atchison, had reluctantly taken up arms against the Union. His brother-in-law John C. C. Thornton enrolled in the Confederate Army and became a lieutenant colonel. Several other friends and relatives served in the Confederate military during the war. Why not Doniphan? Despite the pull of the South, Doniphan tried to maintain a middle position. He attended the unionist convention in Jefferson City on July 22, 1861, in which Hamilton R. Gamble became governor to replace the now exiled Confederate government of Claiborne Fox Jackson. He also declared loud and long that he would not fight against the flag under which he had served, nor would he raise his hands to subdue his friends in the South. He wished to remain neutral in a land where neutrality could not be found. Doniphan's inner conflict was probably never fully resolved, but he recalled in later years that his Christian beliefs prevented him from either rebelling against the Union or fighting against those in rebellion. It may have been a more difficult choice than declaring for one side or the other.[30]

The years of the Civil War broke the spirit of Doniphan. He had worked so hard through the summer of 1861 to preserve peace and to secure the rights of all sides in the sectional conflict. This effort had come to very little. Missouri did not secede, and he believed that was the right decision, but it brought no serenity to his soul. With a foot in both camps, passionately in favor of the Union and believing in its highest ideals while maintaining his proslavery leanings, Doniphan wrestled with his conscience over the crisis and his response to it. In the end, all he could do was to declare neutrality, work for justice as he understood it, and long for peace. By the time the war was over, Doniphan was chagrined by politics and jaded by life and retreated into private business activities and social relations.

Because of his desire to remain neutral in the sectional conflict, Doniphan faced distrust from both sides. They each suspected that his

29. *Liberty Weekly Tribune,* June 21, 1861; Snead, *Fight for Missouri,* 195–97; Castel, *General Sterling Price,* 25–47.

30. Francis B. Heitman, *Historical Register & Dictionary of the U.S. Army,* 2:96; Parrish, *History of Missouri,* 3:30–33; A. W. Doniphan to D. C. Allen and members of the Christian Church, February 3, 1865, Doniphan Papers; *History of Clay and Platte Counties,* 200, 280.

sympathies truly lay with the other. Confederate newspapers charged that the once-respected Doniphan had become a "pet lamb" that had even voted for the "abolitionist" Hamilton R. Gamble as governor of the loyal government of Missouri. If he was southern in sentiment, correspondents shook their heads at Doniphan's unwillingness to lead secessionist forces in western Missouri. On the other side, Federal leaders questioned Doniphan's loyalty because of his well-known hatred of Republicans and abolitionists, whom he considered synonymous with one another, and because he was friendly with avowed secessionists.[31]

If both sides questioned his loyalties, over a period of several months Doniphan showed everyone that he stood with the Union and opposed rebellion. For example, in February 1862 Sterling Price, now a major general in the Confederate Army and responsible for operations in the West, sent Colonel John Taylor Hughes, the self-appointed historian of Doniphan's expedition, into the western part of the state to recruit soldiers and destroy railroads and communications infrastructure. Somehow, probably because his brother-in-law John C. C. Thornton was a lieutenant colonel in Hughes's regiment, Doniphan learned of the plan. Accordingly, he rode through a snowstorm to the headquarters of Union forces at Plattsburgh and informed Colonel James H. Birch about the plan. Doniphan reported to Birch:

> Colonel, I have reliable information that John T. Hughes intends to cross the Missouri River at Camden, six miles west of Lexington, and after crossing to tear up the Hannibal & St. Joseph Railroad from Macon to St. Joseph and burn the bridges. He will then recruit a brigade and recross the river with it before the Federal troops can be brought in. Now this alone would not trouble me, for he would take out of northwest Missouri hundreds of men the absence of whom would tend to give us a greater degree of peace. But the force of Hughes would doubtless commit some depredations, and when the Federals came in again the devil would be in supreme command in this particular country. I know John T. Hughes well; he was in my regiment in Mexico; and he is the most ambitious and daring officer in Price's army, and if effective steps are not taken at once he will execute his purpose, and you know as well as I do what will follow.

Armed with this intelligence, Birch went to St. Louis and requested Union military reinforcements to meet Hughes. When the Confederate commander arrived at Camden, Birch thus had a superior Federal force and ran off the Confederates with only a few shots exchanged. Doniphan's aid had blunted a Confederate surge from the South.[32]

31. *Liberty Weekly Tribune*, August 9, 1861; *War of the Rebellion*, Series 1, 3:601.
32. Connelley, ed., *Doniphan's Expedition*, 55–57. As an interesting sidelight, at the Battle of Independence on October 22, 1864, Hughes was killed. A kinsman of Sterling

Doniphan also demonstrated his commitment to the Union in other ways as well. In April 1862 he addressed a rally in Liberty in favor of voluntarily taking a loyalty oath to support the United States Constitution. He told the audience that secession sentiments were a delusion for Missourians and those who harbored them should understand the reality of the situation. Allegiance to the government of the United States was the only answer, despite what one might think of it at the present, and in time reform could be secured.[33]

He also involved himself in the debate over how to deal with the issue of slavery. Beginning in the fall of 1862 and especially in 1863, Abraham Lincoln transformed the war between the United States and the Confederacy from a struggle to preserve the Union into one to secure the freedom from bondage of chattel slaves. When Lincoln issued the Emancipation Proclamation, he freed the slaves in the Confederacy but not in slave territories that had not seceded and not in those areas under Union occupation. Even so, slavery would not be allowed to continue indefinitely anywhere in the United States for long after the end of the war. Missouri political leaders considered how to implement emancipation in their state, since it was unaffected by Lincoln's proclamation. Men of Doniphan's moderate ilk believed that if they did not do so on their terms, the Republicans would take steps to abolish it with provisions inimical to owners.[34]

To deal with this issue, Governor Gamble recalled the convention in which Doniphan had served in 1861. At this meeting on June 15, 1863, Doniphan voted for a bill freeing all slaves in the state beginning on July 4, 1870. The bill provided for slaves over the age of forty at the time of emancipation to remain for life with their former masters, those under twelve to remain in servitude until the age of twenty-three, and those between the ages of twelve and forty to serve until July 4, 1876. No blacks were to be sold after 1870, and they would not be considered taxable property. During the period before these former slaves left their masters, they were to be humanely cared for and to serve what amounted to an apprenticeship for freedom. This bill passed rather easily, and Doniphan considered it a great victory to have convinced proslavery Missourians to take this important step.[35]

Price, Hughes had been a trusted commander in Price's Confederate Army since the battles of Wilson's Creek and Lexington in the summer of 1861. See Monaghan, *Civil War on the Western Border*, 325–26; and Webb, *Battles and Biographies*, 86, 111–18, 282.

33. *Liberty Weekly Tribune*, April 11, 1862, April 18, 1862.

34. On Lincoln and the Emancipation Proclamation, see John Hope Franklin, *The Emancipation Proclamation*; Benjamin Quarles, *Lincoln and the Negro*; James M. McPherson, *The Struggle for Equality: Abolitionists and the Negro in the Civil War and Reconstruction*; and LaWanda Cox, *Lincoln and Black Freedom: A Study in Presidential Leadership*.

35. Bill R. Lee, "Missouri's Fight over Emancipation in 1863"; Walter B. Stevens, "Lincoln and Missouri"; Marvin R. Cain, "Edward Bates and Hamilton R. Gamble"; Parrish, *History of Missouri*, 3:87–97, 101–2, 116–17, 144–45.

Doniphan was not entirely in agreement with the provisions of this gradual emancipation plan. As he wrote to his friend and agent D. C. Allen, during the period of servitude prior to July 4, 1876, Doniphan had wanted no "restriction as to selling, Deportation or free ownership during the whole of that time." The committee preparing the plan, however, compromised in favor of the bill as passed. The convention had discussed dates for full emancipation ranging from "1867 to 1900 but that 1876 [date] had been the result of a compromise of these conflicting opinions." The convention, and especially its leadership, felt the pressure of radical Republicans breathing down their necks on this issue. Doniphan also allowed that the Republicans were "corrupt office seekers" who could not be trusted. He added, "you cannot count corrupt office seekers at any time very long in the same position—but in a revolution where motion is so greatly accelerated and where morals are lost sight of—they cannot be held longer than a man can hold a live eel by the tail." He also correctly gauged the nature of the war, commenting that slavery "cannot survive the continuance of such a war—carried on as this is & has been for the last year—for even two more years." In many respects, therefore, Doniphan's support of gradual emancipation represented a recognition that politics would force the end of the "peculiar institution" and that Missouri should take action on its own terms.[36]

In addition to understanding the political divisions over slavery in the state, Doniphan supported gradual emancipation for a practical reason. He wanted to remove the issue as a rationale for violence. Some antislavery zealots, apparently, were illegally aiding in the removal of slaves from their masters. He told Allen,

> we have authentic accounts written to the members here from various counties of the stealing of more than 1200 negroes since our session commenced—many of them have been mustered into the service—twenty five such soldiers went down on the same train with the Govr Saturday—I saw a letter from Henry County that a band of 25 negroes & some whites had come into that County & that probably they would get all of them in a week—no kind of opposition is offered to this by anyone civil or military—So you may see the negro is played out for all useful purposes—it only remains as an excuse to inaugurate murder—and theft—or rather

36. A. W. Doniphan to D. C. Allen, June 22, 1863, Doniphan Papers. DeWitt Clinton Allen, or Clint as Doniphan called him, served as Doniphan's agent in Clay County for more than twenty years after the outbreak of the Civil War. A native of the county, Allen graduated from William Jewell College and read law with Doniphan. When Doniphan went to Fort Leavenworth in the latter 1850s, Allen went with him and remained there to read law with Richard R. Rees. He returned to Missouri in 1860. Allen served as attorney for the Fifth Judicial Circuit for a time, but left office on December 17, 1861, rather than take the Union loyalty oath. He continued in private law practice thereafter ("DeWitt Clinton Allen," in Conard, ed., *Encyclopedia*, 1:23–24).

to continue them for in many localities they have been in full blast
for many months.

Doniphan closed his discussion of the convention's doings with a prophetic statement: "may the thunderbolt not descend in its fury upon all
the interests of Missouri is my prayer but not my hope."[37]

The nuances of Doniphan's support for gradual emancipation were
lost on some of his neighbors in Clay County. When he returned home,
having voted to end slavery, they criticized his position. In early July
1863 Doniphan spoke in Liberty where he gave his rationale for supporting gradual emancipation, noting that it was the least dangerous of the
possible answers to the question. He feared alternative plans, he said, especially those for immediate abolition proposed by Republicans. He then
discussed his desire to prevent civil war, and especially its debilitating
effects on his beloved Missouri. He had always stood up for compromise
and had urged everyone to avoid plunging the state into the maelstrom
of rebellion and desolation. Those of other persuasions, he advocated,
should leave Missouri and take up arms elsewhere rather than make the
state's green hills a battlefield. As a slaveholder himself, as well as a long-
standing proslavery advocate, Doniphan told the assembled multitude
that he still felt gradual emancipation the only answer to the crisis.[38]

At the same time that Doniphan legislated the end of slavery he also
took stock of the wider political scene in Missouri and expressed discom-
fort about how it shaped up. Hamilton Gamble was leaving the Missouri
governorship and a successor had to be found and put into office. The
right person, Doniphan concluded, "is far more important [than even the
slavery issue] as on that depends the restoration & preservation of law
and order." While he had disagreed with Gamble on many occasions,
he commented to D. C. Allen, "he has great influence at Washington &
when the convention & Legislature are not in session he is impressible
by good men & being naturally honest & conservative—he can be used
to influence [Missouri Republican leader Edward M.] Bates & Lincoln."
Willard Preble Hall, the heir apparent in 1863 and ultimate successor to
Gamble, did not comfort Doniphan in the slightest. He thought Hall "a
gambling politician" willing to do whatever it took to gain power. Even
so, Hall might be better than an alternative, especially a Republican. Such
a person might be "a tyrant elected by a corrupt faction—aggressive
& revolutionary would of course do much harm—and his reign would
be Robespirian." He noted that "in the avalanch of red republicanism
the whole people would be first overrun then demoralized, then finally

37. Doniphan to Allen, June 22, 1863, Doniphan Papers.
38. *Liberty Weekly Tribune,* July 10, 1863.

corrupted so that no negative roothless politician is the most debasing & demoralising of any functionary."[39]

Like in many regions of the South, the crucible of the war broke down the old party divisions in the state. Before 1861 Doniphan could not bring himself to support anyone identified with the Democrats, despite his respect for them personally and his acceptance of their political positions. Now all that was gone. Whigs and Democrats were swept before the tide of extremism. Thus old Whig Doniphan could willingly associate with old Democrats in a party committed to moderation. But neither Doniphan's actions nor those of his fellow Conservative Unionists could stem the tide of radical Republicanism. In 1864 radicals gained control of the state government and promptly voted for slavery's abolition in the state effective January 11, 1865. This preceded by only a month Congress's passage of the Thirteenth Amendment ending slavery nationwide. Consequently, Doniphan's moderate position fell to the resolute and hard-edged extremism of radicals.[40]

Even as these issues arose, Doniphan faced hardship in Liberty. Western Missouri was rife with contention between Confederate and Federal forces fighting it out in a brutal war. The regular forces of both sides created plenty of trouble, and battles between organized units throughout western Missouri during the first two years of the war were certainly desperate; however, members of guerrilla organizations on both sides caused even more trouble. The border ruffians of both sides, practiced in the art of terrorism from years of fighting over Kansas, produced a level of violence in western Missouri not present anywhere else in the nation.[41]

On the Union side, Charles Jennison's Jayhawkers, sometimes known as the Mound City Sharp's Rifles or the Seventh Kansas Cavalry, periodically swept into western Missouri from Kansas to loot, burn, murder, and sometimes even to engage Confederate forces. More brigands than authorized troops, Jennison's men attacked indiscriminately. In November 1861 Margaret Hays of Westport commented on one raid by the Jayhawkers:

> We have been overrun with Jayhawkers . . . and they have robbed us and harassed us, and our neighbors have suffered a great deal from them. Uncle Jimmie has lost upwards of ten thousand dollars worth; they came to his house one night and took eight negroes, a fine carriage, a two-horse wagon, some horses and mules, and robbed his house of all bed clothing and everything valuable. In a

---

39. Doniphan to Allen, June 22, 1863, Doniphan Papers.
40. *Liberty Weekly Tribune,* October 30, 1863; Parrish, *History of Missouri,* 3:116–30.
41. War in western Missouri has been documented in Goodrich, *Black Flag,* a popular account; more fully and with great insight in Michael Fellman, *Inside War: The Guerrilla Conflict in Missouri during the American Civil War;* and with a flare for both detail and drama in Richard S. Brownlee, *Gray Ghosts of the Confederacy: Guerrilla Warfare in the West, 1861–1865.*

few days they came to the same house, took about seventy head of sheep and 45 or 50 head of the finest stock there was in the county. In a few days after they went to another neighbor some two miles off, took the negroes, went to the beds and rolled them up saying they would take them to their wives. . . . I am looking every hour for everything I have to be taken, and my house destroyed by these Jayhawkers.[42]

By the fall of 1862 the situation was even more desperate. Margaret Hays complained to her mother that "Times here are very hard: robbing, murdering, burning and every other kind of measure on every side. Every man has to join the Federal Army or hide out in the country and have his property taken from him. And if they are not shot on the spot they are banished from this country."[43]

Confederate outriders were even more brutal than their Union counterparts. For example, William C. Quantrill led a fierce raid on the antislavery stronghold of Lawrence, Kansas, on August 21, 1863. Charging into town at daybreak, 450 riders dispersed into small groups to work from house to house in search of booty and men. Quantrill directed them to "Kill every male and burn every house." They followed his order with passionate zeal, killing 182 men and boys and burning 185 buildings. Slipping out of town just ahead of Union troops the irregulars rode like hell for the Missouri border where they dispersed to masquerade as peaceful Missourians who only wanted to remain neutral.[44]

At his home in Clay County, Doniphan expressed dismay at the brutality taking place on the western border. He and a lot of other people in the county only wanted to be left alone to pursue their lives, and they could not do so. As early as August 1861 one citizen wrote to the governor that "Horse stealing and house burning are the common occurrences that mark the way."[45] Daniel H. Moss wrote to Doniphan in October 1863 that "the entire military force in Clay and Platte was nothing more or less than an armed mob and a portion of them in full fellowship with the Kansas Redlegs."[46] Another resident wrote in 1864 that "this once beautiful and peaceable land is forsaken and desolated, ruined, and only fit for bats, owls, & cockralls to inhabit."[47]

42. Margaret J. Hays to Mother, November 12, 1861, typescript in "Extracts from War Times Letters," Albert N. Doerschuk Papers, Jackson County Historical Society, Independence, Mo. An excellent account of Jennison's campaigns is in Stephen Z. Starr, *Jennison's Jayhawkers: A Civil War Cavalry Regiment and Its Commander*.

43. Margaret J. Hays to Mother, November 24, 1862, Doerschuk Papers.

44. See Monaghan, *Civil War on the Western Border*, 274–89; Goodrich, *Black Flag*, 77–95; Brownlee, *Gray Ghosts of the Confederacy*, 110–57; and Albert Castel, *A Frontier State at War: Kansas, 1861–1865*, 124–41.

45. J. R. Carter to Governor Hamilton R. Gamble, August 29, 1861, Gamble Papers.

46. Daniel H. Moss to A. W. Doniphan, October 3, 1863, Gamble Papers.

47. J. Freeman to W. A. Brannock, May 30, 1864, W. A. Brannock Family Letters, Jackson County Historical Society.

Doniphan complained in 1864 that Missouri was an enormous battle-field where no one could carry on a normal life. He wrote to W. H. Jennings that it was

> in as great commotion as when you left—the guerrilla[s] generally have the country and the soldiers the towns—but every few days we hear of some town being taken by the *whackers,* and now we are all in the *qui vive* for [Confederate General] Marmaduke to make a raid from Arkansas into the central counties—I hope it may prove false as that and the consignment march of the army to oppose them would between them ruin the country effectually & cause hundreds of innocent women & children to be murdered.[48]

As this savage border war took place in western Missouri, it became increasingly difficult to carry on a peaceful existence. Doniphan did not want to be away from home for fear that raiders might arrive during his absence. As a strong Union man he felt harassment from proslavery Missouri ruffians as well as ostracism from some of his oldest friends. His law practice, accordingly, went to ruin. So too did his land, insurance, rail-road, and banking businesses. By January 1864 he was virtually destitute of cash: Although he still owned property, it was essentially worthless given the volatile situation on the western Missouri border.[49] Obviously, he had to do something to get himself and his wife out of the line of fire in the guerrilla war.

He decided to move across the state to St. Louis, a city relatively untouched by the fighting in the countryside. The new governor, Willard Preble Hall, gave him the excuse he needed in 1863 when he appointed Doniphan a special claims agent for victims of the war in the state.[50] He set up offices in downtown St. Louis, entering into a partnership with William S. Field, another displaced Unionist from Lafayette County. Doniphan had

48. A. W. Doniphan to W. H. Jennings, September 2, 1864, Civil War Papers, Missouri Historical Society.

49. *Liberty Weekly Tribune,* October 30, 1863; interview with Louise Darneal, August 1972, cited in Maynard, "Alexander William Doniphan, the Forgotten Man," 102. Some of Doniphan's Clay County property was sold for back taxes in January 1864 because he was unable to pay them (*Liberty Weekly Tribune,* January 29, 1864, February 19, 1864).

50. A. W. Doniphan to D. C. Allen, "Sketch of Life," 6, Doniphan Papers; "General Assembly, 23rd, 1864–1865, Senate Resolutions," January 1865, Collection #2154, fld. 12409, Missouri Fire Documents Collection. The report noted: "Resolved by the Senate—The House of Representatives concurring—That Alexander W. Doniphan the special agent appointed by the governor of the state under and by virtue of an act entitled an act to provide for the appointment of a special agent to forward and prosecute the claims of the widows and orphans of deceased soldiers, and for soldiers of Missouri disabled in the military service of the United States approved February 13, 1864, and he is hereby requested to make to this General Assembly his report of requirements by the 2d session of the above named act at his earliest convenience."

known Field for years, having served with him in the state legislature and practiced law at the same courts with, and sometimes against, him.[51]

Doniphan's appointment as claims agent was a part-time position helping victims of the fighting. Compensated by the state, the work involved pressing claims, bounties, and pensions for widows, orphans, and disabled soldiers. It also gave him an important boost in income as he tried to build a law practice in the city. The whirl of state claims kept him relatively busy for several months. Doniphan's letter to D. C. Allen demonstrates the nature of the work:

> Will you see Jimmy Burns as to Rebecca Jane Goodins pension—you say she is married—all right—it is a poor man that is not better than 8 dollars a month to a buxom young widow—but she is entitled to pension up to the date of her marriage—she must return her pension certificate with the papers—she is entitled probably to $200 or $250. If she has any children by Goodins I can have the pension turned over to it until it is 16 years old—there must be a guardian appointed & application by him—write me if there is a child & I will send you a form & directions make them pay out the money—I will send it to your care.
>
> Dont let the deputy clerk sign as deputy—Tom Murray always does. It is played out in the military. The child will draw from date of her marriage.[52]

The details of his work for the claims commission are not readily apparent, but this letter suggests that it involved processing paperwork for the state and acting as an advocate for those entitled to recompense.

He seemed frustrated with the slowness of this process. In December 1864 Doniphan wrote to D. C. Allen that although determined to be legitimate and deserving of payment, "the Govt does not have a dollar for months past. There are $14,000,000 of vouchers on the In & Crns, Depts. held in this City alone, about $7,000,000 each." Because the government was not paying them, many of those with outstanding claims were trading them like commodities on the open market. Doniphan wrote, "They are hawking on the streets at 15 per cent off & can not be sold at that—they will be paid—but where?" Doniphan knew it was no way to help widows,

51. "Civil War Claims Records Books," passim, Civil War Papers; *Liberty Weekly Tribune*, January 29, 1864, February 19, 1864, April 15, 1864, April 29, 1864, June 3, 1864; Williamson, "Colonel Alexander W. Doniphan," 184. A city directory for 1864 notes: "Doniphan & Field, Attorneys and Counselors at Law. Room 5, Kennett Building, south side Chestnut street bet. Third and Fourth. Government Claims Prosecuted, Bought and Sold." Doniphan and his wife boarded at several locations, all on Olive Street in downtown St. Louis, during their stay through 1876. See *Edwards' St. Louis Directory*, 1864 copy in Missouri Historical Society; and *Liberty Weekly Tribune*, April 15, 1864.

52. A. W. Doniphan to D. C. Allen, n.d., Doniphan Papers.

orphans, and disabled veterans, and has far as he knew, it spoke to the corruptness of the radicals.[53]

Perhaps in part because of this criticism, certainly because of his moderateness and anti-Republican stance, when the new Missouri governor, Republican Thomas C. Fletcher, was elected in the fall of 1864, he removed Doniphan as state claims agent. In Doniphan's place Fletcher appointed stalwart abolitionist George Hillgaertner as the new claims agent. Doniphan left office on January 25, 1865, turning over his clients to Hillgaertner along with the offer to assist if any questions arose about the status of outstanding actions. This assistance seemed necessary, for Doniphan continued to press claims for clients accepted before his resignation. As late as August 1866 he still had underway several claims for pensions from widows and orphans.[54]

Doniphan was also successful in building some semblance of a law practice in St. Louis, and found himself in moderate demand from businessmen with pro-southern leanings. He wrote to W. H. Jennings in the fall of 1864 that "Business keeps us pretty fair for summer and especially tobacco is still active . . ."[55] By 1866 he was pleading again before the Missouri Supreme Court. For instance, in the October 1866 term he appeared for the plaintiffs in two indemnity suits against the Union Pacific Railroad. He lost those cases, but was back before the Supreme Court in the March 1867 term to represent individual citizens against the North Missouri Railroad. Legal scholar Hugh P. Williamson concluded that because of his location in the antislavery unionist stronghold of St. Louis, his pro-southern sympathies, his now-discredited moderation, the strangers he was among, and his struggling law practice, "these years in St. Louis must have been hard and lonely ones for Doniphan." Although busy throughout this period, he did not make a good living and all of the moderate and patriotic values he had engendered seemed to have gone by the wayside.[56] He had to have been disheartened.

The experience of war in Missouri did something to Doniphan that more than twenty-five years of political involvement had not accomplished. It made him into a Democrat. By the summer of 1864 he began to make noises about the upcoming presidential election and the opportunity to throw Republicans out of office. When the peace advocates within the Democratic Party captured the convention and nominated Union general

53. A. W. Doniphan to D. C. Allen, December 14, 1864, Doniphan Papers.

54. "Civil War Claims Record Books," Civil War Papers. Doniphan and Field to D. C. Allen, June 6, 1866, June 29, 1866, July 17, 1866; A. W. Doniphan to D. C. Allen, March 2, 1865, November 3, 1865, June 14, 1866, August 9, 1866, all in Doniphan Papers.

55. Doniphan to Jennings, September 2, 1864, Civil War Papers; *Missouri Reporter* (1864–1866), 39:115, 40:304, 41:126.

56. A. W. Doniphan to D. C. Allen, January 4 [no year]; A. W. Doniphan to D. C. Allen, December 14, 1864, December 29, 1864, March 2, 1865, all in Doniphan Papers.

George B. McClellan for the presidency in a platform calling for the end of the war, Doniphan got interested. As he wrote:

> not that I often engage in politics or feel much interest in political conventions: never haveing been a member of one—but this is a crisis of more than ordinary interest and so much of the future wellfare of the Country and the world depended upon the harmony and success of its proceedings that even I could not resist its influence, and arouse myself somewhat from daily routine of business. The nomination of Genl McClellan does not give entire satisfaction to the peace Democrats—or men of Southern sympathies—but all concur that he was the most judicious choice all things considered—that he was almost certain to carry the large free states—and that the border States would swallow him on the principle that children swallow nauseating medicines—that it must be done or they die—it is McClellan or death in the opinion of border state democrats.[57]

In the midst of the presidential campaign Doniphan witnessed the St. Louis draft riots, and noted "how easily the interests of Lincoln & McClellan could be lost sight when a few days ago civil war seemed to be impending between their respective partrizans [sic]."[58]

Of course, McClellan did not defeat Abraham Lincoln for the presidency. Lincoln ensured that the members of the Union army voted in the election, and that margin carried him to victory. By the spring of 1865 Republicanism was triumphant throughout the United States, if not at the ballot box then through the force of arms and the resultant conquest of the Confederate States of America. For Doniphan the end of the war passed without specific reference, but he undoubtedly felt both relief and disgust with the conflict. Relieved that it was finally over, Doniphan was also disgusted that it had come and bitter over what it had portended. He had tried mightily to effect compromise and preserve the peace but had failed, his efforts to find a peaceful solution played out ad infinitum during the brutal, bloody conflict on the border.

With the war ended, Doniphan sought to rebuild his life, but it would not be easy. He had much to overcome, and his increasing bitterness and hard-bitten cynicism about government made it more difficult for him to function. His belief in the positive liberal state of the Whigs in the 1840s seemed to be replaced in the 1860s with a fear of a centralized government that tyrannized a population.[59]

57. Doniphan to Jennings, September 2, 1864, Civil War Papers.
58. A. W. Doniphan to D. C. Allen, September 20, 1864, Doniphan Papers.
59. A. W. Doniphan and D. C. Allen to the Citizens of Clay County, February 3, 1865, Doniphan Papers. On the absentee balloting of the troops, see T. Harry Williams, "Voters in Blue: The Citizen Soldiers of the Civil War."

13

Businessman and "Bourbon"

THE CIVIL WAR changed everything. It altered social, political, economic, and race relations throughout the United States. Alexander William Doniphan did not think those changes for the better. He believed that Missouri had suffered enormously because of the havoc of war. Not only had a lot of good people suffered and died, but those who remained had to remake their place in a world foreign from what they had known before. Starting over presented Doniphan with unique challenges after the four years of savage fury.[1]

Doniphan was more than fifty-five years old by the time the Civil War ended in the spring of 1865. Set in his whiggish ways, he seemingly became more conservative with every passing year. He knew that the war had destroyed the Missouri he had loved, causing the deaths of thousands of its inhabitants and setting slave-owning society at odds with postwar reality. Chagrined and bitter at the new reality, Doniphan believed deep in his bones that the Republicans had been responsible for all of those catastrophic changes. It had been their extremism that had forced ruin upon the nation, on Missouri, and on Doniphan. As he wrote to his nephew and close confidant, John Doniphan, "I have had enough to try the patience of a better man than I am since the war commenced."[2]

---

1. On Reconstruction in the South, see Eric Foner, *Reconstruction: America's Unfinished Revolution, 1863–1877*. On the experience of Missouri, see Fred DeArmond, "Reconstruction in Missouri"; William E. Parrish, *Missouri under Radical Rule, 1865–1870*; Thomas S. Barclay, *The Liberal Republican Movement in Missouri, 1865–1871*; and Parrish, *History of Missouri*, 3:116–69. A comparison of Missouri with other border states can be found in Richard O. Curry, ed., *Radicalism, Racism, and Party Realignment: The Border States during Reconstruction*.

2. A. W. Doniphan to John Doniphan, February 18, 1873, Doniphan Collection.

While the human suffering of war had not directly affected Doniphan, in retrospect he might have more easily accepted that than constant humiliations associated with survival in a new regime where his old ideas and accomplishments had little weight. The anger Doniphan felt at the sectional crisis did not abate the rest of his life. He reflected a bleak perspective on the Civil War and Reconstruction for D. C. Allen in 1874: "The past 14 years has been an *episode* in the history of our country dark & saddening, ruins every where . . . the times have changed & with them all our political surroundings. Thus nothing was requisite to ensure defeat or victory but a few magic Shib[b]oleths, *rebellion, loyalty, negro equality*—when thousands of our best citizens were imprisoned and hundreds shot for that mythical & undefinable something called Southern Sympathy." Doniphan always condemned the Republican radicals for their vindictiveness, and never forgave them for fomenting war with their extremist positions in the antebellum period.[3]

During the Reconstruction era Doniphan expressed skepticism and demoralization at virtually every turn. He believed the Republicans were involved in a bald-faced attempt to gather power to themselves in Missouri and to punish those who might oppose them for crimes both real and imagined. This came out clearly in a speech he gave in Liberty, while attending the April 1866 term of the Clay County Circuit Court. After the judicial proceedings had closed for the day, a Democratic Party meeting began in the courtroom without so much as a supper break. Doniphan took to the stump to reemphasize the only remaining points of his increasingly cynical but still persistent whiggery: patriotism to the Federal union and moderation and charity toward the fellow citizens of the nation who had rebelled against the national government.[4]

Doniphan eloquently defended President Andrew Johnson, the vice president who had succeeded Abraham Lincoln after his assassination in April 1865. While Tennessean Johnson had affiliated with the Republican Party during the Civil War, he had been an antebellum Democrat whose perspectives on secession, the Union, and the host of other issues swirling around the conflict closely allied with those of Doniphan. As a senator from Tennessee on December 18–19, 1860, Johnson had gained fame and great respect from such men as Doniphan for his denial of secession's constitutionality at the same time that he defended southerners' rights. Johnson's sympathies assured that he ran afoul of the radical wing of the Republican Party, who thought of southerners as rebels deserving punishment for secession. In February and March 1866, just before Doniphan gave his defense of Johnson, the president had vetoed the Freedmen's

3. A. W. Doniphan to D. C. Allen, November 10, 1874, Doniphan Papers.
4. *Liberty Weekly Tribune,* April 27, 1866.

Bureau Bill and the Civil Rights Act, formally breaking any remaining ties with Republican radicals and starting a process that eventually led to his impeachment and near removal from office in 1867.[5]

Doniphan's impassioned defense of Johnson and his policies thrilled the packed courtroom. The speech of his nephew John Doniphan, who also defended moderate political policies concerning Reconstruction, did much the same. The Doniphans' speeches resonated so fully in Clay County that the night after the rally the Liberty Cornet Band serenaded them at their hotel in the town.[6]

Doniphan's appearance at a Democratic Party gathering signaled his acceptance of new political realities. Like a lot of fellow old Whigs, Doniphan united with the Democracy as a means of continuing to influence public policy along lines more moderate than that of the Republicans. It was, in essence, the only politically viable place for him to go. Collectively, such men as Doniphan affected the Democratic Party toward a course that moderated the radicalism of the Republicans. For their efforts, they were labeled "Bourbons" by their opponents. This name invoked an image of the ruling family of France at the time of the French Revolution—arch-conservative, rigid, and elitist. In reality, the Bourbon Democrats incorporated many of the ideals of whiggery into their attitudes with their emphasis on industrialism, business, and economic growth. As one historian described Bourbons:

> Their function was to prevent control of the government by farmers, wage earners and inefficient, irresponsible, corrupt officeholders. The Bourbons believed governmental interference with the natural laws of economics imposed a check on progress and thus government regulation and government aid should be limited to the barest necessity. Because taxation was a drag on the economy, it was to be kept to a minimum. Hence the managers of the public purse must be efficient, economical, honest; opposed to spending money for paternalism and special privilege.

While Bourbons did not seek a wholesale retreat from the radical Republican agenda, they used every possible avenue to moderate social revolution. Most important, they preached the blessings of the modern

---

5. The Andrew Johnson presidency, and the differences over how to relate to the states of the former Confederacy, has engendered significant historical study. Some of the key works on the subject, although they do not agree on interpretation, include James E. Sefton, *Andrew Johnson and the Uses of Constitutional Power;* Michael Les Benedict, *The Impeachment and Trial of Andrew Johnson;* David Warren Brown, *Andrew Johnson and the Negro;* Albert Castel, *The Presidency of Andrew Johnson;* Eric McKitrick, *Andrew Johnson and Reconstruction;* and Hans L. Trefousse, *Impeachment of a President: Andrew Johnson, the Blacks, and Reconstruction.*

6. *Liberty Weekly Tribune,* April 27, 1866.

industrial state and advocated the expansion of manufacturing, railroading, and other industrial activities.[7]

This perspective squared well with Doniphan's new cynical perspective on government. Instead of the "positive liberal state" of the Whigs, embracing Federal action to bring about a better society and nation, Doniphan had seen what the full weight of Federal power could accomplish when marshaled for the accomplishment of a specific political and social agenda—the Republican efforts then underway—and it terrified him. Earlier, Doniphan had viewed the power of the national government as a tool to effect positive change; after the Civil War he perceived it as something deserving circumscription because of the horrors it had inflicted on the people of Missouri. Doniphan summarized his perspective in an 1872 letter to his nephew; "I would not give one cent for the Gov't."[8] His position did not improve in the five years that followed: "I always entertained an exalted opinion of the purity of judges of our highest courts,—I have known for many years that the other two departments were steeped in the seething cauldrons of political corruption, but I had clung to the judiciary with great tenacity as the best hope of the republic; but that delusion had passed—the government is as rotten as a pear."[9]

Doniphan spoke publicly to these concerns in June 1867 when the Missouri radical Republicans tried to impeach Judge Walter King, in charge of the Fifth Judicial Circuit in western Missouri. King had decided neither to take an "iron-clad" loyalty oath required in a new 1865 state constitution ramrodded by the Republicans nor to resign his post. The trial took place before a special session of the state senate, and while conviction was virtually assured, the proceedings took nearly a month and summoned fierce rhetoric on all sides. Doniphan traveled to Jefferson City to defend King, delivering the finest speech of his career, at least in the view of the editor of the *Liberty Weekly Tribune*.

In it he defended King personally, but also took the opportunity to lecture the Republicans sitting in judgment on the excesses and abuses arising from "ruthless" pursuit of political objectives. He declared that in a free society such as the United States difference of opinion not only inevitably flowed from the society at large but must be stimulated as a positive good. "It is as impossible for all men to think alike, as it is for all men to look alike, and it is very wisely so," he said. "There are thousands of different positions to be filled in this world, and it requires men of different tastes to fill them. It would not do for all men to turn their

7. Horace Samuel Merrill, *Bourbon Leader: Grover Cleveland and the Democratic Party,* 44–45. See C. Vann Woodward, *Origins of the New South, 1877–1913;* and T. Harry Williams, *Romance and Realism in Southern Politics,* 17–43.

8. A. W. Doniphan to John Doniphan, May 24, 1872, Doniphan Collection.

9. A. W. Doniphan to Emma Doniphan, February 13, 1877, Doniphan Collection.

attention to agriculture, nor to any other one particular avocation. Nature has provided us with different tastes and inclinations that we supply each others wants." Individuals of integrity and honesty and reverence for the Constitution can differ over important issues, Doniphan avowed. That does not, and should not, make them enemies to be vanquished but rather opponents who talk and work together to achieve decisions that represent popular consensus and justice for all.

Doniphan then scolded the Republicans for breaking down the process of thesis/antithesis/synthesis. Doniphan nagged, "Whenever the Legislative department, holds the rod of party terror, and the Judiciary truckles willingly to it, we are in a fair way to tyranny and oppression," adding, "whenever the Legislative branch absorbs the Judiciary, then farewell justice, farewell Republican liberty." What the Republican radicals proposed, he explained, subsumed the courts under the thumb of the legislature and demolished the cherished checks and balances that assured liberty. Doniphan concluded, "I tell you here, that if I for one moment thought the Judge would condescend to enter into any compact with lawyers outside of his Court, I would not stand here to defend him, and would gladly see you hurl him from his judicial position." But such was not the case, and the old Whig ended his defense by demanding King's acquittal.[10]

When the conviction and removal from office of Walter King came down later in the month, it crystallized Doniphan's skepticism about the unbridled power of the Republican radicals. Doniphan's political activities for the rest of the decade aimed at replacing the radicals with Democrats. To accomplish this, after having moved to Richmond from St. Louis, in August 1868 he presided over the Democratic convention for the Sixth Congressional District when it met in Lexington, Missouri. It endorsed the Democratic platform, including the goals of restoring the former Confederate states to full rights in the Union, amnesty for all past political offenses associated with the Civil War, and "expulsion of corrupt men from office, the abrogation of useless offices, the restoration of rightful authority to and independence of the executive and judicial departments of government." In an articulate speech Doniphan declared that their cause required unity, for "their free institutions were in danger, and many shed tears at the picture he drew so accurately of the times."[11]

While the election of 1868 went firmly in favor of the Republicans, the Democrats made a strong showing and two years later ousted the radicals from most of the state's offices. It came none too soon for Doniphan. He believed that the Republicans had succeeded only in changing the South from the "most prosperous portion of the union," into "a waste, destitute

10. *Liberty Weekly Tribune,* June 14, 1867.
11. *The Conservator,* August 22, 1868; Parrish, *History of Missouri,* 3:233.

of commerce, agriculture or money—insulted and down-trodden by military tyrants & federal bayonets."[12]

Even in a victory absolutely necessary for his state's welfare, Democrats grated on Doniphan's still whiggish sensibilities. He wrote to his nephew John Doniphan in 1872 about the "old wooden-headed Democrats who think they are as strong as when old Jackson was a candidate. It is annoying to hear such asses—such words as 'the time-honored usages of the Democratic Party—the principles of the old Democracy' are a stench in my nostrils. I never wish to hear them again."[13] Democratic victories were mere shadows for Doniphan of what political campaigns had been before. By this time his vision of the Democratic governmental agenda, in contrast to the positive role government could formerly have played, was to make it transparent in the lives of citizens. Perhaps it was appropriate that Doniphan, though still interested in political developments both within the state and at the national level, increasingly found himself on the sidelines of political campaigns, venting about the elections to his relatives and friends but not significant in shaping their outcomes.[14]

The last great political hurrah for Doniphan came when he chaired the Missouri delegation to the Democratic National Convention in St. Louis in 1876. Convening on June 27, the meeting eventually nominated Samuel J. Tilden for the presidency, a decision that Doniphan endorsed because Tilden had long been identified with efforts in New York State to clean up the corruption of the Tammany Ring. Doniphan's participation in the convention proved more ceremonial than representative of his actual place in the political process. A long-respected moderate, a war hero, a native son, he appropriately attended the convention when held in his home state. He even received favorite-son status for the presidency early in the balloting. But Doniphan was at best a bit player in the convention—his increasing sourness about the political process perhaps making him a less-than-useful political ally—and he returned quietly to his home afterward to prepare for a trip to the Rocky Mountains where he would sit out the election.[15]

12. A. W. Doniphan to D. C. Allen, November 10, 1874, Doniphan Papers.
13. Doniphan to John Doniphan, May 24, 1872, Doniphan Collection.
14. See the letters of Doniphan reproduced in McGroarty, ed., "Letters from Alexander W. Doniphan," 26–39; and Culmer, "Snapshot of Alexander W. Doniphan," 25–32. See also A. W. Doniphan to John Doniphan, August 23, 1872; A. W. Doniphan to Emma Doniphan, May 3, 1876, September 12, 1876, all in Doniphan Collection; A. W. Doniphan to D. C. Allen, April 9, 1874, April 21, 1874, August 21, 1874, October 27, 1874, November 10, 1874, December 16, 1874, May 4, 1875, May 29, 1882, August 25, 1883, August 30, 1883, September 15, 1883; A. W. Doniphan to Henry C. Routt and D. C. Allen, April 9, 1874, all in Doniphan Papers; and "For the Missouri Republican—Genl. Alexander Doniphan," March 3, 1879, Darby Family Papers, Missouri Historical Society. Finally, see Conservator, November 14, 1879, May 28, 1880, October 17, 1884, October 31, 1884.
15. Conservator, June 2, 1876, June 9, 1876, June 16, 1876, July 7, 1876, August 11, 1876; A. W. Doniphan to Emma Doniphan, September 12, 1876, Doniphan Collection.

If Doniphan's general skepticism about the role of state and Federal institutions in effecting positive change emerged from the war years, he also resented what the war had done to his life personally. Because of the border warfare he had lost thousands of dollars in property which took him years to recover. In the antebellum era he had invested heavily in real estate and business enterprises that he was sure would make him financially secure in the long term. All of these made him cash-poor in the short term, but whatever appreciation they might have enjoyed fell to the disjointedness and rancor of the war years. With the coming of war land in western Missouri, where considerable guerrilla fighting took place, was suddenly worth almost nothing. Who would want it with the disruption of the countryside? It was not even good for farming, for the guerrillas destroyed or took the crops. Railroads, banks, insurance companies, and the like also suffered from the desolation and disruption of the war. In addition, early in the war Doniphan readily helped old friends who needed money, and gave several loans that he could not collect later when he needed cash himself. Accordingly, Doniphan's St. Louis years became a desperate attempt to maintain solvency and to pay debts owed others. Ultimately unable to do so, Doniphan went hat in hand to Cyrus Brashear to borrow cash to keep his other creditors at bay. He secured a note for four hundred dollars from Brashear but had to mortgage some of his Clay County property to do so. By late December 1864, Doniphan had to ask his business agent and friend in Liberty, D. C. Allen, to sell the mortgaged property to pay off Brashear, even "if it only sells for one fourth."[16]

This transaction represented only the beginning of a financial avalanche that nearly buried Doniphan between 1864 and 1867. The government of Clay County seized some of his local property and sold it for back taxes when he could not meet the payments.[17] In the spring of 1865 he tried to sell a large tract of land in war-ravaged western Missouri as a means of paying off his debts. He received an offer of nine thousand dollars for the property, much less than it had been worth in the antebellum era, but he could not sell because he owned it in partnership. Unfortunately, his partner had disappeared and he could only sell after foreclosure on the partnership. He asked Allen to "file the petition[.] I will appear & answer— and let judgment go on all debts. You can swear to the petition—perhaps it would be as well to issue a writ & let there be contest—bring it on the copy it will be good[,] as Ned will bring up & file the original at court[.] We will both be there. I must get out of debt. . . . And will pay all as soon as I can sell & that will be immediately after court." By April Doniphan

16. A. W. Doniphan to D. C. Allen, December 29, 1864, Doniphan Papers.
17. *Liberty Weekly Tribune,* January 29, 1864, February 19, 1864, September 15, 1865, January 26, 1866.

had still been unable to make the sale, or to collect on any debts that he held.[18]

Doniphan summarized his wretched financial situation in a letter to D. C. Allen on November 3, 1865.

> I have been so embarrassed with old debts that I often anticipate my income to pay them to avoid the notification of continued duns. I have paid off my debts as rapidly as I could and my friends from Liberty & other places seeing my condition & constant labor were ashamed to present their claims in person—but left them with shoemakers, grocery keepers & gamblers to be presented as soon as they got out of town. I thank God thus far I have met them all—although I have been unable to collect one Dollar of all my old debts, or sell one acre of land.[19]

In the spring of 1867 this situation began to turn around when he received a fee that had been due him since 1850. These had been tied up to secure a debt of D. I. Adkins, but finally Adkins had been able to pay. This freed his securities so Doniphan asked Allen to use the money to pay off Brashear and other creditors in the county. His situation grew more advantageous the next year when he sold a significant parcel of land he owned near Council Bluffs, Iowa. As the local newspaper reported, "One piece of land adjoining the city, which he vainly tried to sell for less than $2,000 some time since; he is now offered $50,000 for in cash. 'Fortune favors the brave.'" Doniphan knew that bravery had not brought this fortuitous conclusion, the economy of the western border had started rebounding from the desolation of the war and in hanging on—even if by his fingernails and not declaring bankruptcy and losing everything—he had positioned himself to recover as well.[20]

Never happy in St. Louis, always longing to return to western Missouri, Doniphan took the opportunity afforded by his financial recovery to relocate across the state. He did not return to Liberty, however. In February 1868 Doniphan moved to Richmond, Ray County, Missouri, about fifty miles east of Liberty but still near the Missouri River. It would be Doniphan's home for the rest of his life. He and his wife purchased a home near the center of town on what is now South Camden Avenue. Although modest on the outside, the local residents remembered it as well furnished with fine mahogany furniture, elegant and comfortable.[21]

18. A. W. Doniphan to D. C. Allen, March 2, 1865, Doniphan Papers; *Liberty Weekly Tribune,* June 28, 1865.

19. A. W. Doniphan to D. C. Allen, November 3, 1865, Doniphan Papers.

20. *Liberty Weekly Tribune,* April 2, 1867; *Council Bluffs Nonpareil,* quoted in *Liberty Weekly Tribune,* June 19, 1868.

21. Interview with Louise Darneal, Richmond, Mo., August 1972, niece twice removed of Doniphan, cited in Maynard, "Alexander William Doniphan, the Forgotten Man," 107; Williamson, "Colonel Alexander W. Doniphan," 184.

In Richmond Doniphan opened a law practice, as he had done for more than thirty years, and began to rebuild his career. A local advertisement read: "A. W. Doniphan (late of St. Louis), C.[hristopher] T. Garner, Attorneys at Law, Will practice in the courts of the 5th Judicial Circuit & the Courts of Lafayette and Caldwell Counties, Collections and general agency business."[22] Garner was a distant cousin of Doniphan's wife so the relationship was a natural one.

Doniphan caught the essence of his practice with Garner in an 1871 memorandum to business associate and friend D. C. Allen:

> I wrote you a letter some weeks ago about having an Execution issue on the case of John Crowley vs Fuller & Majors—but not having heard from you I fear you never received it.
>
> Fuller we think is worth nothing[,] his land being all covered with mortgages Majors sold to John Linn after our judgment—we wish his land levied on & Linn garnished for he still owes him— my former letter was full & hoping you received it I will not report myself.[23]

The two worked together until 1875, when they dissolved the partnership so that Garner could enter practice with his son James. Not long thereafter Doniphan retired from the practice of law; he had pretty much completed his legal career by the time the Missouri Supreme Court decided on several cases he presented at its May 1876 term. By that time he was nearly sixty-eight years old and declining in health. Even though he did not practice law thereafter, Doniphan consulted with former colleagues and offered advice to young hopefuls until the mid-1880s.[24]

While practicing law, Doniphan also quickly expanded his business dealings to include banking, a pre-war activity that had intrigued him. Doniphan refused to allow himself and his family to come so close to financial ruin again. He would make a lot of money during the rest of his life, and he would enjoy a comfortable life. To this end, he helped to charter and operate the Ray County Savings Bank, formed in 1869 with T. D. Woodson as vice president and Doniphan as president. A notice in the local newspaper indicated that the new "Bank is now prepared to do a general banking business and will buy and sell Eastern and St. Louis exchange, gold, silver, uncurrent money, Government securities, &c. Loans negotiated, collections made in favorable terms and deposits received."[25]

22. *Conservator,* February 3, 1868.

23. A. W. Doniphan to D. C. Allen, June 20, 1871, Doniphan Papers.

24. *History of Ray County, Missouri,* 524, 569; *Missouri Reporter,* 62 (1871): 565; A. W. Doniphan to Gov. C. H. Hardin, April 12, 1875, October 3, 1875, "Governor, Hardin, Charles H. Correspondence: Patronage, Coal Oil Inspectors," Missouri Fire Documents Collection; W. B. Napton to W. E. Connelley, October 14, 1907, Napton Letters.

25. *Conservator,* August 7, 1869. On the banking system, see Timothy W. Hubbard and Lewis E. Davids, *Banking in Mid-America: A History of Missouri's Banks,* 108–24.

Since Richmond, a town of about one thousand residents, had only one small bank in 1868, another seemed a reasonable venture. When chartered its capitalization stood at a hundred thousand dollars, and its only branch operated during regular business hours at the corner of College and Main Streets in Richmond. Although not a full-time job, Doniphan put considerable effort into building up the investments of the bank and presiding over its expansionistic financial dealings. Indeed, he and Garner's law office occupied the rooms on the second floor above the bank and Doniphan was in and out of the business on virtually a daily basis for many years. However, to keep it on a firm financial footing— something that required long hours of work that the increasingly elderly Doniphan could not sustain—he stepped down as president in early 1880. T. C. Woodson replaced Doniphan as president and the old president took a seat on the bank's board of directors.[26]

Doniphan's retirement from most activity in the 1870s came because he increasingly felt his age (he turned seventy in 1878) but also in response to intense emotional upset. Early in May 1873 he attended a session of the Missouri Supreme Court and then met his wife, Jane, for an extended trip to New York City. Never fully healthy, she had been ill for some time and Doniphan believed that a visit to two of her sisters in the city might be good for her. The scheme worked. Though they had planned to return to Missouri in mid-June 1873, Jane was having such a fine time that she decided to stay with her sisters a while longer. Accordingly, Doniphan boarded the train alone for the lengthy trip back to Richmond. He resumed his business and legal activities, and took time out on the Fourth of July to participate in a reunion of Mexican War veterans. Shock overcame him only two weeks later, however, when he received a telegram from his relatives in New York City that his wife had suddenly taken a turn for the worse and was gravely ill. Doniphan prepared to return East, but before he could depart on July 19 he received a second telegram that Jane had died. The physicians pronounced the official cause of death as a hemorrhaging of the lungs. Heart-stricken, Doniphan had his wife's body returned to Missouri and buried in Liberty. They had been married for more than thirty-five years; also, she was much younger than he, and her passing made Doniphan feel his mortality all the more.[27]

In 1875 Doniphan opened a remarkable correspondence with a second cousin, Emma Doniphan, of Washington, D.C., wherein he frankly wrote of his feelings for his departed wife. In his first letter Doniphan told her that "I was once blessed with a lovely wife," but that it "pained" to discuss

26. *Conservator,* January 30, 1880, May 7, 1880; A. W. Doniphan to Emma Doniphan, May 6, 1878, Doniphan Collection; *History of Ray County,* 495.

27. *Conservator,* May 7, 1873, May 24, 1873, July 12, 1873, July 26, 1873; *Columbia Statesman,* August 1, 1873.

"my heart-rending loss." He also described her demise: "But death spares neither the gentle and lovely any more than the less lovely; three years ago my wife died of heart disease—suddenly; she was on her feet talking to her sister when she ceased to breathe; she was talking and died with a smile on her face."[28] "My own wife was such a gentle loving woman," he wrote later, "yet with an intellect a man of culture might have envied; the loss is the misery of my life. I trace much of my suffering although physical to suffering—the agony of the heart."[29]

Perhaps his sorrow over Jane's loss affected his physical well-being, for within weeks Doniphan's health began to fail and he never really recovered. Bronchitis kept him bedridden, or at least housebound, most of the time. The winter of 1873–1874 passed amid equal parts illness and boredom. He told two of his correspondents, "My health is simply such as to wholly preclude the idea of any business for a time[,] perhaps forever— that last most probably." He added, "I cannot live long unless I can find in some other climate a rejuvenating power to at least *patch* me up—this is all I anticipate at the best."[30] He wrote later in the year, "My health is all I care for—dying is something of course but not so much compared to the suffering of a sick bed—and my spells are so long & suffering so intense." So persistent did the bronchitis and subsequent pain and suffering become, that Doniphan took to the use of quinine for the rest of his life.[31]

Because of these developments, Doniphan saw no reason, and probably had little desire, to continue living at his home in Richmond. In the fall of 1873 he moved to a boarding house located one block from his bank. Proprietor William B. Huggins ran what he considered the finest boarding house in the county, advertising that it had the "best sample rooms on the road for only two dollars per day."[32] It was a difficult adjustment. "After living at my own home more than thirty years, having every comfort and delicate attention," he wrote to a cousin, "I am now boarding at a Hotel with no one of my family in the county. It is a great change but far better than to live in the family of another. You can make a hotel a sort of home by using money and being quiet and conciliatory—and the family are old acquaintances and very kind to me." Some of his wife's relatives had asked Doniphan to live with them but he refused, saying he did not want to be

28. A. W. Doniphan to Emma Doniphan, [no month and day] 1875, Doniphan Papers.
29. Ibid., May 6, 1878.
30. A. W. Doniphan to Henry L. Routt and D. C. Allen, April 9, 1874, Doniphan Papers. See also A. W. Doniphan to D. C. Allen, April 21, 1874, Doniphan Papers; and *Conservator*, April 4, 1874, April 25, 1874.
31. A. W. Doniphan to D. C. Allen, August 21, 1874, Doniphan Papers; A. W. Doniphan to Emma Doniphan, February 13, 1877, February 22, 1878; A. W. Doniphan to Sister Caroline, August 3, 1878, all in Doniphan Collection.
32. *Missouri State Gazetteer & Business Directory*, 547.

Alexander William Doniphan as an old man in Richmond, Missouri. Photo accession no. 009110, courtesy of the State Historical Society of Missouri, Columbia.

an imposition on anyone.[33] As he told his sister Caroline in a statement that spoke volumes about Doniphan, "a hotel & a negro is best for me when sick—I can order what I please and pay for all extra trouble."[34] The boarding house proprietor and his wife treated Doniphan well, and he rewarded them handsomely by paying admirably and by leaving Mrs. Huggins five hundred dollars in his will in "gratitude for her uniform friendship in sickness and in health."[35]

Also because of his persistent sickness, Doniphan began to travel in search of a climate and lifestyle that would improve his health. In 1873 he had suggested to his nephew that the arid, elevated climate of the Rocky Mountains might be just the ticket in curing one of their friends, and the next summer Doniphan took his own advice. Accordingly, in early May 1874 a large number of friends accompanied Doniphan to the local train station for a farewell that would see him to Denver and the health spas of the Rocky Mountains. When he returned to Missouri in the fall of the year Doniphan's health had improved somewhat, but the journeys to Colorado became something of an annual pilgrimage thereafter.[36]

These were generally pleasant and relaxing trips to the West, offering an opportunity to see anew country visited during the Mexican War and to renew acquaintances with old friends and colleagues and sometimes rivals. Doniphan had recovered financially from his Civil War difficulties, and he could spend and enjoy as he saw fit. And he saw fit to do so in elegant style, staying in high-class hotels, traveling first class in sleeping cars on trains, enjoying luxury, and perhaps spending to extravagance. His manner might have put some of the locals aback, but he apparently enjoyed the impression that he made on those he met. In 1874, for instance, he traveled through the passes of the mountains from Denver into the valley of the Great Salt Lake. There he renewed acquaintances with Mormon leaders known forty years earlier, and received a hero's welcome for his stand in 1838 not to execute Joseph Smith.[37]

Two years later, just after the Democratic National Convention in St. Louis, Doniphan took a summer trip to his Mexican War stomping grounds. Leaving in the middle of July, he wrote to a cousin of the trip and the recollections it summoned and the sorrows it invoked:

> I desired to travel over the route of my march in 1846—for four hundred miles they are almost identical—the railroad crossing the old trail many times—and although the progressing column

33. A. W. Doniphan to Emma Doniphan, [no month and day] 1875.
34. A. W. Doniphan to Sister Caroline, August 3, 1878, Doniphan Collection.
35. "Will of A. W. Doniphan," 79, Ray County Courthouse, Richmond, Mo.
36. A. W. Doniphan to John Doniphan, February 18, 1873; A. W. Doniphan to Emma Doniphan, September 17, 1877, both in Doniphan Collection; *Conservator*, May 9, 1874.
37. *History of Caldwell and Livingston Counties*, 137.

of civilization has changed the physique of the country greatly, towns, villages and cities having taken the place of the wigwam, yet the highlands and water courses are much unchanged and easily recognizable. Each trip was in July, thirty years apart and at one point—Bents Old Fort just thirty years to a day, there is only one marked difference, then we wended our slow march on horseback at twenty miles per day, encumbered by several hundred waggons, now in a palace sleeping car, gliding over the smoothest grade on the Continent at twenty miles per hour at least; . . . I was then young, hopeful and ambitious—my position novel and exciting—everything was before me—great responsibility, a wide field of notoriety if successful—to say nothing of fame. All these I fully realized—I had the ambition of most young men, had children to inherit my fortunes, great and small—now Alas? I am only seeking an asylum.[38]

Doniphan stayed in the Rockies for seven weeks in 1876, enjoying the health resorts, climate, and sites, and followed up thereafter with more trips.[39]

Doniphan spent the rest of his life enjoying himself as best he could with his increasingly suspicious perspective on politics and his flagging health. At his best, he could be both charming and reflective. On some days, however, he could be both obnoxious and domineering. He expressed his opinions with increasing vehemence as time passed, perhaps thinking that his age gave him the right to voice whatever thoughts he wanted. Discretion, which had been so much a part of his earlier moderateness, seemingly slipped away as he grew older and more infirm. Perhaps it was just ill-health, his bad physical feelings influencing his communication. Whatever the reason, people found it more difficult as time passed to associate with him for extended periods. As this happened, concerned about his reputation for future generations, Doniphan increasingly wrote to friends and researchers about the "good old days" before the war when he had been a war hero and a major player in state politics, as well as a much sought after attorney and a valued husband and father.[40] All that was gone now and Doniphan's writings reflect that development. He told his cousin in 1877: "Early life is the time for enjoyment—in age neither

38. A. W. Doniphan to Emma Doniphan, September 12, 1876, Doniphan Collection.

39. A. W. Doniphan to Editor *Plattsburgh (Mo.) Lever,* September 1, 1876, Doniphan Collection; A. W. Doniphan to D. C. Allen, August 25, 1883, Doniphan Papers; Connelley, ed., *Doniphan's Expedition,* 585–91.

40. As examples, see A. W. Doniphan to D. C. Allen, "Sketch of Life," Doniphan Papers; A. W. Doniphan to D. C. Allen, February 4, 1874, April 9, 1874, October 27, 1874, May 14, 1883, May 31, 1883, September 10, 1883, September 19, 1883, September 20, 1883, all in Doniphan Papers; A. W. Doniphan to Emma Doniphan, February 22, 1878, Doniphan Collection; "The Testimony of General A. W. Doniphan to the Character of Early Mormon Leaders in Missouri," LDS Archives; and Doniphan, *Address.*

fortune or fame can bring happiness—the aroma of life ebbs away, perhaps slowly, but certainly."[41]

Alexander William Doniphan's most reflective piece of correspondence emerged from the angst and ardor of his seventy-fifth birthday. On July 9, 1883, he wrote to longtime friend D. C. Allen about his life of action in Missouri:

> Looking back at a glance the time seems short—and when I esti-mate the few things I have done worth recording and remembering the time seems even shorter. The events in the life of the average man are poor megre things. I am aware that I have some admiring friends who regard my professional life to have been active and successful—and it would be unpardonable—if not contemptible affectation not to agree with them, that in some departments of the practice, it was creditable. But what of that?—if I had trusted less to native resources and delved deeper into the mines of learning, that others have dug up and prepared to my hands—it would have been more like a jurist. The episodes of my life, mere lucky accidents mainly[;] my only ambition in truth was to be esteemed the best jury lawyer & advocate in the counties where I practiced—this was too limited an ambition—but the book is closed—"what is writ is writ" & cannot be changed. This is candid truth. As far as moral honor and true manhood is concerned I have no twinges of conscience—not what I have done but what I have failed to do, causes my regrets. It is a grand but peaceful thought—that although the lamp of life will soon be extinguished the work that has been done or failed to do, will continue through eternity.

Doniphan closed his letter to Allen, and perhaps said much about why he failed to write a memoir of his life, thus: "Blessed is the man who having nothing to say, abstains from giving us wordy evidence of the fact, especially in writing. So farewell."[42]

It was a fitting summation. Doniphan lived another four years after writing that letter to Allen. He died at his boarding house in Richmond on Monday, August 8, 1887, with a few old friends and relatives surrounding him. For instance, during his last few days his nephew John Doniphan came to visit him. If he might have been difficult to visit in his latter years, with Doniphan near death those who were dear to him returned.[43] Three days after his death, Doniphan's body was transported from Richmond to its final resting place in the Liberty cemetery. He was buried in the family plot next to his wife and two sons. By all accounts the funeral proved an elegant affair, presided over by the Reverend J. A. Dearborn, the minister of the local Christian church where Doniphan had worshiped before

41. A. W. Doniphan to Emma Doniphan, February 13, 1877, Doniphan Collection.
42. A. W. Doniphan to D. C. Allen, July 9, 1883, Doniphan Papers.
43. *Conservator,* August 11, 1887; "Will of A. W. Doniphan," 79–81.

moving to St. Louis in 1863. Doniphan's pallbearers were all members of his Mexican War regiment, and that more than anything punctuated the end of his life. His tombstone said of Doniphan, and this too seemed quite appropriate for a man of his inclinations and accomplishments, "An Orator, Jurist, Statesman, Soldier, and a Christian."[44]

As might be expected, Doniphan's death brought forth a wide response from those who remembered him. As is the case with all eulogies, and perhaps fittingly so, they remembered him not for all he had done but for the best that he had ever done. The Ray County Bar Association wrote a series of resolutions praising his long list of accomplishments, and noting that he was "true to his convictions of duty and right; a sincere friend, frank open and magnanimous to those with whom he differed—as a lawyer he occupied the very front in his profession as an orator, gifted brilliant and captivating, the peer of most gifted speakers, impressive and convincing."[45] During his funeral, several of his old friends stood and told of Doniphan's finest attributes, but D. C. Allen's remarks encapsulated better than any the principles upon which his friend had tried to live. "I never knew any one whose perception of right and wrong was so strong," he said. "I never knew of his doing or saying an unworthy thing, and never knew a better man."[46]

In many respects Doniphan's life was an American success story on a par with any Horatio Alger ever envisioned. Alexander William Doniphan was also a man of many dimensions. Certainly, he was one of the most impressive individuals of nineteenth-century Missouri and a man of considerable talents even when compared to elite leaders of the nation. He enjoyed remarkable stature in Missouri but was largely ignored outside its borders. He succeeded admirably in three distinct arenas of leadership—politics, law, and the military—for which he earned numerous plaudits but never national fame. He symbolized reason, understanding, and moderation on several divisive issues when too many other leaders of his caliber advocated extreme solutions, but his common sense and practical approach to these matters remain underappreciated.

Doniphan, in short, represents in all too many instances a neglected man. This is true in spite of his standing within his own state between the 1830s and the Civil War. Few men had more prestige. In his varying capacities he built a reputation that made him an idol of small boys, a considerable influence among men, and a model of circumspect leadership for all. As an attorney in western Missouri, as a soldier and commanding officer of the famed First Missouri Mounted Volunteers during the Mexican War, and as a politician, Doniphan exemplified the best attributes of his era.

44. *The Gazette*, August 12, 1887; *Conservator*, August 18, 1887.
45. *Conservator*, August 11, 1887.
46. *Gazette*, August 12, 1887.

Doniphan helped to bring law and stability to his adopted Missouri through legal practice, where he became one of its most respected courtroom orators. He cowrote the legal code for New Mexico, which did much the same in that newly acquired territory. He also stood for legal and moderate measures in dealing with such crises as the Mormon war of 1838 and the secession question in 1860–1861.

As a politician Doniphan embodied valued qualities in the American political tradition. His whiggery aimed for the reformation of society along lines that recognized government's role in the betterment of society. He served for many years as a state legislator, bringing to his duties a commitment to fairness and compromise in his effort to satisfy all quarters of society. Always, he preferred to see change handled with accommodation and after due deliberation and with the consent of all concerned. As a force in Missouri politics during the antebellum era Doniphan displayed this sense of proportion and moderation repeatedly. He stressed the necessity of continuous, cooperative action to accomplish the moral improvement of society in general and Missouri and the Union in particular.

This same attitude permeated his defense of the Union in the secession crisis and his participation at the Washington Peace Conference. He was a representative, albeit one of the more capable, of the group of American politicians who embraced practical actions seasoned with principle and integrity. The brutality displayed in western Missouri and Kansas deeply troubled him and his reaction expressed persistent whiggish moderation. His chagrin at the extremism that led to the Civil War confirmed a logical extension of his perspective, and he felt it necessary to abandon his belief in strong government action because of a fear of forcing tyranny on others.

As a military leader Doniphan showed remarkable leadership ability and grasp of tactical nuances. First glimpsed in the Mormon war of 1838, he demonstrated these capabilities with remarkable flair in the Mexican War. Pressed into military service, Doniphan commanded the First Missouri Mounted Volunteers during an epic march of thirty-six hundred miles through the Southwest. He led his troops to victory against two separate armies of Mexican regulars. Doniphan's military victories at El Brazito and Sacramento were complete and unquestioned. John Taylor Hughes, a member of Doniphan's regiment who died in the Civil War, stated what most might agree was the most important accomplishment made by Doniphan in 1847. "The history of this expedition will be Colonel Doniphan's most lasting monument," he wrote.[47] As a slaveowner, a Missourian, a Whig, a military commander, a political moderate, and an American, however, Alexander William Doniphan's life represented what historian Arthur M. Schlesinger Jr. referred to as "the vital center."

47. Hughes, *Doniphan's Expedition*, 128.

The statue of Alexander William Doniphan that stands in the courthouse square of Richmond, Ray County, Missouri, taken in 1994. Photo by the author.

A place Doniphan believed necessary to occupy, he found it increasingly difficult as time and circumstances changed. In the fractious age of the late twentieth century, it is from that "vital center" that he still speaks across time and a sea of social change to his fellow citizens of the republic that he loved and sought to defend against the forces of extremism.[48]

48. Arthur M. Schlesinger, *The Vital Center.*

Bibliography

MANUSCRIPT COLLECTIONS

Church of Jesus Christ of Latter-day Saints, Archives,
Salt Lake City, Utah (LDS Archives)
Britton, Rollin J. "General Alexander W. Doniphan." February 20, 1914.
Doniphan, Alexander William. Letters.
Missouri Circuit Court (5th Circuit), Legal Proceedings of *Edward Partridge v Samuel D. Lucas et al.*, MS 899. Photocopy. Original in the Huntington Library, San Marino, Calif., Identification number HM 25795.
Partridge, Edward, v Samuel D. Lucas et al. Amended Declaration to the Circuit Court of February Term, 1834, n.d., MS 629.1.
Phelps, W. W. Collection of Missouri Documents, MS 657.
Robinson, George W. "The Scriptory Book of Joseph Smith, Jr., President of the Church of Jesus Christ of Latter-day Saints in All the World."
Smith, George A. History.
State of Missouri. "Subpoena of Missouri Circuit Court for Samuel D. Lucas." November 3, 1835, MS 2966.
"The Testimony of General A. W. Doniphan to the Character of Early Mormon Leaders in Missouri." N.d. [ca. 1885], MS 559.
Woodruff, Wilford. Journal.

Harold B. Lee Library, Special Collections,
Brigham Young University, Provo, Utah
Cooper, Dudley H. Papers.
Doniphan, Alexander William. Letters.
Huntington, Oliver B. "History of the Life of Oliver B. Huntington, also His Travels and Troubles."

Mace, Wandle. "Journal of Wandle Mace." Typescript.
Tracy, Nancy Naomi Alexander. "Autobiography of Nancy Naomi Alexander Tracy." Typescript.

Missouri Historical Society, St. Louis

Bradford, Thomas G. Correspondence.
Britton, Rollin J. "General Alexander W. Doniphan."
Butterfield, Josiah. Letters.
Civil War Papers.
Clemens, James. Collection.
Darby, John F. Papers.
Doniphan, Alexander William. Papers.
Edwards' St. Louis Directory (1864).
Gamble, Hamilton R. Papers.
Hughes, John Taylor. "Diary of John T. Hughes."
Kearny, Stephen Watts. Diary and Letter Book, 1846–1847.
Lane, William Carr. Collection.
Link Family Papers.
Mexican War Files.
Miller, Robert H. Papers.
Missouri Tax Lists, 1836–1839.
Missouri Tax Lists, 1840–1845.
Sibley, George C. Papers.
Smith, George R. Papers.
St. Louis History Papers.
Turner, Henry S. Collection.

Missouri State Archives, Jefferson City, Mo.

Missouri Fire Documents Collection.
Missouri State Supreme Court, RG 600, Case Files.
Platte County Deed Book A. Platte City, Mo. Microfilm in County Records, C5382.
Platte County Deed Books J–P. Platte City, Mo. Microform in County Records, C5379.

National Archives, Washington, D.C.

Clay County, Mo., Population Schedules for the Sixth Federal Census, 1840, National Archives, Washington, D.C., microfilm located in the Missouri State Archives, Jefferson City, Mo.
Clay County, Mo., Slave Schedules for the Eighth Federal Census, 1860, National Archives, Washington, D.C., microfilm located in the Missouri State Archives, Jefferson City, Mo.
Correspondence Received, 1829–1841–1842 to 1844, U.S. Consulate General, Mexico City, Mexico. RG 84.

Kearny, Stephen Watts. Letters. War Records, Adjutant General's Office, Letters Received. RG 94.

Mason County, Ky., Population Schedules for the Third Federal Census, 1810, National Archives, Washington, D.C.

Records of Army Commands, Office of the Adjutant General, Letters Received. RG 94.

Records of Army Commands, Office of the Quartermaster General, Consolidated Correspondence. RG 92.

Records of the Adjutant General, Vol. 42 1/2, General Orders and Special Orders, 1846–1848, Army of the West and 9th Military Department, RG 94, National Archives, Washington, D.C.

Records of the Adjutant General Office, Letters Received. Microcopy 567, roll 319.

Western Historical Manuscript Collection, Columbia, Mo.

Alvord Collection.

Atchison, David Rice. Papers.

Aull, Robert. Collection.

Doniphan, Alexander William. Collection.

Dunklin, Daniel. Papers.

Gist Family Letters.

Hardin, Charles H. Papers.

Leonard, Abiel. Collection.

Napton, W. B. Letters.

Pomeroy, E. V. Letters.

Rollins, James S. Collection.

Other Manuscript Collections

Jackson County Historical Society, Independence, Mo. W. A. Brannock Family Letters. Albert N. Doerschuk Papers.

Kansas State Historical Society, Topeka. William E. Connelley Collection.

Latin American Collection, University of Texas Library, Austin. Justin Harvey Smith Papers.

Marriott Library, Special Collections, University of Utah, Salt Lake City. Reed Peck Diary, 1839. Photocopy.

Museum of New Mexico, Archives and Library, Santa Fe. James Austin Letters. Battle of Brazitos, Typescript of Documents Relating to Battle, 1846.

Reorganized Church of Jesus Christ of Latter Day Saints, Library-Archives, Independence, Mo.

Southern Historical Collection, University of North Carolina, Chapel Hill. McClanahan-Taylor Papers.

State of New Mexico Records Center and Archives, Santa Fe. Alexander William Doniphan Letter. Gov. Stephen Watts Kearny Papers.

William Jewell College, Special Collections, Curry Library, Liberty, Mo.
    Raymond W. Settle Collection.

NEWSPAPERS

The Anglo Saxon (Chihuahua City, Mexico), 1847.
Boon's Lick Times (Fayette, Mo.), 1839.
Carthage (Ill.) Republican, 1856–1858.
Columbia (Mo.) Statesman, 1844–1873.
Congressional Globe (Washington, D.C.), 1845–1861.
Congressional Record (Washington, D.C.), 1917.
The Conservator (Richmond, Mo.), 1868–1887.
Daily National Intelligencer (Washington, D.C.), 1834.
Evening and Morning Star (Independence, Mo.), 1832–1833, (Kirtland,
    Ohio), 1834.
The Gazette (St. Joseph, Mo.), 1887.
Jefferson City (Mo.) Inquirer, 1850.
Jeffersonian Republican (Jefferson City, Mo.), 1833–1847.
Kansas City Journal, 1881.
Kansas City Star, 1916.
Kansas City Times, 1947.
Latter-day Saints' Millennial Star (Salt Lake City, rep. ed.), 1860–1867.
Liberty (Mo.) Weekly Tribune, 1847–1887.
Louisville (Ky.) Journal, 1848.
Missouri Argus (St. Louis), 1836–1840.
Missouri Examiner (Jefferson City, Mo.), 1855.
Missouri Intelligencer and Boon's Lick Advertiser (Boonville, Mo.), 1833–
    1834.
Missouri Register (St. Louis), 1843.
Missouri Reporter (St. Louis), 1843.
Missouri Republican (St. Louis), 1833–1861.
Missouri Statesman (Columbia, Mo.), 1843.
Niles Weekly/National Register (Baltimore), 1833–1844.
New York Daily Tribune, 1847.
New-York Herald, 1846–1847.
New York Tribune, 1846–1854.
The Picayune (New Orleans), 1847.
The Return (Davis City, Iowa), 1889–1891.
St. Louis Democrat, 1856.
Saints' Herald (Plano, Ill.; Lamoni, Iowa), 1881–1891.
Santa Fe Republican, 1846–1847.
Squatter Sovereign (Atchison, Kans.), 1855.
Times and Seasons (Nauvoo, Ill.), 1839–1946.
Weekly Reveille (St. Louis), 1846–1847.

Western Emigrant (Boonville, Mo.), 1839.
Western Star (Liberty, Mo.), 1838.

REFERENCES

Abert, 2d Lt. J. W. "Notes of Lieutenant J. W. Abert." House Executive Document No. 41, 30th Cong., 1st Sess., Vol. 4.

Abstract of Infantry Tactics; Including Exercises and Manoeuvres of Light-Infantry and Riflemen; for the use of the Militia of the United States. Boston: U.S. War Department, 1830 and later editions.

Address Delivered in the Chapel at West Point . . . by the Hon. Ashbel Smith, of Texas, and Col. A. W. Doniphan, June 16, 1848. New York: W. L. Burroughs, 1848.

Alcaraz, Ramón, et al. *The Other Side: Notes for the History of the War Between Mexico and the United States.* Ed. Albert C. Ramsey. New York: John Wiley, 1850.

Allen, James B., and Glen M. Leonard. *The Story of the Latter-day Saints.* Salt Lake City: Deseret Book Co., 1976.

Anderson, Richard L. "Atchison's Letters and the Causes of Mormon Expulsion from Missouri." *Brigham Young University Studies* 26 (summer 1986): 3–47.

————. "Jackson County in Early Mormon Descriptions." *Missouri Historical Review* 65 (April 1971): 170–93.

Andrews, Horace, Jr. "Kansas Crusade: Eli Thayer and the New England Emigrant Aid Company." *New England Quarterly* 36 (1962): 497–514.

Armstrong, Andrew. "The Brazito Battlefield." *New Mexico Historical Review* 35 (January 1960): 63–74.

Arrington, Leonard J. "Church Leaders in Liberty Jail." *Brigham Young University Studies* 13 (autumn 1972): 20–26.

Arrington, Leonard J., and Davis Bitton. *The Mormon Experience: A History of the Latter-day Saints.* New York: Alfred A. Knopf, 1979.

Atherton, Lewis E. *The Frontier Merchant in Mid-America.* Columbia: University of Missouri Press, 1971.

Baldwin, P. M. "A Short History of the Mesilla Valley." *New Mexico Historical Review* 3 (July 1938): 315–30.

Baltimore, Lester B. "Benjamin F. Stringfellow: The Fight for Slavery on the Missouri Border." *Missouri Historical Review* 62 (February 1967): 14–29.

Bancroft, Hubert Howe. *Chronicles of the Builders of the Commonwealth.* San Francisco: History Co., 1891.

————. *History of Arizona and New Mexico, 1530–1888.* San Francisco: History Co., 1889.

Barclay, Thomas S. *The Liberal Republican Movement in Missouri, 1865–1871.* Columbia: University of Missouri Press, 1926.

Barry, Louise. *The Beginning of the West: Annals of the Kansas Gateway to the American West, 1540–1854.* Topeka: Kansas State Historical Society, 1972.

Bauer, K. Jack. *The Mexican War, 1846–1848.* New York: Macmillan, 1974.

———. *Zachary Taylor: Soldier, Planter, Statesman of the Old South.* Baton Rouge: Louisiana State University Press, 1985.

Benedict, Michael Les. *The Impeachment and Trial of Andrew Johnson.* New York: Norton, 1973.

Benson, Lee. *The Concept of Jacksonian Democracy: New York as a Test Case.* Princeton: Princeton University Press, 1961.

Benton, Thomas Hart. *Return of the Missouri Volunteers: Address of the Hon. Thomas H. Benton to Col. Doniphan and his Regiment, at their Reception in St. Louis, Upon Their Return from Mexico, and Col. Doniphan's Reply, St. Louis, July 2d, a.d., 1847.* Broadside. Missouri Historical Society, St. Louis.

———. *Thirty Years' View, or, A History of the Working of the American Government for Thirty Years, from 1820 to 1850 . . . by a Senator of Thirty Years.* 2 vols. New York: D. Appleton and Co., 1854–1856.

Bent's Old Fort. Colorado Springs: State Historical Society of Colorado, 1979.

Berwanger, Eugene H. *The Frontier against Slavery: Western Anti-Negro Prejudice and the Slavery Extension Controversy.* Urbana: University of Illinois Press, 1967.

Beveridge, Albert J. *Abraham Lincoln, 1809–1858.* 4 vols. Boston: Houghton Mifflin, 1928.

Billington, Ray Allen. *The Far Western Frontier, 1830–1860.* New York: Harper and Row, 1956.

Bingham, George Caleb. "Letters of George Caleb Bingham." *Missouri Historical Review* 31 (October 1937): 17.

Bloom, John P. "New Mexico Viewed by Anglo-Americans, 1846–1849." *New Mexico Historical Review* 34 (July 1959): 165–98.

Boggs, William M. "Sketch of Lilburn W. Boggs." *Missouri Historical Review* 4 (January 1910): 106–8.

Boorstin, Daniel J. *The Americans: The National Experience.* New York: Random House, 1965.

Britton, Rollin J. "Early Days on the Grand River and the Mormon War." *Missouri Historical Review* 13 (January, April, and July 1919): 112–34, 287–309, 388–98, and 14 (October 1919, January, April, and July 1920): 86–116, 233–45, 459–73.

Brown, David Warren. *Andrew Johnson and the Negro.* Knoxville: University of Tennessee Press, 1989.

Brown, Dwight H., ed. *Corporations Chartered or Organized under the Territorial Laws and by Act of the General Assembly of the State of Missouri, 1803–1865.* Jefferson City, Mo.: Midland Printing, 1934.

Brown, Thomas. *Politics and Statesmanship: Essays on the American Whig Party.* New York: Columbia University Press, 1985.

Brownlee, Richard S. *Gray Ghosts of the Confederacy: Guerrilla Warfare in the West, 1861–1865.* Baton Rouge: Louisiana State University Press, 1958.

Burnett, Peter H. *Recollections and Opinions of an Old Pioneer.* New York: D. Appleton and Co., 1880.

Cable, John Ray. *The Bank of the State of Missouri.* New York: Columbia University Press, 1923.

Cain, Marvin R. "Edward Bates and Hamilton R. Gamble." *Missouri Historical Review* 56 (January 1962): 146–55.

Captain of Volunteers. *Conquest of Santa Fe and the Subjugation of New Mexico.* Philadelphia: Caray and Hart, 1847.

Carr, Lucien. *Missouri: A Bone of Contention.* Boston: Houghton Mifflin, 1894.

Carr, Marion Lucille. *Marriage Records of Clay County, Missouri, 1822–1852.* Kansas City: n.p., 1957.

Carroll, E. Malcolm. *Origins of the Whig Party.* Durham: Duke University Press, 1925.

Carroll, Stephen. "Loyalty or Secession?" *Bulletin of the Missouri Historical Society* 29 (October 1972): 20–31.

Castel, Albert. *A Frontier State at War: Kansas, 1861–1865.* American Historical Association, 1958; Lawrence: Kansas Heritage Press, 1992.

———. *General Sterling Price and the Civil War in the West.* Baton Rouge: Louisiana State University Press, 1968.

———. *The Presidency of Andrew Johnson.* Lawrence: Regents Press of Kansas, 1979.

Chalfant, William Y. *Dangerous Passage: The Santa Fe Trail and the Mexican War.* Norman: University of Oklahoma Press, 1994.

Chambers, William N. *Old Bullion Benton: Senator from the New West.* Boston: Little, Brown, 1956.

Clark, Dwight L. *Stephen Watts Kearny: Soldier of the West.* Norman: University of Oklahoma Press, 1961.

Clark, Kimball. "The Epic March of Doniphan's Missourians." *Missouri Historical Review* 80 (January 1986): 134–55.

Clift, G. Glen. *History of Maysville and Mason County, Kentucky.* 2 vols. Lexington, Ky.: Transylvania Printing Co., 1936.

Cole, Arthur C. *The Whig Party in the South.* Washington, D.C.: American Historical Association, 1913.

Conard, Howard L., ed. *Encyclopedia of the History of Missouri.* 6 vols. New York: Southern History Co., 1901.

Connelley, William Elsey, ed. *Doniphan's Expedition, and the Conquest of New Mexico and California.* Topeka, Kans.: Crane and Co., 1907.

Cooke, Philip St. George. *The Conquest of New Mexico and California: An Historical and Personal Narrative.* New York: G. P. Putnam's Sons, 1878.

Cooper, William J., Jr. *Liberty and Slavery: Southern Politics to 1860.* New York: Alfred A. Knopf, 1983.

———. *The South and the Politics of Slavery, 1828–1856.* Baton Rouge: Louisiana State University Press, 1978.

Corrill, John. *A Brief History of the Church of Christ of Latter Day Saints (Commonly Called Mormons, Including an Account of their Doctrine and Discipline, with the Reasons of the Author for Leaving the Church).* St. Louis: n.p., 1839.

Court Record E. Jackson County Courthouse, Independence, Mo.

Cox, LaWanda. *Lincoln and Black Freedom: A Study in Presidential Leadership.* Columbia: University of South Carolina Press, 1981.

Crofts, Daniel W. "The Union Party of 1861 and the Secession Crisis." *Perspectives in American History* 11 (1977–1978): 327–76.

Culmer, Frederic A. "A Snapshot of Alexander W. Doniphan, 1808–1887." *Missouri Historical Review* 38 (October 1943): 25–32.

Curry, Richard O., ed. *Radicalism, Racism, and Party Realignment: The Border States during Reconstruction.* Baltimore: Johns Hopkins University Press, 1969.

Cutler, William G. *History of the State of Kansas.* Chicago: Historical Publishing Co., 1883.

Cutts, James Madison. *The Conquest of California and New Mexico.* Philadelphia: Carey and Hart, 1847.

The Daily News History of Buchanan County and St. Joseph, Missouri. St. Joseph, Mo.: St. Joseph Publishing Co., 1898.

Dawson, Joseph G., III. "American Civil-Military Relations and Military Government: The Service of Colonel Alexander Doniphan in the Mexican War." *Armed Forces and Society* 22 (summer 1996): 555–72.

DeArmond, Fred. "Reconstruction in Missouri." *Missouri Historical Review* 41 (April 1967): 364–77.

DeVoto, Bernard. *The Year of Decision: 1846.* Boston: Little, Brown, 1943.

Document Containing the Correspondence, Orders, &c. In Relation to the Disturbances with the Mormons; and the Evidence Given Before the Hon. Austin A. King. Fayette, Mo.: Office of the Boon's Lick Democrat, 1841.

Donald, David, ed. *Why the North Won the Civil War.* New York: Collier Books, 1962.

Doniphan, Alexander William. *Address by Col. Alexander W. Doniphan, Delivered in Liberty, Mo., June 5, 1872, on the Occasion of the Celebration by the People of Clay County, of the 50th Anniversary of the County's Establishment.* Liberty, Mo.: Advance Book and Job Printing House, 1883.

Duchateau, Andre Paul. "Missouri Colossus: Alexander William Doniphan, 1808–1887." Ph.D. diss., Oklahoma State University, 1973.

Durham, Reed C. "The Election Day Battle at Gallatin." *Brigham Young University Studies* 13 (autumn 1972): 36–61.

Edmunds, R. David. "Potawatomis in the Platte Country: An Indian Removal Incomplete." *Missouri Historical Review* 68 (July 1974): 375–92.

Edwards, Frank S. *A Campaign in New Mexico with Colonel Doniphan.* Philadelphia: Carey and Hart, 1847.

Eisenhower, John S. D. *So Far from God: The U.S. War with Mexico, 1846–1848.* New York: Anchor Books, 1989.

Elliott, R. Kenneth. "The Rhetoric of Alexander W. Doniphan." *The Trail Guide* (Kansas City Posse, The Westerners), 14 (December 1969): 3–14.

Emory, Lieutenant William H. *Notes of a Military Reconnaissance from Ft. Leavenworth in Missouri, to San Diego, in California, including parts of the Arkansas, Del Norte, and Gila Rivers.* Senate Executive Documents, 30th Cong., 1st Sess., no. 7, 1848.

Ershkowitz, Herbert, and William G. Shade. "Consensus or Conflict? Political Behavior in the State Legislatures during the Jacksonian Era." *Journal of American History* 58 (December 1971): 591–621.

Executive Documents, House Reports No. 458, 30th Cong., 1st Sess. (1847).

Fehrenbacher, Don E. *The Dred Scott Case: Its Significance in American Law and Politics.* New York: Oxford University Press, 1978.

———. *Prelude to Greatness: Lincoln in the 1850s.* Stanford, Calif.: Stanford University Press, 1962.

Feldberg, Michael. *The Turbulent Era: Riot and Disorder in Jacksonian America.* New York: Oxford University Press, 1980.

Fellman, Michael. *Inside War: The Guerrilla Conflict in Missouri during the American Civil War.* New York: Oxford University Press, 1989.

Finnie, Gordon E. "The Antislavery Movement in the Upper South before 1840." *Journal of Southern History* 35 (August 1969): 349–62.

Fitzgerald, Fred. "Daniel Dunklin." *Missouri Historical Review* 21 (April 1927): 395–403.

Foner, Eric. *Free Soil, Free Labor, Free Men: The Ideology of the Republican Party before the Civil War.* New York: Oxford University Press, 1970.

———. *Reconstruction: America's Unfinished Revolution, 1863–1877.* New York: Harper and Row, 1988.

Franklin, John Hope. *The Emancipation Proclamation.* Garden City, N.Y.: Doubleday, 1963.

Frederickson, George M. *The Black Image in the White Mind.* New York: Harper and Row, 1971.

Fuller, J. D. F. *The Movement for the Acquisition of All Mexico, 1846–1848.* Baltimore: Johns Hopkins University Press, 1936.

Gardner, John C. "Election of Lincoln to the Presidency in 1860." In *Great Events from History: American Series,* ed. Frank N. McGill. 3 vols. Englewood Cliffs, N.J.: Salem Press, 1975.

Gardner, Mark L., ed. *Brothers on the Santa Fe and Chihuahua Trails: Edward James Glasgow and William Henry Glasgow, 1846–1848.* Niwot: University Press of Colorado, 1993.

Gentry, Leland H. "The Danite Band of 1838." *Brigham Young University Studies* 14 (summer 1974): 421–50.

———. "A History of the Latter-Day Saints in Northern Missouri from 1836 to 1839." Ph.D. diss., Brigham Young University, 1965.

George, Isaac. *Heroes and Incidents of the Mexican War, Containing Doniphan's Expedition.* Greensburg, Pa.: Review Publishing Co., 1903.

Gibson, George R. *Journal of a Soldier under Kearny and Doniphan, 1846–1847.* Ed. Ralph P. Bieber. Southwest Historical Series, vol. 3. Glendale, Calif.: Arthur H. Clark, 1935.

Goodrich, Thomas. *Black Flag: Guerrilla Warfare on the Western Border, 1861–1865.* Bloomington: Indiana University Press, 1995.

Goodson, W. H. *History of Clay County, Missouri.* Topeka: Historical Publishing Co., 1920.

Gordon, Joseph F. "The Political Career of Lilburn W. Boggs." *Missouri Historical Review* 52 (January 1958): 121–22.

Greene, John P. *Facts Relative to the Expulsion of the Mormons or Latter-day Saints, from the State of Missouri, Under the "Exterminating Order".* Cincinnati: R. P. Brooks, 1839.

Greene, Lorenzo J., Gary R. Kremer, and Antonio F. Holland. *Missouri's Black Heritage.* St. Louis: Forum Press, 1980.

Gregg, Josiah. *The Commerce of the Prairies.* Ed. Milo M. Quaife. Chicago: R. R. Donnelley, 1926.

———. *The Diary and Letters of Josiah Gregg.* Ed. Maurice Garland Fulton. 2 vols. Norman: University of Oklahoma Press, 1941–1944.

Grimstead, David. "Rioting in Its Jacksonian Setting." *American Historical Review* 77 (April 1972): 361–97.

Grossman, Michael. "Institutionalizing Masculinity: The Law as a Masculine Profession." In *Meanings for Manhood: Constructions of Masculinity in Victorian America,* ed. Mark C. Carnes and Clyde Griffen, 133–51. Chicago: University of Chicago Press, 1990.

Gunderson, Robert Gray. *The Log Cabin Campaign.* Lexington: University of Kentucky Press, 1957.

———. *Old Gentleman's Convention: The Washington Peace Conference of 1861.* Madison: University of Wisconsin Press, 1961.

Hamilton, Francis Frazee. *Ancestral Lines of the Doniphan, Frazee, and Hamilton Families.* Greenfield, Ind.: Mitchell Pub. Co., 1928.

Hansen, Klaus J. *Quest for Empire: The Kingdom of God and the Council of Fifty in Mormon History.* East Lansing: Michigan State University Press, 1967.

"The Heatherly Family of Missouri." *Bulletin of the Missouri Historical Society* 13 (January 1957): 156–60.

Heitman, Francis B. *Historical Register & Dictionary of the U.S. Army.* 2 vols. Washington, D.C.: Government Printing Office, 1903.

Henry, Robert Selph. *The Story of the Mexican War.* Indianapolis: Bobbs-Merrill Co., 1950.

Hill, Jim Dan. *The Minute Man in Peace and War: A History of the National Guard.* Washington, D.C.: National Guard Bureau, 1964.

Hill, Marvin S. *Quest for Refuge: The Mormon Flight from American Pluralism.* Salt Lake City: Signature Books, 1989.

Hinkle, S. J. "A Biographical Sketch of G. M. Hinkle." *Journal of History* 13 (October 1920): 449.

Historical Listing of the Missouri Legislature. Jefferson City: Published by Roy D. Blount, Secretary of State, 1988.

History of Andrew and DeKalb Counties, Missouri. 2 vols. St. Louis: Goodspeed Publishing Co., 1888.

History of Caldwell and Livingston Counties, Missouri. St. Louis: National Historical Co., 1886.

History of Clay and Platte Counties, Missouri. St. Louis: National Historical Co., 1885.

History of Clinton County, Missouri. St. Joseph, Mo.: National Historical Co., 1881.

History of Jackson County, Missouri. Topeka, Kans.: Hickman Historical Publishing Co., 1920.

History of Ray County, Missouri. St. Louis: Missouri Historical Co., 1918.

Holman, Hamilton. *Prologue to Conflict: The Crisis and Compromise of 1850.* Lexington: University of Kentucky Press, 1964.

Holt, Michael F. *The Political Crisis of the 1850s.* New York: John Wiley, 1978.

Horgan, Paul. *Great River: The Rio Grande in North American History.* New York: Farrar, Strauss, and Giroux, 1954. Reprint, Hanover, N.H.: University of New England Press for Weslyan University Press, 1984.

House Executive Document 60, 30th Cong., 1st Sess. Washington, D.C.: Government Printing Office, 1846.

House Report 458, 30th Cong., 1st Sess., 1848.

House Reports, 23d Cong., 2d Sess., Document 107.

Howe, Daniel Walker. *The Political Culture of the American Whigs.* Chicago: University of Chicago Press, 1979.

Hubbard, Timothy W., and Lewis E. Davids. *Banking in Mid-America: A History of Missouri's Banks.* Washington, D.C.: Public Affairs Press, 1969.

Hughes, John Taylor. *Doniphan's Expedition.* Cincinnati: U. P. James, 1847.

Hughes, Willis B. "The Heatherly Incident of 1836." *Bulletin of the Missouri Historical Society* 13 (January 1957): 161–80.

Hurt, R. Douglas. "Planters and Slavery in Little Dixie." *Missouri Historical Review* 91 (July 1994): 397–415.

Hymen, Harold M., and William M. Wiecek. *Equal Justice under Law: Constitutional Development, 1835–1875.* New York: Harper and Row, 1982.

Instruction for Field Artillery, Horse and Foot. Baltimore: Board of Artillery Officers, 1845.

Jennings, Warren A. "The Expulsion of the Mormons from Jackson County, Missouri." *Missouri Historical Review* 64 (October 1969): 41–63.

————. "Importuning for Redress." *Bulletin of the Missouri Historical Society* 27 (October 1970): 15–29.

————. "Zion Is Fled: The Expulsion of the Mormons from Jackson County, Missouri." Ph.D. diss., University of Florida, 1962.

Jesse, Dean C. " 'Walls, Grates, and Screeching Iron Doors': The Prison Experience of Mormon Leaders in Missouri, 1838–1839." In *New Views of Mormon History: Essays in Honor of Leonard J. Arrington,* ed. Davis Bitton and Maureen Ursenbach Beecher, 19–42. Salt Lake City: University of Utah Press, 1987.

Jessee, Dean C., ed. *The Papers of Joseph Smith.* Vol. 1, *Autobiographical and Historical Writings.* Salt Lake City: Deseret Book Co., 1989.

————. *The Personal Writings of Joseph Smith.* Salt Lake City: Deseret Book Co., 1984.

Johannsen, Robert W. *The Frontier, the Union, and Stephen A. Douglas.* Urbana: University of Illinois Press, 1989.

————. *Stephen A. Douglas.* New York: Oxford University Press, 1973.

————. *To the Halls of the Montezumas: The Mexican War in the American Imagination.* New York: Oxford University Press, 1985.

Johnson, Clark W., ed. *Mormon Redress Petitions: Documents of the 1833–1838 Missouri Conflict.* Provo, Utah: Religious Studies Center, Brigham Young University, 1992.

Johnson, Samuel A. *The Battle Cry of Freedom: The New England Emigrant Aid Company in the Kansas Crusade.* Lawrence: University of Kansas Press, 1954.

————. "The Emigrant Aid Company in the Kansas Conflict." *Kansas Historical Quarterly* 4 (February 1937): 21–32.

————. "The Genesis of the New England Emigrant Aid Company." *New England Quarterly* 3 (January 1930): 118–30.

Johnston, Abraham Robinson, Marcellus Ball Edwards, and Philip Gooch Ferguson. *Marching with the Army of the West, 1846–1848.* Ed. Ralph P. Bieber. Southwest Historical Series, vol. 4. Glendale, Calif.: Arthur H. Clark, 1936.

Johnston, Richard Malcolm, and William Hand Browns. *Life of Alexander H. Stephens.* Philadelphia: J. P. Lippincott, 1878.

Journal of the House of Representatives of the State of Missouri at the First Session of the Seventh General Assembly, 1832–1833. Bowling Green, Mo.: Office of the Salt River Journal, 1833.

Journal of the House of Representatives of the State of Missouri at the First Session of the Ninth General Assembly, November 29, 1836. Bowling Green, Mo.: Office of the Salt River Journal, 1837.

Journal of the House of Representatives of the State of Missouri, 1840–1841. Jackson, Mo.: Southern Advocate, 1841.

Journal of the House of Representatives of the State of Missouri, 1854–1855. Jefferson City, Mo.: State Printers, 1855.

Journal of the Senate of the State of Missouri, 1854–1855. Jefferson City, Mo.: State Printers, 1855.

Journal of the Senate, Extra Session of the Rebel Legislature, Called Together by a Proclamation of C. F. Jackson. Jefferson City, Mo.: State Printer, 1865–1866.

Karnes, Thomas L. "Gilpin's Volunteers on the Santa Fe Trail." *Kansas Historical Quarterly* 30 (spring 1964): 1–14.

———. *William Gilpin: Western Nationalist.* Austin: University of Texas Press, 1970.

Kennerly, William Clark. *Persimmon Hill: A Narrative of Old St. Louis and the Far West, as told to Elizabeth Russell.* Norman: University of Oklahoma Press, 1948.

Kirkpatrick, Arthur Roy. "Missouri in the Early Months of the Civil War." *Missouri Historical Review* 55 (April 1961): 235–66.

Knight, Newel K. "Autobiography." In *Scraps of Biography.* Salt Lake City: Juvenile Instructor Office, 1883.

Knight, Vinson. "Autobiography." In *Classic Experiences in Restoration History.* Salt Lake City: Juvenile Instruction Office, 1893.

Lamar, Howard Roberts. *The Far Southwest, 1846–1912: A Territorial History.* New Haven: Yale University Press, 1966. Reprint, New York: W. W. Norton and Co., 1970.

Langsdorf, Edgar. "S. C. Pomeroy and the New England Emigrant Aid Society, 1854–1858." *Kansas Historical Quarterly* 7 (August, November 1938): 227–45, 379–98.

Launius, Roger D. *Zion's Camp: Expedition to Missouri, 1834.* Independence, Mo.: Herald Publishing House, 1984.

Launius, Roger D., and Linda Thatcher, eds. *Differing Visions: Dissenters in Mormon History.* Urbana: University of Illinois Press, 1994.

Lavender, David. *Bent's Fort.* Garden City, N.Y.: Doubleday, 1954.

Laws of the State of Missouri, Passed at the First Session of the Ninth General Assembly, Begun and Held at the City of Jefferson, November 21, 1836. St. Louis: Chambers and Knapp, Republican Office, 1841.

Laws of the State of Missouri, Passed at the Regular Session of the 21st General Assembly, Begun and Held at the City of Jefferson, December 31, 1861. Jefferson City, Mo.: W. G. Cheney, Public Printer, 1861.

Lee, Bill R. "Missouri's Fight over Emancipation in 1863." *Missouri Historical Review* 45 (April 1951): 256–74.

Leopard, Buel, and Floyd C. Shoemaker, eds. *The Messages and Proclama-tions of the Governors of the States of Missouri.* 22 vols. Columbia: State Historical Society of Missouri, 1922.

LeSueur, Stephen C. "The Danites Reconsidered: Were They Vigilantes or Just the Mormons' Version of the Elks Club?" *John Whitmer Historical Association Journal* 14 (1994): 1–15.

———. *The 1838 Mormon War in Missouri.* Columbia: University of Mis-souri Press, 1987.

———. " 'High Treason and Murder': The Examination of Mormon Pris-oners at Richmond, Missouri, in November 1838." *Brigham Young University Studies* 26 (spring 1986): 3–30.

Leyes del Territorio de Nuevo Mejico: Santa Fe, a 7 de octobre 1846. Santa Fe: Printed by Order of the Governor, 1846.

Lightfoot, B. B. "Nobody's Nominee: Sample Orr and the Election of 1860." *Missouri Historical Review* 60 (January 1966): 127–48.

Littlefield, Lyman O. *Reminiscences of Latter-day Saints.* Logan, Utah: Utah Journal Co., 1888.

Lyon, William H. "Claiborne Fox Jackson and the Secession Crisis in Missouri." *Missouri Historical Review* 58 (July 1964): 422–41.

Magoffin, Susan Shelby. *Down the Santa Fe Trail and into Mexico: The Diary of Susan Shelby Magoffin, 1846–1847.* Ed. Stella M. Drum. New Haven: Yale University Press, 1926.

The Magoffin Papers. Santa Fe: Publications of the Historical Society of New Mexico, No. 24, 1921.

Malin, James C. *John Brown and the Legend of Fifty-Six.* Philadelphia: Amer-ican Philosophical Society, 1942.

———. "LeCompte and the 'Sack of Lawrence,' May 21, 1856," *Kansas Historical Quarterly* 20 (November 1953): 465–94.

———. *The Nebraska Question, 1852–1854.* Lawrence, Kans.: n.p., 1954.

———. "The Proslavery Background of the Kansas Struggle." *Mississippi Valley Historical Review* 10 (1923): 285–305.

March, David D. "The Campaign for the Ratification of the Constitution of 1865." *Missouri Historical Review* 47 (April 1953): 323–32.

Maynard, Gregory P. "Alexander W. Doniphan: Man of Justice." *Brigham Young University Studies* 13 (summer 1973): 462–72.

———. "Alexander William Doniphan, the Forgotten Man from Mis-souri." M.A. thesis, Brigham Young University, 1973.

McCandless, Perry. *Constitutional Government in Missouri.* Davenport, Iowa: Market Publishing, 1984.

———. *A History of Missouri.* Vol. 2, *1820 to 1860.* Columbia: University of Missouri Press, 1972.

McClure, Clarence H. "A Century of Missouri Politics." *Missouri Historical Review* 15 (January 1921): 315–32.

———. "Early Opposition to Thomas Hart Benton." *Missouri Historical Review* 10 (April 1916): 151–96.

———. *Opposition in Missouri to Thomas Hart Benton.* George Peabody College for Teachers Contributions to Education, no. 37, Nashville, 1927.

McCormick, Richard P. "Suffrage Classes and Party Alignments: A Study in Voter Behavior." *Mississippi Valley Historical Review* 46 (December 1959): 397–410.

McDougal, Henry Clay. *Recollections, 1844–1909.* Kansas City: Franklin Hudson, 1910.

McGaw, William Cochran. *Savage Scene: The Life and Times of James Kirker, Frontier King.* New York: Hastings House, 1972.

McGroarty, William B., ed. "Letters from Alexander W. Doniphan." *Missouri Historical Review* 24 (October 1928): 26–39.

———. "William H. Richardson's Journal of Doniphan's Expedition." *Missouri Historical Review* 22 (January, April, July 1928): 193–236, 331–60, 511–42.

McKee, Howard I. "The Platte Purchase." *Missouri Historical Review* 32 (January 1938): 129–47.

McKiernan, F. Mark, Alma R. Blair, and Paul M. Edwards, eds. *The Restoration Movement: Essays in Mormon History.* Lawrence, Kans.: Coronado Press, 1973.

McKiernan, F. Mark, and Roger D. Launius, eds. *An Early Latter Day Saint History: The Book of John Whitmer.* Independence, Mo.: Herald Publishing House, 1980.

McKitrick, Eric. *Andrew Johnson and Reconstruction.* Chicago: University of Chicago Press, 1960.

McLaws, Monte B. "The Attempted Assassination of Missouri's Ex-Governor, Lilburn W. Boggs." *Missouri Historical Review* 60 (October 1965): 50–62.

McLear, Patrick E. "Economic Growth and the Panic of 1857 in Kansas City." *Bulletin of the Missouri Historical Society* 26 (October 1970): 144–56.

McNitt, Frank. *The Navajo Wars: Military Campaigns, Slave Raids, and Reprisals.* Albuquerque: University of New Mexico Press, 1972.

McPherson, James M. *Battle Cry of Freedom: The Civil War Era.* New York: Oxford University Press, 1988.

———. *The Struggle for Equality: Abolitionists and the Negro in the Civil War and Reconstruction.* Princeton: Princeton University Press, 1964.

McWhiney, Grady, and Perry D. Jamieson. *Attack and Die: Civil War Military Tactics and the Southern Heritage.* Tuscaloosa: University of Alabama Press, 1982.

Meinig, D. W. *The Shaping of America: A Geographical Perspective on 500 Years of History.* Vol. 2, *Continental America, 1800–1867.* New Haven: Yale University Press, 1993.

Mering, John V. "The Political Transition of James S. Rollins." *Missouri Historical Review* 53 (April 1959): 217–26.

———. "The Slave State Constitutional Unionists and the Politics of Consensus." *Journal of Southern History* 43 (fall 1977): 395–410.

———. *The Whig Party in Missouri.* Columbia: University of Missouri Press, 1967.

Merk, Frederick. *Manifest Destiny and Mission in American History: A Reinterpretation.* New York: Vintage Books, 1963.

———. *Slavery and the Annexation of Texas.* New York: Alfred A. Knopf, 1972.

Merrill, Horace Samuel. *Bourbon Leader: Grover Cleveland and the Democratic Party.* Boston: Little, Brown, 1957.

Missouri State Gazetteer & Business Directory. St. Louis: S. L. Polk and Co., and A. C. Danser, 1881.

Monaghan, Jay. *Civil War on the Western Border, 1854–1865.* Boston: Little, Brown, 1955.

Moore, Glover. *The Missouri Controversy, 1819–1821.* Lexington: University of Kentucky Press, 1953.

Moorhead, Max L. *New Mexico's Royal Road: Trade and Travel on the Chihuahua Trail.* Norman: University of Oklahoma Press, 1958.

Morgan, Dale L. *Jedediah Smith and the Opening of the West.* Indianapolis: Bobbs-Merrill, 1953.

Nevins, Allan. *The Emergence of Lincoln.* Vol. 2, *Prologue to Civil War, 1859–1861.* New York: Charles Scribner's Sons, 1950.

———. *Ordeal of the Union.* Vol. 2, *A House Dividing, 1852–1857.* New York: Charles Scribner's Sons, 1947.

Newhard, Leota. "The Beginning of the Whig Party in Missouri, 1824–1840." *Missouri Historical Review* 25 (January 1931): 254–80.

The New York City Co-Partnership Directory, for 1844 & 1845. New York: John Dogett, Jr., 1844.

Nichols, Roy Franklin. *The Disruption of American Democracy.* New York: Macmillan, 1948.

———. *Franklin Pierce: Young Hickory of the Granite Hills.* Philadelphia: University of Pennsylvania Press, 1958.

———. "The Kansas-Nebraska Act: A Century of Historiography." *Mississippi Valley Historical Review* 43 (September 1956): 187–212.

Oates, Stephen B. *With Malice toward None: The Life of Abraham Lincoln.* New York: Harper and Row, 1977.

Oliva, Leo E. *Soldiers on the Santa Fe Trail.* Norman: University of Oklahoma Press, 1967.

Overdyke, W. Darrell. *The Know-Nothing Party in the South.* Baton Rouge: Louisiana State University Press, 1950.

Parkin, Max H. "A History of the Latter-Day Saints in Clay County, Missouri, from 1833 to 1837." Ph.D. diss., Brigham Young University, 1976.

Parkman, Francis. *The Oregon Trail*. Garden City, N.Y.: Doubleday, 1946.

Parish, William J. "The German Jew and the Commercial Revolution in Territorial New Mexico, 1850–1900." *New Mexico Historical Review* 35 (January 1960): 1–29.

Parrish, William E. *David Rice Atchison of Missouri: Border Politician*. Columbia: University of Missouri Press, 1961.

———. *A History of Missouri*. Vol. 3, *1860–1875*. Columbia: University of Missouri Press, 1973.

———. *Missouri under Radical Rule, 1865–1870*. Columbia: University of Missouri Press, 1965.

———. *Turbulent Partnership: Missouri and the Union, 1861–1865*. Columbia: University of Missouri Press, 1963.

Parrish, William E., Charles T. Jones Jr., and Lawrence O. Christensen. *Missouri: The Heart of the Nation*. Arlington Heights, Ill.: Forum Press, 1980.

Paterson, Thomas G., J. Garry Clifford, and Kenneth J. Hagan. *American Foreign Policy: A History*. Lexington, Mass.: D. C. Heath, 1977.

Paxton, William M. *Annals of Platte County, Missouri*. Kansas City: Hudson-Kimberly Pub., 1897.

Pessen, Edward. *Jacksonian America: Society, Personality, and Politics*. Rev. ed. Urbana: University of Illinois Press, 1985.

Peterson, Norma L. *Freedom and Franchise: The Political Career of B. Gratz Brown*. Columbia: University of Missouri Press, 1965.

Pohl, James W. "The Influence of Antoine Henri de Jomini on Winfield Scott's Campaign in the Mexican War." *Southwestern Historical Quarterly* 77 (spring 1973): 85–110.

Potter, David M. *The Impending Crisis, 1848–1861*. New York: Harper and Row, 1976.

Potts, Louis W. "The Old Men of Clay County, 1870." Unpublished paper presented at Missouri Conference on History, April 15, 1995, Jefferson City, Mo.

Primm, James Neal. *Economic Policy in the Development of a Western State: Missouri, 1820–1860*. Cambridge: Harvard University Press, 1954.

Quaife, Milo Milton, ed. *The Diary of James K. Polk during His Presidency, 1845–1849*. 2 vols. Chicago: A. C. McClurg and Co., 1910.

Quarles, Benjamin. *Lincoln and the Negro*. New York: Oxford University Press, 1962.

Randall, James G., and David Donald. *The Civil War and Reconstruction*. 2d ed. Lexington, Mass.: D. C. Heath, 1969.

Rawley, James A. *Race and Politics: "Bleeding Kansas" and the Coming of the Civil War*. Philadelphia: Lippincott, 1969.

"Record Book 2," Circuit Court, Clay County Courthouse, Liberty, Mo.

Remini, Robert V. *Andrew Jackson and the Bank War.* New York: Norton, 1967.

Report of the Special Committee Appointed to Investigate the Troubles in Kansas; with the Views of the Minority of Said Committee. House Report no. 200, 34th Cong., 1st. sess. Washington, D.C.: U.S. House of Representatives, 1856.

Richards, Paul C. "Missouri Persecutions: Petitions for Redress." *Brigham Young University Studies* 13 (summer 1973): 520–43.

Richardson, William H. *Journal of Doniphan's Expedition.* Baltimore: Robinson, 1847.

Rigdon, J. Wickliffe. "I Never Knew a Time When I Did Not Know Joseph Smith." Ed. Karl Keller. *Dialogue: A Journal of Mormon Thought* 1 (winter 1966): 36.

Riggs, Michael S. "The Economic Impact of Fort Leavenworth on Northwestern Missouri 1827–1838: Yet Another Reason for the Mormon War?" In *Restoration Studies 4,* ed. Marjorie B. Troeh and Eileen M. Terril, 124–33. Independence, Mo.: Herald Publishing House, 1988.

Robinson, Jacob S. *A Journal of the Santa Fe Expedition under Colonel Doniphan.* Portsmouth, N.H.: Portsmouth Journal Press, 1848.

Roed, William. "Secessionist Strength in Missouri." *Missouri Historical Review* 72 (July 1978): 412–23.

Ruxton, George Augustus Frederick. *Adventures in Mexico and the Rocky Mountains.* 1847. Reprint, Glorieta, N.M.: Rio Grande Press, 1973.

——. *Ruxton of the Rockies.* Ed. Clyde Reed, Mae Reed, and LeRoy R. Hafen. Norman: University of Oklahoma Press, 1950.

Schindler, Harold. *Orrin Porter Rockwell: Man of God, Son of Thunder.* Salt Lake City: University of Utah Press, 1966.

Schlesinger, Arthur M., Jr. *The Age of Jackson.* Boston: Houghton, Mifflin, 1945.

——. *The Vital Center.* Boston: Houghton, Mifflin, 1962.

Sefton, James E. *Andrew Johnson and the Uses of Constitutional Power.* Boston: Little, Brown, 1980.

Senate Documents, 30th Cong., 1st Sess., Vol. 1 (1847).

Settle, Raymond W. *Alexander William Doniphan: Symbol of Pioneer Americanism.* Liberty, Mo.: William Jewell College Bulletin, 1947.

Settle, Raymond W., and Mary Lund Settle. *War Drums and Wagon Wheels.* Lincoln: University of Nebraska Press, 1966.

Shade, William G. *Banks or No Banks: The Money Question in Western Politics, 1832–1865.* Detroit: Wayne State University Press, 1972.

Shalhope, Robert E. "Jacksonian Politics in Missouri: A Comment on the McCormick Thesis." *Civil War History* 15 (March 1970): 210–25.

——. "Thomas Hart Benton and Missouri State Politics: A Re-Examination." *Bulletin of the Missouri Historical Society* 25 (April 1969): 171–91.

Sharp, James Rogers. "Gov. Daniel Dunklin's Jacksonian Democracy in

Missouri, 1832–1836." *Missouri Historical Review* 61 (April 1962): 217.

Shoemaker, Floyd C. "Clay County." *Missouri Historical Review* 52 (October 1957): 25–34.

———. "Missouri's Proslavery Fight for Kansas, 1854–1855." *Missouri Historical Review* 48 (April, July 1954): 221–36, 325–40, and 49 (October 1954): 41–54.

———. "Some Colorful Lawyers in the History of Missouri." *Missouri Historical Review* 53 (June 1959): 711–24.

Shortridge, James R. "The Expansion of the Settlement Frontier in Missouri." *Missouri Historical Review* 75 (October 1980): 64–90.

Skinker, Thomas K. "The Removal of the Judges of the Supreme Court of Missouri in 1865." *Missouri Historical Society Collections* 4 (1914): 243–74.

Smith, Elbert B. *Magnificent Missourian: The Life of Thomas Hart Benton.* New York: J. B. Lippincott, 1958.

Smith, Joseph, Jr. *The History of the Church of Jesus Christ of Latter-day Saints,* Ed. B. H. Roberts. 7 vols. 2d ed. Salt Lake City: Deseret Book Co., 1976.

Smith, Ralph A. "The 'King of New Mexico' and the Doniphan Expedition." *New Mexico Historical Review* 38 (January 1963): 29–55.

Snead, Thomas L. *The Fight for Missouri, From the Election of Lincoln to the Death of Lyon.* New York: Scribners, 1888.

Snow, Eliza R. "Letter from Missouri, February 22, 1839." *Brigham Young University Studies* 13 (summer 1973): 547.

Stanton, William. *The Leopard's Spots: Scientific Attitudes toward Race in America, 1815–1859.* Chicago: University of Chicago Press, 1960.

Starr, Stephen Z. *Jennison's Jayhawkers: A Civil War Cavalry Regiment and Its Commander.* Baton Rouge: Louisiana State University Press, 1973.

A Statement of Facts and a Few Suggestions in Review of Political Action in Missouri. Broadside. N.p., 1856.

State of Missouri v Orrin Porter Rockwell. County Court Records. Clay County Courthouse, Liberty, Mo.

Stevens, Walter B. *Centennial History of Missouri (The Center State): One Hundred Years in the Union, 1820–1921.* 2 vols. St. Louis: S. J. Clarke Publishing, 1921.

———. "Lincoln and Missouri." *Missouri Historical Review* 10 (January 1916): 63–119.

Stewart, A. J. D., ed. *The History of the Bench and Bar in Missouri.* St. Louis: Legal Publishing Co., 1898.

Stokes, Durwood T., ed. "The Wilson Letters, 1835–1849." *Missouri Historical Review* 60 (July 1966): 495–517.

Strozier, Charles B. *Lincoln's Quest for Union: Public and Private Meanings.* New York: Basic Books, 1982.

Temin, Peter. *The Jacksonian Economy.* New York: Norton, 1973.

Thomas, Benjamin P. *Abraham Lincoln: A Biography.* New York: Alfred A. Knopf, 1952.

Thorp, Judge Joseph. *Early Days in the West: Along the Missouri One Hundred Years Ago.* Liberty, Mo.: Liberty Tribune and Liberty Advance, 1924.

Tocqueville, Alexis de. *Democracy in America.* Trans. Henry Reeve. 2 vols. New York: Vintage Books, 1973.

Trefousse, Hans L. *Impeachment of a President: Andrew Johnson, the Blacks, and Reconstruction.* Knoxville: University of Tennessee Press, 1975.

Trexler, Harrison A. *Slavery in Missouri, 1804–1865.* Baltimore: Johns Hopkins University Press, 1914.

Tucker, Phillip Thomas. "Above and Beyond . . . African-American Missourians of Colonel Alexander Doniphan's Expedition." *Password* 35 (fall 1990): 133–37.

———. "The Missourians and the Battle of Brazito, Christmas Day, 1846." *Password* 34 (winter 1989): 159–70.

Turner, Henry Smith. *The Original Journals of Henry Smith Turner: With Stephen Watts Kearny to New Mexico and California, 1846–1847.* Ed. Dwight L. Clarke. Norman: University of Oklahoma Press, 1966.

Twitchell, Ralph Emerson. *The History of the Military Occupation of the Territory of New Mexico from 1846 to 1851 by the Government of the United States.* Danville, Ill.: Interstate Printers and Publishers, 1909.

———. *The Leading Facts of New Mexican History.* 2 vols. Cedar Rapids, Iowa: Torch Press, 1911–1912.

Wallace, Doris Davis. "The Political Campaign of 1860 in Missouri." *Missouri Historical Review* 70 (January 1976): 162–83.

The War of the Rebellion: A Compilation of the Official Records of the Union and Confederate Armies. Series 1 and 2. Washington, D.C.: U.S. War Department, 1880.

Webb, James Josiah. *Adventures in the Santa Fe Trade, 1844–1847.* Ed. Ralph P. Bieber. Southwest Historical Series, vol. 1. Glendale, Calif.: Arthur H. Clark, 1931.

Webb, William Larkin. *Battles and Biographies of Missouri.* Kansas City: Hudson-Kimberly Pub. Co., 1900.

Wellman, Paul I. *The House Divides.* Garden City, N.Y.: Doubleday, 1966.

Wells, Eugene T. "The Growth of Independence, Missouri, 1827–1850." *Bulletin of the Missouri Historical Society* 16 (October 1959): 33–46.

Wells, Junius F. "A Prophecy and Its Fulfillment." *Improvement Era* 6 (November 1902): 8.

Wetmore, Alphonso, ed. *Gazetteer of the State of Missouri.* St. Louis: n.p., 1837.

Williams, James. *Seventy-five Years on the Border.* Kansas City: Standard Printing Co., 1912.

Williams, T. Harry. *Romance and Realism in Southern Politics.* Baton Rouge: Louisiana State University Press, 1966.

————. "Voters in Blue: The Citizen Soldiers of the Civil War." *Mississippi Valley Historical Review* 31 (September 1944): 187–204.

Williamson, Hugh P. "Colonel Alexander W. Doniphan—Soldier, Lawyer and Statesman." *Journal of the Missouri Bar* 8 (October 1952): 180–85.

"Will of A. W. Doniphan." Probate Court of Ray County, Mo. Record Book E-6, pp. 79–81. Ray County Courthouse, Richmond, Mo.

Winn, Kenneth H. *Exiles in a Land of Liberty: The Mormons in America, 1830–1846.* Chapel Hill: University of North Carolina Press, 1989.

Wislizenus, Frederick Adolphus. *Memoir of a Tour to Northern Mexico, Connected with Col. Doniphan's Expedition.* Senate Miscellaneous Document No. 26, 30th Cong., 1st Sess. Washington, D.C.: Tippin and Streeter, 1848.

Woodward, C. Vann. *Origins of the New South, 1877–1913.* Baton Rouge: Louisiana State University Press, 1951.

Wyatt-Brown, Bertram. *Southern Honor: Ethics and Behavior in the Old South.* New York: Oxford University Press, 1982.

Wyman, Walker D. "The Military Phase of Santa Fe Freighting, 1846–1865." *Kansas Historical Quarterly* 1 (1932): 415–26.

Young, William. *Young's History of Lafayette County, Missouri.* 2 vols. Indianapolis: B. F. Brown and Co., 1910.

Zornow, William Frank. *Kansas: A History of the Jayhawk State.* Norman: University of Oklahoma Press, 1957.

Index